Hopewell Village

A Social and Economic History of an
Iron-Making Community

Hopewell Village

*A Social and Economic
History of an
Iron-Making Community*

JOSEPH E. WALKER

Philadelphia
University of Pennsylvania Press

Library of Congress Catalogue Card Number : 64–24506

7474

Printed in the United States of America

To
Rachael

Acknowledgments

ONE OF THE PLEASURES OF RESEARCH IS THE DISCOVERY OF the large number of persons who will give many hours of their valuable time for no apparent reason except that they are kind, generous and helpful to aspiring writers.

The author is deeply grateful for the detailed and valuable suggestions made by Dr. Harry M. Tinkcom and Dr. John M. Mickelson in the development of this study. He is particularly indebted to Dr. James A. Barnes for the constant guidance and help and the many hours of constructive criticism which he gave during the weekend visits to his home.

The writer is also debtor to the personnel of the Hopewell Village National Historical Site for their assistance with the research work. Mr. Robert Ronsheim and Mr. Joseph Prentice first suggested a history of Hopewell Furnace; Superintendent Benjamin Zerbey, Mrs. Charlotte Fairbairn and Mr. Leland Abel gave valuable aid at several critical points; and Mr. Earl Heydinger generously shared the product of his own research and worked almost daily to fill in needed areas of background. Mr. Ronald Lee and Mr. Frank Barnes of the Philadelphia Regional Office of the National Park Service were also most cooperative.

Valued help on certain technical matters was supplied by Dr. C. M. Myers, Dr. and Mrs. V. A. Champa, Dr. David Voigt, Mr. William Caulwell, Mr. Henry Kauffman, Col. Wayne Homan, Mrs. Freas Downing, Mr. Richard Murr, Mr. Edward Smuck, Mrs. Esther Turner and Mrs. Betty Meyers. Much assistance was also received from the persons who are responsible for the records and manuscripts at the Berks County Historical Society, Berks County Court House, Chester County Historical Society, Historical Society of Pennsylvania, Lancaster County Historical Society, Lancaster County Law Library and Millersville State College Library. All photographs unless otherwise specified are reproduced through the courtesy of the National Park Service.

Finally the author is under obligation to his wife Rachael and sons Bob, Sam and Wally for absorbing his frustrations and sharing his enthusiasms and particularly to Sam for his help with tabulating the statistical data and to Rachael for her suggestions for improvements on style and form.

Millersville State College
Millersville, Pa.

J.E.W.

Contents

Tables

Introduction

IN THE CENTURY AND THREE QUARTERS OF THE CHARCOAL IRON industry in Pennsylvania, several hundred little furnaces dotted the wooded areas from the Delaware River to the Ohio line. One of these in Union Township, Berks County—but only a few hundred yards from the Chester County line—was named Hopewell Furnace. Mark Bird was displaying no originality in thus naming his iron works. Hopewell was a common name in the iron industry of Pennsylvania, and other states as well. Mark Bird and his father William Bird had owned a forge by that name before the furnace was built. The Grubb family operated a Hopewell Forge in Lancaster County, and there were Hopewell Furnaces in New Jersey and Ohio.

Why should this one out of so many furnaces be the subject of intensive study? Hopewell missed by more than half a century the right to claim the distinction which Colebrookdale bears as the first Pennsylvania furnace. Warwick Furnace had a larger productive capacity and a longer history. Joanna Furnace was in operation after Hopewell's last blast had ended. Hopewell records did not note such distinguished visitors as George Washington and Benjamin Franklin who were reported to have accepted the hospitality of nearby Warwick Furnace. Hopewell had its bankruptcies and its periods of prosperity. So did many other furnaces. Hopewell made good iron and attracted a distant market. So did others.

Hopewell may have been typical of charcoal-iron furnaces, or it may have been quite distinctive. It will not be possible to make this judgment until comparisons can be made with other

13

furnaces. In this account of one community comparisons and contrasts have been made with other furnace and forge communities in a few instances where it seemed that the Hopewell story was made more meaningful. But no comparative research in depth was attempted. The full history of the charcoal iron manufacture in Pennsylvania, especially in the nineteenth century, has not yet been written. This work presents some aspects of the history of one furnace. If others will continue this effort by investigating other furnaces, the story of early iron-making will emerge.

Perhaps the greatest advantage in selecting Hopewell as the subject for research of an iron-making community was the opportunity to use the extremely valuable collection of documents and microfilm available to students and scholars at the Hopewell Village National Historical Site. Journals, ledgers, time books, molders' books, transportation books, letters and business papers are in this collection which has been compiled by the professional staff members of the National Park Service. Facilities and opportunities for its use are made available through the employees on permanent duty there to the fullest extent compatible with their other responsibilities.

This book is not a technical study of iron-manufacturing. Possibly some one else may wish to use the Hopewell records as material for this kind of presentation. However, there exists a fairly extensive literature on techniques of which a sampling is included in the bibliography. Emphasis here has been directed not to iron but to people—the men, women and children of the community where iron was made.

The furnace was a dominating influence in the life of the village. The flare from the stack cast a dim light over the village at night. The roar of the blast, the squeak of the water wheel, the peal of the cast-house bell, the rumble of wagon wheels were comforting sounds of production and prosperity. Quiet in the furnace area was a sign of hard times. But the furnace operation was the backdrop against which the life of the people was enacted, and the actors rather than the background are the cynosure of this account.

The title chosen is Hopewell Village rather than Hopewell Furnace. In part this choice was made because the National Park Service Historical Site has given meaning to the former term to the more than one million persons who have visited there. But, more important, the term "village" emphasizes social and economic factors rather than industrial ones. "Village" is used in a somewhat unnatural way, however, as meaning the much wider community of all those who were tied together by their common interest in and concern for the prosperity of Hopewell Furnace. Not only the residents of the ironmaster's mansion and the tenant houses along the road to Warwick, but also the woodcutters and colliers in their forest cabins, the miners at several miles distance, the local farmers who provided a part-time labor force and sold provisions at the Furnace, the storekeepers in Birdsboro or Morgantown, and even the merchants in distant cities became at times a part of this wider Hopewell community.

The book is divided into different sections to call attention to several aspects of the interassociation of the people concerned with Hopewell. Chief emphasis is placed upon the first half of the nineteenth century because it was at this time that the Furnace reached its peak of prosperity and also because the records are more complete for this era. The end of stove casting at Hopewell in 1844 began a period of decline which culminated in the final blast-out in 1883. The Civil War and the growth of the railroads created demands for iron which postponed, but could not prevent, the demise of the charcoal furnaces. Hopewell history began before 1800 and continued after 1850. These earlier and later periods are included in the historical sketches and in some references in the social and economic studies, but a major part of the material is taken from the half century of concentration.

In the era of charcoal iron the furnace plantation was a strange hybrid of agriculture and industry. The voracious consumption of fuel tied the furnace to the proximity of extensive forest holdings. Food for the workers provided an outlet for farm products. While both forest and farm offered employment to many workers, their economy was tied to the prosperity of the furnace. The author has attempted to recreate the interrelationships among these different kinds of workers through the scattered bits of information which are buried in the business records, the letters and the recorded reminiscences of people who once lived at Hopewell.

A brief history of the Hopewell Furnace is given in three chapters, each chapter devoted to a fairly distinct era. The economy of the community is examined through the furnace product, the market, management and labor relations, the operation of the store and the product of farm and forest. Social life of the community is investigated with particular attention given to the colored population, women, children, education, religion, and the influence of the outside world upon the furnace enclave.

Finally, answers are sought to these questions about the village and its people : Why did the Furnace struggle, prosper and decline? How did the people live? How did the owners manage the business? Was the company store a monopoly, or was an attempt made to keep the workers in debt at the store? What working conditions were maintained? Were wages comparable to those paid on other jobs? What were the labor needs of Hopewell Furnace? How was social rank determined in the village? Was racial discrimination practiced? Was Hopewell a "feudal," "self-sufficient" community?

Part One
The Historical Village

1   An Uncertain Youth, 1771-1800

MARK BIRD BUILT HIS NEW FURNACE ON THE EDGE OF A meadow where French Creek flows between Mount Pleasant and Brushy Hill in Union Township, Berks County, Pennsylvania, close to the Chester County line. Proof that the location was a good one was demonstrated by the production of iron on this site for more than a century. But there must have been times when Bird and his successors wondered whether a successful business was possible here. The first half century of the history of Hopewell Furnace was replete with crises— financial, legal and physical. It was shut down and reopened. The stack was rebuilt and extensively repaired. The sheriff was a frequent visitor. There were disputes over land owner- ship. Partnerships were formed and dissolved. Water was too abundant or in too short supply. However, despite all of the troubles, there were always those individuals who believed that Hopewell Furnace could be made to produce iron profit- ably.

The French Creek Valley offered many advantages to the person who hoped to make iron in a charcoal furnace. Some specific ingredients for this business in the eighteenth century were four natural resources: iron ore near the surface of the ground, abundant woodland to supply the fuel, fast-flowing water to provide power to the blast bellows at the furnace and a quantity of limestone to serve as the "flux" in the smelting process.[1] It was also desirable to have a hill against which to anchor the charging bridge, an available supply of common labor, housing for the workers and capital for building on the site.[2]

Hopewell Furnace had one serious fault in its location: the meadow in front of it was marshy.[3] Because water around the foundation interfered with proper operation of the furnace, the area had to be dry. This problem was controlled at Hopewell by placing the structure higher than the bank of the creek and by digging ditches along the side of the road which passed by the workers' houses. Eventually, too, the slag piles built up a porous plateau around the furnace.

The other needs of the furnace also were met by the energetic Bird. On August 23, 1770 he was granted rights to a little more than 157 acres in "Eastnantmill Township," Chester County,[4] upon which he developed the Old Hopewell Mine, also called Birdtown. Three and a half years later he recorded a deed for nearly 40 acres known as the Jones Good Luck mine tract.[5] These two areas would provide for much of the ore needs of the furnace although later owners secured mining rights in the Warwick mine holes.

The land upon which the furnace and nearby homes were built was included in a purchase of 33 acres from Owen Hugh in 1769 for £76 10s. and subject to a quitrent due to the

[1] Edna M. Handwork, "First in Iron-Berks County's Iron Industry, 1716 to 1815," *Historical Review of Berks County,* XXV, 4 (Fall 1960), p. 121.

[2] E. N. Hartley, *Ironworks on the Saugus* (Norman: University Press, 1957), p. 100.

[3] Leland Abel, "Archeological Report of Hopewell Furnace Site" (unpublished study, 1962). Hopewell Village Library.

[4] *Berks County Deed Book,* AA, Vol. 11, p. 140. Berks County Court House.

[5] *Ibid.,* B. Vol. 2, p. 530.

provincial proprietors of a half penny sterling per acre.[6] Apparently the quitrent payment did not prove burdensome, for Bird's name seldom appeared on the list of those who paid this fee.[7]

Reports existed that Mark Bird was a sharp dealer in acquiring title to lands. He was said to have ejected Clement Hughes from a house he had built earlier on the furnace plot.[8] Peter Cox testified under oath in 1811 that he, also, had been forced off a piece of land upon which he had a house partially built.[9]

Charcoal for the furnace came from forest lands, valued at almost £13,000, which had been inherited by Bird from his father William Bird who died in 1761.[10] Mark was in possession of 8,050 acres of land in Union Township in 1763,[11] and he had added to these holdings by the time the furnace was built.[12]

Despite its location Hopewell Furnace did not at first use the water of French Creek for its power supply. Instead water was brought from springs on the mountain side in an east headrace one mile long and a west headrace twice that length. The west ditch crossed land which did not belong to the Furnace, a circumstance which was later the cause of an eviction suit and the building of a dam on the creek not far from the iron works.[13]

Limestone was available locally. The Furnace records over

[6] *Ibid.*, A. Vol. 6, p. 237.

[7] Charles B. Montgomery, "Report on Hopewell Furnace in Berks County, Pa." (unpublished report, 1941). Hopewell Village Library.

[8] Albert Painter Interview, 1950. Hopewell Village Library.

[9] *Berks County Court Continuance Dockets*, 1800–1820. *Penn Lessee v. Kahler*, tried 1810, and *Buckley et al v. Kahler*, tried Jan. 16, 1811, Berks County Court House.

[10] *Alden's Appeal Record*, 93, Pennsylvania 182, Philadelphia, 1878, p. 119.

[11] *Union Township Assessment Records* for 1763. Microfilm, Hopewell Village Library.

[12] The nature of some of Bird's land titles were to plague his successors with suits at law. See chapter 2 for discussion of these.

[13] Harker A. Long, *A Short History of the Hopewell Furnace Estate in Union Township, Berks County* (Reading: Reading Eagle Press, undated).

a number of years show that lime was bought from neighbors or hauled from furnace land.

The availability of laborers and housing for them will be discussed in later chapters.

The capital for Hopewell came from several sources. One was the paternal inheritance already mentioned. When in 1764 Mark Bird transferred Berkshire Furnace to his mother and her new husband John Patton,[14] he may have secured additional funds for investment. Apparently the inheritances of a sister and two brothers were used by Mark for on November 18, 1772 he gave a mortgage to Mary Bird, William Bird and James Bird for their shares in their father's estate.[15] The mention of Hopewell Furnace in this mortgage was one of the earliest specific references to it found in any extant document.

The absence of early Furnace business records caused a long controversy over the date of the founding of the works at this site. Morton L. Montgomery, historian of Berks County, wrote that Hopewell Furnace was built in 1759 by William Bird;[16] but later in the same volume he said it was erected about 1765.[17] Since this latter date was after the death of William Bird, the furnace could not have been built in that year by him. Other writers followed Montgomery in giving the 1759 date.[18] In support of an earlier date a diary left by a visitor to Hopewell in 1837 recorded that Manager Clement Brooke told the writer that the furnace had been in operation for 80 years.[19] If taken literally, that statement would have dated the founding in 1757; but Brooke was certainly mistaken. Much evidence exists to support a later date.

[14] *Alden's Appeal Record, op. cit.,* p. 119.
[15] *Berks County Court Pleadings,* 1770–1785, November 18, 1772. Berks County Court House.
[16] Morton L. Montgomery, *Historical and Biographical Annals of Berks County, Pennsylvania* (2 Vols.; Chicago: J. M. Beers and Company, 1909), I, p. 27.
[17] *Ibid.,* pp. 309 and 326.
[18] For example: *Industrial Berks County,* 1748–1948 (Reading: Textile Machine Works, 1948), p. 6.
[19] Otis Cary, *Diary of A Trip from New York to Pennsylvania in 1837* (unpublished, Berks County Historical Society), Feb. 17, 1837.

An inventory of the estate of William Bird did not mention Hopewell Furnace.[20] Since it was unlikely that so valuable a possession would have been overlooked, it is probable that there was no such establishment in his possession at the time of his death in 1761. In sworn testimony a witness in a suit tried in 1811 stated that he had cut wood on land next to the furnace tract in 1770. He thought that the furnace had been erected a year or two earlier.[21] In 1787 an advertisement for the sale of the furnace noted that it had been operating for seventeen years[22] Evidence in another law suit noted that Mark Bird was in possession of the furnace tract in January 1770, and that he had had it surveyed during April and May of that year.[23]

On more direct evidence the tax records show that Mark Bird's property tax in Union Township increased sharply for the year 1768 and took another jump in 1770. It then remained the same through 1773. In the absence of a general tax increase, which did not appear for other tax payers, it seems probable that Bird's valuation was increasing in those years. The furnace itself witnesses to a later founding date. A stone at the edge of the cast arch has the date 1771 cut into its face.[24] The oldest known product of Hopewell Furnace is a stove, owned by the Birdsboro Y.M.C.A., bearing on its surface the name of the Furnace and the date 1772. It seems probable, therefore, that Mark Bird built the furnace in 1771 on land he had recently acquired.

Specific events at Hopewell in the next thirteen years are not too clear because of the absence of Furnace books and records. Stoves were cast with the inscriptions "Hopewell

[20] *Hopewell Furnace Papers* (uncatalogued documents at Hopewell Village National Historical Site).
[21] Evan Lewis in Ejectment Suit of *Buckley et al. v. Kahler, op. cit.*
[22] *Pennsylvania Gazette,* April 11, 1787.
[23] *Peregrin Pickle Les. of Penn and Richard Penn Esq. v. Mathew Brooke, Pleadings and Miscellaneous Old Papers, 1752–1843* (Prothonatory's Office, Berks County, Reading, Pennsylvania), Case tried March 5–8, 1811.
[24] Photographed in 1962 by Archeologist Leland Abel.

Six-Plate Stove Made in 1772, Oldest Known Product of Hopewell
Furnace

Furnace" or "Mark Bird." One patriotic model appeared with
the motto, "Be Liberty Thine."[25]

Hopewell, like many of its neighboring furnaces, was used
to help with arming the American military forces in the
Revolutionary War. Surviving papers contain one specific
reference to munitions at Hopewell and considerable support
for the contention that cannons were made here. Sam Hodg-
don, Commissary General of Military Stores, left a record of
"the Shot and Shell at the Several Furnaces." The document,

[25] Committee on Historical Research, *Forges and Furnaces in the
Province of Pennsylvania* (Philadelphia: Pennsylvania Society of the
Colonial Dames of America, 1914), p. 154.

undated but bundled with others for 1781, listed "Hopewell (Mark Bird) 10 Inch Shells 517."[26] The importance of this contribution to the war effort was emphasized in the following action of the Continental Congress:

> The Board of War reported June 23: "That eleven workmen employed by Colonel Mark Bird at his Cannon and Nail Rod works in Berks County, Pennsylvania, be discharged from the Militia into which they are drafted, as Congress are of opinion they are of more extensive uses to the continent in their employment as artificers, as it is represented that the works must stand still if these workmen march out with the Militia."

> Tuesday, June 24, 1777.

> The Board of War having recommended, that eleven workmen employed by Colonel Mark Bird in the cannon foundry and nail works . . . carried on by him for the use of the United States, be discharged from the militia into which they are now drafted,

> Ordered, That this matter be referred to the Supreme executive council of the State of Pennsylvania.[27]

The *Journals of the Continental Congress* contained a number of references to Bird's cannon. He was advanced $2,000 on August 22, 1776 because of his contract ". . . to cast cannon for the United States."[28] Twice he was issued powder ". . . to prove the cannon he has made. . . ."[29] In 1778 he was allowed ten pounds Pennsylvania currency per ton more than the original contract for his cannon ". . . in consideration of his loss sustained by the additional quantity of powder required to be used in the proof of the said cannon. . . ."[30]

On April 8, 1780, payment was authorized to Mark Bird in the amount of $125,691.60 ". . . for sundry quantities of

[26] *Knox Papers* (Colonial National Park, Yorktown, Virginia). Photocopy at Hopewell Village.

[27] *Journal of the Continental Congress* (34 Volumes; Philadelphia: Government Printing Office, 1904–1937), VIII, pp. 495–496.

[28] *Ibid.*, V, p. 695.

[29] *Ibid.*, IV, p. 355 and VI, p. 860.

[30] *Ibid.*, XI, p. 473–474.

Mark Bird's Property as Listed in the Berks County Tax Book for 1779

military stores . . . the . . . contracts have been compleated,
and the stores proved and accepted. . . ."[31] But Bird must
have had some cannon on hand when the war ended; for on

[31] *Ibid.*, XVI, p. 338–339.

August 12, 1784 he sold to John Pasmore "2 great guns wt. 2T : 8C : @ £5–12/6 = £13–10."[32]

There was no mention in these journals of Hopewell Furnace in connection with the manufacture of cannon for the Continental Army. But the old Hopewell residents were familiar with a story that cannon were buried near the furnace after the Battle of Brandywine when the British Army advanced up the Schuylkill Valley.[33] In 1858 Hopewell Furnace sold six old cannon weighing 18,600 pounds to the railroad for scrap iron at twenty-four dollars per ton.[34] The Furnace journal did not report when these cannon were cast, but it might have been during the Revolution. The museum at Hopewell Furnace now contains a part of an old cannon which, according to tradition, was uncovered at Hopewell during the Civil War. In 1935 a cannon ball was recovered from the slag pile, and three more were found in excavations in the furnace area in 1962.[35]

If Hopewell Furnace worked for the American cause in obscurity, its owner was frequently mentioned for his activities. He was probably not in active management at the Furnace during this time, for as early as 1772 he was listed as a citizen of the county of Philadelphia.[36] He rented his furnace to William Hays sometime in the 1770's, and Hays was probably the manager during the Revolutionary period.[37]

Before the outbreak of the war Mark Bird served on the Committee on Observation and the Committee of Correspondence and was chosen to the Provincial Conference of 1775.

[32] *Hopewell Furnace Day Book, 1784–1794*, p. 70. There are 76 volumes of Hopewell Furnace Ledgers and Journals available for use. They have been named by the historians at Hopewell Village as source material, and each one has been assigned a number. They are referred to as SM 1, etc. The above named book is SM 41. Subsequent references to these books will be by the SM numbers.

[33] For example, the Thomas Hoffman Interview, November 22, 1940.

[34] SM 60, p. 69.

[35] Appleman, *op. cit.*, p. 8; Report of Archeologist Leland Abel.

[36] Arthur Cecil Bining, *Pennsylvania Iron Manufacture in the 18th Century* (Harrisburg: Pennsylvania Historical Commission, 1938), p. 194.

[37] Ejectment Suit of *Buckley et al. v. Kahler, op. cit.*

When the war came, he was Lieutenant Colonel of the Second Battalion of Berks County militia and later became its Colonel. He was credited with providing uniforms, tents and provisions for three hundred men at his own expense.[38] He was a member of the Pennsylvania Assembly;[39] chairman of the General Committee of Berks County which selected eight members, including himself, to serve in the Provincial Convention of 1776;[40] and judge of the Berks County Court.[41]

Perhaps the most important services that Mark Bird performed for the American cause were those executed while he was deputy quartermaster general. He may have advanced some of his own money to obtain supplies, for Congress voted on February 8, 1776, that he be paid $5.80 for necessities provided for several prisoners. The next month he was granted $50,000 for which he was accountable.[42] In February of 1778 he took advantage of high water on the Schuylkill River to ship 1000 barrels of flour to Washington's army at Valley Forge.[43] Earl J. Heydinger wrote of this action, "The timely shipment . . . was only the minimum for four or five days requirements, but those four or five days . . . enabled Washington's army to survive. . . ."[44]

The end of the war found Mark Bird a creditor of the government of the United States. On September 15, 1783 he requested that he be given the chain ". . . which was prepared to throw across Hudson River. . . ."[45] But this request was denied ". . . as the memorialist being a creditor of the United States may obtain a settlement of his accounts in common

---

[38] Montgomery, *op. cit.*, I, p. 326.
[39] Bining, "Early Ironmasters of Pennsylvania," reprint from *Pennsylvania History*, XVIII, 2 (April 1951), p. 12.
[40] James E. Gibson, "The Pennsylvania Provincial Conference of 1776," *The Pennsylvania Magazine of History and Biography*, LVIII, 4 (October 1934), p. 326.
[41] *Reading Eagle*, July 27, 1930. Article by C. M. Montgomery.
[42] *Journals of the Continental Congress*, IV, pp. 119, 243–244.
[43] *Ibid.*, X, p. 189.
[44] Earl J. Heydinger, "The Schuykill, Lifeline to Valley Forge," *Bulletin of the Historical Society of Montgomery County, Pennsylvania*, IX, 3 (October 1954), p. 161.
[45] *Journals of the Continental Congress*, XXV, p. 585.

with others under similar circumstances, it is unnecessary to give any particular order in his behalf."[46]

Bird at this time was 44 years of age,[47] brother-in-law to two signers of the Declaration of Independence, George Ross and James Wilson;[48] and a businessman with broadly scattered interests. Beside owning Hopewell Furnace and Birdsboro Forge, Slitting Mill and Steel Furnace, he was partner in a number of other iron works: Gibraltar Forge[49] and Spring Forge[50] in Berks County and the Delaware Falls Iron Works near Trenton. In this last business he had James Wilson as his partner.[51]

That he was willing to invest in hazardous ventures was indicated by his presence among the owners of the *United States,* which was one of the first ships to leave this country to trade with China. There were six other owners, including James Wilson. This investment was probably no success, because the ship and cargo were seized upon their return to Philadelphia by the creditors of some of the partners.[52]

However, failure in the China trade was not the only sign of financial difficulty for the Bird enterprises. In 1784 he appealed for a reduction in his taxes on Hopewell Furnace property on the plea that his iron works had not operated for some time. The tax records showed that his taxes already had been sharply reduced in the preceding two years.[53] Apparently he was caught in the post-Revolution depression and inflation. A letter from Mark Bird to an unknown creditor on October 14, 1785 said ". . . as my misfortune has been, as it now is, I

[46] *Ibid.,* XXV, p. 626

[47] *St. Gabriels Episcopal Church Records,* Douglasville, Pennsylvania, lists his baptism on February 4, 1739, p. 103. Berks County Historical Society.

[48] *Ibid.,* p. 70.

[49] Bining, *Pennsylvania Iron Manufacture in the 18th Century, op. cit.,* p. 189.

[50] Committee on Historical Research, *op. cit.,* p. 158.

[51] Bining, *op. cit.,* p. 109.

[52] Samuel W. Woodhouse, "Log and Journal of the Ship *United States* on a voyage to China in 1784," *The Pennsylvania Magazine of History and Biography,* LV, 3 (July 1931), p. 226–227.

[53] *Union Township Tax Records,* 1782–1784. Berks County Historical Society.

have no money otherwise would have paid you Long since but if I was to a Been Crusified I could get none. . . ."[54]

Post-war business for the ironmasters was slow with imports creating a surplus of bar iron. The Pennsylvania Assembly, when asked to adopt an import tax to protect the industry in this state,[55] voted against a bill which would have imposed a forty shilling per ton tariff on bar iron.[56]

Nature also conspired to complicate Bird's problems when floods did extensive damage in southeastern Pennsylvania in the fall of 1786.[57] Both Hopewell and the Birdsboro properties suffered,[58] and a fire at Birdsboro caused further loss.[59]

Mark Bird and James Wilson were in partnership in the Delaware Falls iron works. They had built rolling and slitting mills, a forge, a grist mill and a saw mill. But by 1785 their capital was exhausted, and in a final attempt to recover, Wilson tried unsuccessfully to borrow 500,000 florins in Holland.[60] One reason why the partners found it difficult to borrow was that they had already overextended their credit. On March 29, 1785, they had given to John Nixon, a Philadelphia merchant, a mortgage on about 8000 acres of Hopewell and Birdsboro land in Berks and Chester Counties and on the Delaware Falls property in Bucks County. In return they received from Nixon "200,000 fine Spanish milled Silver Dollars."[61] Another debt to the Bank of North America was of concern to the directors of that institution as shown by at least six separate entries in the minutes of their meetings from 1784 to 1789. Possibly more forceful action to collect was

---

[54] *Montgomery Manuscripts,* book 3, p. 1. Hopewell Village Library.
[55] *Pennsylvania Gazette,* February 1, 1786.
[56] *Ibid.,* April 21, 1787.
[57] *Ibid.,* November 22, 1786.
[58] Appleman, *op. cit.,* p. 8.
[59] Jackson Kemper, III, "The Making of Charcoal," *The Historical Review of Berks County,,* II, 4 (July 1937), n. p.
[60] *James Wilson Papers,* Vol. 3, p. 24, Historical Society of Pennsylvania. Letter dated July 16, 1785.
[61] *Berks County Surveyor. General Draughts and Miscellaneous Old Papers, 1700 to Early 1800* (Prothonotory's Office, Berks County Court House, Reading), March 29, 1785.

accounts, to settle the same immediately, with either of them, otherwise they will be proceeded against as the law directs.

JACOB PAUL, Abington,
¶   CORNELIUS COMFGYS Philadelphia,   } Assignees.

To be Sold by Public Auction,

On MONDAY, the 15th day of May next, and the succeeding days, till the whole shall be sold,

SEVEN tracts of Land in Union and Robinson townships, in the county of Berks; they contain from 150 to 200 acres each, six of them have fronts on the river Schuylkill, on one of them is the Birdsborough house, with the numerous and valuable improvements around it, on four others are houses, barns, orchards and other improvements, the remaining two consist chiefly of woodland; the soil is good, and there is a great proportion of watered meadow.

The vendue will be held on the premises, and the terms will be made known at the time of sale. It is probable that three other Tracts, adjoining the foregoing seven, will be exposed to sale at the same time.

To be Sold by Private Sale,

Hopewell Furnace, the Birdsborough Forges, and Spring Forge, all in the county of Berks. To Hopewell Furnace will be allotted 4000 acres of land, to the Birdsborough Forges 1500 acres, all well timbered, and extending three miles on Hay Creek, to Spring Forge 800 acres. Along with the Furnace will be sold 3 banks of good iron ore, all within a reasonable distance. It will be a term of the sale of the Furnace to supply, during four years, all the foregoing Forges with a certain quantity of pig iron at a stipulated price. Bar iron and castings will be received in payment for the whole iron work estate.

To any person inclining to purchase, the lands, lines and works will be shewn, from the 8th to the 15th day of May, by the subscriber, who will attend at Birdsborough for that purpose. The Furnace will be in blast, with a provision of five thousand cords of wood, and eight hundred loads of ore. Two thousand cords of wood are cut for the Birdsborough Forges, and two thousand and two hundred for Spring Forge. Five teams compleat may be purchased along with the Furnace.   MARK BIRD.

Cumberland county, State of New-Jersey, April 17, 1786.

THE Creditors of David Joslin and Jonas Mullica, debtors, confined in the goal of said county, are requested to appear

Hopewell Furnace Offered for Sale in the *Pennsylvania Gazette* for April 26, 1786

not taken because Wilson had been a member of the board of directors from 1781 to 1784.[62]

Bird tried to sell part of the property in an effort to save the rest. A public sale was advertised of Hopewell Furnace with 4000 acres of land, 5,000 cords of wood and 800 loads of ore. Birdsboro and Spring Forges were also offered for sale at the same time.[63] Perhaps the bids were insufficient, for no sale was consummated. Nixon insisted on payment; and on August 16, 1786 he received from Mark Bird and James Wilson a release of "all rights to the Equity of Redemption."[64] This in effect was a quitclaim deed to permit Nixon to sell the properties named in his mortgage at public or private sale to recover the amount of his note.

In 1788 Nixon brought suit for recovery of his money. This was apparently a preliminary action to a forced sale; and in April of that year a sheriff's sale was held of "Hopewell plantation."[65] The furnance and 5163 acres of land were purchased by Cadwallader Morris with one third interest and James Old with two-thirds interest.[66]

With this sale Mark Bird temporarily passed out of the picture of Hopewell Furnace history. Financial problems continued to plague him. He left Pennsylvania for North Carolina and in 1790 appealed to the legislature of that state for bankruptcy relief. On November 17, 1790 the House of Commons of the North Carolina Legislature heard the following report :

The committee of propositions and grievances to whom we referred the petition of Mark Bird, report—On information before the committee, it appears that the said Mark Bird became bankrupt when a citizen of the state of Pennsylvania— that he has since that time become an inhabitant of this State,

[62] *Minutes and Letter Book of the Bank of North America.* November 2, 1781, to January 21, 1792, *Montgomery Manuscripts,* Book 3, p. 92.

[63] *Pennsylvania Gazette,* April 26, 1786.

[64] Box on Iron Industry, *Miscellaneous Manuscripts,* Mortgage Book G, p. 299. Historical Society of Pennsylvania.

[65] *Berks County Pleadings, op. cit.,* 1788.

[66] Morton L. Montgomery, *History of Berks County in Pennsylvania* (Philadelphia : Evorts, Peck and Richards, 1886), p. 89.

and wishes the legislature to substantiate the said bankruptcy, —your committee having duly considered the circumstances, are of opinion that the legislature have nothing to do in the business, therefore reject the petition.[67]

In 1796 James Wilson paid all the debts owed by the firm of Bird and Wilson to the Bank of North America "in notes satisfactory to the Directors."[68] This action may have relieved some of the pressure on Bird, because he was back in Berks County in 1796[69] for a short stay. Two letters written by him from Rutherford County, North Carolina on June 1, 1807, revealed much of his life and position in the South. One was written to Dr. Benjamin Rush of Philadelphia and indicated a hope of recovering his fortune. In it he asserted:

> . . . I was Bankrupt by the Vile unnatural war, and never has been Able to get anything of Acct. in my hands since . . . There is no doubt my principle ruin, was by the Warr and Depretiation . . . I had three Nagroes, one of which Died, the other Two I was obliged to sell . . . They brought there Value, but the land would not bring a quarter of the Value, so I thought it most prudent, to sell them, as the Land would not dye. If all my friends and acquaintance would send as much, as will buy three Nagroes, as I still hold my land, I can get along, the Laybourers here will do Nothing, there is no getting a long with them . . . You have I expect a number of welthy acquaintance . . . If they are Informed that I have been a friendly Man, and a good Whig, and ruined by the Warr, they will give me a lift.

Dr. Rush wrote on the back of the letter: "declined soliciting relief for him as all his friends of 1776 were dead or reduced."[70]

The second letter was addressed to Mathew Brooke, who was by this time one of the partners at Hopewell Furnace, pleading:

[67] *Colonial and State Records of North Carolina* (Vol. XXI; Department of Archives and History, Raleigh, North Carolina), pp. 933–934. Photocopy at Hopewell Village Library.
[68] *Montgomery Manuscripts*, book 1, p. 80.
[69] *Berks County Deed Books* 15, pp. 216, 382; 20, p. 139.
[70] *Dr. Benjamin Rush Collection*, Vol. B2–2, p. 10. Historical Society of Pennsylvania.

It is long since I have heard from Penn[a] and my lims are so Faled, that I am under the Necessity of moveing on Cruches, and Cannot ride on Horseback, so I think, I shall never see Penn[a] any more, when I was last there by the Best observations I could make, you and your sister Mrs. Buckley, shewed the most friendly countnance to me, and seem[d] to feel the most sensibly, for my situation, then any others I met with in the state—I wrote to Mr. Coleman [probably Robert Coleman of Cornwall Furnace] two years ago or near it, but he has never answered, I shall not think well of the Iron masters, when they come to know my Situation, if they do not fall on some mode, in some measure, to relieve me, either by lone, or other wise, they know I was Ruined, by the Warr, it was not, Drunkenness, Idleness, or want of Industry, that I was ruined, and Labour, cannot be had, in this Country, or I should have done very well, small as my Capital was, but I have been unfortunate, whether, for want of sence or what, I cannot say, with all that, if I had had, 10 or 12 Negres to have kept a long the Business, I should have done well—Can I prevale on you to spend a little time for me by going to the Iron Masters, who is now, I am told grown Verry welthy, in general to get me a poor Cripple along and not be quite reduced to Beggery—The person I expect will hand you this is a neighbor of mine . . . who will bring your answer. . . ."[71]

There was no indication what reply was made to this letter. Mark Bird died in 1816 and was buried in the cemetery of the Concord Baptist Church near Bostic, North Carolina.[72] The Bird family connection with Hopewell was revived very briefly when Mark's son George Bird visited the Furnace on June 9, 1847, and was presented with $25.[73]

Hopewell Furnace should have enjoyed prosperity in the twelve years after its sale to Morris and Old. This was a prosperous period for the iron industry. Many old furnaces were being reopened and new ones erected.[74] Hopewell, with

[71] *Brooke Family Papers,* Historical Society of Berks County, Mark Bird to Mathew Brooke, June 1, 1807.
[72] *Kemper Papers,* Genealogical Notes. Hopewell Village Library.
[73] SM 31, p. 34.
[74] Victor S. Clark, *History of Manufactures in the United States, 1607–1860* (Vol. I; New York, Peter Smith, 1949), p. 500.

post-war production costs about the same as those at Warwick Furnace and only a little higher than costs at Cornwall Furnace,[75] was the second largest of the fourteen Pennsylvania furnaces in 1789 with a listed capacity of 700 tons annually.[76] But this was an uncertain period for the Furnace, and the number of changes of owners indicated business troubles. Absentee ownership may have been one of the problems.

In 1790 Cadwallader Morris sold his share in the furnace to his brother Benjamin. A year later Benjamin Morris bought the share of James Old to become the sole owner of Hopewell Furnace.[77] But James Old had not lost interest in Hopewell, for two years later he bought it from Benjamin Morris for £14,000 in gold or silver money of Pennsylvania. Payment was to have been made in four annual installments.[78] As this price was more than $37,000, Hopewell was a valuable property despite its problems.

Old may not have intended to operate the furnace, for two months later he sold it to James Wilson for £2,000 down payment and a mortgage in the amount of £11,901 9s. 6d.[79] Since Wilson also acquired the Birdsboro Forge in the same year,[80] his chief interest in Hopewell was as a source of pig iron for his forges. Not intending to manage these properties personally, he entered into an agreement with three men, John Lewis Barde of Berks County, John René Barde of Philadelphia and Paul Henry Mallet Prevost of New Jersey, to

[75] Samuel Gustof Hamerlin, *Report About the Mines in the United States, 1783* (Philadelphia: John Morton Memorial Museum, 1931), p. 67.
[76] John B. Pearse, *A Concise History of the Iron Manufacture of the American Colonies up to the Revolution and of Pennsylvania Until the Present Time* (Philadelphia: Allen, Lane and Scott, 1876), p. 88.
[77] *Hopewell Village Cataloged Documents,* 8730407, "Brief of Title of Hopewell Property." (The catalogued collections of some 8000 documents at Hopewell Village are identified by number which represents the date on the document. The above number means 1873, April 7. Subsequent references to these documents will use this numbering system.)
[78] *Montgomery Manuscripts,* "Indenture for sale of Hopewell Furnace," December 1, 1793.
[79] *Brooke Family Papers,* Mortgage from Wilson to Old, February 3, 1794. Berks County Historical Society.
[80] John C. Wetzel, *200th Anniversary of Birdsboro, Pennsylvania* (Birdsboro: The Executive Committee, 1940), p. 77.

lease ". . . All . . . the said James Wilson's Works called Hopewell Furnace, Birdsborough Forges and Gibraltar Forges and the Messuages, Mills, Plantations or Tracts or Pieces of land thereunto belonging. . . ." Wilson reserved for his own use a house and thirty acres of land. The lessees agreed to furnish at least eight hundred tons of cast iron from the furnace each year which Wilson contracted to buy at a price of six pounds per ton of pig iron, £9 10s. per ton for "country and forge castings" and £14 per ton for "hollow ware or flask work." If Wilson should default, the partners were free to sell iron at the market price.[81]

Once again floods ravaged Birdsboro Forge in the periodic overflow of Hay Creek in 1795. Hopewell Furnace escaped at this time, but the damage to the forge property weakened Wilson's financial position.[82] In 1796 he sold the forges and 2,200 acres of land to John Lewis Barde.[83] Later that year the following advertisement appeared in a Reading newspaper:

Sheriffs Sale
. . . Sale by *Public Vendue,* . . . on Monday the Seventh Day of November next, at Two o'Clock in the Afternoon, at the House of George Flieger Innkeeper in the Borough of Reading and the County of Berks, viz.
All those Tenements, Messuages, and Furnace for casting of Iron commonly called or known by the Name of Hopewell Furnace, with the lands appertinent thereto, situate in the Townships of Union and Caernarvon, in the County aforesaid, containing About Four Thousand Acres . . . seized and taken in the Execution as Late the Estate of James Wilson Esqr.[84]

Wilson did not long survive the failure of his businesses. He moved to New Jersey in 1797 to avoid arrest for debt, and early the next year moved to Edenton, North Carolina where

---

[81] HV 7950501A, Lease Agreement.
[82] *Gratz Collection, American Clergy,* Case 9, Box 23, Historical Society of Pennsylvania. Letter from Bird Wilson in Birdsboro to William Wilson in Philadelphia, n. d.
[83] Montgomery, *History of Berks County,* op. cit., p. 894.
[84] *The Weekly Advertiser,* (Reading, Pennsylvania), October 15, 1796.

he died on August 21, 1798.[85] His wife wrote concerning his last days, ". . . his mind had been in such a state for the last six months, harassed and perplexed, that it was more than he could possibly bear, and brought on a violent nervous fever. . . ."[86]

James Old purchased Hopewell Furnace for a third time, and again it was involved in a financial failure. A notice appeared in December 1799 that Sheriff Nicholas Dick would sell on January 6, 1800, "that well known Estate called Hopewell Furnace with the Mine and Lands appurtenant containing upwards of Three Thousand Acres of Land . . . the property of James Old."[87]

During the time between these two sheriff's sales, Hopewell was under the active management of John Bishop[88] and Mathew Brooke.[89] At the sale in 1800 the Hopewell Furnace property was purchased by Benjamin Morris once more.[90] Later in the year Morris sold it to a partnership consisting of Daniel Buckley of Lancaster County and his two brothers-in-law Thomas Brooke of Montgomery County and Mathew Brooke, Junior of Berks County.[91]

Now after so many changes of ownership, several sheriff's sales and the financial ruin of at least three of its owners, Hopewell had come into the possession of the Buckley and Brooke families who would nourish it through many lean years and at last reap a rich reward from its prosperous period of production. Hopewell remained in the possession of descendants of these men until the property was sold to the United States Government in the 1930's.

[85] *Dictionary of American Biography,* "James Wilson" (Volume XX; New York: Scribners, 1936), pp. 326–330.
[86] *James Wilson Papers,* Business Correspondence, Historical Society of Pennsylvania, Volume 6, p. 12.
[87] *Brooke Family Papers,* Copy of Notice of Sheriff's Sale.
[88] HV 7980603, Farm Agreement.
[89] *Montgomery Manuscripts,* book 3, p. 46.
[90] Berks County Prothonotory Office, *Old Book* 2, p. 162.
[91] *Berks County Deed Book* 17, p. 219.

2   Growth to Prosperity, 1800-1845

THE NEW PARTNERSHIP OF DANIEL BUCKLEY, THOMAS Brooke and Mathew Brooke, Junior, provided active and personal management for Hopewell Furnace. Except for a few years during the first decade of their ownership, a member of one of these families was manager in residence at the "Big House," overseeing Furnace operation for more than half a century. Thomas Brooke's son Clement held this place for forty years, and it was he who finally proved that Hopewell could be made a profitable enterprise.

Success was not immediate for the new owners. They were plagued by debt, general business conditions and legal contest to protect title to the land they had bought. During one period of more than seven years the furnace hearth was cold, and little more than maintenance work was conducted at Hopewell. When the furnace was put back in blast, it was hampered by the business panic beginning in 1819. One law suit was contested for a quarter of a century before the courts affirmed the Buckley-Brooke title. Prosperity followed these troubled times, and for twenty years Hopewell Furnace played its part in the rapid expansion of the charcoal iron industry of

Daniel Buckley, Hopewell Partner 1800–1828

Pennsylvania. Then a new threat came from technological advances in iron-making.

The deed from Benjamin Morris and his wife Francis to Buckley and Brooke listed seven different tracts of land with a total area of about 5,360 acres. Among these were the Birdstown and Jones Good Luck mines. The deed mentioned that possession was given, in addition to land, to ". . . all houses—outhouses — buildings — improvements — mines — minerals, quarries—woods—waters—watercourses— rights, liberties, etc."[1] The purchase price was £10,000.

The new owners made extensive alterations in the furnace area. Beside rebuilding the hearth walls, they changed the direction of the original north-south water wheel to one running east-west. The west headrace was built to bring water from French Creek and thus supplement the older east headrace. A new "colehaus" for the storage of charcoal was constructed. This was the earliest mention in the furnace books of such a structure at Hopewell although possibly an older one was being replaced.[2]

In order that the purchasers might have a definite record of what they had bought beside land and buildings, an appraisement of movable property was made by Robert May, Thomas Bull and John Buckley. It was also possible that these items belonged to John Bishop, manager under James Old, and were bought from him in a separate transaction. Among the items listed were the following:

One Bay hors and gairs combleat
1 Rone fifth hors
1 Bay hind hors
1 Sarl mare
One Wagon and Body all Readey to hidch in to hale mine
Black Backer Team
Foylan Team

[1] *Berks County Deed Book* 17, p. 219 ff.
[2] Richard P. Donahoe, "The Charcoal House and Shed, Hopewell Village National Historic Site" (unpublished study, 1956). Hopewell Village Library.

About 11 tons of hay
437 bundles of straw
6 cows and 2 heffers
10 hogs
125 tons of ore on the bank
25 loads of lime
90 coal baskets
2 2/3 hogsheads of Beef wt. 17½ hundred
200 lb. Borck
1 stelyard
2 Coal Barows and one Bank borrow
New coal body without iron and one old one with iron
1 large woden skayles
About ½ bbl of Tar
1 Timber Schain wt. 42 lb.
6 Peces of furnace tuls
Leatel moal weight about one hundred
Worck man Beds
85 Patterns of wood
Other Patterns, Suntry furnace tuls, 17 mine Baskets
3 wire Riddle, 3 old hand Belleses
Pair woffel mole
1 Potters Brush
3 Weel Borows more than half worn at mine hols
3 picks
3 shuffels
1 sledch
1 Crow Bare
1 Coberd in Room
5 old winser chars
1 Dresser and his Contents
2 Buckets
1 Tup
1 Coal Raike
1 Dung forck and pidch forck
1 Pat lock
1 Load of Pot sand—2 loads of sand stone
10 stofs and one franklin
1909 cords wood in Rank
6 loads mine

There were many more items, but "the sums adtet all together" totaled £223 19s. 2½d.[3] With some use of phonics and a little application of German, it is possible to get from this list an impression of the complex operations which constituted a little rural iron foundry and its auxiliary agencies.

On July 19, 1800, Mathew Brooke paid to one Frederick Reikard $400 "on acct of Stock at Hopewell" and received a receipt signed by John Bishop.[4] The Furnance books also showed that on March 10, 1803, John Bishop was paid "for Stock" the sum of £1200 4d. These sums did not quite cover the appraised total but came close to doing so.

The purchase price paid to Morris for the furnace was paid almost entirely in bonds for future redemption. Payments on these bonds constituted a complex of transactions over many years. Interest mounted. Bonds were transferred to other owners. Payments were made from time to time until 1806, and then stopped except for redemption of one bond and interest to George Kerst in 1810.[5] Five years later Mark John Biddle threatened to go to court to collect about $122.00 due him on a Hopewell bond.[6]

In 1816 when the Furnace was being readied to resume operation after a long shutdown, it was necessary to make some settlements with creditors. The following summary of the payments and amounts due was prepared at that time:

Bonds outstanding April 1, 1800	£21,437.33
Paid to Sept. 24, 1806	13,300.00
Paid interest to Jan. 10, 1806	956.00
"Deduct for a tract of Land not recovered from Mathias Kaler–239 acres @ $6"	1,434.00
Interest total to October 1, 1806	7,801.21
Payments in 1805 and 1806	13,300.00
Balance due Sept. 24, 1806	13,581.16
Interest from Oct. 1, 1806 to Jan. 10, 1816	7,560.00

[3] *Brooke Family Papers*, Appraisement of John Bishop at Hopewell to Brooke and Buckley, 1800–March 20.
[4] *Brooke Family Papers*, Receipt.
[5] HV 8100121A.
[6] HV 8150116.

Paid on Jan. 10, 1816	8,500.00
Balance Due	12,641.16
Paid on Feb. 2, 1816	8,000.00[7]

Finances were a worry to the partners and a threat to the continued operation of the furnace. In the spring of 1802 Daniel Buckley wrote to Mathew Brooke.

> Mathew Davis[8] has been here and has let me know his Situation at the furnace Respecting Money it is Bad but not at all different from mine here [Brooke Forge in Lancaster County] it is with the utmost Difficulty I can get as much money as will keep off the Constable . . .
> Whether the furnace Blows or not altogether Depends upon you and Thomas as you have there all the former Produce of it . . .[9]

A month later Buckley wrote again to report on a trip to Lancaster where he had proposed a partnership to "Mr. Grubb," who it was hoped would put some cash into the business. He had also made a similar proposal to William Coleman. He cautioned Brooke to keep these negotiations very quiet as Grubb and Coleman were bitter rivals.[10] Nothing came of these hopes. A year later the same Coleman refused to give Buckley and Brooke any more pig iron from Cornwall Furnace until they paid for what they had already received.[11]

The Furnace was probably losing money at this time. A study of labor costs for the years 1805–1807 shows that the total value of the iron produced in two blasts was less then $1,000 more than wages and salaries paid. Other expenses would certainly have netted an operating loss.[12]

Notations by the Clerk in 1803 indicated trouble at the

[7] HV 8160110A, 8160110B, 8160110C, 8160110D, 8160205.
[8] Davis was employed to manage the Furnace after Thomas Brooke had been manager in 1800–1801.
[9] HV 8020418.
[10] HV 8020520. "Mr. Grubb" was probably ironmaster Henry B. Grubb.
[11] *Brooke Family Papers*, Wm. Coleman to Buckley and Brooke, July 22, 1803.
[12] See Appendix B.

furnace and probably with the founder as well : "August 12
. . . This day at 2 o'clock quit Putting mine on the Furnace
working bad." The blast was back in after a new hearth was
installed. Seventeen days were lost. In the interim Frederick
Meck agreed to blow the furnace,[13] replacing William Templin
as founder. A possible explanation for the change was this
observation, "This day WM Templer [sic] went hoam not fit
to work."[14] This wording was often used in the clerk's books
when a workman came on the job drunk. Meck had been
founder at nearby Changewater Furnace.[15] In August of 1804
the furnace had to be stopped again for one week because of
malfunction.[16]

The dam was a source of difficulty in 1807 when it was
broken by a flood on April 29. Repairs were begun, but another break took place on July 27. Two months later lightning
struck the dam wall and knocked it to the bottom.[17]

The partners maintained a faith in the eventual success of
Hopewell through this discouraging period. In 1803 they built
a log house[18] and in 1806 a stone tenant house and a spring
house.[19]

An air of excitement and expectancy surrounded the beginning of a blast. Final repairs were rushed to get back into
operation as soon as possible. Men were taken from other jobs
to facilitate the work. Here was the sequence of events which
led to the beginning of the blast of 1805 :

April 23—Millwright began work on the wheel in the
           afternoon.
           C. Remley reported to dress the bellows.
May   4—The millwright finished the furnace wheel.
May   5—Put fire to the Furnace about 7 o'clock and 40
           Minnets in the Evening.

[13] SM 1, p. 36.
[14] Ibid., p. 37.
[15] Ibid., p. 39.
[16] Ibid., p. 59.
[17] SM 45, under dates April 29, May 22, July 27, September 14, 1807.
[18] SM 2, p. 104.
[19] SM 4, p. 127.

May   7—Put Mine on the Furnace about 9 O'clock in the
       Morning in expectation of a prosperous Blast.
       Wind east SE.
May   9—This Morning about 6 O'clock and 40 Minnets
       Blew.[20]

The Furnace business continued but in a most precarious
condition in 1807 and 1808. There were numerous letters to
the partners demanding money for unpaid bills and some
threats of suits to collect.[21] Daniel Buckley wrote to Mathew
Brooke on December 22, 1808 that he had discussed with
". . . Mr. Tench Cox the possibility of entering a bid for
making cannon balls from 4 lb. to 32 lb." Buckley suggested
that they place a bid; and if they were to get a contract,
". . . it might answer to make another Blast at hopewell if not
we may be no worse."[22]

This attempt must have failed because Hopewell Furnace
was out of blast from 1808 to 1816. Activity at the village was
sharply reduced. Peter Turner, a Negro teamster, drew his
wages for hauling and for farm work. Mathew Brooke,
manager, and Frederisk Meck, founder, were paid their wages
to date. Meck later did some wood-cutting and hauling of
mine.[23] Wages from 1809 forward were usually for work
which was essentially maintenance. The Birdsboro Forge books
showed that some Hopewell men were given employment elsewhere by the Buckley and Brooke Company, included were:
Adam Johnston, Thomas Cuthbert, Thomas Rutherford,
George North, George Moyers, Henry Jacobs, John Richards,
Samuel Richards, Philip Shaffer and Henry Minker. Among
these were several miners, a molder and a blacksmith. Henry
Jacobs was a Negro laborer.[24] With Hopewell out of blast, the
forge found it necessary to turn to other sources for its pig iron.
One supplier was William Coleman at Cornwall and Elizabeth

[20] SM 1, May 4–9, 1805.
[21] Brooke Family Papers for these years.
[22] Brooke Family Papers.
[23] SM 5, p. 78–109; SM 4, p. 235.
[24] Birdsboro Forge Time Book, 1809–1810. Hopewell Village Library.

M. Brooke Buckley, Hopewell Partner 1827–1853

Furnaces.[25] Mt. Vernon Furnace exchanged pig iron for nails.[26]

The furnace store closed out its business in food and cloth early in 1809. The last normal day of activity at the store was December 16, 1808. In January, February, and March of 1809 there were only 45 purchases noted and nothing more after that except some cast iron items. The smith shop also stopped its active business of horse-shoeing and farm-machine repairing.[27]

The shutdown of the furnace left many workers with wages due them. These were settled in many ways. Some got cash or store goods from Hampton Forge, another Buckley-Brooke operation. Nicholas Hunter, Robert Gilmore and John Benson, all of them miners, settled their accounts by living in houses at the mines and paying no rent until their accounts were evened.[28] Thomas Wynn sued to collect his account and was paid his wages plus court costs by Hampton Forge on May 12, 1812.[29]

Laverty and McFarland, wholesalers, had a balance due to them when the store closed in the amount of £381 15s. This debt was also paid by Hampton Forge in three installments over the next three years.[30] Hampton Forge accounts paid many Hopewell bills, including taxes and interest on bonds in an apparent effort of the partners to prevent loss of Hopewell by sheriff's sale. The Hopewell ledger for these years closed with the note for November 9, 1812, that Hopewell Furnace owed Hampton Forge $25,507.35.[31]

Hampton Forge received in return some iron from the only industrial activity which continued at Hopewell Furnace, the operation of a stamping mill. This machine was erected in

[25] *Brooke Family Papers*, Wm. Coleman to Buckley and Brooke, 1810, Several Letters.
[26] *Ibid.*, H. B. Grubb to Buckley and Brooke, October 13, 1809.
[27] SM 4, pp. 251–254.
[28] SM 5, pp. 68, 84, 92.
[29] SM 5, p. 56.
[30] SM 5, p. 95.
[31] SM 5, p. 133.

Clement Brooke, Hopewell Manager 1816–1848, Partner 1827–1861

1805 at a cost of a little more than $100[32] to crush pieces of slag in order that beads of iron might be recovered. Clement Brooke was given the job of running the stamping mill for at least the period from 1809 to 1814.[33] Good iron was obtained from the stamping mill, according to Daniel Buckley, who wrote Mathew Brooke on February 23, 1808, "Pray have the stamping mill repaired and let it go on with Spirit, as that stamt stuff would Impove the Quality of the Iron . . . I would be glad to have some of it . . . and when it can be got with so little trouble why is it neglected?"[34] The price received for the

[32] SM 2, July 22, 1805.
[33] *Hopewell Papers*, Buckley and Brooke a/c with Clement Brooke, 1809–1814. Hopewell Village Library.
[34] HV 8080223.

stamped iron varied from $10 per ton to $20 per ton, with Hampton Forge buying most of it at $18 per ton.[35] As late as 1816 Edward Hughes was paid for running the stamping mill.[36]

Why did Hopewell Furnace close its business? Why was it not making iron during the War of 1812 when the demand was great? The general business conditions, financial problems and technical difficulties were certainly a part of the cause. But perhaps the most compelling reason was the one recorded in a notation made by a lawyer for the Buckley and Brooke Company. He placed the blame for the Furnace's problems on the law suits in which the partners had tried to defend their land titles. He declared that:

> The ejectment . . . claim was not terminated after re-peated tryals till 1815. The defendants during the term from the fall of 1808 to which time, was prevented from the use of the furnace for want of sufficient wood, and were oblidged to expend large sums of money to defend and carry on the tryals against the Penn Claim.

> During which time the works etc. went into decay and after the Decision of the cause Cost near $8000 to repair before the furnace could be of any use.[37]

The Penn Claim case referred to in this note was one of a great many suits at law which involved the Hopewell partners for years after they assumed ownership. Some were minor actions to recover wages, to collect tavern or grocery bills, and for trespass or damage suits. The court records do not disclose the nature of many of these suits.[38] There were, however, three cases which dragged on for many years and involved major claims against Hopewell property.

In the April,1801, term of the Berks County Court Matthias

[35] HV 8097227; 8140321; SM 4, p. 241; 8160416.
[36] SM 9, p. 137.
[37] *Brooke Family Papers.* "Memorandum: Points to be made and proven at the Reading Court, April, 1818."
[38] *Berks County Court Appearances Dockets,* April, 1800–April, 1811.

Edward S. Buckley, Hopewell Partner 1853–1895

Kahler challenged the title of a part of the Hopewell lands and received a verdict to eject Buckley and Brooke from 50 acres of arable and 300 acres of wood land in Union Township.[39] The defendants appealed the case. In 1806 Kahler asked for arbitrators.[40] Four years later the matter was adjudged by five men in favor of Kahler, and again Mathew Brooke appealed.[41] The final verdict awarded Kahler 239 acres of woodland.[42]

Daniel Buckley's reaction to the outcome of the Kahler action was noted in a letter to Mathew Brooke while this final appeal was still pending:

> I observe you have not suceeded in Kellers [sic] Suit and I think it very proper to Renew the Suit . . . God only knows what [wil]l be the Consequences . . . I am endeavoring to reconcile myself to the most Disastrous Consequences . . . my Business ever since I have been concerned in Berks County has been going Backwards and unless someting meraculous turns up I fear I shall be Ruined . . . My mind has almost sunk under my Trouble. . . .[43]

A complex suit called *Leasee of John Penn and Richard Penn Esqr v. Mathew Brooke* ("Penn Claims Case") tied up the use of woodland and was blamed for the inability of Hopewell Furnace to operate until title was cleared, as noted earlier in this chapter. This claim was entered on behalf of Warwick Furnace owners for "one house, one barn, and one thousand acres of land with the appurtenances situate in Union Township . . ."[44] The argument involved the disputed wording of an old grant from the Penns to Reading Furnace on September 14, 1742. A jury decided in favor of the defendant in 1809, and the judge upheld this decision on appeal in 1811. But further appeals delayed settlement until 1815.[45]

[39] *Berks County Court Pleadings,* August, 1800–September, 1801.
[40] *Ibid.,* January, 1806, Number 74.
[41] *Berks County Court Records,* Term of January, 1806–July, 1810.
[42] *Berks County Court Pleadings,* January, 1810–May, 1813.
[43] HV 8110206.
[44] *Berks County Court Pleadings and Miscellaneous Old Papers,* 1752–1800.
[45] *Ibid.,* 1802–1817.

The case with the record for continuance was one referred
to as the *Bishop-Smith Case*. John Bishop had been manager
of Hopewell Furnance before its purchase by Buckley and
Brooke, and John Smith was the manager of Dale and Joanna
Furnaces. They probably wished to get control of Hopewell
Furnance, and certainly they wanted a large tract of woodland for the use of Joanna Furnace. The first intimation of
trouble from this quarter appeared in a letter from Daniel
Buckley to Mathew Brooke in May, 1802 :

> . . . Mr. Morris and those who hold our Bonds have sold
> them to a Company of whom Bull Smith at Joanna and Smith
> the Cashier of the Bank of Pennsylvania and Frazier the
> Lawyer of Phila^d are some of them and that Mr. Morris has
> turned against us to favor them and keep the land not sold at
> Sherrifs sale. Should these things be true I think that the Idea
> of Just Dealings is Departed from him, and that we must
> Imediately take some measures to counteract their Inten-
> tions . . .[46]

On the same day this letter was written, Bishop and Smith
purchased Hopewell bonds from Benjamin Morris. Smith then
ordered Hopewell workers to avoid trespassing on land
claimed by Joanna Furnace, and Mathew Brooke assumed
responsibility for any of his workmen who cut wood or dug
for ore in the disputed area.[47] Bishop and Smith announced the
sale of 1876 acres of land which had been part of the Hopewell Furnace property and then bid it in for themselves on
June 18, 1802. Buckley and Brooke gave public notice at the
sale of their claim to the land and offered to pay all money
owed to Bishop and Smith ". . . Provided Bishop and Smith
would convey all the lands to which the[y] pretended claim
and complete our title."[48] Three days later Bishop and Smith
sent the sheriff to Hopewell to levy on personal property of
Buckley and Brooke, but Sheriff Nicholas Dick refused to

[46] HV 8020510.

[47] *Brooke Family Papers,* Draft of Papers Relating to Jones Mine Hole.

[48] *Ibid.,* Memorandum : Points to be made and proven at the Reading
Court, April, 1818.

make the levy until Mathew Brooke had a chance to talk to him.[49] However, on June 23 he seized 50 tons of pig iron, 4 teams with wagons, 10 head of "Horned cattle" and 3,000 cords of wood. The total value was £2,535.[50]

In the autumn the dispute moved into court with a suit in ejectment from 1876 acres in Union, Robeson and Caernarvon Townships of Berks County. Mathew Brooke was ordered to appear before the court and present any claims he had to the property.[51] No settlement was reached at this time. In 1805 Buckley wrote to Mathew Brooke:

> . . . I have had several Conversations with Mr. Frazier on the Hopewell Business. . . . He offers to Extinguish the Claim of Bishop Smith and Co to the part of the Estate put in Dispute Provided that the money Remaining due, which he says by his Calculating amounts to $10,440—or something more, be paid in three Equal parts . . . within the next year.[52]

A month later Buckley wrote that he was convinced that the object of Bishop and Smith was to get control of the Hopewell property. He urged his partner to raise all the money he could to pay off the bonds.[53] Some payment was evidently made, as it was noted on January 1, 1807, "Paid Bishop and Smith at sundry times £2743–2/6."[54]

Soon after this, all payment on the bonds was suspended until settlement was reached on the title to the disputed land. In 1815 Buckley and Brooke were trying for some kind of decision so they could reopen the Furnace. Smith and Bishop had both died recently, and there was apparently more hope of a settlement with the heirs. Buckley wrote on September 15, 1815:

[49] *Ibid.*, William Brown to Mathew Brooke, June 21, 1802.
[50] *Ibid.*, Sheriff's Levy, June 23, 1802.
[51] *Hopewell Papers,* Notice of Suit in Berks County Court.
[52] *Brooke Family Papers,* Daniel Buckley to Mathew Brooke, February 18, 1805.
[53] *Ibid.*, March 20, 1805.
[54] SM 4, p. 132.

". . . As the tryal of the Dispute about the Hopewell property will I suppose soon come on I have sent Clement over to make Inquiry of Thomas Smith what mesures he is likely to take to have the Business terminated. Clement is not much engaged at this time I wish that he might Employ himself in Endeavouring to Descover which of the tracts have not been patented . . . Any other Business which you may think Clement can be of service at . . . you will Inform him of and he will attend to it.[55]

There were numerous references to this action in the Berks County Court in the years 1816–1818. In November of the latter year a jury ruled in favor of Buckley and Brooke.[56] The case was appealed, and the courts ruled again for them in an application for a writ of mandamus in 1820.[57] Another appeal was tried in the Pennsylvania Supreme Court sitting in Lancaster in May 1824. James Buchanan was the lawyer for the Bishop and Smith Estates and the firm of Baird and Hopkins represented Buckley and Brooke.[58]

The summary of the evidence presented to the Supreme Court gave a review of the entire dispute. It showed that the title given by Benjamin Morris to part of the land was disputed by Matthias Keller (sic) and others. In 1806 Buckley and Brooke brought an action of ejectment against Keller and lost. They then refused to pay the bonds, representing a mortgage on the property, held by John Bishop and John Smith until there should have been an adjustment in the purchase price by Morris. The basis of this action was that Morris had not given a valid title to all of the lands. Morris, acting for the executors of Bishop and Smith, brought action against Buckley and Brooke to collect the principal and interest on the bonds. But the Supreme Court upheld the decision of the Berks County Court in favor of Buckley and Brooke.[59]

[55] Brooke Family Papers. Daniel Buckley to Mathew Brooke.
[56] Berks County Court Appearance Docket, 1815–1817.
[57] Hopewell Papers, Sam Barde to Daniel Buckley, May 21, 1820.
[58] Thomas Sergant and William Rawle (Editors), Reports of Cases Adjudged in the Supreme Court of Pennsylvania (Volume VIII; Philadelphia: Abraham Small, 1824), p. 211–214.
[59] Ibid., Volume IX, pp. 168–176.

The *Bishop-Smith Case* was apparently closed for all time by this action, but a curious revival came seventy years later. Edward S. Buckley planned to sell his interest in Hopewell in 1895 and discovered that there was an unsatisfied mortgage for £9,000 standing on record against Hopewell Estates for the purchase money in 1800. He had the record cleared by the county court.[60]

On March 20, 1816, business began again at Hopewell, at least in the store. It is not clear exactly when the furnace was put back in blast. But in July a letter from a customer stated, "Mr. Buckley was to let us know whether he could not supply our whole quantity now he has the furnace in blast . . ."[61] And in September Amos H. Slaymaker of Columbia wrote that he had Hopewell stoves in his store.[62] A new bookkeeping series began with Journal A, and the first two entries on March 20, 1816 read :

Paid for two a/c Books	4.00
Paid M. Richards Collector for Lisence	15.00

There followed then a number of entries for the sale of store goods.[63]

The postwar market for iron was good. In 1815 charcoal pig iron sold for an average price of $53.75.[64] This price may have been one of the biggest inducements for putting the furnace in operation. Some hope for expanded molding at Hopewell was indicated by the construction in 1816 or early in 1817 of a cupola to make use of pig or scrap iron for molding.[65] There were a number of references to the cupola for several years, and then mention of it ceased. So it was probably not a great success.[66]

[60] HV 8950223, E. S. Buckley to Maria T. Clingan.
[61] *Brooke Family Papers*, Whitestone Manufacturing Company to Matthew Brooke, Esq., July 24, 1816.
[62] HV 8160906.
[63] SM 8, p. 1.
[64] Birkinbine, *Manufacture of Pig Iron in Pennsylvania, op. cit.*, p. 37.
[65] SM 7 and SM 8, *passim*.
[66] *Ibid.*

Furnace business was not very firmly established when the severe business depression of 1819 struck. In the two blasts extending from 1818 into 1820 the Furnace may have shown a small profit. The iron produced was worth about $5,000 more than the wages and salaries paid.[67] Because the journals for the depression years have disappeared, the full effects of the depression cannot be assessed; but the Furnace weathered the panic and emerged into a period of great prosperity. In the blasts of 1825–1827 the value of iron produced over labor costs was more than $36,000. For the period 1835–1837 it was about $83,000.[68] Another evidence of growth was an inventory of stock on hand at Hopewell in 1820 giving a total valuation of $27,009.34. Included in this total were furnishings for the ironmaster's home to the value of $550, store goods of $387, beef and pork of $480, thirteen horses worth $925 and eleven milch cows valued at $220.[69]

Under the shrewd management of Clement Brooke, Hopewell Furnace found new markets for its products, took advantage of the improvements in transportation and profited from the demands for new products of iron. Stoves became the largest item of Furnace produce and the source of its greatest profit.[70] New mine property and forest lands were purchased as they came on the market. Five tracts were bought at sheriff's sales in 1825 and two in 1826. Additional woodland was bought at private sales in 1832 and 1833.[71]

The death of members of the firm forced several changes in the partnership organization. The reorganized company in 1816 was known as Daniel Buckley and Company. Until the time of his death some twelve years later Daniel Buckley drew profits from the firm to the amount of $31,301.40.[72] Part of this was in pig iron sent to the Brooke Forge in Lancaster

[67] See Appendix B.
[68] *Ibid.*
[69] HV 8200307A and 8200307B.
[70] These items will be discussed in detail in subsequent chapters.
[71] SM 46, p. 64; SM 12, pp. 13, 125; SM 6, pp. 6, 36.
[72] HV 8270517.

County which was operated by his sons Clement and M. B. Buckley. On May 15, 1827, these two men were included in the Hopewell partnership, owning with their father a one-half share. The other half was shared by Clement Brooke, his brother Charles and his sisters Tacy and Ann. The firm name was then changed to Buckley and Brooke.[73] The women had a share worth $3,000 each and drew interest on that amount but probably were not regarded as active partners.[74]

The company was reorganized once more in 1831. M. Brooke Buckley paid $40,000 to the estate of his father for the half interest the Buckleys owned. Then he sold to Clement and Charles Brooke one third of the Buckley interest for $13,333.33. Each of these men now owned one third of a firm known as Clement Brooke and Company. An appraisal of the stock at the Furnace at this time placed its value at $13,562.93½, not including real estate.[75]

A survey of the iron industry made in 1829–1830 gave these statistics for Hopewell Furnace: "Employees—168; wood used—15,000 cords; produced—1,000 tons of pig iron and 700 tons of castings over past three years."[76] The Louis McLane report to the national House of Representatives in 1832 listed for Hopewell:

Men employed—168
Supposed No. of dependants—800
No. of Horses—84
Pig Metal—1,000 Tons
Castings—700 Tons[77]

The most prosperous period for Hopewell was from 1830 to 1838. In one blast from January 3, 1836, to April 10, 1837, the furnace operated continuously for 445 days and

[73] *Ibid.*
[74] SM 17, p. 2.
[75] HV 8310111.
[76] Pearse, *op. cit.*, p. 155.
[77] *Hazard's Register of Pennsylvania*, XIV, 18 (November 1, 1834), p. 350.

produced 1,169 tons of mixed castings.[78] But trouble was not
far ahead in the forms of technical improvements in the iron
business and another severe business depression beginning in
1837. Clement Brooke was full of confidence when he wrote
in 1836 :

> . . . if you wish us to furnish you with castings the next
> year, be Punctial in meeting us in Philad[a] on Tuesday the
> 3rd Jany. next, as it will be necessary for us by that time to
> know who we may Contract with, the supposed Price of stove
> Castings will be from $100 to $110 per ton . . . We presume
> castings will be very scarce in the marked next season, Pig Iron
> is now selling on the Furnace Banks from $50 to $60 per ton
> and a Supply cannot be got at any Price, we intend making a
> winter Blast and must know who we are to supply . . .[79]

Four years later the Furnace was making castings for which it
had no contract and was offering to fill orders immediately.[80]

In 1836 the Pennsylvania legislature authorized the forma-
tion of corporations to make iron with coke and in 1838 added
anthracite coal.[81] The coal-operated furnaces proved to be
advantageous, and their expansion began the period of decline
for the charcoal furnaces. The end of an era took place at
Hopewell when stove-casting was halted in 1844. Some small
castings were made after that date, but the Furnace operated
then primarily to produce pig iron. It survived on this basis for
almost forty years.

---

[78] Dennis C. Kurjack, *Hopewell Village National Historical Site* (Washington: National Park Service Handbook Series, Hamberg, 1950), p. 28.
[79] HV 8361207A.
[80] HV 8400309.
[81] Pearse, *op. cit.*, p. 272.

3 Decline, Shutdown and Survivals, 1845-1963

THE END OF STOVE-MAKING AT HOPEWELL BROUGHT MANY changes in the business. The skilled, well-paid molders left for employment elsewhere. The Furnace was dependent upon the sale of pig iron for its operation, but the expansion of the country and the Civil War created so great a demand for iron that Hopewell Furnace continued to operate at a profit for many years.

Most of the iron communities had been formed in the eighteenth century. Many of them continued well into the nineteenth, but by the middle of the latter century they were feeling the effects of the competition from larger iron works which were located nearer the centers of population. The large capitalistic enterprises and consolidations after the Civil War made it impossible for these small local iron works to continue.[1] Charcoal iron was better suited for agricultural castings, blacksmiths' bars and nails than was anthracite iron. But anthracite and coke iron were preferred by the roller-mills producing iron for the railroads and industry.[2]

[1] Bining, *Pennsylvania Iron Manufacture in the 18th Century, op. cit.*, p. 29.
[2] Harold F. Williamson (Editor), *The Growth of the American Economy* (New York: Prentice-Hall, 1946), p. 216.

There were other factors unfavorable to the small charcoal furnaces : the depletion of forests and ore deposits in the East, the development of the hot blast, the new iron ore mines in the midwest, and the movement of the center of population west of the mountains.[3] At midcentury, however, charcoal furnaces still outnumbered anthracite furnaces in Eastern Pennsylvania by 103 to 100.[4]

Hopewell, like many of its competitors of Berks and Chester Counties, gave up its attempt to compete in the market for finished products. It sold its stove patterns to a small foundry at Parkersford, and many of the Hopewell molders moved there to find employment. Others went to furnaces which were still making castings. For some years former Hopewell molders worked at Rock Furnace in Lancaster County.[5]

The Triennial Assessment in 1846 gave a view of Hopewell in this period of transition :

Owner—Clement Brooke and Company
Seated Acres—3,800
Valuation—$66,000
12 Horses—$600
6 Cattle—$72
1 Pleasure Carriage—$150
Occupation—Ironmaster
Occupation Tax valuation—$200
Yearly income above $200 @ 1% Tax. Ironmaster $500
Public Loan or Stock Owned $240
1 Gold Watch $75
14 Tenants on C. Brooke Property.
  [8 others may have been Brooke tenants and 5 single men gave Hopewell as their place of residence].[6]

Hopewell suffered a great loss from the decision of Clement Brooke to retire from active management in 1848. He re-

---

[3] Gemmell, *op. cit.,* p. 116.

[4] Victor S. Clark, *History of Manufactures in the United States* (Volume I; New York: Peter Smith, 1949), p. 329.

[5] Long, *op. cit.,* p. 9–10.

[6] *Triennial Assessment Book,* Berks County, Union Township, 1846. Berks County Court House.

Doctor Charles M. Clingan, Hopewell Manager 1849–1859

mained as a partner until his death in 1861, but after 1849 he was living in his home in Pottstown. For one year Hopewell was managed by John Church, nephew of Clement Brooke's wife, who had been the clerk under Brooke. After Church's short tenure active management was taken over by Charles M. Clingan who had married Maria Brooke six years before.[7]

In 1852 the partnership of Clement and Charles Brooke and Mathew Brooke Buckley was formally dissolved by the Court of Common Pleas of Berks County upon the petition of Clement Brooke. The reason for this action was apparently to remove Charles Brooke from the company. The Furnace valua-

[7] SM 32, *passim*.

tion was placed at $87,833.00, and Clement agreed to pay one third of that amount to each of the others. The Furnace lands were listed in various tracts which totaled 3958 acres and 123 perches.[8] Clement resold a half interest to Mathew Brooke Buckley for $43,916.50.[9] The latter died in 1853 bequeathing his share of Hopewell Furnace to his son Edward S. Buckley.[10]

Charles M. Clingan was the manager for ten years, after which he entered the banking and provision businesses in Philadelphia. He made frequent visits to Hopewell until his death in 1875, but he entrusted the supervision to hired managers.[11] Two of these last managers were John R. Shafer[12] and Harker A. Long.[13]

Clement Brooke was too good an ironmaster not to recognize the advantages of the new anthracite fuel for his furnaces. Overman, writing in 1849, asserted, ". . . good anthracite is undoubtedly the most perfect of all fuels for the manufacture of iron. Its application is simple; its hardness prevents it from falling into slack; and the small amount of hydrogen it contains makes it advantageous for the blast furnace operation."[14] The saving on labor over charcoal iron was phenomenal. In 1848 it cost $12.35 per ton for labor to produce charcoal iron,[15] but the labor cost for anthracite iron was only $2.50 per ton.[16] For the blast periods from 1851 to 1853 the labor cost at Hopewell was $15.44 per ton of pig iron.[17]

Clement Brooke had had experience with an anthracite

[8] *Berks County Deed Book* 59, p. 529.

[9] *Stokes Collection, Hopewell Papers,* Deed of Sale, December 6, 1853. Hopewell Village Library.

[10] *Berks County Deed Book* 76, p. 64.

[11] *Reading Eagle,* February 11, 1917. Article by Cyrus Fox.

[12] H. F. Bridgens and A. R. Witmer; *Atlas of Chester County, Pennsylvania* (Safe Harbor, Pennsylvania; A. R. Witmer, 1873), p. 55.

[13] HV 8761110.

[14] Frederick Overman, *The Manufacture of Iron* (Philadelphia: Henry C. Baird, 1854), p. 99.

[15] *Documents Relating to the Manufacture of Iron in Pennsylvania* (Philadelphia: Published by the General Committee of the Convention of Iron Masters, 1850), p. 90.

[16] Overman, *op. cit.,* p. 183.

[17] See Appendix B.

operation at Robesonia Furnace which he purchased in 1841 and where he helped to erect an anthracite furnace in 1845. This experience, plus the discovery in 1846 or 1847 of a large body of sulphur ore at the old Hopewell Mines, may have been the reason for the decision to build an anthracite furnace at Hopewell. Possibly Charles Brooke opposed this venture and thus precipitated the dissolution of the partnership in 1852. At any rate the new partnership built an anthracite furnace at Hopewell in 1853.[18]

The anthracite operation at Hopewell was very brief. The new ore was not usable unless mixed with other ore which was not available at Hopewell,[19] and the cost of hauling the coal from the Schuylkill Canal to the Furnace and the iron back to the canal was too great. After less than four years the furnace machinery was moved from Hopewell to Monocacy on the canal, where smelting operations began in 1857.[20] Hopewell records show that ore was hauled from 1857 to 1859 to what was at first called "the new furnace" and later "the Teresa Furnace."[21] In the latter year this furnace was sold to another firm and was then operated as the Monocacy Furnace.[22]

With this upstart rival removed, the old Hopewell charcoal furnace resumed its place as the center of industrial activity for the community. In 1850 it was listed among the cold blast charcoal furnaces with this data :

Post Office—Douglasville
Owner—Clement, Brooke and Co.
Kind of Ore used—Magnetic
Largest Product—1,150 tons
Actual Make in 1849—1,000 tons
No. of men and boys employed—80
    „ „ Oxen, horses and mules—50

[18] Benjamin J. Zerbey and Earl J. Heydinger, "Anthracite Furnace, Hopewell National Historic Site" (unpublished study, 1962). Hopewell Village Library.
[19] Wilmer W. MacElree, *Around the Boundaries of Chester County* (West Chester, Pennsylvania : Published by the Author, 1934), p. 556.
[20] Zerbey and Heydinger, *op. cit.*
[21] *Kemper Manuscripts*, "Book of Ore Hauling."
[22] *Montgomery Manuscripts*, Book I, p. 108.

Blast—Cold
Tuyeres—1
Pressure—3/4 lb
Stack—Bosh—6½ feet
          Height—30 feet
Kind of Power—Water
Kind of Metal Made—No. 1
Market for Sales—Philadelphia
Capacity—1,150 tons[23]

There was evidence that the owners continued to have faith in the old furnace in the purchase of additional tracts of land in 1849 and 1857.[24] They also may have found a new source of income in the sale of charcoal, for in 1851 Edward Gault was paid $555.45 "for hauling charcoal to the canal."[25]

The Civil War brought new activity to the charcoal-iron industry. The price of pig iron rose so rapidly that cost of production was no longer a worry. Iron which in normal times had sold for $30 per ton was bringing $80 in 1864[26] and touched $99 before it began its decline.[27] Prices remained high after the war largely because of the demands of the expanding railroads. Most Hopewell iron was purchased at this time by a Philadelphia manufacturer of railroad car wheels.[28] Because of the strain placed upon them and the need for reliability, a special quality of iron was used in casting car wheels. Uniformity of contraction was obtained by slow cooling for several days in modified annealing furnaces.[29] This casting and annealing were not done at Hopewell, however, but in Philadelphia. This new business encouraged extensive repairs to the furnace in 1869 according to this report by the clerk:

[23] *Documents Relating to the Manufacture of Iron in Pennsylvania,* op. cit.
[24] SM 31, p. 89 and SM 65, August 19, 1857.
[25] SM 32, p. 119.
[26] HV 8640629.
[27] Long, op. cit., p. 12.
[28] "Hopewell Village," *International Molders and Foundry Workers' Journal,* 94, 10 (October 1958), p. 6.
[29] Clark, op. cit., p. 504.

Repaired old Stack and put in new inwals the inwalls of new fire brick—Started on an iron ring Seven feet wide with a regular taper to the top which is twenty two inches—the new inwall was 9 inch brick backed by 12 inches of fire brick bats, and a Space of four inches between them and the Stone Wall which was filled with Sand.[30]

Another new customer was the Reading Railroad Company which agreed to try 10 tons of Hopewell iron in 1876 at $33 per ton.[31] More orders came from the railroad after this initial trial.[32]

But there were signs of approaching death for the Furnace. The Hopewell Mines were leased by the Patterson Iron Company.[33] The furnace was out of blast in 1874[34] and again in 1877–1878. In 1877 the mules were sold. But a rise in the price of iron postponed the decease and encouraged the owners to make the necessary repairs to resume operations in 1880.[35] E. S. Buckley wrote to Long:

. . . Get all the wood cut off the property that it is possible to get out by paying as much wages as any one else in the neighborhood; and blow the furnace *as early in the Spring as it may be possible to get coal made from our own wood, say by 1st of May* and keep her going until all our own coal is consumed and then blow out. Proceed steadily with this view in mind, and do not think of any project, as I have never entertained any others, and will not. In relation to wood choppers do the best you can, *but keep the men at work.* Do not let a man leave who is doing good work.[36]

During the next winter a severe cold spell froze the water wheel and forced the furnace to shut down for lack of a blast. To insure against a recurrence of this mishap, a boiler was

[30] SM 60, p. 7.
[31] HV 8760201. Edward S. Buckley to Chas. M. Clingan.
[32] SM 60, p. 201.
[33] *Jeffersonian*, West Chester, Pennsylvania, March 30, 1872.
[34] *Daily Local News*, West Chester, Pennsylvania, November 22, 1874.
[35] Long, *op. cit.*, p. 13.
[36] HV 8800214A.

installed to run a steam engine as auxiliary power to the water wheel. Water was heated in the boiler by the hot gas from the furnace stack.[37] Another technical improvement, installed in 1882, was an ore roaster to remove impurities and improve the texture of the ore for use in the furnace.[38] Buckley had opposed spending money for these improvements. "Hopewell is about 'played out,' and next years blast is probably the last she will ever make, and there is no use of spending any more money on her," he wrote.[39]

The company did not operate a store at Hopewell for some years before the furnace closed. Sally Care Boone said that she and her husband came to Hopewell in 1875 and opened a store in one of the tenant houses. Business was good so long as the furnace was in operation, but after the shutdown the villagers could not pay their bills. The Boone store closed in 1891.[40]

The last blast at the Hopewell Furnace ended on June 15, 1883. After this no more iron was produced.[41] In the year the operation ceased, the Union Township tax collector raised the assessment on the property from $58,000 to $84,600.[42] As recently as 1877 the assessment had been $32,369.[43] Buckley expressed the view that this increase was outrageous and that he intended to protest.[44]

While there might have been reason to sympathize with Mr. Buckley for an assessment which almost tripled in six years and was levied on an inactive business, the future records show that there was still much value in the Hopewell property; and

[37] Harker A. Long Interview, August 13, 1936.

[38] Franklin Kemper, "J. Lincoln Palsgrove" (unpublished study, n.d.), p. 6. Hopewell Village Library.

[39] *Kemper Manuscripts,* Edward S. Buckley to Harker A. Long, November 8, 1880.

[40] Sally Boone Interview, March 22, 1941.

[41] SM 61, p. 206.

[42] *Hopewell Papers,* Edward S. Buckley to Maria T. Clingan, April 25, 1883.

[43] SM 34, April 1, 1877.

[44] *Hopewell Papers,* Edward S. Buckley to Maria T. Clingan, April 25, 1883.

several sources of income were derived from it. As late as 1886 there were 360 tons of pig iron on hand. On September 14 of that year the Reading Railroad bought 100 tons of this at $26 per ton.[45] The Furnace books were kept until March 23, 1896. During this period there were records of the sale of pig iron, ore and wood; payments of freight bills; farm operations; rental of houses; and royalty on stone quarried on the property. The last pig iron was sold in 1888;[46] the horses and mules had gone a year earlier.[47]

At the time the furnace closed, it was owned in equal shares by Edward S. Buckley as the heir of M. Brooke Buckley and Maria T. Clingan, daughter of Clement Brooke and widow of Charles Clingan. Buckley frequently expressed a lack of hope for income from Hopewell in letters to his partner. In 1886 he said he had been spending his own money on taxes and repairs and proposed that they divide the remaining pig iron between them to realize what they could on it.[48]

Five years later he wrote of his disappointment in failing to lease ground for a stone quarry. He was not at all hopeful that a buyer of the property could be found,[49] and the next year he said he would take $25,000 for his half interest if anyone would make an offer[50] In 1894 Mrs. Clingan proposed to trade her share in two store buildings on Front Street in Philadelphia for Buckley's half of Hopewell.[51] Buckley agreed to the trade, and his part of the partnership was transferred to Mrs. Clingan's children Charles B. Clingan, Alan Hunter Clingan and A. Louise Clingan Brooke.[52]

The Clingans found a number of uses for Hopewell. The old mansion house served as a summer home until 1915. The rear wing, however, was occupied by Harker A. Long and later by

[45] *Hopewell Papers,* Record book of Maria T. Clingan.
[46] SM 61, pp. 206–241.
[47] HV 8870314.
[48] HV 8860710.
[49] HV 8911008.
[50] HV 8920219.
[51] HV 8941124.
[52] *Berks County Deed Book* 209, p. 22.

Remains of Anthracite Furnace at Hopewell Village

Nathan Care, who acted as caretakers.[53] Fence posts and rails were cut from the woodland under the direction of the Clingan sons and sold in carload lots. The records indicate that this was a major operation.[54] Charcoal was again a Hopewell product, but this time it was sold instead of being used for furnace fuel.[55]

In 1894 Richard Humphreys signed an agreement to quarry stone on Hopewell property.[56] There was no record of the extent of this quarrying. But in 1906 A. Louise C. Brooke and

[53] *Hopewell Papers,* File H 3019.
[54] HV 8980817.
[55] HV 9030928.
[56] *Hopewell Papers,* "Agreement between E. S. Brooke and Maria T. Clingan with Richard Humphreys, Jr."

her husband Edward Brooke sold quarrying rights on 3,000 acres, of which 2,829 acres were Hopewell Furnace property, to the Schuylkill Stone Company for $157,000.[57] This transaction alone justified the faith of the Clingans. In another kind of "quarrying" the Pottstown Iron Company was continuing to mine iron ore from the old Hopewell Mine. As late as 1913 a carload per day was going to the Eastern Steel Company at Pottstown.[58]

Most of the activity described involved the land and not the buildings at Hopewell Furnace. Repairs were neglected. One of the tenants described the house in which he lived as in a bad state of disrepair—fences rotting, porch falling off and roof leaking.[59] The furnace was deteriorating. Some of the machinery installed there was thought to have historical value, and Mrs. Brooke offered it to the Franklin Institute in Philadelphia. They accepted the gift, dismantled the wooden working parts and in 1930 built a shed to house them pending removal to Philadelphia. They were still at Hopewell when the National Park Service decided to restore the old furnace, and the Franklin Institute gave permission for the machinery to be reinstalled in its original place.[60]

Renewed activity came to Hopewell Village in 1935 and thereafter. The United States Government purchased about 6,000 acres of land from A. Louise Brooke and others. Mrs. Brooke received $86,970.82 for the main tract of 3,781.34 acres[61] and $11,301.62 for an additional 458.95 acres. John T. Dyer Quarry Company sold 1,217 acres for $17,211.60. There were also other smaller purchases.[62]

In 1935 two Civilian Conservation Corps camps were located in the area with a total of about 400 men. They did

[57] Berks County Deed Book 330, p. 449.
[58] West Chester (Pennsylvania) Star, November 20, 1913.
[59] HV 8990418, H. A. Care to Hunter Clingan.
[60] Roy Edgar Appleman, "Historical Report, French Creek Area" (unpublished study, n. d.). Hopewell Village Library.
[61] Berks County Deed Book 768, p. 642.
[62] Hopewell Papers, Abstract of Deeds to Hopewell Property, February 11, 1938.

repair work at Hopewell Village and constructed some road-
ways. A Works Progress Administration program was also
engaged in restoration work from 1935 to 1939.[63]

The original reasons for the government purchase of this
property were given as:

> . . . the lands are being acquired for use as a public park
> and recreational area, for the restoration of structures of
> historic interest, the conservation of natural resources, the
> preservation of scenic beauty, forestation and reforestation and
> for use in connection with the construction of certain improve-
> ments necessary and appropriate to provide public facilities
> for the purposes of the project.[64]

In 1938 a new purpose was stated for the Hopewell Furnace area:

> *Whereas* certain lands and structures in Hopewell Village,
> Pennsylvania, including the old furnace, mansion house,
> blacksmith shop, etc., by reason of their relationship to the
> colonial history of the United States, have been declared by
> the Advisory Board of National Parks, Historic Sites, Build-
> ings, and Monuments to be a historic site of National signifi-
> cance . . . *Now, therefore,* I, E. K. Burlew, Acting Secretary
> of the Interior . . . do hereby designate the following
> described lands, with the structures standing thereon, to be a
> national historic site, having the name "Hopewell Village
> National Historic Site. August 3, 1938."[65]

In 1947 the national government deeded to the Commonwealth of Pennsylvania about 5,000 acres of the land purchased and retained 848 acres for the Hopewell Village site.[66]
On this area the National Park Service has been engaged at
restoration work aimed at making the life of an old iron plan-

[63] Roy Edgar Appleman, "Memorandum Respecting the Historical and
Archeological Importance of the French Creek Recreational Demonstration Area, Pennsylvania, and the Proposal that it be made a National
Monument" (unpublished study, 1939). Hopewell Village Library.
[64] *Hopewell Papers,* Abstract of Deeds to Hopewell Property, *op. cit.*
[65] *Ibid.*
[66] *Birdsboro* (Pennsylvania) *Dispatch,* June 13, 1952.

tation come alive. In 1963 alone more than 100,000 visitors came to look and listen to the story of charcoal iron and of the people who made it. The target date for completion of the restoration is 1966.

Part Two

The Physical Village

4 The Ironmaster's Mansion

IN THE HEYDAY OF CHARCOAL IRON THE SUCCESSFUL OPERATOR
of one or more furnaces and forges was a man of affluence
and power. He lived well in the mansion, or "big house,"
which he built close enough to the iron works that he could
supervise the industrial activity of his establishment. His house
may have lacked something of the advantage of setting enjoyed by the Philadelphia merchant at his country seat or the
Southern planter in the midst of his cotton fields, but it did
not suffer by comparison in size or elegance of appointment
with the homes of other entrepreneurs of the era. A number
of the homes of the ironmasters, including the one at Hopewell Village, survive to our day as evidence of the scale of
living their occupants enjoyed.

There are differences of opinion about the quality of the
architectural style of the Hopewell mansion house. One observer called it one of the "three best examples of country homes
of the Revolutionary period in existence in Pennsylvania."[1]
Another said, "The mansion house at Hopewell is of a not
very interesting colonial style."[2] It is large, and probably it
was utilitarian in the day it was built.

Parts of this house were constructed at three different times.

[1] Cyrus Fox in the *Reading Eagle*, February 25, 1917.
[2] Appleman, "Historical Report," *op. cit.*, p. 28.

Front View of Hopewell Mansion

Northeast Corner of Hopewell Mansion, Basement Dining Area and
Bake Ovens

North Side of Hopewell Mansion, Bathroom in Frame Addition in Center

South Side of Hopewell Mansion

The northwest wing of the T-shaped house may have been built about 1771 when the furnace was constructed. The east-wing corner was probably added next, and the southwest corner last. It was possibly completed essentially in its present form by 1830, but the porches were certainly added much later.[3] The east wing may have been built in 1802 when Thomas Lloyd sold "40 logs for raising the kitchen."[4] Architect Gustavus Mang thought the rear wing was built about 1820.[5]

As it stands today, the mansion is a four-storied stone house built against the side of a hill. The door from the front porch opens into the second-floor entry hall. The rear court has direct access to the first floor. This ground floor includes three cellars, a dining room and a kitchen; the second contains four large rooms; the third consists of six bedrooms, a bath and a hallway; the fourth has two non-communicating suites of two rooms each. The building's three chimneys served seven fireplaces which are still visible and possibly two more which are no longer open on the top floor. From the entry hall a broad stairway leads to the third floor. Steep, narrow stairs join all the floors at the rear of the house. Separate service stairs also lead from the first to the second and from the third to the fourth floors at the front of the house.[6]

The original part of the house is separated from the later additions by a stone wall two feet thick extending from the basement floor to the roof. A wide, open area around the east wing lies lower than the basement floor. Its purpose was apparently to facilitate the admission of light to the basement kitchen and dining room where the molders and some other

[3] Information from National Park Service architect Norman Souder.
[4] SM 2, p. 26; SM 1, p. 13.
[5] *Kemper Manuscripts*, Report of Gustavus Mang, April, 1935. Harker Long thought this last section of the house was completed in 1849. In 1964 Archeologist Leland Abel reported to the National Park Service that physical evidence within the house indicates that it was built in three sections between 1820 and 1846. He said it could have replaced an older house on the same site.
[6] Parts of the first and second floor are open to visitors.

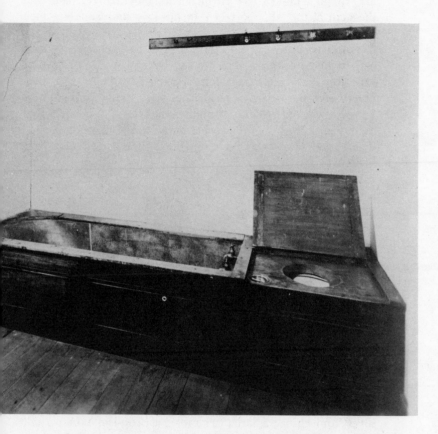

Bathroom Appointments in Hopewell Mansion

workmen ate. A ten-foot wide veranda was built across the entire west side of the house, and porches were added on each side of the rear wing.[7] A bathroom was installed in a frame addition above the north rear veranda in 1870. Probably at the same time the windows of the first story in the west wing were extended to the floor. The overall dimensions of the house

[7] Mang, *op. cit.*

are: main wing 53 feet 10 inches long by 28 feet wide and the stem of the "T," 35 feet 2 inches long and 22 feet 1 inch wide.[8]

Water was brought into the house at an early period. The earliest known date is a record for December 23, 1816, that "the Repairs acount paid John Hagen $30.70 for 168′ pipe bored and pump from spring house to house."[9] That this amount was charged to "repairs" may have indicated that there was a pipe from the spring house to the mansion earlier. The spring house was built in 1806.[10] It enclosed what one of its users declared was "one of the finest springs that ever came out of the earth."[11] At some later, but unknown, date a wooden pipeline was run from the house to a large spring about 2,000 feet away. This conduit was made by boring holes approximately two inches in diameter through the length of 16 foot to 18 foot logs, each about ten inches in diameter. A section of this old pipe was uncovered by Civilian Conservation Corps workers in the 1930's.[12] Perhaps some modernization of the water system was made in 1850 when the Furnace paid $43.80 to install "Hidraulic Ram, pipes, Etc."[13]

How were the rooms furnished? Unfortunately little information is available. Alterations would have been made with changing style, obsolescence and the taste of the several mistresses of the mansion. Violet Care remembered the southwest room as containing a large pedestal table surrounded by eight cane-seated chairs; a large chest for storage of linens, silver, and china; a large tier table; a drop-leaf table; a tall whatnot; a corner cupboard made in two parts and the parts used separately; a piano and a rocking horse which had belonged to the Clingan children.[14]

When the National Park Service was beginning its work of

[8] *Ibid.*
[9] SM 7, December 23, 1816, n. p.
[10] SM 4, December 20, 1806, n.p.
[11] *Kemper Manuscripts,* H. A. Long's Notes on Hopewell.
[12] Appleman, "Historical Report," *op. cit.,* p. 28.
[13] SM 31, p. 18.
[14] Violet Care Interview, January 15, 1941.

Bedroom Furnishings in Hopewell Mansion

restoration, J. C. Fisher Motz took advantage of an offer from the Brooke Family to purchase a large collection of furniture and furnishings which were identified by the family as having been associated with Hopewell. No government money was available; so Motz put up the necessary sum from his own funds to prevent this collection from being dispersed at public sale. He was later reimbursed by the government. Francis Brinton, an antique dealer from West Chester, established the approximate dates for the various items listed. The inventory of the Motz purchase contained the following:

Four Poster Bed	Mahogany	1860's
Double Wardrobe	,,	1850
Serving Stand	,,	?
Arrow Back Chair	Pine	1840
Wash Stand—2 Faucets	,,	1870
Double Sleigh Bed	Possibly Walnut	1850
Urn-Back Rocker	Painted	1830
Wash Stand—Faucets and 4 Drawers	Walnut	1870
Sofa—Red Plush	Mahogany	1840
Four Poster Bed	,,	1850
Sewing Stand	,,	1830's
Four Poster Bed	,,	1830's
Wardrobe	,,	1830's
Armchair	Walnut	1850's
Tilt-Top Table	Possibly Mahogany	1860's
2 Matching Wardrobes	Mahogany	1830's
Single Sleigh Bed	Possibly Walnut	1830
Spool Bed	Soft Wood	1850's
6 Chairs—Red Plush Seats	Mahogany Veneered	1830
Drop-Leaf Table	Mahogany	1815
8 Chairs—Red Plush Seats	Mahogany Veneered	?
Sideboard	Mahogany With Marble Top	?
2 Matching Sofas— Red Silk	Rosewood	1850
Whatnot	Mahogany	1850
Chest of Drawers Chippendale	Walnut	1770
Upholstered Armchair— Red Silk	Rosewood	1850
2 Matching Sofas— Ribbed Red Plush	Walnut	1840's
Mirror in Gilt Frame		1830
Whatnot—with Drawer	Mahogany	1840
Desk—with Book Cupboard	Mahogany Veneered	1840
Cradle	Mahogany	?
Cradle	Pine	?
Serving Stand—Marble Top	Mahogany	?

Sitting Room of Hopewell Mansion

Wash Stand—Marble
   Top   ,,   ?
Five Oil Paintings :
   Charles Brooke, Jr.
   Charles Brooke
   Dr. Charles Clingan
   Clement Clingan
   Mrs. Charles Clingan[15]

[15] *Hopewell Papers,* Furniture Cataloguing, D6215.

It was not possible to determine whether all of these items had been used at Hopewell. The dates indicated purchases spanning a century of occupation. By searching the Furnace record books, the following purchases of furniture for the mansion were discovered, but details were usually lacking or were too incomplete to make possible positive identification with articles on the Motz list:

August 14, 1802	6 Winser Chairs @ 11/3. Made by William Bird.	
December 5, 1802	1 Spinning Wheel	£1-2/6
August 20, 1803	A Breakfast Table	£1-17/6
November 19, 1803	1 Cupboard	60/
November 20, 1817	1 doz Chairs received last spring	$19.50
July 17, 1819	2 bed cords	$ 1.00
July 28, 1819	A spinning Wheel	$ 4.50
March 7, 1820	Furniture for Big House valued at $550.00 in furnace inventory of this date.	
October 31, 1822	Pair Andirons	$ 5.00
	Pair Tongs and Shovel	$ 3.50
	2 Candlesticks	$ 1.00
August 28, 1828	A Clock Case	$25.00
	Bureau	$12.00
April 26, 1830	Large Looking Glass	$44.00
April 27, 1830	12 Fancy Cane seat Chairs from Philadelphia	$46.00
? 1831	A Bureau	$14.00
April 23, 1832	looking glass	?
? 1835	Dining Room Table	$ 9.00
	Ward robe	$30.00
April 30, 1835	2 pair of beadsteads	$20.00
	1 doughtrough	4.00
August 12, 1841	cleaning the clock	$ 1.00
November 29, 1847	Parlor rocking chair from Philadelphia	?
March 3, 1853	Bench Table	$3.58
November 4, 1854	Sideboard	$20.00[16]

[16] Items collected from the journals and cash books for these dates.

More frequent mention was made of purchases for the dining table and of bedroom china at the Big House :

July 11, 1803	2 Qt. Decanter	8/8
	Large White pitcher	2/9
	½ doz. Knives and forks	8/3
October 6, 1803	1 doz Knives and forks	17/0
February 10, 1806	½ doz tea spoons	1/10½
	½ „ knifs and forks	10/6
January 31, 1820	Plates tumblers and Snuffers	$1.75"

Mrs. Brooke must have acquired a new set of dishes in October 1822. A bill from Patrick Ryan of Philadelphia listed the following purchases by Clement Brooke :

1 Doz handled Grecian Teas	1.50
3/4 „ blue print plates	1.05
½ Doz blue print Twifflers	.62½
½ „ „ „ Muffins	.55
1 Pitcher „ ½ gallon	.50
2 Blue print Bakers	.80
2 egd „ „	.50
3 blue „ Bowls	.56½
1 egd dish	.33
½ doz Tumblers Ground bottoms	.75
1 C C Chamber	.31¼
1 Decanter	.50
Box etc.	.31¼
	———
	$8.29½[18]

"Blue print" ware was mentioned in many of these items, and in 1825 two small pitchers were added.[19] In an archeological dig made under the direction of Archeologist Leland Abel in 1962 many pieces of Chinese-made "blue willow" patterned dinnerware were found. Perhaps these broken bits identified the "blue print" dishes bought in 1822.

Purchases continued from time to time of dishes, pottery and eating utensils :

[17] *Ibid.*
[18] HV 8221031.
[19] HV 8250615A.

March 18, 1825	6 knives and 6 forks	$2.50
May 19, 1825	Silver Spoons in City	?
May 29, 1827	1 8/11 Damask Table Cloth	$4.50
	1 „ (Nail Holes)	$2.50
	¼ Doz Napkins	1.37½

Bought of John Reed and Co., Philadelphia[20]

April 13, 1831 Bought of R. Tyndale, Philadelphia

	1 Chamber Sett	$3.00
	1 Cut Cellery	1.50
	1 Doz Cut Tumblers	2.00
	1 pr. sma. Dishes	1.00
	2 „ Muffins	5.00
	1 pr. fruit baskets	3.00
	1 sma. Ireg.	1.00
	1 Doz cup plates	.37½
	1 pr. sma. dishes on foot	1.25
	1 horsradish	.25[21]

Bought of Carey and Preston, Philadelphia

	1 Doz Silver Desart	$25.00
	1 Pair [————?] and	
	Silver B. Knives	5.00
December 4, 1823	Table Linen	$3.75
	½ Doz Tea sps	5.00

June 27, 1838 from R. Tyndale, Philadelphia

	1 Doz Canton Cups and	
	saucers	$4.50
	1 „ „ Plates	1.75
	1 „ tumblers	1.75
	1 Pr. glass dishes	3.00
	1 „ Butter Dishes	1.00
	1 „ China Cake plates	.20[22]
January 6, 1841	China Ware	$80.87
? 1841	1 Sett Bratania ware	14.00
January 29, 1850	China Ware	11.25
	Spice Box	1.25
April 29, 1850	Table linen	6.75
October 21, 1851	Table Linen	16.47[23]

[20] HV 8270529.
[21] HV 8310413A.
[22] HV 8380627.
[23] Unless otherwise identified the items are from the journals of the appropriate date.

Fireplace in Hopewell Mansion

Family Dining Room in Hopewell Mansion

Heat and light were items of cost and concern in a house as large as this one. The seven or nine fireplaces constituted the means of heating the house for much of its history. Probably when stoves became a principal article for sale by the company, one or more of these would have been installed in the mansion. Stove purchases probably did not appear on the earlier Furnace books because no cash payment was made for them. Just about the time stove-casting ended at Hopewell, a new kind of heating system must have been installed somewhere in the house. Clement Brooke bought from Francis McIlvain, Philadelphia, "Mfg. of Warm Air Furnaces,"

One 11 in. Cast Radiator and Urn	$18.00
piece of Line	1.50
2 Elbows and 2 joints of Russia Pipe	1.75[24]

Ten years later "1 Hathaway Stove" was purchased for $12.84.[25] Mrs. Clingan had heat in her bedroom radiated from a large drum through which passed the smoke pipe from a stove in the first floor dining room.[26]

Lights of many kinds were used in the house. In the southwest room a candelabra held eight candles and could be lowered to make lighting easier. The front-hall light was made of wrought iron, the sides covered with red glass. It had a small tin oil fount to hold the fuel.[27] In 1802 the Furnace purchased "3 large lantrens."[28] These might have been used for work around the furnace or barn rather than in the house. More decorative lighting appliances were bought in 1831 : "1 Astral Lamp" at $11.00, "1 Entry Lamp" at $3.50[29] and "A Lamp" $16.00.[30] The lamp purchased in 1838 for twelve and one half cents[31] and the "Kitchen Lamp, Lamp

[24] HV 8430925.
[25] SM 32, p. 140.
[26] Sally Boone Interview, March 22, 1941.
[27] Violet Care Interview, February 13, 1941.
[28] SM 2, p. 67.
[29] HV 8310413E.
[30] SM 28, p. 65.
[31] HV 8380627.

Kitchen in Hopewell Mansion

wicks and Chimneys" bought for eighty cents in 1850[32] were probably of a strictly utilitarian nature.

Since whale oil was regularly available at the village store, it was doubtless the fuel used in the lamps before the 1850's. But the march of progress was shown when the Furnace bought:

November 11, 1858   1 Carasene Lamp $2.75
                     Oil, Bottle Wicks, etc   1.42
                     One Shade   .50[33]

[32] SM 31, p. 120.
[33] SM 65, November 11, 1858, n. p.

A startling circumstance about this purchase was that it dated from the year before Colonel Edwin Drake drilled his famous pioneer oil well at Titusville.

All rooms at the Big House were papered and most were carpeted, according to the memory of one resident of the village.[34] This recollection was supported by two items for the purchase of wall paper in the 1840's and two bills for "Painting and Papering the House."[35] In the late years of Furnace operation the paper in the hallway showed English hunting scenes.[36] There were many purchases of carpet, and sometimes carpet was made for the mansion. Maria Brooke wrote to a Mr. Davis in Morgantown, "I have sent you more yarn to finish the carpet I left with you some time ago—Please weave 34 yds. full yard wide (for room) and $9\frac{1}{4}$ yds. to be $1\frac{1}{4}$ yds wide (for Entry) the same pattern that you wove for us some time ago. . . ."[37]

The windows, at least after 1830, were fitted with window shades[38] and covered with curtains.[39] The most costly of decorative touches in the house were two marble mantels. In 1829 the Furnace "paid Magers for Marble Mantle $75.00, paid for hauling and putting up $6.00."[40] Eight years later Clement Brooke reimbursed Charles W. Warnick $78.75 for a marble mantel.[41]

The Big House was not all for show or even for living quarters for the ironmaster's family. It had its part to play in the iron business as well. There was a reason, too, for its size; it was home for a considerable number of workers. There were often relatives of the family in residence, as Ann and John Church spent much of their early lives at Hopewell mansion. Maids and apprentices lived there. It is possible that the

[34] Sally Boone Interview, March 22, 1941.
[35] SM 28, pp. 18, 154; SM 31, pp. 88, 106.
[36] Violet Care Interview, February 13, 1941.
[37] HV 8321129.
[38] SM 14, p. 89 and SM 31, p. 105.
[39] SM 65, December 3, 1858, n. p.
[40] Cash Book, July 17, 1829, Berks County Historical Society.
[41] SM 21, p. 195.

Cook Stove in Hopewell Mansion

divided attic, reached by separate stairways, was used for quarters by servants of both sexes.

The censuses showed sizable groups in residence under the name of the ironmaster. In 1810 Clement Brooke was listed as having had a household of two males and four females.[42] Since at that time he was a bridegroom of two years,[43] it is unlikely that these persons were all members of his family. The population in the mansion may have reached a peak in 1830 when Brooke enumerated nine males and six females in his household. Four of the females were Negroes[44] who were doubtless maids or cooks.

The basement of the mansion served as a dining area for the single men of the community. They slept in one of the tenant houses set aside for them.[45] The molders also took their meals in the basement dining room, perhaps because it was close to their work at the cast house. They slept elsewhere. Beds were kept in the wheelwright shop for single molders or for any of them who needed a place to rest while they waited for the founder to begin casting. Some molders were married and lived at home.[46]

A rumor persisted in the village to recent times that the dirt floor of the cellar had served as the burial place of an employee who died in the winter when the ground outside was frozen too hard to dig and the roads were impassable.[47]

The food served to the workmen in this basement dining area was reported to have been very good; one molder said that the meals were the equal of "the best that could be gotten at the best Hotels."[48] If this report were the general opinion of the boarders, it was in contrast with reports from other furnaces

[42] *United States Census of 1810,* Berks County, Union Township, p. 679.

[43] *St. Mary's Episcopal Church Record,* p. 185. March 4, 1808. Berks County Historical Society.

[44] *Census of 1830,* p. 515. See Appendix B for more census reports on residents of the Hopewell mansion.

[45] *Kemper Manuscripts,* H. A. Long Interview, November 9, 1936.

[46] H. A. Long Interview, December, 1935.

[47] Grace Styer Interview, June 1, 1941.

[48] *Kemper Manuscripts,* Notes on Hopewell.

Outdoor Bake Ovens, Front View

Outdoor Bake Ovens, South Side

of beans, bacon and fried mush as the regular fare.[49] Martha Furnace in New Jersey had several food riots in its dining room in protest against the meals.[50] However, food delivered to the Hopewell mansion indicated that someone ate, and drank, well; but the journals did not reveal what food was served in the basement to the workers and what was on the table in the upstairs dining room where the family and their guests were eating.

The outdoor bake oven produced bread and pastries and was also used to dry apples, peaches and corn.[51] Hams, flitches and shoulders came from the smoke house.[52] Oysters and cranberries were bought at Christmas time in sufficient quantities to indicate that they were for many people.[53] Sweet potatoes were frequently mentioned in the journals as having been purchased from outsiders. Large quantities of Irish potatoes were raised on the farm, and more were purchased from neighbors. In the fall melons were brought to the village and become the basis for feasts for everyone. Cabbage was a regular purchase; turnips and beets were sometimes bought and were probably raised also on the plantation. Pork, beef, veal and fowls were produced on the farm and bought from neighbors. The amount used indicated that everyone ate meat with regularity.[54] In 1831 the furnace purchased a keg each of brandy and Lisbon wine and an unspecified quantity of "A Very Superior old real Cognac."[55]

The store ledgers and journals showed no purchases of food by the manager or the clerk. Nor did these men pay for boarding, as did the people who ate in the basement. Free room and meals would appear to have been a fringe benefit of the management class at the Furnace.

[49] Rowe, *op. cit.*, p. 19.
[50] *Martha Furnace Diary*, Microfilm in Hopewell Village Library, *passim*.
[51] Sally Boone Interview, March 22, 1941.
[52] SM 35, p. 74.
[53] SM 31, p. 136.
[54] *Passim* in store journals.
[55] HV 8310601A.

Spring House at Hopewell Village

Outside of the mansion there were several utility buildings and a garden. The spring house, the smoke house and the bake oven have been mentioned previously in this chapter. In addition to supplying water the spring house cooled milk and butter, and a fireplace in the south end heated water for laundering and butchering. Milk pails and equipment were also cleaned here.[56] The smoke house, to the east of the Big House, was 30 feet square and built of stone below and logs above.[57] This building could have provided for a large supply of meat. The bake oven was behind the kitchen.

On terraces to the north of the house was the garden, within which stood a building with a multiple purpose. Above ground

[56] Violet Care Interview, February 13, 1941.
[57] Appleman, "Proposed Restoration Plan," op. cit.

it was an open summer house, shielded with lattice-work and topped by an eight-gabled roof. A wide path led from the house[58] to this shaded area where the summer breezes made life more pleasant, and possibly a courting couple could have found welcome seclusion. Beneath the floor of the summer house was the ice house. During the winter ice was cut from a nearby pond and placed in the underground storage area. This space, 15 feet square and 20 feet deep, was insulated with a lining of rye straw.[59] A supply of ice was thereby insured with which to cool drinks and preserve food during the summer months. Ice was cut from January to March when it had frozen thick enough to make good blocks.[60]

A most important auxiliary building was the latrine, dating from about 1876, at the east end of the garden area. It was about six by eight feet and partitioned in the middle. A path ran from the front of the house to the north half of the privy which was used by the ironmaster's family. Another path ran from the rear of the house to the south, or servant, portion of the outhouse.[61] A lattice-work screen covered with trumpet vine concealed the family door.[62]

A greenhouse was built about 1829 to the north and east of the mansion where its remains are still visible. It was about 80 feet long, and more than half of its space was used to grow grapes.[63] It was also used to start plants for spring transfer to outdoor beds.[64]

The terraces north of the Big House were occupied by the garden. It was useful for producing asparagus, strawberries and raspberries in beds[65] and grapes on an arbor.[66] Rosemary, migonette, sage and thyme were grown for their fragrance or

[58] *Ibid.*
[59] *Ibid.*
[60] SM 32, p. 84 and SM 35, pp. 97–98.
[61] *Kemper Manuscripts*, H. A. Long's Notes on Hopewell, *op. cit.*
[62] *Hopewell Papers*, H3015, Map of the Garden by M. A. Krewson.
[63] *Kemper Manuscripts*, H. A. Long's Notes on Hopewell, *op. cit.*
[64] SM 67, December 12, 1808, n.p. and SM 31, p. 113.
[65] *Kemper Manuscripts*, H. A. Long's Notes on Hopewell, *op. cit.*
[66] H. A. Long Interview, August 13, 1936.

flavor. Bee hives rested near the summer house to provide honey for the mansion tables. But the chief purpose for the garden must have been decorative.[67]

There were two terraces with a stone wall separating them. Areas on each terrace were marked with rows of boxwoods.[68] At the east end were daffodils, poppies, foxgloves, yellow roses, red and pink ramblers, violets, blue bells and hyacinths in their individual beds. Snow ball, lilac, orange blossom and rose of sharon bushes shared the guardian duties with boxwoods.[69] Pinks, lilies and hollyhocks added their heads to the colorful array.[70] Pavilions and benches lined the paths for any who desired to rest and enjoy the flowers.[71]

Somewhere about the house or garden there must have been some bird boxes; for in the 1830's Ann Brooke wrote, ". . . I am writing to you by [sic] side the window on my Music book, interrupted occasionally by the chattering of the Martins above my head, harbingers of spring."[72]

The attractions of Hopewell may have been greater in the summer than in the winter. Letters made many references to the ironmasters' families having gone to Philadelphia for the winter months.[73]

The Hopewell mansion was the center of bustling activity for more than a century. Within its walls occurred marriages, births and deaths. The ironmaster and his family, often the clerk and always a number of servants made it their home. Buyers and guests were entertained. Relatives visited. Parties were given for the families of other ironmasters who sometimes came from a distance and stayed for days. Sometimes, too, the

[67] *Hopewell Papers*, H3015, Map of the Garden, *op. cit.*
[68] Appleman, "Proposed Restoration Plan," op. cit.
[69] Map of the Garden, *op. cit.*
[70] Franklin Kemper, *op. cit.*, p. 5.
[71] Samuel Westey Freese Interview, September 21, 1959.
[72] *Stokes Collection*, Ann Brooke to Sarah R. Brooke, May 2, year not given.
[73] For example see *Brooke Family Papers*, John Springer to Edward Brooke, January 11, 1833.

families of the Village were invited to special festivities at the Big House.[74]

For the people of Hopewell Village, then, the ironmaster's mansion served many purposes as residence, dining room, seat of authority and center of social life.

[74] More details on the entertainments at the mansion will be given in Chapter 20.

5   Homes for the Workers

THE OPERATION OF A CHARCOAL FURNACE DEMANDED THE services of a fairly large force of workmen who would usually have been required to live in an area remote from towns. Hopewell Furnace was about five miles from Birdsboro or Douglasville and eight from Morgantown. These villages had stores which furnished Hopewell workers with many things not stocked by the company store. But they were too far away to provide homes for many of the workers. Some of the Furnace employees were needed near the furnace; others worked at the mines, the coaling pits or the wood lots. Since some of these areas were several miles from the furnace, it was more convenient for these men to live near their work than close to the stack. Besides the regular employees the Furnace had need of many part-time workers, especially wood cutters during the winter months. It was helpful to have neighboring farmers and their sons available to lend a hand for such work.

All of these workmen needed places to live. Some were married and required a house for a family; others were single and wanted a place to eat and sleep. The Furnace management had to make certain that living quarters were available to all of their workmen. Lodgings at Hopewell took many forms. They were neither luxurious nor pretentious. In some cases they were decidedly makeshift; other dwellings were solidly built. Purchases of furnishings indicate that at least a part of the families lived well above the level described by Arthur C. Bining and other historians of the eighteenth century iron villages.

Some workers lived in homes they owned; others rented houses from the Furnace or local landlords. They were scattered over many square miles in Union, Robeson and Caernarvon Townships of Berks County and East Nantmeal, West Nantmeal and Warwick Townships of Chester County. Even this area may not have encompassed the entire population. When one writer stated that 200 people lived in the village,[1] the immediate area of the furnace could scarcely have been considered "the village." The largest number of company-owned tenant houses in the Union Township tax records before the end of the Civil War was 14 in 1855.[2] In other representative years the tax records showed the numbers to have been 10 in 1837, 11 in 1840 and 1843, 12 in 1852, 10 in 1864,[3] 10 single and one double in 1867, 10 in 1873,[4] 9 in 1877[5] and 5 in 1883.[6] Harker Long remembered 14 tenant houses "near the furnace" when it was closed in 1883,[7] although at another time he said there had been 15.[8] He reported that the molders' families lived elsewhere and that the tenant houses near the furnace were occupied by laborers who worked around the furnace.[9] In 1936 three tenant houses survived in the furnace area and three others in the immediate vicinity.[10] The restoration area under the National Park Service includes two double and two single tenant houses.

[1] Committee on Historical Research of the Colonial Dames of America, op. cit, .p. 155.
[2] Tax Records, Berks County, Union Township.
[3] Ibid.
[4] Triennial Assessments, Berks County, Union Township.
[5] SM 34, tax evaluation for April 1, 1877, n. p.
[6] Hopewell Papers, Assessment, April 25, 1883.
[7] Long, Historical Sketch, op. cit., p. 17.
[8] H. A. Long Interview, August 13, 1936.
[9] Long, Historical Sketch, op. cit., p. 17.
[10] H. A. Long Interview, August 13, 1936.

View of Four Surviving Tenant Houses in Hopewell Village

Group of Tenant Houses about 1940

The Furnace also owned some homes in the neighborhood of the mines. In 1866 Haskebiah Clemons rented three company-owned houses at Hopewell Mine. The office house at the Jones Mine was rented as late as 1872.[11] An atlas for 1873 showed five buildings at the "Hopewell Iron Mines" belonging to Dr. Charles M. Clingan, a building of Clingan and Buckley along the creek near the Baptist Church in Warwick Township and two buildings listed as belonging to Dr. Chas. M. Clingan along the county line about two miles west of the furnace.[12] Presumably other homes occupied by the workers belonged to owners other than Hopewell Furnace.

Appleman believed that the surviving tenant houses dated from the Revolutionary Period,[13] but this seems rather improbable considering the changes in the number of houses which existed in different years. In 1941 an old resident visited Hopewell and identified 23 buildings or sites of buildings which he claimed had been used at some time as tenant houses. They ranged from the brick structure originally built as a kiln to the respectable duplex, the "boarding house," the Nathan Care House and the Houck House, all of which are still standing. It is not known how many of the 23 houses were occupied at any one time. Some may have burned or have been torn down before others were built. Several were built after 1883. The area covered was from beyond the lake on the west to beyond the public highway on the east.[14]

The Furnace records show payments for new tenant houses in 1803[15] and 1826. At least the latter one had an excavated cellar.[16] In 1878 John Roberts paid rental on the brick kiln for a residence at the rate of one dollar per month.[17] If this appears to be an insignificant rental by present standards, we should

[11] SM 34, p. 200.
[12] Bridgans and Witman, *op. cit.*, p. 55.
[13] Appleman, "Proposed Restoration Plan," *op. cit.*, p. 11.
[14] Reginald Smith Interview, March 16, 1941.
[15] SM 2, p. 148.
[16] SM 59, p. 5.
[17] SM 34, May 5, 1878, n.p.

Tenant House Number 1

note that the same amount was paid for quite respectable houses.

There is now no way of knowing whether the houses presently surviving were typical of all the tenant homes. Perhaps they survived because they were better houses in original construction. But the best idea of the workers' housing is to be gained by examining the ones which still stand.

The house nearest the furnace is called for identification purposes by the National Park Service Tenant House Number 1. It is built of native stone and currently contains four rooms. Its outside dimensions are 28 feet by 18 feet plus a stone shed built against the south wall measuring 13 feet by 10 feet. The large fireplace in the southwest corner of the lower floor of the main structure was the principal source of heat when the house was built. The two upper floor bedrooms are reached by a steep circular staircase.

Tenant House Number 2 is very similar to its next-door neighbor. It has a porch along its east side and a two-part shed, one of stone and one of frame. The next house in line is the duplex previously mentioned. It is 26 feet by 30 feet with a 6-foot porch running the entire length of the east side. There is a divided cellar under the entire house. Each apartment has a front and a rear door, two rooms on the first floor, two on the second and one on the third. Each side also has its stairway near the center of the house from the cellar to the third floor and a chimney serving a first floor fireplace. This structure was sometimes called the Shaffer House.

Last of the houses along this "street" is the Nathan Care House. Care was one of the founders and probably built this home for himself and his family. It is not then properly a tenant house, but it is an example of a worker's domicile. This residence is built of stone and measures 29 feet by 22 feet and has an 8-foot porch running across the front of the house. There is a single room cellar under the entire house. Above it are two rooms on the first floor, three on the second and one on the third. The stairway connecting all floors is located in

Tenant House Number 2

the southwest corner. A first floor fireplace is served by a chimney on the west end of the house. A well in the front yard provided water which was drawn by a bucket and windlass.

Across the Warwick Road from the tenant houses already described is a structure called by the old inhabitants "the boarding house." It is stone and measures 50 feet by 20 feet plus a stone shed built against the west end of the south section of the house. The other section has a small frame porch at the west entrance. The front of the house has two entrances, and there are separate stairways connecting the first and second floors which would have made possible the use of this dwelling as a duplex. The west end was built about

Interior of Tenant House

Interior of Tenant House

Duplex Tenant House One Mile from Village

1830, and the east end was added about a decade later. The older section has two rooms on each floor and a central chimney for the first floor fireplace. The newer part of the house has but a single room on each of the two floors and a first floor fireplace on the east side. Between the house and the road is a well with an old wooden pump. This was the source of water for the families in the tenant houses.[18]

Behind the duplex house is a stone barn 20 feet by 14 feet with a frame shed 20 feet by 20 feet. This is the only surviving tenant barn; but probably the other houses also

[18] Details for descriptions of the houses come in part from J. C. F. Motz, "Historical Base Map," (unpublished study, 1941). Hopewell Village Library.

Nathan Care House and Barn

had had some kind of shelter for pigs, poultry, cows and horses. Outside each house was formerly a yard and garden surrounded by a picket fence which served the purpose of keeping cows and chickens from the flowers and vegetables. The children had the job of whitewashing the fence.[19]

The animals and children enjoyed playing in the water in a ditch which ran along the west side of the Warwick Road carrying water from springs on Mount Pleasant. Each house on this side of the road had a little foot bridge across the ditch and a path to the front door.[20]

[19] Albert Painter Interview, May 9, 1958. The picket fences probably were of a comparatively recent date.
[20] David Care Interview, March 22, 1941.

How large were the families which lived in these houses? Unfortunately it is not possible to tell which specific worker resided in any one of these tenant houses at any definite time. The houses identified by the clerk with particular families were usually those away from the furnace where a descriptive association seemed more necessary. Some who were listed as renting houses in this area were checked in the census reports to obtain some idea of family sizes. John Mills, who rented in 1807,[21] had a family of ten members by 1810.[22] Jacob Cramp had a family of four in 1810[23] and eight by 1820.[24] David Hart in 1830 had a family of seven.[25] A boarding housekeeper, although it was not certain that he lived in "the boarding house," was John Wert with a family of three in 1830.[26]

Purchases of furniture and home furnishings by workers indicate that their houses were provided with normal pieces and in some cases a luxury or two. Tables and chairs, and doubtless many other items such as beds and cupboards were usually home made.[27] Mattresses were made from ticking purchased at the store and filled with straw or feathers. It must have required eight yards of material for a mattress, for that specific quantity was frequently sold. In 1818 it cost $62\frac{1}{2}$¢ per yard.[28] Random items selected from the journals show purchases of mirrors, bedsteads, "doughtroughs," chests, "beaurows," desks, dishes, chairs, trunks, rugs, cradles, tubs, clocks, cupboards, tables, stoves, coverlets, comforters and sheets.[29]

There were many notes on purchases of tableware and

---

[21] SM 4, p. 39.
[22] *Census of 1810,* p. 682.
[23] *Ibid.*
[24] *Census of 1820,* p. 98.
[25] *Census of 1830,* p. 515.
[26] *Ibid.*
[27] H. A. Long Interview, December, 1935.
[28] SM 9, p. 116.
[29] See Appendix B for more purchases for their homes by Hopewell workers.

Windlass and Bucket at Nathan Care Well

cooking utensils. Some idea of the kind of furnishings needed in the home can be gained from examining an order placed in 1844 by Jacob Winings at the Eli Keen Store in nearby Warwick. This purchase may have represented the outfitting of a newly married couple who were setting up housekeeping or one that had just moved into the community. Here is the list of their needs:

1 Tea Canister	.12½	½ doz. plates	.28
1 Sald Celler	.10	2 small ,,	.08
1 Pepper Box	.08	I Large Tin Bucket	.62½
1 Sugar Bowl	.15	1 ,, ,,	.50
½ doz. spoons large	.31	2 Candle Sticks	.25
½ ,, ,, small	.16	3½ yds. Crash	.31½

1 Cream jog	.15	4 „ Table diaper	.60
2 round deep dishes	.48	2 Bowls	.14
1 long dish	.14	1 Butcher Knife	.20
2 „ „	.32	½ lb. Pepper	.10
1 Pitcher	.28	Small Deep dish	.09
1 Doz. cups and saucers	.40	1 White Wash Brush	.31¼
½ „ knives and forks	.87½	1 Coffee Mill	$1.25
1 Hand Brush	.12½	Pair Snuffers	.12½[30]
½ doz. plate	.31		

Since the workers bought relatively little food from the company store, they must have raised much of what they ate. There were records of sales of melons, potatoes, turnips, turkeys, much pork, veal and beef and a little mutton; shad, herring and mackerel; pickles, peaches, sweet potatoes, beans, cherries and cabbage. Corn meal was a regular item of store purchase before 1808 and seldom appeared after that. Rye and wheat flour were the more common bases for baked items in later years. Sugar, tea, coffee, chocolate, salt, pepper and spices were kept in regular stock at the store.[31]

Preserving of meat was a problem before freezing was available. The workers used the smoke house at the mansion, or they might have had their own. Pickling meat in a salt brine was another method used. A formula for that process read: "10 gal water, 15 lb. of salt, 5 lb. of sugar and 5 oz. salt petre. Boil until no more scum appears."[32] Spoilage was a not uncommon occurrence. A large loss was recorded by the clerk in 1817: "Note: there was 13 shoulders weighed 146 lbs. which was intirely Spoiled which can not be allowed for —we agreed with David Hart to take them for $7. in case he could make any use of them and if not he was to have them for nothing."[33]

[30] *Eli Keen's Storebook,* 1844–1845, pp. 9, 10. 25.
[31] Appendix C gives complete purchases at the company store for twenty-six accounts covering a period of fifteen months. Much detail on items purchased and quantities consumed may be obtained from this source.
[32] James L. Morris, *Diary or Daily Notes,* December 17, 1841. Berks County Historical Society, Reading, Pennsylvania.
[33] SM 7, August 22, 1817, n. p.

Boarding House

The fireplace began to give way to the stove in the homes of Hopewell workers at a fairly early period. In 1784 several workmen bought ten-plate stoves at £5 5s. each.[34] This style was a cook stove which probably was first introduced to America about 1765 at the Mary Ann Furnace. The sale of stoves to workers continued during the entire period of stove making at Hopewell Furnace. The usual fuel was wood, and the journals showed many purchases of cordwood from the Furnace. There were also instances of agreements for rental of Furnace houses which included either wood or the right to cut wood on Furnace property as a part of the contract.[35]

Homes were lighted partly by the open fire from the fire-

[34] SM 41, p. 20.
[35] Examples will be noted later in this chapter .

place; but candles were sold at the store, even as late as 1850 the sale was good.[36] Doubtless many housewives made their own candles. "Lanthorns" were stocked at the Hopewell store as early as 1803,[37] and lamps were on sale before the middle of the century.[38]

Homes required maintenance and repair. In 1803 the Furnace paid John McGowan £5 1s. 6d. for work he had done on the house in which he lived.[39] There were payments for plastering, painting and whitewashing in or on Furnace-owned houses at various times.

Housecleaning was a semi-annual disruption of household routine. One husband wrote this account of the autumn cleaning at his house in 1842:

> Things are torn upside down, furniture displaced, beds and bedding thrown out of the house, closets and wardrobes turned inside out and not a nook or cranny or hiding place on or in premises, but what has to give up its secrets and its contents. . . . Order has fled from the house and happy is the man who has had the good fortune or good sense to fly with them . . . dirty handkerchiefed turbaned heads, slip shod shoes, smutty faces, angry looks and pinned up petticoats are the marks of the house cleaning woman . . .
> The very victuals, the only stay and support of the animal economy under such great affliction, is grudgingly doled out to you with complaints of the loss of time in making them ready. The coffee looks the very impersonification of the sloppy water under your feet, the beefsteak is done black on one side and not done at all on the other and your cake, if not all dough is pretty near it. And even these are served up to you . . . most likely on the bare dough trough in the kitchen corner. . . .[40]

Fires were a threat and a calamity in all rural areas. On July 12, 1803, the clerk recorded, "This night J. McColasters

[36] SM 31, p. 130.
[37] SM 2, p. 154.
[38] SM 31, p. 130.
[39] SM 2, p. 148.
[40] *Morris Diary, op. cit.,* pp. 237–239.

Barn Behind Tenant House

Restored Church House Now a Home

Hous Burnt."[41] One of the tenant houses burned in the 1870's.[42] Chimney fires were frequent and often dangerous because of wind-borne sparks. In the 1840's steps were built at the south end of the mansion house to enable workers to climb to the chimney quickly when it caught on fire.[43]

Not all houses had their own wells, because drilling a well was expensive. To reduce the risk of drilling without finding water, many people hired an expert to locate an underground stream before they began drilling. James Morris wrote on October 4, 1842:

> Today father had the famous old Dutch water smeller from near Adamstown searching for water round about his new house. The old man uses no rod or witch hazle as the other "water smellers" do, but depends entirely on a peculiar sensitiveness in his legs—a slight twitching of the muscles which he feels on passing over the underground course of a spring or stream of water. . . . He charged $1 for locating water at 30-35 feet.[44]

Rent for Furnace houses was usually from $12 to $25 per year. In 1840 John Miller paid $45 per year for a "house and lot at Hopewell Mines," and others were paying from $25 to $35 for houses at Hopewell Mines and Jones Mineholes.[45] The Furnace rented two houses at the Jones Mineholes from Daniel Uble in 1819 and used them to house miners. The owner received $67.[46]

Renting a house to a workman must have been a condition of employment in some instances. Two examples are quoted below to show rental terms:

> Rented to Isaac Danfield the house in which Isaac Hoffman now resides adjoining land of John Fries for One year to Commence the first of April next . . . for the sum of twelve

[41] SM 1, p. 33.
[42] Charles Sheridan Painter Interview, February 16, 1957.
[43] Rose Sands and Catherine Rhodes Interview, May 13, 1941.
[44] *Morris Diary, op. cit.*, pp. 233–234.
[45] SM 32, p. 103.
[46] SM 9, p. 6.

South End of Main Wing of Hopewell Mansion Showing Step Roofline
(Courtesy of William Caulwell)

dollars per year for house and fire wood. Danfield is to cut no thriving timber but old decayed timber, he is likewise to assist in haymaking and harvest if Called upon, he is likewise to take care of the pruning and see that there is no hoop poles, rails or any timber taken of the land by people that has no Authority so to do.

Hopewell, January 26th, 1824[47]

Rented to Samuel Steel the house at Joneses Mineholes now occupied by Mary Phillips for One year from 1st April next insuing for the sum of Ten dollars. Saml Steel is to raise or wash ore during the time that the rest of the hands are employed and to get the customary wages—Steel is to be Constant at the work except two weeks in harvest and he is to find his own fire wood. Hopewell January 22*nd* 1825[48]

Single men and molders made arrangements for sleeping quarters as best they could. Sometimes several men rented a house and hired a woman to care for them;[49] sometimes they stayed in the home of a married worker. Bunks were provided in a plastered room in the attic of the wheelright shop for the use of the molders when off duty or while waiting for the next run of iron from the furnace. The founder had the bell on the cast house rung when he was ready to run off the iron.[50]

Because no taverns or ordinaries were near enough to furnish meals, providing food for the men without families was an extensive business throughout the history of the Furnace. In the preceding chapter it was related that some of these men ate in the basement dining room of the mansion. Sometimes they left this arrangement and "went to housekeeping" or "left the house and went to board himself."[51] Charges for boarding at the mansion varied from $4 to $6 per month.[52] In 1800 a board bill stated that the charge was 2s. per day "with liquor."[53] Later accounts did not mention liquor with the

[47] SM 46, page not readable.
[48] *Ibid.*
[49] Hunter Care Interview, January 26, 1941.
[50] David Boone Interview, March 22, 1941.
[51] SM 1, p. 37.
[52] Furnace journals from 1802 to 1851.
[53] HV 8000116.

meals. Meals may not have been served on Sundays. At least when the clerk calculated the meals eaten, there was no count for Sundays until about 1851 when the month was 30 days. All meals were charged at the same rate per meal.[54]

At times the Furnace paid someone else to board its hands. This could have been when the work was at a distance from the furnace—for example at the mines[55]—or when someone was hired to do special work such as rebuilding the hearth at the furnace.[56] In the 1850's when Ann Parliman was running a boarding house, the Furnace paid her to board Alexander Church, the company clerk.[57] A strange entry in 1851 showed that the Furnace also paid Mrs. Parliman for boarding her own son Edward Parliman.[58] Apparently at that time boarding was a part of the wage or the cost of boarding was withheld from the wage and paid to the keeper of the boarding house.

Another manager of a boarding house was John Wert who was also a keeper at the Furnace. One of his boarders was his father-in-law Thomas Care, founder and molder. Wert had married Rebecca Care,[59] and her father came to board with them soon after. Care may have helped the young couple when finances were low, for he bought food and was later repaid by Wert.[60] At Wert's death in 1832, Care paid for a coffin in which to bury him.[61] When Doctor Clingan was Furnace manager, more workers were boarded in private homes; and few men ate in the basement of the mansion.

How did prices at Hopewell compare with boarding charges at other furnaces? William Sullivan said that there was not much change from furnace to furnace between 1800 and 1840 with the usual charge for boarding having been $1 to $2 per week.[62] Hopewell was within that range.

---

[54] For example see SM 46 for 1822.
[55] SM 12, p. 136.
[56] SM 59, p. 19.
[57] SM 32, p. 122.
[58] SM 32, p. 113.
[59] *St. Marys Episcopal Church Record, op. cit.,* p. 195.
[60] SM 59, p. 25.
[61] SM 21, p. 25.
[62] Sullivan, *op. cit.,* pp. 61–62.

Housing at Hopewell Furnace varied widely from the luxury of the ironmaster's mansion to the makeshift accommodations of John Roberts in the brick kiln. Available evidence, however, does not show squalor or starvation. Food was plentiful and reasonably varied. Homes were provided with essential furniture and furnishings, and some had mirrors, clocks, silver spoons and stoves to show that living was above the subsistence level.

6   The Farm and Forest

A CHARCOAL FURNACE IN PRODUCTION NEEDED LARGE QUAN-
tities of food and fuel for man, beast and furnace hearth; and
these requirements necessitated the ownership of large areas of
land for farm crops, gardens, orchards and forests. In 1833 a
report was submitted to the national House of Representatives
on the cost of producing cast and bar iron. One interesting
section of this study showed the consumption of farm products
and depreciation of animals per ton of metal produced to have
been : 20 bushels of wheat and rye, 57 pounds of pork, 43
pounds of beef, 10 pounds of butter, 2 bushels of potatoes, $\frac{1}{2}$
ton of hay, $1.00 in fruits and vegetables and $1.43 depreciation on the purchase value of horses. The total cost of farm
produce and live stock was $27.35 per ton of castings or bars.
The same report noted that the mortality among horses
averaged one of seven per year.[1]

No similar estimates were given for the agricultural costs
of producing pig iron; so it was not possible to make an
exact application of these figures to Hopewell Furnace. But
there were years when Hopewell was making over 700 tons
of castings plus a quantity of pig iron; and, therefore, some
idea of the consumption of food could be obtained from the
general figures quoted for the industry.

[1] *Hazard's Register of Pennsylvania*, XI, 7 (February 16, 1833), p. 103.

The operators of Hopewell Furnace owned farm land close to the furnace and at a distance from it. Rental agreements mentioned several different farms. But not all of the needs of the people of the village were supplied by the partner-owned farms; for the records showed many neighboring farmers were trading grain, fruits, vegetables, meats, dairy products and animals for store goods, castings or the services of the blacksmith and wheelright. Grain, flour and feed were purchased at grist mills a number of miles distant from the furnace. It was not possible to determine the acreage of land cultivated for Hopewell Village consumption, but the area would necessarily have been large.

Two writers reported that in New Jersey a charcoal furnace required 20,000 acres of timber land to furnish wood for charcoal. A common practice was to divide the forest into tracts of 1,000 acres each with one tract being cut each year. At the end of twenty years the first section would have grown enough to cut again, and thus a continuous supply of wood was provided.[2]

Forest lands in southeastern Pennsylvania must have been more productive than those in New Jersey, because none of the furnaces in the former region possessed a domain approaching 20,000 acres. Representative furnaces in the Hopewell area were listed as owning in the eighteenth century the following estates, in acres: Elizabeth 10,124; Cornwall 9,669, Reading 5,600 and Warwick 1,796.[3] The land associated with Hopewell Furnace varied in different periods from about 3,900 to about 8,000 acres. All of these figures included both farm and forest lands with the greater amount devoted to producing wood for charcoal.

The history of the Hopewell farms showed several different kinds of agreements between proprietor and farmer. In 1814

[2] Robert J. Sims and Harry B. Weiss, *Charcoal-Burning in New Jersey from Early Times to the Present* (Trenton: New Jersey Agricultural Society, 1955), p. 11.

[3] *Pennsylvania Archives*, Third Series (Volume XII; Harrisburg: Wm. Stanley Ray, 1897), pp. 65, 295; *Aliens Appeal Record, op. cit.*, p. 189.

Buckley and Brooke agreed to pay Matthew Foy $65 per year
and to provide him a house, in return for which Foy agreed
to do the farming and other work as required of him.[4] Ten
years later Clement Brooke preferred a straight cash rental
basis on two of his farms. Henry Shick rented the farm which
was "formerly William Thomas' " for $135 for 1824. The
next year the payment was $150 and remained the same
through 1830.[5] James Reperts paid Clement Brooke $212 in
1832 "For 1 year Rent of Farm and Tenant House in East
Nantmeal Township . . ."[6]

The more common arrangement between farm owner and
tenant was a formal share-crop agreement. John Bishop and
Samuel Cox signed a contract in 1798 which required Cox
to clear a field, fence, plow and sow it "upon his own expense;"
and he was to have "two thirds of the corn above the furnace
race and half below, and half the buckwheat, or any other
kind of summer grain, . . . the winter grain [was] to be sowd
and seed found by Cox—for which he [was] to have two
thirds in the shock." . . ." Cox was also to be permitted to
mow the meadow "to the Haves."[7] Later a farmer paid $50
in cash for the use of the meadow.[8]

The specific obligations of both parties were detailed in this
farm contract between Clement Brooke and Isaac Hayer in
1829 :

> ". . . Said Hayer is to sow thirty acres of winter grain and
> Sumer grain in proportion according to the rules of farming
> and deliver Said Brooke the one half of all the grain in the
> bushel to Birdsborough Mill and likewise to make and repair
> all the fences and make all the rails at his own expense, the
> rails to be made on the wood land belonging to the premises
> and he is to haul six hundred bushels lime . . . and spread
> it on the land in a farmer like maner and likewise to find all
> the clover seed that may be wanted—Said Brooke is to pay

[4] *Hopewell Papers*, Agreement, January 4, 1814.
[5] SM 12, p. 136; SM 59, p. 22; SM 14, pp. 53, 92.
[6] SM 21, p. 25.
[7] HV 7980603.
[8] HV 8361228B.

for the lime and be at the expense of the one half of all the
seed grain—Said Hayer is to have one half acre of ground for
Potatoes and one half acre for flax to sell no hay or straw of the
premises—Said Hayer is to have firewood for the use of the
mansion house but no fire wood for the tenant house and to
pay the road tax for said Farm."[9]

When the time of year came to renew or cancel the rental
agreements, there must have been some anxiety on the part of
the farmer. Note the tenor of this letter:

> Sir this is to let you now that you did not let me now
> according to promise you promised to let me now between
> Chrismus and New Year before witness and I am resolve to
> stay anther year and I will make you satisfaction as good as
> anny man and you may cum down and let me now how it is
> wether I can stay or now and your grain is all thraght . . ."[10]

One of the farmers recorded the way he and his two sons
had used their time during a part of the year. It may have
been that Mathew Brooke was to pay them extra for some
kinds of work done beyond the usual farming activities. A
sampling of the jobs listed tells something of the work of a
farm family in 1804:

May	1	Sowd the front lot with flax
May	2	Hauld dung in garding
May	30	Hauld Brush out young orchard
June	11	Plowed petatoes in garding
July	4	Hauld clover out the orchard
July	18	Hauld his part of the wheat to the Barn
July	28	Sowed Buckwheat
August	2	Cross plowed Barn lot
August	4	Sowd flax lot and Barn lot with turnip seed and sowd meadow grond with turnip seed
August	6	Hauld a load Brush and wood from Young Orchard to Big House
August	13	Hauld a load of oats

[9] HV 8290112A.
[10] *Brooke Family Papers,* John Bohn to Mathias Brooke, January 1,
1803.

August	27	Moad clover in Young Orchard
August	31	Hauld a load of hay
September	10	Hauld a load flour from Stichters to Big House
September	18	Threshed 15 bushels
September	25	Hauld sill for sider press
September	26	Hauld Beam post—1 Sill Sweep
September	29	3/4 of a day thrasht and John helped to clean 6 Bushels
October	3	Hauld load Corn from Bishops Mill to Big House
October	11	Hauld Rails to fence turnip ground
October	13	Laid the worm for the fence and hauled Stone for Trunnels
October	16	Made fence
October	18	killd 2 Beefs at twise Black and Red Cows
October	23	hauld 1 load from Bishops Mill to Hopewell and 1 load of Stoves back
October	27	hauld 1 load Stoves to Reading and a load flour and feed . . . back. killed Beef Cut up and Salted
October	28-29	to 2 days Riding of a hors when Jack Run away
November	30	to 1 day Cleand Ditch
December	13	hauld fire wood to Big House half a day Self and Mark
December	17	killed hoggs and Cut and Salted
December	21	hauld wood for . . . forgemen
December	22	hauled hoggshears from hofmans
December	17	hauld load feed and pork from Reading[11]

The usual grain crops of wheat, corn, oats, buckwheat and rye were sold directly from the farm to people of the village or were taken to the mill to be ground into flour, meal or feed The miller took his pay in a percentage of the grain ground. An important byproduct of the grain crops was straw which was sold in bundles at $5 per hundred bundles.[12] Straw had uses as bedding for animals, possibly as a cover for dirt floors

[11] *Brooke Family Papers,* Account Pages, Mathew Brooke to Elishu Bard, 1804.
[12] SM 4, p. 224. This was in 1808.

and certainly as filler for mattresses. Potatoes, turnips, Indian corn and hay were other products of the Furnace farms.

Before 1820 farming was a hand-tool operation for the most part. A hoe, rake, axe, scythe, sickle, flail and plow, costing from $15 to $20, put a family in the farming business.[13] But the next forty years brought inventions of expensive farm machines such as drills, planters, reapers, mowers, horse rakes, threshers, feed grinders and plows of many kinds.[14] These new tools provided Hopewell with new markets for its iron[15] and lightened the work of the farmers. Among the new machines put into operation on the Hopewell farms were: A horse-drawn rake in 1819; a winnowing mill, improved plow and a "revolving rake" in 1827; a threshing machine by 1849. An inventory of farm tools at Hopewell in 1876 listed a mowing machine, a grain drill, a roller, single and double "Hoca plows," spike and hoe harrows, a fodder cutter and a portable engine.[16]

The farmers of the nineteenth century had their troubles with nature when unusual numbers of locusts and grasshoppers appeared and cutworms destroyed the young corn stalks. The Hessian fly damaged the wheat; smut and mildew took their toll both in wheat and in rye. Potatoes rotted in the ground when the weather was too wet to harvest them.[17]

Hopewell owners were conscious of the necessity of maintaining the fertility of their lands and wrote into their farm agreements specific requirements upon the tenants for good farm practices. James Wilson demanded that not less than 1,000 bushels of lime be put on the arable Furnace lands each year and that clover be planted.[18] Daniel Buckley and Company bought clover seed which was presumably sown on

[13] Williamson, *op. cit.*, p. 136.
[14] *Ibid.*, p. 117.
[15] See chapter 7.
[16] HV 8760401.
[17] *Morris Diary, op. cit.* Many references to the problems of area farmers.
[18] *Hopewell Papers*, Rental Agreement, May 1, 1795.

their farms.[19] Ground plaster and manure were used for ferti-
lizers.[20]

Before the introduction of tractors and other power
machinery, farming required work animals. Horses, mules and
oxen were used around the furnace and for transportation to
the distant markets. Poultry, cows, hogs and sheep were kept
to provide meat, eggs, milk, leather and wool. Dogs were
used in farm work as well as in providing companionship to
the isolated rural families. The animals were in turn consumers
of much that the farm produced, and they returned a portion
to the soil in nitrogen-rich manure. Providing for the needs
of the animals was costly in labor and money to build shelter
and fences, to feed and water, to milk and butcher and to
care for them when they were ill.

Hopewell had its animal population in profusion of numbers and of kinds. Mark Bird reported to the Union Township tax collector in 1779 that he was the possessor of 16
horses, 21 cows and 46 sheep.[21] He may have possessed other
animals as well, but these were the only kinds which were
included in the tax return. In 1832 Hopewell Furnace was
reported to have had 84 horses,[22] and in 1850 the draft animals
at the Furnace were 50 oxen, horses and mules.[23] The business
records of the company contained many references to the
purchase or sale of animals or to some other expense or income from the possession of beasts and fowls.

There were at least two buildings in the immediate area of
the furnace for the sheltering of the nonhuman population.
Below and to the south of the mansion was a large barn which
contained 6 sets of stalls, each capable of holding 6 horses,
mules, cows or steers. Above the stalls were three haymows

[19] Examples are found in HV 8210409B and 8260323B.
[20] *Hopewell Papers*, Farm Rental Agreement, May 20, 1805.
[21] *Pennsylvania Archives*, Third Series, XVIII, Berks County, Union
Township Tax Return for 1779.
[22] McLane Report in *Hazard's Register*, XIV, 18 (November 1, 1834),
p. 350.
[23] *Documents Relating to the Manufacture of Iron in Pennsylvania*,
op. cit., "Table on Cold Blast Charcoal Furnaces."

North Side of Restored Hopewell Village Barn

which, among them, could hold enough hay to feed 36 horses or mules for a year.[24] Obviously this barn alone was not sufficient to shelter all the draft animals when the Furnace owned 84 or even 50. Some livestock may have been kept at other farms, or teamsters may have cared for their own teams. In the late years of Furnace operation the east end of

[24] H. A. Long Interview, August 13, 1936.

West Side of Restored Hopewell Village Barn

the barn was used for cattle and the west end for horses and mules.[25]

East of the barn was a large pen, about 40 feet square, used to house hogs and chickens. It had two separate sections for its different kinds of denizens.[26]

The price of horses remained remarkably stable in the first

[25] Violet Care Interview, February 13, 1941.
[26] *Kemper Manuscripts*, H. A. Long's Notes on Hopewell.

half of the nineteenth century. A good sound horse in the prime ages was never very far from $100 in price. There were many sales at that exact price and numerous others at a range from $90 to $120 each. Animals lost rapidly in value when they were past their best work years or when they were impaired in some way. "An old horse" brought only $20 in 1807,[27] and a blind mare was sold for the same price in 1818.[28] Horses were priced much higher when there was a special reason for their value, as in 1820 the Furnace received "$150 in part for the Stud horse."[29] The total price was not reported. When horses were bought or sold, they were usually identified in the records by color. Other means of identification included names of the animals or of the teamster who had driven them.

Horses involved their owners in other kinds of expense beside purchase and shelter. Horseshoes at the blacksmith shop were priced at about 20¢ to 30¢ each, and there was an additional charge of 10¢ for removing the old shoe. In 1827 the Furnace purchased from a harnessmaker for $13 : 5 horse collars, 6 blind bridles, 1 back band and 1 creeper.[30] Thomas Care, the founder, paid $15.00 "for keeping horse,"[31] but the record did not report whether he was paying for feed in addition to shelter.

Oxen seldom appeared in the Hopewell records, but that they were used was verified by the purchase of a pair in the summer of 1818 for $20.[32] Cattle for milk and meat, however, were often mentioned. As proof that many of the village families had their own cows, frequently the purchase price of "a cow" or "a milch cow" was charged against the account of a workman. Prices varied widely for the cows which changed hands. In 1808 the going price was about $16.00,[33] in 1818

[27] SM 4, p. 198.
[28] SM 9, p. 18.
[29] SM 10, p. 51.
[30] SM 59, p. 22.
[31] SM 54, p. 117.
[32] SM 9, p. 145 and SM 6, p. 24.
[33] SM 4, p. 250.

from $17.00 to $32.75,[34] in 1825 about $16.00,[35] through the 1830's about $15.00 and in 1850 about $20.00.[36] Age again was a factor in price, for in 1852 Henry Ammon bought "1 old cow" from the Furnace for only $6.[37]

Cattle were purchased for butchering by the Furnace and by individuals. Through the 1840's there were many references to "store cattle" and to "fat cattle." Store cattle were bought for $17 each in 1845,[38] for $27 each in 1847[39] and the same in 1850. This last purchase was made from Timothy Parker, a drover, who spent the night at the Furnace and paid $1.50 for pasturing his herd in the meadow. The Furnace also sold him eleven "Fat cattle at $40 per head."[40]

About 20 steers were butchered each autumn to provide beef for the employees and their families.[41] South of the Furnace office was an iron ring fastened to a large rock and called by the old Hopewell residents "the bull ring." A steer for butchering was tied here so that its head could be drawn down into a position where it was easy to hit the forehead with a sledge hammer to stun the animal before its throat was cut.[42]

Butter making at the Furnace was indicated by the purchase in 1846 of a set of "milch pans and bowls."[43] These containers were used to hold the milk while the cream gathered at the top to be skimmed and placed in the churn. Women of the village also made butter to sell to the company store.

Hogs were raised by both the Furnace and the Village families to furnish the large quantities of pork sold at the store and in private sales. Probably most of the tenant houses had

[34] SM 10, pp. 14–40.
[35] SM 14, pp. 67–70.
[36] SM 32, p. 97.
[37] SM 32, p. 120.
[38] SM 28, p. 162.
[39] SM 31, p. 41.
[40] SM 31, p. 132.
[41] Charles Sheridan Care Interview, February 24, 1941.
[42] Charles E. Stevenson Interview, September 23, 1940.
[43] SM 31, p. 10.

pigpens on the premises. On at least one occasion the Furnace provided shelter and food for a hog belonging to one of the workmen when David Griffith paid three dollars "for keeping and fattening his hog from last Spring."[44] The price of pigs depended upon their size. "Little pigs" sold for 75¢ each,[45] but "Shoats" brought $4 each.[46]

Sheep were seldom mentioned in the office records of the Furnace. They were reported among Mark Bird's assets for most years for which the tax records were available.[47] A note in 1834 stated that the Furnace had sold 20 head of sheep to Charles Brooke, Senior.[48] Although mutton appeared at rare intervals among the meats sold by the store, sheepskins were frequently recorded among the sales.[49]

The value of animals made the breeding of livestock an important part of rural life. One clerk made note of the dates when a mare was "Put . . . to Horse," and when he "Put the Pony to Wallys Black Horse." The foaling of colts also received official report.[50] In the same period of the 1850's the record of the breeding of dogs[51] was one of the few references to pets at Hopewell, although several years earlier a "puppy" had been sold for two dollars.[52]

Most families kept some fowls for eggs and meat. The store did not often sell these items; but scattered references, mostly from the 1850's, mentioned the presence at the Furnace of chickens, turkeys, ducks and geese. The clerk of this era was again the source for much of the surviving information about the animals and birds around the Furnace grounds. In his detailed record for 1857 and 1858 appeared evidences that these four varieties of fowls were a part of the picture of the

[44] SM 7, December 7, 1816.
[45] SM 31, p. 121.
[46] SM 59, p. 17.
[47] Pennsylvania Archives, op. cit., XVIII.
[48] SM 21, p. 104.
[49] For example in 1830 Thomas Care paid $7.47½ for one. SM 14, p. 89.
[50] SM 35, pp. 80–82.
[51] SM 38, pp. 126–127.
[52] SM 31, p. 110.

life of Hopewell Village. Judging from the following notes, some of them must have had freedom from confinement: "Set a turkey in the Spring House," "two hens with Duck Eggs in Carage and under hog house," "Set a hen in Coal House," "Set a Hen in Chicken House 13 Eggs," "Set a hen Sunday 21st," "Set 2 hens in Chick House," "Set a Goose," "Set a Hen with 7 duck Eggs," "Set a duck at Window," "Set a hen 6 turkey Eggs," "Set a duck in Calf Stabel," "Set a Hen Turkey Eggs in Spring House Loft."[53]

Confining animals to the areas where they belonged and paying costs when they did not remain there were sometimes the causes of expenses for the owners. Rails and fence posts were cut in each year for which the labor study was made from 1805 to 1853. In 1832 Samuel Peirce was paid $91.20 "for cutting . . . and Putting up 420 Panniels five rail fence on the Property that Roberts now lives on."[54] Clement Brooke paid 50¢ to a man who had caught and kept a horse which had run away at the mineholes.[55] Jacob Felman was credited with $7 for damage done his corn by a neighbor's cattle.[56] And a reward was paid in 1828 by the Furnace for "giving information of our Black Horse when stolen last fall."[57]

Veterinary expenses appeared in the record after 1828. Several journal items showed that $5 was paid "for Doctoring Horses." Several other payments were made for "altering Swine" and for medicine for ailing horses.[58]

Farming at Hopewell included vegetable gardens and orchards as well as the previously mentioned field crops. Two sizable garden plots were remembered by Harker Long. One, about a quarter of an acre in area, was located to the west of the barnyard. Stray animals were kept out of the beans and cabbage by a whitewashed picket fence. Another half acre

[53] SM 35, pp. 108–128
[54] HV 8321117A.
[55] SM 44, August 21, 1806.
[56] *Lewis Evans Ledger, 1801–1840,* November 27, 1826. Hopewell Village Library.
[57] SM 14, p. 67.
[58] See for example SM 28, pp. 107–109.

plot near the brick kiln was used for vegetables.[59] This space grew potatoes in 1857, and in the same year potatoes were raised "in Back field."[60] Other vegetables common in gardens of the Village area were onions, beets, radishes, lettuce, cauliflower, tomatoes, salsify, peas, cucumbers, squash and egg plant.[61]

Most of the fruit used in Hopewell Village also was produced in local orchards. The company store was a market for orchard products for the neighborhood, although it is not clear whether purchases were made because the Furnace orchards did not produce enough or because a kind of barter was carried on for store goods. Quantity purchases were made of apples, plums and prunes, quinces, peaches, cherries, cider and vinegar. Dried apples and peaches were bought by the bushel as well as being dried in the outdoor oven at the Big House. One customer requested that his payment be a barrel of rye whiskey or a barrel of "apple whiskey."[62]

There was at least one peach orchard at Hopewell, because a notation in 1835 stated that wood was being hauled "from old peach orchard."[63] Apple orchards were planted at several different times in Furnace history, but these may have been replacements for overage trees rather than the opening of new ground. The advertisements for the sale of Hopewell Furnace in 1787[64] and also in 1788[65] mentioned an excellent young orchard of 250 apple trees. In 1804 Elishu Bard reported that he had "Hauld Brush out Young Orchard."[66] The Furnace bought 160 apple trees in 1829 at 10¢ each[67] and two years

[59] H. A. Long Interview, December, 1935.
[60] SM 35, p. 108.
[61] Morris Diary, op. cit., passim.
[62] Brooke Family Papers, Lewis Wohr to Mathew Brooke, November 5, 1810.
[63] SM 21, p. 127.
[64] Pennsylvania Gazette, April 11, 1787.
[65] Pennsylvania Packet and Daily Advertiser, March 22, 1788.
[66] Brooke Family Papers, Account Pages. Mathew Brooke to Elishu Bard.
[67] Cash Book for 1828–1830, April 10, 1829, n. p. Berks County Historical Society.

later paid Samuel Peirce "for Triming the young orchard."[68]
An additional 304 young apple trees were purchased in 1834
at 12½¢ each.[69] Another "Young Orchard" was mentioned in
1844.[70]

What kind of apples were grown in the orchard? The
journals just called them apples without further identification.
Hopewell Historian Robert D. Ronsheim made inquiry of S.
W. Fletcher, author of *Pennsylvania Agriculture and Country
Life, 1840–1940,* about the varieties of apples grown in
Pennsylvania in the first half of the nineteenth century.
Fletcher replied that about half of the orchard was probably
in three kinds of apples: Baldwin, Northern Spy and Rhode
Island Greening.[71] In 1916 Cyrus Fox saw trees in the Hope-
well orchard producing Baldwins and Northern Spies.[72] Other
varieties grown nearby were: Rusty Coats, Rambos, Pippins
and Grindstones.[73]

Fletcher also said there was little or no pruning of the
orchards, but at Hopewell payments were made in both 1807
and 1827 for trimming the apple trees.[74]

The Furnace paid for 1,289 grafts in the young orchard in
1844.[75] During the same spring James Morris of Morgantown
had had eighty grafts made to his fruit trees. Possibly the same
persons did the work in both orchards, for the price to each
customer was 4¢ per graft. Morris reported that he had gotten
grafts of Pound, Eollowalter, Bellflower, Black Apple, Smoke-
house, Jones Apple and Summer Iwen.[76] Perhaps these same
kinds of apples grew at Hopewell.

One other kind of fruit which was certainly grown at Hope-

----

[68] SM 15, p. 59.
[69] *Hopewell Papers,* Bill from Isaac Hambleton to Clement Brooke,
1834.
[70] SM 58, June 10, 1844.
[71] *Hopewell Papers,* Fletcher to Ronsheim, March 19, 1958.
[72] *Reading Eagle,* February 25, 1917.
[73] *Morris Diary, op. cit.,* p. 161.
[74] SM 4, p. 137 and SM 59, p. 19.
[75] SM 58, June 10, 1844, n. p.
[76] *Morris Diary, op. cit.,* p. 115.

well was grapes. Twice in 1832 and once in 1857 the journals
showed payments for dressing the vineyard."

A great part of the land was used for growing wood for the
production of charcoal for the furnace. The furnace manager
who failed to take care of his wood supply did not stay in
business very long. England had stopped making charcoal iron
by 1775 "except for a few isolated furnaces, mainly in remote
regions" because of the scarcity of wood."[78] Salford Forge ceased
to operate in 1810 because of the depletion of its timber, and
Green Lane Forge was inactive for twenty years after 1813
while a new stand of timber grew in its area."[79] An acre of land
in Southeastern Pennsylvania grew cn an average about a
cord of wood per year."[80] Matthew Cary reported in 1837 that
Clement Brooke had told him that Hopewell Furnace burned
6,000 cords of wood per year, "and the growth of his land is
4,000 cords per year."[81] But the furnace did not depend
entirely upon company owned land for its wood supply. Wood
"leave" or "leif" was bought to permit wood cutting on the
land owned by neighbors. The usual fee was from 70¢ to $1
per cord. Some men cut wood on their own land and sold it
to the Furnace, but apparently most of the wood came from
Hopewell property.

As was evidenced by several memoranda, the Hopewell
managers were aware of the importance of protecting their
own growing timber. The word "sprouts" used in the following
excerpts meant the new growth in a cut-over area of woodland :

1836   Henry Sheets was paid $9.75 "for Sundry work and
         saving sprouts."[82]

[77] SM 17, pp. 16, 27 and SM 65, April 17, 1857, n. p.
[78] H. R. Schubert, *History of the British Iron and Steel Industry* (London : Routledge and Kegan Paul, 1957), p. IX.
[79] Gemmell, *op. cit.,* p. 99.
[80] *Ibid.,* p. 109.
[81] *Cary Diary, op. cit.,* February 17, 1837, n. p.
[82] SM 21, p. 184.

1851   A fence was built "around the Sprouts near Geigertown."[83]

1863   "Levi Keller and J : Bland have been getting Stone off our land and done considerable damage to Sprouts." A note beside this said, "paid."[84]

The thousands of acres of land associated with Hopewell Furnace served many purposes in providing food and fuel. Although land was used generally for auxiliary production to facilitate the making of iron, possibly some grain was sold off the premises, and in the last years of the Furnace's history charcoal and cordwood were marketed in Pottstown and Philadelphia.

[83] SM 32, p. 119.
[84] *Kemper Manuscripts,* C. W. Clingan Pocket Note Book, n. p.

Part Three
The Industrial Village

7 The Furnace Product

THE CENTER OF ACTIVITY AND THE RAISON D'ETRE FOR
Hopewell Village was the little stone furnace in which iron was
smelted. While relatively few people worked right at the
furnace, the entire labor force was engaged in service to its
needs and was subject to its whims. The old charcoal furnace
was called a fickle mistress by those who served her and who
were dependent upon her operation for their economic well-
being. Many of the villagers were constantly aware of the
evidences of furnace operation, for as Bining wrote:

> The intermittent roar of the forced blast could be heard a
> long distance away. From the top of the furnace stack a stream
> of sparks was occasionally emitted as the flames rose and fell.
> At night the almost smokeless flames cast a lurid glare upon
> the sky, visible for miles around which illuminated the sur-
> rounding buildings.[1]

The furnace operation required a coal shed where the coal
was kept until all danger of fire from it was past and a coal
house where 30,000 bushels of charcoal were stored. To put
hot coal into the coal house too soon would endanger the
entire supply on hand. Between the coal house and the furnace

[1] Bining, *Pennsylvania Iron Manufacture in the 18th Century, op. cit.,*
p. 33.

Hopewell Furnace Group in 1887

Hopewell Furnace and Bridgehouse After Shutdown

stack was the bridge house upon which were stored the ingredients for charging the furnace for the next few hours and from which the fillers dumped the fuel, ore and flux into the charging hole. On a lower level was the casting house into which the molten iron flowed through its trenches of sand. Nearby, too, were the blacksmith shop and the cleaning shed. Around the furnace were the piles of ore and limestone and the slag heaps of furnace waste. This was the industrial heart of Hopewell Village. To it came the wagon loads of raw materials; and from it went the wagon loads of pig iron, gate metal and cast products which constituted the source of income to pay the wages of the several hundred men and women who worked for the owners of Hopewell Furnace.

About 25 men were employed on each of two shifts at the furnace.[2] This did not include the blacksmith, the wheelwright or their helpers. It did include a founder, a keeper, fillers, guttermen, and molders as well as men who did the jobs described as "putting in the mine," "putting in the night stock" or "stocking coal." In later years there was also a "banksman."[3]

The furnace was charged about every half hour with 15 bushels of charcoal, 400 to 500 pounds of ore and 30 to 40 pounds of limestone. In the two year period from May 1, 1880, to May 17, 1882, Hopewell Furnace consumed 352,365 bushels of charcoal in 23,491 charges.[4] The consumption of charcoal was always higher in the first week of the blast, perhaps 50 to 100 charges more than in the second week,[5] because of the necessity of heating the inwalls before the charge was put in. In normal operations it required about 160 bushels of charcoal to make a ton of iron.[6] The annual requirements for charcoal at Hopewell consumed 5,000 to 6,000 cords of wood.[7]

[2] Atwood Lacey Interview, October 17, 1940.
[3] For the various classifications of furnace workers see Appendix B.
[4] SM 34, p. 175.
[5] SM 60, *passim*.
[6] Overman, *op. cit.*, p. 168.
[7] *Morris Diary, op. cit.*, p. 4

Abandoned Hopewell Furnace

The iron ore for Hopewell Furnace came from three mines owned in whole or in part by the furnace proprietors. In addition there was a reciprocal arrangement in 1802 with Changewater Furnace by which Hopewell obtained ore and Changewater received castings.[8] The earliest source of ore was the mine called Hopewell, or sometimes Birdtown, opened about 1770.[9] Ore from this mine was reported in 1883 to contain 37.85 per cent metallic iron, but it may have produced richer ore at an earlier period of its operation. It contained

[8] *Changewater Furnace Account Books,* 1802. Microfilm at Hopewell Village Library.
[9] Charles William Heathcote, "The Iron Industry of Northern Chester County" (*Bulletin of the Chester County Historical Society,* 1936), p. 50.

Unique Wooden Blowing Tubs and the Water Wheel in Deteriorating Furnace

two veins each about 7 feet thick at the top and as much as 25 feet at a lower level.[10]

Jones Mine was operated for more than one hundred years in Robeson and Caernarvon Townships of Berks County not far from Morgantown. Hopewell owned a section of this mining land. The metallic content of the Jones ore was apparently fairly high, for in 1824 Hopewell used about 4,500 pounds of ore per ton of iron produced.[11] An additional source of income was derived from the Jones Mine after 1843 when an English company leased the right to the copper at ten dollars per ton raised.[12]

As early as 1821 Hopewell was receiving some of its ore from the Warwick mines near St. Mary's Episcopal Church in Chester County. This mine was opened before 1760 and had numerous veins varying in thickness from 1 to 17 feet. It averaged about 45 per cent metallic iron.[13] Royalty was paid on the ore used, based on the tonnage of iron produced by the furnace, at rates ranging from $.87½ to $1.12½ per ton of iron.[14] In 1829 Hopewell became part owner of Warwick by the purchase of 1/11 of 1/8 of the mines from Miss Martha Rutter for a price of $350, and 5/11 of 1/8 from John P. Rutter for $800.[15] For the very profitable blast of 1837 the royalty on ore from Warwick Mine amounted to $1,268.76, of which $1,182.23 was paid to other partners, the remainder being the Hopewell share.[16]

About 1840 Hopewell Furnace joined a new kind of partnership called the Warwick Furnace Reserve. Anyone who owned a share could search for ore anywhere in the 20,000 acre reserve in Chester and Berks Counties. Any iron found

[10] *Second Pennsylvania Geological Survey*, 1883, Chester County, pp. 176, 236. (Microfilm.)
[11] HV 8240725.
[12] *Morris Diary, op. cit.*, p. 88.
[13] *Second Pennsylvania Geological Survey, op. cit.*, p. 240.
[14] SM 12, p. 124.
[15] *Cash Book* for 1828–1830, November 20, 1829; SM 14, p. 72.
[16] SM 21, Blast of January 3, 1836, to April 10, 1837.

Another View of Blowing Machinery

Partial Restoration of Furnace Group

could be removed and paid for at the rate of 50¢ per ton, less the proportionate share of the reserve owned."

The limestone for the flux was sometimes obtained from quarries on Hopewell land. More of it was apparently bought from the Christian Mast quarry east of Morgantown. The price paid Mast in 1851 was 50¢ per load for the 169 loads used during the year."

No charcoal furnace could operate continuously. The intense heat, friction and draft gradually wore away the inwalls and hearth, and eventually the furnace had to shut down for repairs. It often happened, too, that the supply of charcoal on hand in the fall was not sufficient to keep the furnace in blast

[17] Long, *Short History of Hopewell Furnace, op. cit.,* p. 7.
[18] SM 37, p. 106.

Partial Restoration of Stack, Front View

over the winter when no new supply of fuel was arriving.[19] When the charcoal was exhausted, the operation ceased until the colliers resumed their work in the spring. During this period of inactivity the necessary repairs were made on the stack and hearth in order to have it in good operating order when the new supplies of charcoal arrived. Probably some repair work would have been necessary about once a year even if there had been no other reason to shut down.

The frequency with which the repair work was done during the winter led one observer to conclude that ". . . they meant to go out of blast every fall, and if they did not there was some extraordinary reason for it. . . ."[20] Many iron men were aware that their furnaces worked better in the clear, dry air of winter than in the moist, humid air of summer. Henry Huse Campbell explained the greater efficiency of winter operation in terms of fuel needs, "On a moist summer day the air holds about 6 grains of water per cu. ft. On a cold winter day it holds 1.7 grains or less. The average for the year is about 3.6 grains."[21] To reduce one pound of water to H^2 and O^2 absorbed the heat produced by burning 0.8 pounds of coke. Thus the moisture in the air on a humid day used fuel not necessary on a dry, cold day[22]

Hopewell Furnace made iron during the winter months when it could do so. A letter in 1823 spoke of an intention to continue the blast all winter.[23] The longest blast in Hopewell history lasted through most of two winters from January 3, 1836 to April 10, 1837.[24] In 1859 the furnace was blown until April 8 before it was shut down "For want of coal" and was back in blast three weeks later.[25] The average blast of

[19] For the problems of charcoal-making see Chapter 11.

[20] *Allens Appeal Record, op. cit.,* p. 96.

[21] Harry Huse Campbell, *The Manufacture and Properties of Iron and Steel* (New York : Hill Publishing Company, 1907), p. 74.

[22] *Ibid.,* p. 48.

[23] HV 8231118A.

[24] SM 21, p. 206.

[25] SM 60, p. 5.

Partial Restoration of Bridge House

Hopewell furnace was eleven and one-half months from 1820 to 1840 and ten and one-half months after 1840.[26] The winter of 1881 presented some unusual difficulties according to a newspaper report:

Owing to the severity of the weather during the present winter the proprietors of Joanna and Hopewell Furnaces have been unable to get their usual quantity of wood cut for burning charcoal for these establishments, and fears are entertained that they will have to close their works in the spring for want of fuel.[27]

[26] Kurjack's Chart of Furnace Operation. Hopewell Village Library.
[27] *Daily Local News*, West Chester, Pennsylvania, February 1, 1881.

Restored Furnace and Bridge House

The end of a blast was a period of hilarity for the furnace crew at whatever time of year it took place. The clerk at Martha Furnace made note of several of these occasions: "Blew the Furnace out at 8 o'clock P. M. All Hands drunk," and again, "All in very high glee." He also chronicled many fights during these celebrations.[28] That Martha was not the only furnace where drinking marked this event was proved by this entry about a Hopewell founder: John Painter was

[28] *Martha Furnace Diary, op. cit.,* January 7, 1809, and January 16, 1811.

charged for ". . . 2 quts. whiskey . . . between you and Jacob when Furnace blowd out."[29]

The purpose of all furnace activity was to get a supply of iron extracted from the ore in a usable form. The product of the furnace was cast iron, but there were many variations of the form and shape it assumed when it cooled. One of the most important jobs at the furnace was to mold the iron into useful articles of commerce. For the first three-quarters of a century the most important finished product of Hopewell Furnace was stoves, but there were many other cast items made. Throughout its history Hopewell also sold pig iron and gate metal to forges where it was further treated to produce yet other commodities of iron.

Pig iron was a raw material for further refinement and was sold wholesale to other iron establishments. One pig now in the Hopewell museum is 48 inches long and about $5\frac{1}{2}$ inches by 2 inches on an end. These pigs were formed by running molten iron into sand trenches to cool. The pieces were broken into convenient size for handling. Pig iron, by chemical definition, was ". . . a granular crystalline compound of iron with carbon, silicon, sulphur, phosphorus, and Manganese, with oftentimes also smaller quantities of other metals. . . ."[30] It contained from 2 per cent. to 4 per cent. of carbon which was either in compound or in mixture with the iron. Quantities of the two forms and the presence of other foreign elements determined the different varieties of pig iron: black, gray, white and mottled. Each kind had special uses.[31]

Gate metal was waste from the casting process. Although it was as good metal as the pig iron, it was not as convenient to handle; so it usually sold for about $2 per ton less than the price of pigs.

During its early history Hopewell sold most of its pig iron to forges owned by partners in the furnace company. Mark

[29] *Lewis Evans Journal, op. cit.,* January 16, 1805.
[30] William Henry Greenwood, *Steel and Iron* (London: Cassell and Company, 1900), p. 62.
[31] Overman, *op. cit.,* p. 140.

Restored Water Wheel at the Furnace

Bird, James Wilson and Buckley and Brooke used it at Birdsboro Forge, and Charles Brooke took most of his share of Hopewell profits in pig iron for his Hibernia Forge. But after the halt of stove-making the production of pig iron was great enough to interest other customers. From 1852 to 1875 the names of 27 different forges, located from Lancaster County to Philadelphia, appeared on the Hopewell records as customers.[32]

Prices for pig iron from Hopewell Furnace ranged from a low of $24 per ton in 1802[33] to a reported $99 in 1865. Charles M. Clingan listed an actual sale September 3, 1864, at $93 per ton to Douglassville.[34] For most of the period of furnace operation the price seemed to have been fairly stable at within a few dollars of $30 per ton.

More profit from the furnace iron was available when the fluid metal was poured into molds instead of the pig beds and marketable finished articles were manufactured. Until about the middle of the nineteenth century Hopewell produced and sold a variety of molded products. Although the kind of articles changed with the demands of a changing economy, some idea of the variety can be obtained from listings of castings, other than stoves which were always of first importance, made in several decades for which records were available. The following kinds of castings were representative:

For the 1780's: Foundry castings, hammers, anvils, forge castings, potts.

For the 1800's: Dutch ovens, hallow ware, riddles, pots [in many sizes], skillets, kettles, lids, bake plates, flat irons, wheelbarrow wheels, French kettles, sash weights, wagon boxes, mill screws, apple mill nuts, tea kettles, and irons, clock weights, forge castings, anvils.

For the 1810's: Backs and jambs, clock weights, sash weights, street grates, stew pans, cambooses, pots, mold boards, mortars, handware, mill gudgeons, bake plates, windmill irons, waffle irons, hollow ware, fire places, mandrels, wagon irons, skillets, anvils.

For the 1820's: Grindstone wheels, mortars and pestals, wing gudgeons, friction wheels, corn-plow machines, mold boards, turning lathe, apple drying kiln, plaster mill, windmill irons,

[32] *Hopewell Papers*, 42215.
[33] SM 1, June 1, 1802, page unreadable.
[34] *C. M. Clingan Pocket Note Book, op. cit.*, n. p.

sash weights, small wheels, tires, shear wings, coulter lays,
land sides, scalleped iron, country iron, finery bottoms,
anvils, rolling mill castings.

For the 1830's : Furnace grates, sash weights, plow castings,
rough castings, mold boards, windmill irons, oil troughs,
bake plates, anvils, mesheinery, threshing machines, griddles,
shelling machines, land sides, sifter grates, wagon boxes.

For the 1850's : Cinder hole plates, plow castings, mold boards,
iron blocks, sand sides, plow handle pieces, beams.

The above tally shows that the invention of farm machinery
brought a demand for new kinds of castings after 1820. Sometimes the market for Hopewell products was quite distant, as
in 1836 when the furnace had a rush order for a large supply
of sash weights to be shipped to New Orleans. Speed was
necessary to get the weights on board a ship about to sail
from Philadelphia.[35]

A letter to Clement Brooke in 1825 mentioned the possibility of a new customer and resulted in the sale of a large
amount of Hopewell iron during the next three years. It
reported :

> I rec[d] a letter from my father the other day stating that
> proposals are to be made to the Commissioners for erecting the
> City Prison for a considerable quantity of Castings and bar
> iron . . . I have business in town and will go tomorrow . . .
> If I can do any thing for you on the subject please inform me
> by letter . . .[36]

It was apparent that this approach was followed up. In
November the Furnace was paid $1,000 for materials sold for
the erection of the "New State Penitentiary."[37] During 1826
and 1827 the molders were making door frames in two sizes,
"peepholes," cones and racks. The price was $65.00 per ton
which was the same as that charged for stoves.[38] Over $3,500

[35] HV 8360109A.
[36] HV 8250411. C. A. Buckley to Clement Brooke.
[37] SM 12, p. 82.
[38] SM 59, p. 11.

Franklin Stove Molded at Hopewell Furnace in the Eighteenth Century

Franklin Fireplace Cast by Buckley and Brooke at Hopewell Furnace

was received for this work in five different payments from June 1, 1826, to April 4, 1827.[39]

A very valuable part of the Furnace product from its founding until 1844 was the stoves molded at Hopewell. Mark Bird was doubtless familiar with casting stoves at his father's iron works. William Bird was making stoves at Berkshire Furnace as early as 1756,[40] and Mark probably continued this work after he became the manager of the Bird enterprises. The number made at Hopewell Furnace must have been relatively small before 1824. The only year before that for which records are available in which Hopewell produced more than one hundred tons of castings was 1783 when cannon and shot were still accounting for a part of the castings total. In 1821 the total weight of castings was sixty-nine tons. Records are not available for the next two years; then in 1824 there were $323\frac{1}{2}$ tons of castings poured. Castings production reached its peak in the celebrated "long blast" of 1836–1837 when $720\frac{1}{2}$ tons of castings were made.[41] Not all of this iron was used for stoves, as we have already noted a variety of castings from this period; but an examination of the labor records showed that the molders were paid for more stoves than for any other kind of castings. To take two examples, in January of 1826 Henry Care was paid for molding $43\frac{1}{4}$ tons of stoves or stove parts and a little more than $7\frac{1}{2}$ tons of all other kinds of castings.[42] Ten years later he was credited with $26\frac{1}{4}$ tons of stoves and less than two tons of other castings.[43] In 1846 the entire weight of cast products was $2\frac{1}{2}$ tons.[44] This last figure demonstrated how little importance castings played after stoves were no longer made.

For most of its history Hopewell did not actually make stoves. It cast the separate plates and shipped them to stove

[39] SM 59, pp. 1, 9, 11, 14, 21.
[40] *Montgomery Manuscripts,* Book I, p. 93.
[41] Kurjack's Chart of Furnace Operation, *op. cit.*
[42] SM 12, p. 108.
[43] SM 21, p. 158.
[44] Kurjack's Chart of Furnace Operation, *op. cit.*

Hopewell Ten-Plate Cooking Stove

Group of Stoves in Hopewell Museum. Note Teakettle in its own base

dealers who supplied the connecting rods, bolts and sheet iron parts. The merchant also did the fine finishing which gave the outside surface its polished look.[45] But a few stoves were finished at Hopewell. The store made retail sales to its customers; and in 1836 this note appeared in the clerk's journal, ". . . stoves are now made on Furnace Bank and not sent off."[46]

As molders were paid during the 1830's from six to twelve dollars per ton for castings made, it was of great importance to have an exact record of what each man had done. Loose papers found in the *Moulders Book for 1832* appear to be

[45] Clark, *op. cit.*, p. 503.
[46] SM 21, p. 159.

daily and monthly records of molding done by each man. The record of weight and kind of casting was later transferred to the *Moulders Book*. Castings were presumably made for orders already received in most cases, for the molders' books also contained the names of the customers for whom the casting was being done.[47] Even with this record at hand it is not possible to determine what a good molder could do in a day. The records seem to have been for a period rather than the day of the dated entry. It is unlikely that George North made 22 stoves on April 2, 1833, as the record credited him with doing.[48]

The work sheet for the molder sometimes noted that he was paid for a number of "half-price stoves." This did not mean the price at which it was sold to a customer but rather that the molder was paid only half of his usual rate because the stove was in some way defective. When these stoves were sold to the customer, the price was about two-thirds of the regular price for a perfect stove.[49]

Stove styles, designs and uses changed over the years, and different names were assigned from time to time. It is a complex task to assemble even a partial list of the Hopewell stoves. Henry C. Mercer described what must have been one of the earliest models as a six-plate stove with a flower design and a ribbon across the top with the inscription, "Mark Bird Hopewell Furnace 1772."[50] Ten-plate stoves in at least three sizes were sold in the early 1800's and also a "Rittenhouse Stove."[51]

When the furnace was reopened in 1816 after seven years of inactivity, it offered more variety along with some more imaginative names for its stoves. The patriotic fervor of the postwar period was evident in such names as New Orleans Victory Stove, Perry Victory Stove, Don't Give Up the Ship

[47] SM 22 and SM 49, *passim*.
[48] SM 22, p. 15.
[49] SM 4, p. 203.
[50] Henry C. Mercer, *The Bible in Iron* (Doylestown, Pa. : Bucks County Historical Society, 1914), p.104.
[51] SM 4, pp. 112, 189–190.

Stove, Ship Stove, Peace Stove, Decatur Flat Front Stove and William Penn Stove.[52] By the 1820's the war motif had been replaced, although the Hulls Victory Stove and the Ship Stove were still being sold in 1827.[53] The new patterns included the Flower Pot, Hornet and Peacock, Shepherd, and Fox Chase.[54]

Ownership pride reappeared, also, when in 1823 stoves were being identified as "Hopewell Stoves" or "D. Buckley Stoves." Many stoves were marked with the name of the merchant who sold them instead of the furnace which molded them. Some of Hopewell's larger customers furnished the molds for the kinds of stoves they found sold most readily.[55] At least one Hopewell customer had a pattern upon which a patent had been issued.[56]

For the late years of stove-making the names given were often descriptive of the shapes or uses for the stoves. A memorandum of the kinds of stoves made in the blasts of 1831 and 1832 showed that the amazing total of 98 different patterns had been molded, distributed as follows:

29 Circular	8 Cabbin
13 Oval	5 Franklin
10 Cannon	8 John J. Hess
2 Square	6 Cornell Cunningham and
9 Cooke	Company
2 Coal grate	2 Henry J. Fougeray
	4 Jacob F. Pliess[57]

The *Moulders Book for 1839* listed the kinds of stoves made in that year and showed several varieties on the same model: Canon Stove No. 1, Cooking Stove No. 8, Cannon Stove No. 1—Back Circular, Cabbin Stove No. 1—New Top, Cabbin Stove No. 1—Plain Top, Franklin Stove No. 4, Circular Stove

[52] SM 8, pp. 14, 56, 59, 62 and HV 8170122.
[53] HV 8270810.
[54] HV 8201006 and HV 8201012B.
[55] HV 8230822 and HV 8270810.
[56] William John Keep, "A History of Stove Making by a man who engaged in the trade for 5 Years," p. 69. Typescript of a manuscript in the Harvard College Library.
[57] *Kemper Manuscripts,* Memorandum of the Weight and Length of Furnace Stoves of Different Patterns.

No. 3—Plain, Cannon Stove No. 1—Bare Cylinder, Cannon Stove No. 1—One Story, Circular Stove No. 3, F. L. Cannon Stove, Premium Stove, Six-Plate Stove, Square Coal Stove, Pagoda Stove, Summer Cook Stove, W. and V. Small Cook Stove, W. and V. Small Heater, J. V. Large Size Stove, Warwick Cook Stove, Radiator Stove and John Volkman Large Stove.[58]

Hopewell stoves must have had a reputation for quality in the region where they were sold, for a firm in West Chester identified for their customers a shipment from this furnace in an advertisement:

> Stoves—The subscribers have just received from Hopewell Furnace an assortment of well finished stoves, which they offer for sale on reasonable terms. November 12.
> Baily and Valintine[59]

Customers for Hopewell stoves were located in an area extending west to York and Harrisburg, south to Baltimore, north to Albany and east to Portsmouth, New Hampshire. Clients of the Furnace in May 1831 numbered 40, ranging from retail buyers of a single stove to large purchasers of hundreds of units.[60] For 1832 orders included one to John J. Hess, Philadelphia, for 543 stoves of 25 different varieties; and on the same day Cornell and Cunningham, New York, ordered 260 stoves in four of their own patterns.[61] A single statement of the account of Morrison and Willard of Portsmouth showed shipments to them of $126\frac{1}{2}$ tons of stoves worth $8,729.63.[62]

Occasionally a stove was ordered for a particular purpose or for a special person. Doctor Joseph Shippen of Philadelphia asked for a "steam stove" to be built for him, and he probably provided the design for the kind he wanted.[63] The Reverend

[58] SM 49, pp. 5–19.
[59] *Chester and Delaware Federalist,* West Chester, Pennsylvania, November 12, 1817.
[60] SM 15, pp. 48–49.
[61] SM 47, May 9, 1832, n. p.
[62] HV 8331218B.
[63] Kurjack, *Hopewell Furnace, op. cit.,* p. 28. This was in 1817.

Mister Samuel Bell of Newark, Delaware, ordered two stoves for his church of the ". . . Largest Square Paterns that one with the Lead Mouldings and Sun on front plate. . . ."[64] The Chester County Courthouse also wanted two stoves; and partner Charles Brooke wrote, ". . . the large Square end and Strate Sides is the kind I think will be best for the place. . . ."[65] The school at Churchtown ordered a stove in September 1825 with the request that it be rushed because it would soon be needed.[66]

One special order must have created a bit of excitement at the furnace, for Hopewell was to serve royalty—even though his royal personage had been unemployed in government for a few years. Daniel Buckley wrote from Philadelphia in 1822,

> . . . old Mr. Fougeray told me a few Days ago he is Coming to the furnace with some patterns for King Joseph Boneparte the price is No object he says, only to have them done well and soon, you will if there is Extra Expense in flasks Put it on the Castings. . . ."[67]

The great merchant, himself, was coming to Hopewell to see that this order was handled properly.

Most sales of Hopewell stoves were at wholesale, and prices were quoted by the ton. Some representative prices were: 1806—$50, 1816—$90, 1822—$70, 1831—$65, 1836—$70 to $90, 1837—$110, 1842—$62.50. The number of units per ton varied with the weight of the kind of stoves ordered. In 1806 the ten-plate stoves varied from 200 to 300 pounds each.[68] Twenty years later stoves were being molded which ranged in weight from a small coal-grate stove weighing 97 pounds to a giant "H A Stove" containing

[64] HV 8221106A.
[65] *Hopewell Papers.* Charles Brooke to Clement Brooke, October 16, 1823.
[66] HV 8220906.
[67] HV 8221010B.
[68] SM 4, p. 113.

691 pounds of iron.[69] Prices quoted usually meant the stoves would be delivered in Philadelphia for that amount. When the merchant sent his own team to pick up his order, he was reimbursed for the cost of hauling.[70] Customers beyond Philadelphia paid the freight from that city. Prices were sometimes quoted to customers in other areas at the Philadelphia rate, as was this one in 1817 to Steinman and Cottrell of Lancaster who were to receive the quantity of stoves they required ". . . not to exceed ten ton of such as are made at Hopewell Furnace at ninety dollars per ton or the phil[a] price . . ."[71] When one customer tried to get a lower price by saying that other furnaces were selling for less, the clerk replied that this was the price from Clement Brooke and Company, and they ". . . did not enquire what others were charging."[72]

An occasional retail sale of a stove at the Furnace gave information on the prices of individual pieces. In 1807 one tenplate stove sold for $14.[73] In 1816 the plain models sold for $11.50–$16, but the patriotic items ranged from $25 for the Don't Give up the Ship to $30 for a Perry Victory.[74] In 1827 a small oval cost $6 and a large circular $12.[75]

Complaints of two kinds came to the Furnace about stoves, defective work and slow delivery. For one letter of the latter kind in 1816 Daniel Buckley noted on the bottom that the stoves were all cast, but he was waiting until he could find a team to go to Wilmington.[76] The demand for stoves was very good in 1836 as indicated by a letter from James H. Deas in Philadelphia, ". . . there is 4 or 5 housekeepers who are harrasing me continually every day and one lady in particular who

[69] SM 12, pp. 108–111.
[70] For examples see SM 21, p. 206.
[71] HV 8170612.
[72] HV 8310222B.
[73] SM 4, p. 189.
[74] SM 8, pp. 40, 59, 62.
[75] SM 59, p. 11.
[76] HV 8161129.

. . . cannot positively have a particle of heat in her house until you send me a cylinder. . . ."[77]

Parts for the stoves were packed in boxes for shipment, and the customer was charged for the box. This item was added to the bill and not included in the prices quoted.[78]

Clement Brooke was still soliciting orders for stoves in 1843,[79] and stoves were sold to nine customers in Philadelphia and one in Quakertown, New Jersey in 1844.[80] But the decision to end stove-making in this latter year was probably forced upon the partners by competition from the new anthracite and hot-blast furnaces. The stove patterns were sold to Isaac Buckwalter for $100.[81] Hopewell would henceforth depend almost completely upon the sale of pig iron for its income from the furnace.

Hopewell Furnace had its golden age to help meet the demand for home heaters and cook stoves in the first half of the nineteenth century. It brought prosperity to its owners for the three decades it was able to compete for its share of the stove market. For forty years longer it showed a profit on pig iron in the years when prices were high.

[77] HV 8361020.
[78] SM 21, pp. 160–164.
[79] HV 8430301.
[80] SM 72, *passim*.
[81] SM 31, p. 42.

8   Management and
       Business Methods

IF WE WERE TO CONTINUE THE METAPHOR OF THE CHARCOAL
furnace as a fickle mistress, we would note that she responded
best when the ironmaster was present and in actual control. A
firm hand, a wide knowledge and an owner's interest in her
success brought a greater reward than the administration of
hirelings. At least the history of Hopewell Furnace showed that
its periods of prosperity coincided with the active management
of one of the owners.

The manager of an iron furnace in the first half of the nineteenth century had a complex and exacting job; he needed an
almost impossible combination of talents and skills to find the
answer to all the problems which faced him day by day. He
was of necessity a technician, a production expert, a personnel
director, a transportation control agent, a salesman, an
expediter, an economist, a market analyst, a currency expert, a
credit manager, a bill collector, a purchasing agent, an investment counselor and a bookkeeper. He had some technical and
administrative help from the founder and the clerk, but the
final decisions were those of the ironmaster.

The ironmaster was a special breed, and relatively few men

met all of the requirements of the position. Those who succeeded were richly rewarded by the profits a little furnace yielded
in the day when charcoal iron was meeting the demands of an
expanding nation. Those who made a wrong guess on the
market, quality of ore, transportation costs or any one of many
problems lost all they had. The roll of bankrupt ironmasters
was long and included such names as Mark Bird, James
Wilson, Matthias Slaugh, James Old, Frederick Delaplank,
John Truckenmiller, Henry William Stiegel and Charles Read.
Eastern Pennsylvania furnaces sold by the sheriff in 1847
numbered 15, in 1848—20, in 1849—30 and in the first four
months of 1850—15. The Walker Tariff of 1846 might have
caused an unusually larger number at this time.[1] The ironmasters, themselves, described their business as a most hazardous one. They related :

> There has been no employment in this State that has met
> with so many revulsions, ruined so many fortunes, impov-
> erished so many families, and in which so few fortunes have
> been made . . . as in the manufacture of Pig Iron. . . .[2]

> Our business . . . is . . . a species of adventure, looked
> upon by the capitalists as more hazardous than any shipping
> or commercial speculation however wild; for in any particular
> enterprise in commerce, even if there should be a loss, there
> remains a balance in cash But to make Iron, there must be
> invested in buildings and machinery, a capital greater than
> many of our merchants employ in their whole business. . . .[3]

> [The ironmaster's expenses include a large sum for the]
> necessary preparation of stock for blast . . . heavy amounts
> in stock in horses, teams and fixtures. These fixtures are almost
> valueless to anyone but the iron master. His stock has to be in
> course of preparation 20 months before it is used; and he lays
> out of the money invested in this way before it is turned into
> Pig Iron, at least an average of 10 months. A years stock is

---

[1] *Documents Relating to the Iron Industry in Pennsylvania, op. cit.*,
pp. 109–110.
[2] *Ibid.*, p. 48.
[3] *Ibid.*, p. 25.

worth $25 to $35,000. It is evident how he would lose if he had prepared stock under one situation of affairs, and before that stock is brought even into a useful shape, an entire change has come over the market, and he may find himself obliged to work this stock up, with loss staring him in the face.[4]

Most of the men who had to face these multiple difficulties had had little opportunity to receive training for their jobs. Most ironmasters before 1850 directed both production and sales; but because they did not understand well either techniques or business, they were poorly prepared to introduce advantageous changes.[5] Overman wrote, ". . . we all well know how difficult it is to eradicate an established prejudice, or even an opinion, among workmen at the iron manufacturing establishments."[6] More improvements in furnaces were brought about by accident than by scientific investigation. For example, the opening at the top of the stack was widened after a furnace in England had had the top give way and was then found to produce more iron of a better quality than before.[7] The first chemical analysis of blast-furnace operation was not made until 1838, and this did not become a common practice in America until after 1860.[8] Obsolete equipment and methods were retained after they were no longer economically advantageous. No clear business records were kept of the exact cost of any part of the process.[9]

What has so far been said about the iron industry in general applied also to Hopewell. Attempts to find information about the cost of labor or of raw materials necessitated sorting the individual payments from the journals and ledgers. Even this was not always possible with complete accuracy because the clerk often lumped many separate payments together and

[4] *Ibid.,* p. 49.
[5] W. Paul Stressman, *Risks and Technological Innovations: American Manufacturing Methods during the Nineteenth Century* (Ithaca: Cornell University Press, 1959), p. 59.
[6] Overman, *op. cit.,* p. 169. This was written about 1850.
[7] Scrivenor, *op. cit.,* p. 248.
[8] Stressmann, *op. cit.,* p. 52.
[9] *Ibid.,* pp. 23, 48.

recorded them as "sundries." No system of maintaining a profit or loss balance for either the furnace or the store was discovered in the extant records.

Some application of science to the iron ore was begun in 1846 when a payment of $15 was made to Thomas Ridgway "for 3 days Geological Surveying at the old Mineholes."[10] Four years later an "analysis of ore" cost ten dollars.[11] Perhaps Charles M. Clingan brought a respect for a scientific approach to the Furnace in the period of these activities. As a medical doctor he would have had training in science before he became an ironmaster.

The ironmaster did not account for his time or the jobs he did, but a little pocket notebook carried by Dr. Clingan contained notes about work done by, and sums of cash paid to, workers. The clerk was doubtless informed of these data to be included in the permanent records. There were lists of hardware items needed and to be purchased when Clingan next went to town. One page had an item concerning labor relations, "To meet choppers on Williams Hill on Thursday Morning."[12] Sally Care Boone said that the manager had to be an expert on the furnace. She remembered several times when her father was recalled hastily from a trip to correct some difficulty with the operation. Usually some "expert tinkering with the tuyere" would bring the furnace back to proper functioning.[13]

One document found among the Hopewell papers, undated but with notations for the tax of 1829, appeared to be an estimate of the operating cost of the furnace for a year. Because it was the only such record which was found, it is quoted below to show the expected operating costs for a year—perhaps 1830:

[10] SM 31, p. 19.
[11] SM 32, p. 111.
[12] *Kemper Manuscripts*, C. M. Clingan pocket note book, n. p.
[13] Sally Boone Interview, March 22, 1941.

5000 Cords Wood @ $1.20	6000.00
Coaling	1500.00
Hauling Wood	500.00
Leaves and Dust	150.00
Hauling Coal	1875.00
[Cost of Charcoal]	10025.00
hauling 1200 loads Mine @ 10/	1600.00
Washing 1200 „ „ @ 1.50	1800.00
	3400.00
Mine Leaf	800.00
[Cost of Ore]	4200.00
Lime Stone	250.00
Workmen [At furnace?]	666.00
Founder	800.00
Repairs, etc.	300.00
[Cost of furnace operation]	2016.00
	42.00.00
	10025.00
[Total Cost]	16241.00[14]

Note that there were no items for depreciation or capital costs. These expenses did not appear except as principal and interest paid on bonds and then never as an operating cost. But if these were the operating figures for 1830, the Furnace should have realized a good profit from the 430 tons of pig iron and 357 tons of castings produced in that year,[15] as the value of this iron would have been about $36,000. By general report Hopewell was averaging about $17,000 per year profit for several years before the blast of 1836–1837. In this blast it

[14] *Hopewell Papers,* H. 2215.
[15] Kurjack's Chart of Furnace Operation, *op. cit.*

was reported to have made over $40,000 "clear of all expenses."[16] In 1842 Clement Brooke wrote to Charles Brooke, a partner, that he expected the profit for that blast would be $9,000.[17] This was during a depression, and 1842 was considered a poor year in the iron business generally. Hopewell profits were down, but the furnace was still making money for its owners.

Hopewell was owned during most of its history as a partnership. Mark Bird built it and hired a "Mr. Markey" as manager; later a "Mr. Lewis" and William Hayes were managers for Bird. Hayes rented the furnace from Bird during the Revolutionary War.[18] From 1787 to 1800 the furnace had a rapid succession of owners and several changes of managers; only James Old was his own manager. After 1800 ownership was a partnership of the Brooke and Buckley families as long as the furnace operated. Thomas Brooke was the first manager for this partnership in the years 1800–1801.[19] Matthew Davis was hired to run the Furnace for two years[20] and was succeeded by Daniel Knabb who served until 1807 when Mathew M. Brooke became ironmaster.[21] When the Furnace reopened in 1816, the partners made Clement Brooke the manager; and he remained in that position for thirty-two years.

The financial arrangments between the partners is not very clear from the records. Clement Brooke was paid a salary, usually about $600 per year, for managing the Furnace. But the distribution of profits did not seem to have had any regular pattern. In the 1840's there were several notations of cash drawn by Clement Brooke in the sums of $5,563, $2,964, $3,945, $7,800, $7,200 and $6,199.95$\frac{1}{2}$ "paid at Sundry times as per his memorandum."[22] Settlement was apparently

[16] *Morris Diary, op. cit.*, May 20, 1837, p. 19.
[17] HV 8421112.
[18] *Montgomery Manuscripts*, Book III, p. 39.
[19] SM 4, p. 251.
[20] SM 1, p. 322.
[21] *Brooke Family Papers*, Mathew M. Brooke to Mathew Brooke, April 23, 1808.
[22] SM 28, pp. 45, 72, 125; SM 31, pp. 9, 31.

balanced among the partners in some way, because in 1842
Clement informed Charles Brooke that his share of the profits
would entitle him to receive 100 tons of pig iron.[23]

A few items in the Furnace papers indicate that relations
were not always smooth among the partners. This note by the
clerk in 1817 was one :

> . . . D. Buckley said he received the Balance in full from
> Ober and Kline Some time last winter the amount of the
> Balance was $393.74 cts and Charles Brooke received from
> D. Buckley at Pequea in February last $240 and the remainder
> $153.74 cts has never Been paid or Received at the
> Furnace . . ."[24]

Possibly that incident represented only an oversight, but the
following letter shows some hostility in the company :

> . . . in reply to yours concerning Charles Brooke's reflec-
> tion, must say that he has not sent any money or Note since
> his return to Hib.[ernia Forge] nor do I expect any under the
> circumstances, the bad humour he was in when he left, merely
> because I asked him to do what was Equal Justice to the parties
> concerned. I tried to reason the matter with him, but his
> replies were curses and harsh Epithets such as no Gentleman
> would use . . . he says there is a conspiracy formed against
> him . . . I mentioned to him what I had written to you when
> I wrote for your note and also your reply that what ever time
> you had extended you to charge you interest. I told him I
> would have to charge him in like manner [for pig iron secured
> from Hopewell].
> He said to Hell with the interest and that you were a rich
> man that I might do with your account as I pleased . . . He
> is a very unpleasant man to do business with or for—the thing
> might of been better arranged had Mr. Clement Brooke of
> been here. He stands in his own light by avoiding Chas.
> Brooke. I think there is but little prospect of their ever settling
> their business unless they meet each other face to face. . . . I
> understand he has no coal to drive on his forge—if he wanted
> Pig Iron he would most likely of made a payment . . ."[25]

[23] HV 8421112.
[24] SM 7, August 23, 1817, n. p.
[25] *Kemper Manuscripts*, 1851 letter to M. B. Buckley, unsigned but
probably from Charles M. Clingan.

During the next year this partnership was dissolved in a court suit to partition Hopewell assets, and Charles Brooke was paid his share of the valuation put upon the property.[26]

Hopewell's period of greatest prosperity was reached under the management of Clement Brooke, son of Thomas Brooke. Clement was an outstanding example of the men who made a success of the iron business—"the shrewd, calculating and trained businessmen who emerged in the first part of the nineteenth century."[27] This assessment by a recent historian was similar to the view of a man who, wanting Clement for a partner in a new furnace, wrote, ". . . I consider you one of the best Iron Masters in Pa.. . . ."[28]

Clement Brooke's success as ironmaster was due in part to his early training in furnace operation and business. He resided at Hopewell as early as 1800 when he was assisting the clerk.[29] A little later Clement secured cash by selling some of his used clothing to four men for a total of £3 5s. 4½d.[30] Two journal entries in 1803 showed that he was paid as a substitute keeper at the furnace.[31] This was a very responsible job for a young man who had not reached his majority, for the keeper was in charge of furnace operation during the night shift. He must certainly have had previous experience around the furnace before being given so much responsibility.

A new relationship between Clement Brooke and Hopewell Furnace apparently began on February 19, 1804, when the clerk recorded, "This day Clement Brooke came to the Furnace."[32] That may even have been his own public notice that he had assumed a new position, for during the next five years the jobs he was doing indicated that he had become the

---

[26] *Berks County Deed Book* 59, p. 529.
[27] Bining, *Early Ironmasters of Pennsylvania, op. cit.,* p. 13.
[28] HV 8361205, John J. Hess to Clement Brooke.
[29] Clement Brooke was born May 10, 1784. Brooke Family Geneological Record, *Hopewell Papers,* H 18 General; SM 43, p. 350 and SM 1, pp. 73, 172, 255.
[30] SM 2, p. 77.
[31] SM 1, p. 31; SM 2, p. 107.
[32] SM 1, p. 47.

company clerk. His expenses were paid "when going to Dowlins, Red Lion, Potsgrove and Sundry other Places;" he went several times to Birdsboro Forge to "post the books;" he both made and received cash payments for the company.[33] These were duties and activities which were usually the work of the clerk. It is not clear what salary Brooke was paid during this time. In a little more than four years there were two payments credited to his account. On May 28, 1804, he received £32½ "for his Time at this place to the 1st of April last."[34] For about six weeks work this was a respectable wage of $58 per month. But four years later the journal contained a curious item which read, "Note Clement Brooke commenced Business 17th of February 1804 and charges to amount of his debt to the 1st April 1808 which is £236–7–3½." He was then credited with that sum to pay off his accumulated debts.[35] One year later he was paid $300 for his work for the preceding year.[36]

When the furnace was out of blast from 1808 to 1816, Clement gained more experience of value to an ironmaster by running the stamping mill and by serving as caretaker at Hopewell. In these jobs he had employees under him, and so he gained experience with personnel problems.[37]

When the furnace reopened, Brooke had had a training period which included both the technical and the business aspects of the work. He was prepared to assume wide responsibilities. He and his family lived well as was indicated by the improvements made at the mansion[38] and by such records as that for November 4, 1825, showing that he had paid $200 and his old "Gigg" for a new one. An apparently related item on the same day said that the Furnace had pur-

[33] SM 44, November 17, 1804, September 16, and October 7, 1805, n. p.
[34] SM 43, p. 370.
[35] SM 5, p. 58.
[36] SM 4, p. 256.
[37] *Hopewell Papers,* Account of Daniel Buckley and Co. with Clement Brooke.
[38] See Chapter 4.

chased for $145 "a cream coloured Gigg horse of Henry High inn keeper in Philadelphia."[39] Clement's salary was $600 per year plus $70 for his wife's services as housekeeper. The use of the mansion house was rent free, and he received food for himself and family at Furnace expense.

Clement Brooke became a man of influence in the business world of Pennsylvania. He owned a share in other iron works beside Hopewell—Black Rock Furnace in Lancaster County, Marion Furnace in Mifflin County, Berlin Iron Works in Union County and Reading Furnace and Robesonia Iron Company in Berks County. At the last-named place he helped to start an anthracite furnace in 1845.[40] He owned shares in the Wilmington and Northern Railroad and in the "New Castle and F. Town Rail Road."[41] He purchased coal land in Schuylkill County,[42] and in 1846 received $13,046.50 in cash and notes of the Bank of Pennsylvania from his son-in-law William R. White as his balance on stocks purchased.[43]

The feeling of the people who worked for him, or perhaps the desire to court his favor, was reflected in the number of Hopewell Village families who named sons for Clement Brooke. The census of 1850 for the nearby townships showed the following names: Clement Hughes, Clement Care, Clement Rutter, Clement Squibb, Clement Russell, Clement Painter, Clement B. Clingan and Clement B. Kephart.

Clement Brooke retired from active management of Hopewell Furnace in 1848. Late in 1849 or early in 1850 he moved into a new house in Pottstown,[44] where he lived until 1859; then he moved to Philadelphia and died there in 1861.[45] His will made special bequests to his wife and son and provided

[39] SM 12, p. 88.
[40] *One Hundred and Twenty-Five Years of The Robesonia Iron Company, op. cit.,* p. 2.
[41] *Hopewell Papers,* Notes on Stock Purchases, December 8, 1838 and September 6, 1841.
[42] HV 8300407A.
[43] HV 8460218.
[44] SM 32, p. 82.
[45] *Richards Scrap Books,* Vol. S, p. 95. Berks County Historical Society.

that the residue of his estate should go to his daughter Maria Clingan and the children of his deceased daughter Ann White.[46] John Church received half of the Berlin Iron Works on condition he pay $100 to Alexander Church.[47]

John Church succeeded Clement Brooke as Hopewell manager for one year before the job was assumed by Dr. Charles M. Clingan. Clingan was twenty-nine years of age and had been the husband of Maria Teresa Brooke for six years when he was given the position of manager by his father-in-law. He had attended West Chester Academy and was graduated from Jefferson Medical College in Philadelphia in 1840. He seemed to have preferred the iron business which his father had followed to his own profession of medicine and had leased Rock Furnace before his marriage.[48]

Clingan continued as manager at Hopewell for ten years, and then he moved his family to Philadelphia where he engaged in the banking and provision businesses. Until his death in 1876 he retained an interest in Hopewell Furnace and came back frequently. The Hopewell records gave no reason for the departure of the Clingan family from the village in 1859, but a heavy loss from the unfortunate experiment with an anthracite furnace at Hopewell[49] could have been one reason. Boredom bred by Hopewell's isolation and limited social activities may have been another cause. But the family still liked food from the farm after they moved to the city. The housekeeper at Hopewell received instructions to send a weekly box of food to Philadelphia containing such delicacies as sauerkraut, doughnuts, smoked meats and fresh eggs.[50] At Clingan's death his estate was valued at $27,483.20 of which $10,000 was the valuation put upon his share of Clingan and Buckley Company, the owners of Hopewell Furnace.

Clingan was remembered by two surviving Hopewell

[46] HV 8620404.
[47] *Hopewell Papers*, H 18 General, Will of Clement Brooke.
[48] *Reading Eagle*, February 11, 1917.
[49] See Chapter 3.
[50] Sally Boone Interview, March 22, 1941.

residents as a good-looking man who was quite popular with the ladies of the community, but "a good and just man" who was "possibly a bit hen pecked" by his wife.[51]

Clingan's departure ended the experience with owner-management at Hopewell. The last twenty-four years of Furnace operation saw hired managers in charge. Nathan Care, John R. Shafer and Harker Long were the managers during this period.[52]

The business assistant to the ironmaster was the clerk who, if capable, could relieve the ironmaster of many of the details of management. Sometimes there was a storekeeper, as in the early 1800's and in the 1830's; but usually the clerk was in charge of the store. He ordered supplies, made the sales and kept track of the store's accounts with the workers.

But this was only a part of the complex job of the clerk; he was also paymaster in a quite complex system. Furnace workers and general laborers had their wages recorded in the journal monthly or quarterly; colliers and molders were paid over longer units of time, sometimes annually or at the end of a blast. Some casual workers were paid in cash, and records of these payments were kept on loose papers and then transferred to the cash book. A daily record was kept of the work done by each molder, but these were grouped into larger units for posting.[53]

The clerk kept track of orders for pig iron and castings, determined the priority for filling orders and took the abuse of customers when orders were delayed.[54] He collected on some of the customers' accounts.[55] He was held responsible when he extended credit to a worker who was already too far in debt to the company.[56]

Money was usually not paid out for wages. The clerk

[51] Rose Sands and Catherine Rhoads Interview, May 13, 1941.
[52] HV 8761110 and Birdgens and Witmer *Atlas, op. cit.*, p. 55.
[53] *Hopewell Papers,* pages of clerks notes on work by molders.
[54] HV 8321103C, HV 8330423A and HV 8320818.
[55] HV 8281016.
[56] SM 2, p. 90.

recorded earnings in the journal and ledger, and the worker drew against this for credit at the store and for the settlement of accounts. The clerk paid for goods bought in other stores and for transactions among the workers or with outsiders. Sometimes such business could become rather complex, for example this notation in 1806 : Frederick Meck was charged $1.50 in favor of Robert Gilmore "for a Debt owed by Adam Johnston and Meck bot a cow from Johnston and is charged with ten dollars on acct. the cow Meck has give Johnston Cr. for $5½ and $1½ is what Johnston owed Gilmore."[57]

The clerk made payments, and usually these were made with mutual trust. But once in a while there was a record of a witness to a payment, as this one: "Peter Geiger Paid him in full on Williams Hill after his wood was taken up in the presence of M. Walters."[58]

The clerk had to be able to differentiate among workers who were credited or debited in the books. Similarity of names was a possible cause of confusion. One John Painter was always identified as "founder" long after he had ceased to work at that job. Others, too, were matched with their occupation. Negroes were identified as such. Juniors and seniors were common, and now present a perplexing problem to the researcher who tries to follow several generations of the same family at Hopewell. The clerk in 1843 did not find any of these usual methods suitable to distinguish between two workers named Joseph Quinter; so he called the one "Black Head" and the other "Red Head."[59]

Most of the clerks were probably of limited training and experience as bookkeepers. It is not too surprising, therefore, to find that they had made errors. Some of these were never corrected, but in the journal for 1818 there were four pages devoted to correcting "errors in journalizing."[60] The prize error

[57] SM 44, November 6, 1806, n. p.
[58] SM 31, p. 7.
[59] Index to SM 29.
[60] SM 8, p. 158 ff.

probably was the £2592 13s. 6d. misplaced by the clerk in 1805.[61]

For all of his multitudinous duties and extensive responsibilities, the clerk was paid a salary ranging from $60 per year paid to Samuel Heister in 1804[62] to $300 per year paid to Thomas Foster in 1837.[63] The most common rate was $200. Most of the clerks had free room and meals at the mansion house, which added considerably to the monetary emolument.

Both the manager and the clerk did considerable traveling on company business and had their expenses paid from company funds. A long list of travel expenses for the years 1818–1820 ranged from $0.37½ for a trip to Reading to $16.57 "for D. Buckley to Baltimore." In addition there are payments for trips to Lancaster, York, Philadelphia, Marietta, Churchtown, West Chester, the Swamp, Columbia, Manheim, Wilmington, Downingtown, Hamburg, Orwigsburg, Evansburg, Conowingo, Harrisburg and "to sundry places." Usually the journal did not say who had done the traveling, but both Daniel Buckley and Clement Brooke as well as Valentine Hoffman, a carter, were named for some of these journeys.[64] Distant customers were not neglected; for the furnace paid a tavern bill for two at Portsmouth, New Hampshire in 1838.[65] Although travel expenses were usually not itemized, a tavern bill in 1834 from the Golden Swan in Philadelphia listed these expenses for "Mr. Brooke":

To 9 Days Board	9.00
Horse	4.50
Washing	.25
2 Lemonades	.25
Postage	.12
	$14.12[66]

[61] SM 44, June 18, 1805, n. p.
[62] SM 1, p. 322.
[63] SM 21, p. 200.
[64] SM 10, pp. 2–60.
[65] HV 8380529.
[66] HV 8340107.

Most business was conducted on credit. One customer wrote that it would not be profitable for him to buy for cash and sell on credit; so he would not buy iron if he could not get it on credit.[67] On one occasion a reduced price was offered by the clerk for payment in twenty days.[68] The more usual payment was in the form of a note to run for 60 days to six months. These notes were often discounted for cash or passed on to someone else in payment for Furnace bills. The Office of Discount and Deposit in Reading was used extensively by Hopewell Furnace to convert its time payments into cash.[69] At the end of the year, however, the company had often received only a small percentage of payment for the castings sold. The ledger on December 31, 1832, showed that ten customers had bought $19,375.56 worth of castings for which the company had received at that date $8,300.[70]

Another method of collecting was to pay Furnace bills by issuing drafts against a customer.[71] The S. V. Anderson Company in Philadelphia which sold storegoods to Hopewell also acted as Furnace agent to receive accounts in the city. Hopewell paid a small fee for this service,[72] but one customer refused to pay a man sent to collect from him because there was no written authorization presented.[73] Drafts were not always honored and were then returned by the person to whom they had been given for some other kind of payment.[74]

Keeping account of the notes the company held, the dates due, by whom issued and whether or not discounted was an important job for the clerk. Several different systems were devised by different clerks to do this as accurately and thoroughly as possible. In 1826 it was done by a separate

[67] HV 8161101A.
[68] *Hopewell Papers,* undated letter to J. and A. Morrison, Portsmouth, N. H.
[69] For example see SM 10, p. 17.
[70] HV 8330227B.
[71] HV 8361018.
[72] SM 21, p. 160 and HV 8260927.
[73] HV 8281028A.
[74] HV 8200512.

account in the regular ledger,[75] and in 1854 a "Bill Book" was begun to record notes both given and received. All notes issued by Hopewell were reported in this record as paid through 1863, but several of those owed to Hopewell were marked "protested and returned" or written off as uncollectable. Beside one of the latter the clerk had penciled "Bad Eggs."[76]

Occasionally barter was conducted—"Pig Mettal on accunt of the Horse."[77] pig iron for castings[78] or whiskey for iron.[79]

Some kinds of castings were made only when an order was on hand, and an advance payment was required on orders of pots and kettles at the time the order was placed.[80]

The price Hopewell Furnace charged for its castings was usually the same regardless of the size of the order. In 1836, John J. Hess wanted $2.50 per ton reduction because he was placing a large order. Smaller customers, however, complained about the competition when they had to pay a higher price.[81]

Under the system of bookkeeping used at the Furnace, payments were often overlooked and were recorded years after the work was done or the obligation incurred. Perhaps the prize delayed payment for labor was the case of Peter Fox who built a chimney in 1808, and payment was recorded in 1822.[82] The Furnace was also on the receiving end of delayed payments. David Hart did not pay his rent for five years between 1832 and 1837.[83]

Although some workers were in debt to the Furnace, a study of the accounts of 14 workers over a period of about twenty-five years showed only four of them were consistently

[75] SM 12, p. 144.
[76] *Kemper Manuscripts,* Clingan and Buckley Bill Book, 1854–1863.
[77] HV 8200526A.
[78] HV 8221219.
[79] SM 1, p. 87.
[80] SM 44, December 8, 1806 and SM 9, p. 97.
[81] HV 8360105 and HV 8360108.
[82] SM 4, p. 262.
[83] SM 21, p. 200.

in debt, and no one of these was never out of debt. The other 10 were on the credit side of the ledger for most of the time.[84] The Furnace carried a quite large balance for some workers as indicated by the withdrawal of $1300 at one time in 1836 by Thomas Care.[85] No interest was paid on these balances, but neither was interest charged on arrears unless an account was unpaid for several years after the worker left employment at Hopewell.

Hopewell never had a payroll, and almost all business at the store was a book transaction. In all probability little money was kept in the office or the store, but what money was used constituted a problem to the managers. In 1784 they were accepting "Doubleoons" and "Johannas"[86] as well as Pennsylvania currency and doubtless that of other States. Even after the United States created a national monetary system, there were often periods of scarcity of species and uncertainty about the currency. In 1817 the editor of a Reading newspaper made a plea for persons who possessed small coins to take them to a bank for notes because of the difficulty of doing business without coins.[87] Coins were again scarce during the depression of 1837. "Shin plasters," or fractional currency, were substituted for scarce coins.[88]

Depreciated bank notes and counterfeit notes were a frequent problem to the Hopewell clerk. A general rule followed was to charge a larger discount on banks located at a great distance. In 1816 "Western paper" was discounted at 10 per cent, but the rate was 8 per cent on paper from banks on "this Side the mountains."[89] There were many references in the next year or two to discount rates on various kinds of paper money ranging from 2 per cent to 10 per cent. The clerk was careful to note the kind of money received and the

---

[84] A summary of this study is found in Appendix B.
[85] SM 21, p. 161.
[86] SM 41, p. 39.
[87] *Berks and Schuylkill Journal,* March 1, 1817.
[88] *Morris Diary, op. cit.,* pp. 59, 102.
[89] SM 8, p. 45.

bank of issue, apparently in case of future question. In one case he even recorded the serial number and date of issue of a $10 note of the Franklin Bank of New York City.[90] One customer included an apology with money sent saying, "I believe the money is all equal to Philadelphia but one 3 dollar note which I would not send if I had other enough. . . ."[91] The furnace also specified that payment for stoves was to be ". . . in York or Lancaster Paper or Good Bank Paper of Maryland or Pennsylvania."[92] Several entries from 1818 to 1823 noted that counterfeit bills had been received and returned to the sender.[93]

Payments by check, frequently posted in the records after 1846, indicated the use of more bank services.[94] The opening of Western mines was probably responsible for the references in 1854 to payments made "in Gold."[95]

A successful ironmaster needed to be a man of many talents and broad experience. Clement Brooke met the requirements because of his background and training for the job, but he was also favored by a generally rising economy while he was manager at Hopewell Furnace. He made a sizable fortune and retired while profits were still being made from charcoal iron. No other Hopewell manager did so well either before or after him.

[90] SM 46, March 10, 1823, n. p.
[91] HV 8160925.
[92] *Hopewell Papers*, Agreement with George Small and Morriss of York. Undated, but probably about 1820.
[93] Examples are: HV 8180210, HV 8181212, SM 9, p. 126.
[94] SM 31, p. 2 ff.
[95] SM 65, p. 1 ff.

Part Four
The Commercial Village

9   The Store

BESIDE THE ADMINISTRATIVE DUTIES MENTIONED IN THE previous chapter, the clerk had complete responsibility for the village store during most of the history of Hopewell Furnace. However, for a few years a storekeeper was employed in addition to the clerk.

The multiple tasks performed by the clerk were conveniently grouped in a single building between the Big House and the furnace in which were located both the company office and the store. This structure had a basement, a main floor, an attic and a lean-to shed on the east side in which bulk grain and feed were stored. The main section was built of stone and the shed of tongue and groove boards. Norman M. Souder, National Park Service architect, found an earlier building concealed by a more recent one. He believed the earlier one dated from the late 1700's, and the more recent alterations appeared to have been made in the 1860's.[1]

In the later building the basement had two rooms, and some crude attempt at insulation with mud and straw indicated that they were used to store perishable goods. A fireplace provided heat to the west end. The packed earth floor in both rooms showed evidence that flood waters of French Creek

[1] Norman M. Souder, "The Office and Store Building" (unpublished study, 1960). Hopewell Village Library.

185

Office-Store Before Restoration

Office-Store from South with Hopewell Mansion in Background

had reached this height. On the main floor were also two rooms with the west one having been used as the office and the other as the store. The walls were plastered directly over the stone. Two fireplaces had been a part of the original construction. But surely when stoves were the chief furnace product, one would have been used to advertise its superior heating ability to customers and visitors to the store. At some time an iron safe had been set into the space where one fireplace had been.[2]

The attic was used as a bedroom for some of the clerks. For a time after the store closed, this building was rented for a residence.[3] Some alterations may have been made in this period.

Although a store was a necessity for the isolated charcoal furnaces, it was often regarded by the owners as more than a convenience to the workers. In fact it was sometimes the only source of profit to the ironmaster.[4] According to a British writer, the system of paying wages in credit at the store ". . . was obviously open to grave abuse; and there is abundant evidence that it was often used as a means of surreptitiously reducing earnings and of increasing profits by exploitation."[5] This study of the Hopewell Furnace store presents evidence upon which it will be possible to arrive at some conclusions as to whether these charges can be applied to this business.

The legal basis for store operation was a state license system for which a fee was paid to the county treasurer. In 1830 the following notation appeared in the treasurer's records of Berks County concerning the Hopewell store:

Clement Brooke Has paid to me for the use of the Commonwealth Six dolls. 67 cts. which entitles him to wholesale or retail Foreign merchandise and Liquors, as a wholesale dealer or a retailer of the Eighth Class, within the County of

[2] *Ibid.*
[3] Charles Sheridan Care Interview, February 24, 1941.
[4] Scrivinor, *op. cit.,* p. 299.
[5] Thomas Southcliffe Ashton, *Iron and Steel in the Industrial Revolution* (Manchester: Manchester University Press, 1951), p. 189.

Rear of Office-Store Restored with Charcoal House in Background

Front of Office-Store Partially Restored

Berks, for Eight months, from the first of September, one thousand eight hundred and thirty.[6]

Annual fees for other years ranged from a low of $7.00 to a high of $10.75.

It is possible that the store was run for a time in the early 1800's by a man who was in private business for himself as well as operating the company merchandising. John Brower was the storekeeper from December 1, 1807 to April 27, 1809 —and perhaps also earlier than this—but at no time in almost a year and a half was there any indication that he was being paid a salary. He received a small sum from the Furnace and "sundries" which could have included some salary. But neither the amount nor the time of payment seem to indicate this. He was also paid by some of the employees with no reason given for the payment. He bought hollow ware and stoves from the Furnace which he apparently sold on his own.[7] If this represented a different kind of arrangement, it was the only time the store was not run by a salaried employee of the Furnace.

The source of supply for goods to be sold was changed from time to time. Until 1807 the chief wholesaler was Samuel Laverty and Company of which Mathew Brooke was one of the partners. He received about $6600 when the partnership was dissolved.[8] For some succeeding years storegoods were supplied through the Buckley and Brooke store in Birdsboro; then in the autumn of 1821 a long association began between the Hopewell store and Samuel V. Anderson and Company in Philadelphia.[9] Thirty years later wholesale purchases were being made from George Lippincott and Company, McFarland Evans and Company, Levick Brothers and Company and Bowlby and Brenner. These wholesalers also were located in Philadelphia.[10] Purchases at times were made locally from

[6] HV 8301126.
[7] SM 5, pp. 87, 119.
[8] SM 44, January 20, 1807, n. p.
[9] SM 6, p. 372.
[10] SM 32, p. 108.

Clerk's Desk in Office-Store

farmers, millers and neighbors. A journal entry in 1819 said the Furnace had purchased "linen at oction."[11]

The clerk kept records of his sales on scraps of paper and later recorded them in the day book, and from this to regular posting in the journal and ledger.[12] Shortage of coins was a problem when the storekeeper had money payments to make. In 1848 Henry Sheets drew his account in full to the amount of $29.23½, but the clerk had no coins. He gave Sheets $30 with the understanding that 76½¢ would be returned, which a later notation showed was done.[13]

The Hopewell store did not try to encourage quantity

[11] SM 10, p. 30.
[12] HV 8350331B.
[13] SM 31, p. 62.

buying, for no reduction in price was given with the purchase
of large quantities. For example the price on 100 "segars" was
25¢, and it was also 6¼¢ for 25.[14]

Interest was not normally charged when purchases ran
ahead of a worker's earnings, but as well as being charged on
accounts which were not settled for some time after the
workers left the employment of the Furnace,[15] interest was
also collected on a purchase by a non-worker when the account
was not paid within a year after the transaction.[16]

The store acted as agent for villagers in the purchase of
goods from other stores. For example John Painter was debited
for six yards of chintz for which the Furnace paid cash to a
city store, possibly through the services of a teamster going to
Philadelphia.[17] The Hopewell store also purchased shad and
mackerel by the barrel on behalf of several of the workers.
Cash was sent by the Furnace teamster to make the purchase.[18]

Considerable informality marked the business done with
neighbors and employees. The journals contained many instances of goods charged to a workman but "delivered" to
someone else. Often the person named as having received the
goods was a son, daughter or wife; not infrequently it was
a housekeeper or neighbor. Apparently women often picked
up orders at the store for men at work when they were making
purchases for their own families. Sometimes the clerk noted
that sales were made "per your order" or "by your written
order," but often there was no indication of anything other
than verbal authorization.

The company lost some money on unpaid accounts. A list
of debtors at the beginning of 1820 included 33 customers who
owed a total of over $4,300. Apparently these were not a
cause of worry, however, for an additional listing was desig-

[14] SM 9, p. 87.
[15] Some examples are found in SM 12, pp. 123, 138.
[16] SM 12, p. 122.
[17] SM 12, p. 113.
[18] SM 9, p. 28 and SM 12, p. 91.

nated "Bad Debts" to the amount of $346 owed by 41 accounts.[19]

The volume of sales at the store never gave evidence of a large operation. Including some payments for blacksmith services and making no attempt to allow for changes in the value of the dollar, the following were the total and average monthly sales for the periods indicated:

Inclusive Dates	Total Sales	Monthly Average
October 1, 1805–September 30, 1806	$ 2,888.19	$240.68
September 1, 1831–August 1, 1832	4,911.25	446.66
March 21, 1853–September 20, 1856	12,018.93	386.16
January 1, 1865–January 1, 1875	17,895.40	135.67[20]

No balance sheet of store profits was found to show what the company made from these sales.

On the next page are shown the per cent markups on some goods sold. The usual range on most common items was 20 per cent to 40 per cent, based upon wholesale prices which did not include the cost of transportation, salary of clerk or storekeeper, or heat and light for the store.

Price Markup at Hopewell Furnace Store

Item	Unit	Wholesale Price	Retail Price	Per Cent Markup
		1802		
Shoes	pr.	$1.00	$1.33	33%
Sugar	lb.	.067	.13½	100
Whiskey	gal.	.60	1.00	67
Coffee	lb.	.24	.267	9
		1817		
Coffee	lb.	.21	.25	19%
Fur Hats	each	3.00	4.00	33
Flour	bbl.	4.125	4.00	–3

[19] *Hopewell Papers,* List of Store Accounts, January 1, 1820.
[20] SM 4, pp. 1–27; SM 21, pp. 4–38; SM 36, *passim;* SM 37, *passim.*

1827

Shoes	pr.	1.25	1.50	20%
Tea	lb.	1.00	1.24	24
Flour	bbl.	3.125	3.24	3
Sugar	lb.	.0975	.125	29

December, 1831—March, 1833

Sugar	lb.	.07¼ –.0834	.125	30–58
Coffee	lb.	.13½ –.15	.16–.17	19–13
Soap	lb.	.06 –.05½	.10	67–75
Molasses	gal.	.48	.56	17
Rice	lb.	.033/4	.05	33
Mackerel, No. 1	bbl.	5.00	7.00	40
„ No. 2	bbl.	4.00	5.50	37½
S. H. Molasses	gal.	.53	.64	21
Salt Petre	lb.	.11	.24	118
Chocolate	lb.	.12½	.20	60
Ground Salt	lb.	.48	.64	33
Oil	gal.	.40	.48–.50	20–25
Potatoes	bu.	.33	.37–.40	12–21
Cheese	lb.	.08	.09–.12½	12½–56
Tea	lb.	.85	1.25	47
Epsom Salts	oz.	.05	.06½	30

Note : Wholesale prices did not include the cost of transporting the goods from Philadelphia.

Based upon these figures, the profit from the store operation would not appear to have been a major factor in the total profit from Furnace operation. Perhaps the store was primarily a convenience for the workers and a medium for purchases of goods used at the Furnace and in the mansion rather than a source of profit to the partners.

Further evidence that the store was not operated on a professional merchandising basis is found in the table of retail price trends at the Hopewell store given on the next page. In the period from 1802 to 1841 for which the prices of a selected group of items were traced, there was a rather remarkable uniformity despite two definite cycles of general American business in this period. The prices on imported goods—such as sugar, molasses, chocolate and coffee—were rather high in the early 1800's. All prices were relatively high in the period following the War of 1812. They dropped in the depression of 1819 and following but seemed little influenced by the depression of 1837 and following:

Retail Price Trends on Selected Items
Hopewell Furnace Store—1802–1841

(All prices in cents per pound except molasses which is per quart.)

Year	Sugar	Molasses	Rye Flour	Choco- late	Pork	Beef	Coffee
1802	13.3c	20c	3c		12c	5.5c	26.7c
1803	13.3	20	2	31c	7	9.3	26.7
1805		20	2.2		5.5	5.5	
1806		20	3	31	7.7	5.5	
1807		19	2.4		6	7.7	35
1808		19	2.4		6.6		33
1809			2		6.7	6.7	
1816	22	31	3		10	9	31
1817	20	22.5	3.5	25		8	25
1818	16	25	2.7		8	8	30
1819	18	22.5	2.7	30	12.5	8	38
1824	12.5	10	1.8	25	10		25
1825	12.5	10	1.8		4.5	4	25
1826	12.5	12.5	1.8	20	8*	5	25
1827	12.5	12.5	2.1	20	4	4	20
1828	12.5	15	1.8				20
1829	12.5	15	3.5	15			20
1830	12.5	15	3.5	20	4		20
1831	12.5	14	2.1	20	5	4.3	16
1832	12.5	14	1.8	20	8	8	16
1833	12.5	16	2.1	20	5	8	17
1834	12.5	16	2.1				17
1835		18			7	5	13
1836	12.5	18	2.1		7	4.8	13.5
1837	13	18	3.5	20	15*	14	17
1838	12.5	17	3	20		10	15
1839	12.5	16	3	20	15*		15
1840	12.5	18	2.3	20	12*		16
1841	12.5	18	2.1			7	16

* Bacon. Others in that column are for "pork."

Note : All prices were taken from as close to January 1 of the year as they could be found in order to eliminate as much as possible the fluctuation during the year.

Note : Missing years have no store journals available to obtain prices. Missing prices indicate the store was not selling the item in that year, or no unit price could be determined.

How did Hopewell store prices compare with those of other furnace stores or of general stores in the neighborhood? A comparison of prices from the *Hopewell Journals* was made with the journals of several other stores where prices of similar goods were found for the same period of time. There was a common difficulty that the clerk often did not give a unit price for the articles sold. For this reason the results of the study are not too conclusive. But Hopewell's prices were not out of line with any of those from the other stores; they were lower in more instances than they were higher. There was not a great amount of difference in price on most items, and in a fair number of cases the price was identical in the two stores being compared. It is also apparent that the furnace stores observed did not charge prices which were noticeably higher than the neighboring general store. That Hopewell workers traded in both stores would have been one guarantee of a fairly uniform pricing at both places. The results of this study are summarized in the following table :

Price Comparison Between Hopewell Furnace Store and Other Stores of the General Area.

Year	Item	Unit	Hopewell Price	Other Store Price
				Changewater Furnace Store
1802	Molasses	qt.	.20	.20
,,	Sugar	lb.	.13	.14$\frac{1}{2}$
,,	Shoes	pr.	1.20–1.33	1.13–2.00
,,	Tobacco	lb.	.20	.27
,,	Whiskey	qt.	.20	.20
,,	Potatoes	bu.	.43	.52

,,	Corn	bu.	.67	.67
,,	Rye	bu.	.80	.87
,,	Beef	lb.	.05½	.05½
				Mt. Hope *Furnace Store*
1806	Shoes	pr.	1.13–1.50	1.50–2.13
,,	Salt	bu.	.73	.80
,,	Nails	lb.	.11–.12	.15
				Mary Ann *Furnace Store*
1837	Coffee	lb.	.17	.19
,,	Flour	lb.	.035	.04
,,	Salt	lb.	.04	.04
,,	Tea	lb.	1.60	1.36
				Lewis Evans *Store*
1827	Coffee	lb.	.20	.25
1828	Sugar	lb.	.125	.125
,,	Molasses	qt.	.15	.14
1832	Coffee	lb.	.16	.18
1833	,,	lb.	.17	.18
,,	Molasses	qt.	.17	.125

Note : Changewater Furnace was a close neighbor; the other two furnaces were farther inland. Lewis Evans operated a store about four miles from Hopewell and sold goods to many Hopewell workers.

The size of the store room and the storage space precluded a large inventory of storegoods at any one time. The kinds of goods carried varied greatly from one period to another. In 1805 sales implied that relatively few articles were carried in stock with flour, beef, "mushmeal," whiskey, nails and salt comprising most of the sales. On October 31 of that year molasses sales resumed after a long lapse. Sales of this item were brisk in the next few days; so probably a new barrel had arrived.[21] There were many other instances when sales

[21] SM 4, pp. 1–9.

records denoted that commodities were sold at the time the store had received a supply rather than from goods kept on hand at all times. The store was also handling the retail sale of stoves for the furnace in 1805 as was shown by the many transactions in which a single stove was purchased.[22] An inventory made in 1820 set the value of goods on hand, except meat, at $387 and of beef and pork at $480.[23]

As the Furnace production increased its tempo in the 1820's and 1830's, the business at the store increased and so did the kinds of merchandise kept in stock. A small booklet in the Hopewell papers enumerates the items sold in 1832. This record appears to have been a memorandum the clerk was keeping for new stock needed rather than an inventory of supplies on hand. A summary of the tabulation with the clerk's descriptions and notations concerning them is listed below:

Memorandum for Storegoods
Nov 5th 1832

Red flannel
Yellow flannel
2 pieces lowpriced Sattinette
1 Ps Sattinett (Steel Mixd) of
  a good quality
Buckskin Mitts
Buckskin Gloves
6 lb Black Pattent thread N 30
White Cotton Balls N 24
Gilt Coat buttons of a good
  quality
Gilt Vest Buttons of a good
  quality (and Plain)
Black bone Suspender buttons
Black do Vest   do
  of different Sizes
Silk flag hdkf of a good quality
Winter Schawls

Russia Sheeting
Apron Tapes
low priced Calicos
dark Calicoes
1 ps Mourning Chince Do
1 doz prs Germantown hose
Ticking
a few pieces Cotton flannels
5 yds dark drab Cloth (Double
  milled)
2 yds Green Cloth (dark) about
  $3 p yd
Horse Rasps
large Files
3 in Butt hinges & Screws
Thumb Latches
2 Blade Buckhorn Handled
  Pocket knives

[22] SM 4, pp. 10, 22.
[23] HV 8200307A.

a Piece of blue worsted Stuff
for Ladies Cloaks
Means Seal Skin Caps
Boys   ditto   do
a few Pieces Worsted binding
of different colors
Shoe Blacking
Writing Paper
Letter   do
Wrapping do
Quills
Black Sand
Brimstone

1 blade   ditto   do
Barlow knives
Curry Combs
Flat bottomed Candle Sticks
1 Paper 12 oz Tacks
1 Paper 6 oz Tacks
Table Spoons
Butcher Knives
Putty
Salt Petre
Wafers[24]

In an effort to discover what the customers of the Hopewell
store bought, a study was made of the purchases of 26 regular
customers for a period of fifteen months from December 1831
through February 1833. The period chosen was one of Furnace prosperity and also one in which James Benson as clerk
made detailed records of sales. The customers included persons
with incomes ranging from a maid earning 75¢ per week to
the manager-owner with an annual income of thousands of
dollars. Because of the bulk of this study the results were
placed in Appendix C. These records show the quantity and
price of each purchase by each of these customers over the
fifteen months, a summary of the various kinds of goods
bought and the total amount spent at the store.

It will be noted by an examination of these accounts that
some customers bought little or no food. They were the people
who boarded at the Big House and had food provided as a
part of their pay, or they paid the Furnace a monthly rate for
boarding. Men with large families spent a high percentage of
their total for food. Bulk purchases of flour, beef, pork and
bacon were common. Molasses was the usual sweetening agent,
with both West India and "sugar house" (maple syrup)
varieties on sale. Sugar was a luxury at a price per pound of
about one fourth of a day's wage for a laboring man. Choc-

---

[24] HV 8321105.

olate was a delicacy usually kept in stock, as also were some spices.

Home clothing fabrication accounted for extensive sales of cloth and notions. Many kinds of cloth were sold with quality ranging widely from the inexpensive buckram, calico, check, flannel, muslin, nankeen and quilting to a type called "blue cloth" which sold at $5 per yard. This latter may have been material for a coat as its sale was usually associated with the purchase of lining, padding and buttons. Needles, thread, scissors, buttons in many varieties, ribbons, tape and patterns were available to the wife, seamstress and tailor who made the Village clothing.

Although some purchases of ready-made clothing were recorded, these were usually stockings, handkerchiefs, suspenders, belts, shoes, cravats, gloves, hats, shawls and similar accessories. Articles for personal care included razors and strops, shaving soap and brushes, medicines and combs. That last commodity included useful pocket combs, decorative side combs for the ladies, and utilitarian fine-toothed combs for combatting head lice.

The purchase of bulk feed was an indication of ownership of one or more domestic animals, probably a horse or a cow. Perhaps there was some social status represented as possession of a horse set one on a higher social level, if the horse served for riding or driving and not just as a work animal.

Pocket knives had a good sale in Barlow, pen and double-bladed varieties. A demand for window glass and putty showed that windows had progressed from the oiled paper stage of the early frontier. Nails, paper, oil, almanacs and plowshares were kept in stock.

The amount of meat mentioned in the records signified that this was a very important part of the diet of the villagers. Steers and hogs were raised on the Furnace farm and by individual families to be butchered for their meat supply. Neighboring farmers sold meat in the Village. For example in

1827 Thomas Care bought 1,269 pounds of pork at 4¢ per pound from Frederick Landis.[25] In addition to such sources the Furnace in 1834–1835 bought the following amount of dressed meat:

Beef	3,576	pounds
Pork	14,480	,,
Bacon	1,447	,,
Shoulder	1,576	,, [26]

Some of the dressed meat was not in the best of condition as was shown by this notation concerning some pork bought from Charles Brooke of Hibernia Forge, "We took off 2 lbs. per cwt. for green rot."[27] Because brine was one of the commonest preservatives for meat, the sale of salt at the Hopewell store was always high in the autumn months when many people were butchering.

Mackerel by the piece or by the barrel were bought for immediate or long-range use. Shad were less commonly available. In 1839 they were selling at 31¢ each; and they were ". . . very high and very scarce at the fishery," according to the Morgantown storekeeper.[28] Tobacco was stocked regularly and was sold in papers and rolls, by the pound or half pound; and after 1818 "segars" were vended.[29]

Some barter was conducted when the villagers or their wives brought butter, cheese, cabbage, "winager," eggs, dried apples and dried peaches, cherries, mutton, potatoes, "cyder," beets, watermelons, homespun linen, beans, cucumbers and chickens to trade for storegoods. Such transactions were usually not recorded in the journal except for any balance remaining; and, therefore, there was seldom a price mentioned.[30] The store rarely resold any of these wares which probably meant that they were used in the Big House.

[25] SM 59, p. 14.
[26] SM 12, *passim.*
[27] HV 8331212B. Charles Brooke was a Hopewell partner.
[28] *Morris Diary, op. cit.,* April 18, 1839, p. 76.
[29] SM 9, p. 85.
[30] *Hopewell Journals,* 1819–1836, *passim.*

The modern housewife would have missed greengoods, baked products and milk. Modern children would probably not have been happy with a choice of confections limited to "liquorice balls and hoarhound candy."[31]

Something of the history of fashions can be learned by a study of the clothing sold over a period of a half century.[32] In the first decade of the nineteenth century men were wearing both wool and fur hats, and a fancy "white hat" cost Frederick Hart $5.[33] Judging from the quantity of "Red Coating" the store was selling,[34] this color was much in style. William Taylor was probably a bit of a dandy about the furnace in his velvet trousers.[35] But velvet was still good ten years later; and equally expensive, at about $2.00–$2.50 per yard, were "sattennett" and "Coburg Cassimer."[36] Charles Brooke paid $37 for four yards of "Blue Cloth" for his best coat.[37] The Furnace was selling some ready-made "great coats" for men at eight dollars each.[38] The most popular item for either men or women was a shawl. Most were a conservative black, but John Keller had "1 red shall."[39] "Perl buttons" were sold at 25¢ for a set of eight to those who wanted such a decoration.[40]

During the 1820's the distinctive new article of dress was the "Roran hat" which was wool on the outside and lined with fur. Prices started at three dollars each in the summer of 1825, but by fall had increased by a half-dollar and then held firmly at that figure.[41] "Blue Cloth" was still fashionable

[31] *Morris Diary, op. cit.,* December 6, 1844, p. 75.
[32] Men's clothing only was considered as women's apparel will be discussed in Chapter 16.
[33] SM 44, November 29, 1806, n. p.
[34] SM 2, p. 60.
[35] SM 2, p. 122.
[36] SM 9, pp. 97–119.
[37] SM 9, p. 171.
[38] SM 8, p. 71.
[39] SM 9, p. 92.
[40] SM 9. p. 97.
[41] SM 12, *passim.*

at $6.50 per yard.[42] Fancy vests were popular with the trimmings selling for 82¢ per set.[43]

In the 1830's the young executive, James Benson, invested $2.50 in "a black silk velvet stock;"[44] and his superior, Clement Brooke, wore a fur collar on his coat.[45] The furnace expected at least five of its customers in 1837 to be interested in silk hats @ $2.75 plus the store profit and also offered to sell "1 white Russia" to someone for more than $3.00.[46] Pantaloons and "Bangup" coats were tailored by George Wert for Hopewell men.[47]

In the 1840's men were wearing wide stripes and very large plaids. Long, single-breasted vests were made to match the pantaloons in figures and colors. Neck stocks were being replaced by "kravats and scarves." The well-dressed man used a buckled waistband instead of suspenders, preferred his shoes to be square toed and had his "pants to button up before and without a fall."[48]

Most children's clothing must have been made at home and probably was handed down from older to younger. There were very few references in the store books to ready-made clothing for children with the exception of shoes.

The storekeeper had to be alert to check new cloth purchases for damage. In 1833 the invoice from Potts, Reynolds and Company was reduced by $7.40 "For a deduction on Sattinett for moth holes, etc."[49]

Furnace workers and farmers needed tools. The Village store supplied them with axes, shovels, copper kettles, mold boards, empty barrels, chisels, rakes, scythes, files, whetstones, screws and screw plates, hinges, steel traps, curry combs, wood saws,

[42] SM 12, p. 103.
[43] SM 12, p. 60.
[44] SM 17, p. 4.
[45] SM 21, p. 152.
[46] SM 21, p. 199.
[47] SM 21, p. 165.
[48] *Morris Diary, op. cit.,* November 12, 1844, p. 169.
[49] SM 21, p. 58.

horse rasps, bellows and casks. For household use there were snuffers, combs, blacking, lamps, cork screws, "Britania table spoons," iron spoons, tea spoons, locks and mouse traps.[50] Whale oil was sold for the lamps.[51]

The store probably did not keep pocket watches in stock but sometimes arranged to purchase one for a villager. These were real luxury items and must have earned their possessors a degree of distinction to warrant a cost which equaled the wages for a working man for more than a month of labor. Philip Shafer, Junior, paid the equivalent of one and one-half months of his 1807 blacksmith's wages for a silver watch;[52] and George Kephart in 1823 paid $20 for a silver watch out of his income of $122.40 for filling the furnace that year.[53] Henry Care was more conservative when he purchased a watch in Reading for 58¢.[54] Others who owned silver watches were: Peter Yocum, woodcutter; Alexander Church, miner; Anthony Steward, stove finisher; Jonathan Jones, teamster; Charles Smith, stove finisher; Joseph McKewen, molder; John Benson, clerk; John Church, manager. The following partners in the firm bought gold watches:

Charles Brooke	1819	$160	
Daniel Buckley	1819	$129.37½ for 2 watches.	
Daniel Buckley	1825	$ 60	for watch, seal and key.
Clement Brooke	1828	$144	for watch, seal, key and chain.
Clement Brooke	1830	$134.50[55]	

Most sales at the store were recorded against the income earned by the worker with no money changing hands. But the cash books did show a few cash sales; most frequently these

[50] Most of these items were on an invoice for hardware bought in 1828, HV 8281104A.
[51] SM 21, p. 143.
[52] SM 4, p. 195.
[53] SM 11, p. 144.
[54] SM 12, p. 84.
[55] SM 9, p. 137; SM 12, p. 135; SM 14, p. 27; *Cash Book* for 1828–1830, March 8, 1830, n. p.

were for products of the molders such as kettles, pots, mold boards or clock weights. In 1818 there were 7 such sales in March, 4 in April, 5 in May, 1 in each of the next months through August and 2 each in September and October.[56]

Hopewell workers were not required to make all of their purchases at the company store. There were frequent references in the journals to bills paid for goods purchased at stores in Morgantown, Reading, Birdsboro and Philadelphia. The store book of the Eli Keen Store, near the St. Mary's Episcopal Church, for the years 1844–1845 showed many Hopewell people were trading there—among the regular customers were Doctor and Mrs. Charles Clingan. For many Hopewell workers this store was closer to their homes than the Furnace store. Keen carried many items that were not ordinarily obtainable at Hopewell: figs, canned peaches, Indian vegetable pills, turpentine, camphor, Swain's Vermifuge, paregoric, curtain paper, matches, tacks, rope, eggs, saleratus, nutmegs, cloves, mintsticks, sulphur, Scots pills, tin basins, sand paper, pie dishes, tooth powder, rosin and cinnamon.[57]

A trip to the store might have been a relief from monotony for the women and children of the village. Its crowded shelves and bins held the produce of the outside world; it smelled of far places. The small volume of trade betokened an absence of rush or hurry in selecting merchandise to be purchased and gave a chance for a little social visiting if several customers happened to be at the store at the same time. The Boone store in the village in the 1870's and 1880's was the loafing place for the men in the evenings,[58] but no evidence was found showing a similar use for the company operated store.

The Hopewell store served a useful purpose in providing a convenient place to secure some of the necessities of life. Its prices were in line with other stores in the area, and the mark-

[56] SM 10, pp. 1–15.
[57] *Eli Keen Store Book, 1844–1845*, Hopewell Village Library.
[58] Sally Boone Interview, March 22, 1941.

up over wholesale prices was moderate. Probably it was not a
source of very great profit to the owners. Trading at the store
was easy because credit was already established through the
record of the workers' wages on the company books, but it
was not necessary for the worker to do his buying there. The
clerk would even make payment for the goods bought by
a Hopewell worker at another store in the neighborhood or
in Philadelphia.

10 Transportation and Sales

A CHARCOAL-IRON FURNACE WAS LOCATED IN A FORESTED AREA to avoid long hauls of the fuel necessary for its operation, but the solution to this transportation problem created other problems of access to markets and sources of supply. As we have seen, the village store was necessary to supply the needs of workers who had to live in locations remote from towns; so storegoods had to be hauled to the furnace site. But of equal necessity were the transportation facilities to take the furnace products to the customers who had use for pig iron and cast items. Transportation costs were a critical factor in determining the success or failure of any furnace and were, in combination with technological improvements, the principal causes for the eventual demise of the charcoal-iron industry. The selection of a site for a new furnace must have taken into consideration the availability of existing transportation facilities and the cost of connecting the furnace with these roads, waterways or railroads. Markets changed as new means of shipping goods were developed. Hopewell Furnace changed its marketing pattern several times in its history because of the opening of roads, canals and railroads.

Mark Bird chose a location for his furnace which was conveniently near an already existing public road; and other roads, public and private, were added during the history of Hopewell Furnace. It never had immediate access to any other means of transportation and was, therefore, always dependent upon wagons to reach its markets or to connect with points on the river, canal or railroad.

In 1758 a public road had been opened from Scarlet's Mill in Berks County to Coventry Forge in Chester County. Hopewell Furnace was built about two hundred yards from that road and was joined with it by a private road. Another private road was built to the Hopewell mines; but a year after operation at the Furnace began, a new public road was opened from the Jones mines to the Schuylkill River. It passed conveniently near to Hopewell and added a new transportation facility. In 1804 a road from Birdsboro to Warwick Furnace passed within a few feet of Hopewell Furnace and formed a street for some of the nearby tenant houses. Five years later a new road was opened to the Jones mines, and a new access road to the Schuylkill River was built from the Birdsboro Road. Connecting roads near Hopewell were built to the Schuylkill Canal in 1827 and 1856.[1] The last one was convenient for reaching the new anthracite furnace at Monocacy, about four and one half miles away.[2]

The road built in 1827 was built in response to a petition to Robert Porter, Judge of the Berks County Court, which presented the necessity of a good road "from Hopewell to Douglass Ford" now that the new canal was going into operation. The petition requested the appointment of a jury to view the old road, declared barely passable for loaded wagons, or to propose a better route for a new road.[3]

In addition to the routes to the river on the north, Hopewell was favored by the opening of roads on the south which connected the Furnace with the best markets in the state. Four

[1] Russel A. Apple, "The Public Roads Serving Hopewell Furnace" (unpublished study, 1955). Hopewell Village Library.
[2] Long, *Historical Sketch, op. cit.*, p. 5.
[3] *Hopewell Papers,* Petition to Honorable Robert Porter, 1824.

miles away was the road from Lancaster to Valley Forge, now Pennsylvania Route 23. The opening of the Philadelphia-to-Lancaster Turnpike in 1794 probably did not aid Hopewell Furnace directly because of its distance, but two connections with it helped to open new markets for Hopewell products. Local iron men were influential in securing a new turnpike which was surveyed from the Lancaster Turnpike "near the Warren tavern, to the base of the Welsh Mountain, near Morgantown; thence to Blue Ball, and thence to Lancaster via New Holland." This road was a failure as a turnpike but was maintained as a public road.[4] In 1819 a public road from Downingtown through Ephrata to Harrisburg was completed.[5] These two roads helped to open markets to the west. Another main route of travel for Hopewell villagers was the river road through Pottstown to Philadelphia. This route was made more favorable about the middle of the century when the Schuylkill was bridged at Monocacy.[6]

The condition of the roads was a matter of great concern to the Furnace manager. Customers could be supplied only when the roads were passable. One of them wrote in 1831, "You will please send me [hollow ware] as Soon as the State of Roads will admit . . ."[7] There were frequent references to Furnace men and teams working at repair of the road, using Furnace slag to fill holes or soft spots. Wages and hauling costs for these repairs were deducted from the road tax owed by the company to the township.[8] Hopewell Village men also worked on the roads to pay for their road tax in lieu of money payments.

To meet the need for wagons and teams for furnace hauling, the manager used three different systems. From 1815 to 1825

---

[4] *Reading Eagle,* February 18, 1917.

[5] James A. Barnes, *Wealth of the American People* (New York: Prentice-Hall, 1949), p. 158.

[6] *Hopewell Papers,* H. A. Long to Roy Edgar Appleman, August 5, 1935.

[7] HV 8310302C.

[8] SM 46, August 28, 1824, n. p.

it was common to contract for some of the hauling with Village men who owned teams. Examples of these pacts were found in the Furnace records:

Agreed with William Thomas for his team by the day from last Monday Morning Being the 16 instant [September,] 1816 @ $2 per day we are to find the horses in feed and Board the Carter Thomas is to pay for shoeing the horses and the Carter his wages.[9]

Agreed with David Shafer February 7th 1823 to haul the wood on Millers hill above the old orchard Computed to be about 2000 c when done Chopping @ 10 cts per cord, and he is to have a collar, one pair traces and back band etc. and to have his horses shod gradis during the time he is employed in hauling the above wood.[10]

Agreed with Fredrick Landis to haul 20 loads sand from near Manor Meeting house at $2 per load and 20 loads Mettal to Hibernia Forge each load to be one and a half tons @ $3 per Load.[11]

A second kind of transportation agreement was to have the customer haul his own castings. Sometimes the Furnace set its price for stoves delivered and then credited the cost of transportation to the customer who hauled his own. In 1818 pig iron prices were set at $33 per ton at Hopewell and $43 in Philadelphia.[12] Later the usual cost for a load of a ton and a half to the city was $7.50.[13] In the 1850's the Furnace charged customers 35¢ per ton to haul pig iron to the "Exit Roads" and one dollar per ton to the railroad. From these points it became the responsibility of the buyer.[14]

The third kind of transportation in and out of Hopewell Furnace was by Furnace teams driven by teamsters who were

[9] SM 7, September 18, 1816, n. p.
[10] SM 46, February 7, 1823.
[11] Ibid., p. 58.
[12] SM 8, p. 149.
[13] SM 14, p. 71 was an example.
[14] SM 32, p. 107.

paid a regular monthly salary. Wages for teamsters ranked above those for ordinary labor but not as high as the skilled molders and colliers. There were other kinds of costs on the trips made by the teamster beside his wages. The expenses of the driver and his team and road or bridge tolls were sometimes more than wages. In 1816 and 1817 typical expenses for trips were listed as Lancaster $3, Wilmington $5, Philadelphia $6, "To the mountain for Stone Coal" $10.[15] Sometimes the driver wanted some cash of his own in addition to Furnace money given him for expenses.[16] When he stayed over night, there were tavern charges. The following bill was submitted from a Unionville tavern for a Negro driver, Samson Coggins, in 1818 :

Hay	.25
1 Bushel Oats	.50
Supper	.25
1 Pint Sider	.06½
1 gill Biters	.06
[Unexplained but probably bed and stable]	2.50
	———
	3.62½[17]

Accidents or bad weather added to the costs. In 1804 a bill for 14s. 3d. was presented to Mathew Brooke for food for a driver and team when a wagon was stuck in the snow on returning from Cornwall.[18] During the same year a Hopewell wagon broke an axle on the outskirts of Philadelphia and had to wait for its repair.[19]

The teamster was apparently alone on his trips most of the time, but an exception was made in 1825 when several journal

[15] SM 7, *passim.*

[16] *Ibid.,* October 4, 1817, n. p.

[17] HV 8181108A.

[18] *Brooke Family Papers,* Michael Valentine to Mathew Brooke, March 5, 1804.

[19] *Ibid.,* Davis and Brooke to Buckley and Brooke, April 20, 1804.

entries stated that the teams hauling stoves had "2 hands with wagon."[20] It would have been natural, too, that once in a while a wife, son, daughter or neighbor would have made a trip to the city or to visit a relative along the way. Hopewell records were silent on this point, but the *Martha Furnace Diary* had a number of such citations.

Turnpike and bridge tolls also added to the cost of travel. In 1806 Birdsboro Forge paid 9¢ for ". . . going Through Ye gate twice."[21] Later the custom was to pay for travel over a period of time on the roads commonly used. In 1817 Hopewell Furnace paid $13.77 for "Passing and Repassing [at] Gate No. 3 on Turnpike" for a period of a little more than three months. Charges were based on the number of horses and the size of the wagon wheels. Hopewell teams consisted of five horses on these trips.[22] Valentine Hofman paid 62¢ for turnpike "tole at Churchtown" for a trip in 1820.[23] On one occasion a customer advanced a Hopewell carter two dollars because he had not been given enough money to pay the tolls.[24]

Use of the turnpikes made possible a form of communication for the Furnace when there was no regular mail delivery. Daniel Buckley wrote to his partner a letter ". . . to be forwarded by Jesse McKnight and to be left at the turnpike gate at Brandywine Meeting House."[25]

The Schuylkill Bridge was a convenience to Hopewell but one which also cost money from 1835 onward. In that year a receipt acknowledged payment of $6.25 "to entitle Brooke and Famelly to pass over the Schuylkill Bridge between the Black and White Horse Taverns one year from the first of January last."[26] In 1855 the Furnace paid $15.00 in advance for the

[20] SM 46, p. 57.

[21] *Birdsborough Forge Cash Book,* December 15, 1806. Hopewell Village Library.

[22] HV 8170426.

[23] SM 10, p. 62.

[24] *Brooke Family Papers,* Whitestone Manfacty Co. to Mathew Brooke July 24, 1816.

[25] *Ibid.,* Daniel Buckley to Mathew Brooke, July 25, 1809.

[26] HV 8350606A.

privilege of crossing the bridge at Douglassville for the year.[27]

The teamsters often performed services for the Furnace and the villagers when they made business trips. They bought articles in the city for which the Furnace made payment and then charged the workers' accounts.[28] Store goods were brought back from the city whenever possible in order to assure a pay load in both directions. At other times the drivers made some purchases on their own and sold them in the Village; for example in 1826 Jacob Mock brought cheese and oysters, and George Marquet sold shad both to the Furnace and to individuals.[29] In 1831 such varied items as oil, tar, sweet potatoes and candlewick were retailed in these private enterprise operations.[30]

Neighbors were accommodated on the trips to Philadelphia. The clerk at Warwick Furnace wrote in 1822 to ask, ". . . Please let me know whether any team load from you to Philad^a this week—the name of the Carters and where they stop. . . ."[31]

Teamsters carried money in both directions to pay bills, and there were at times considerable sums entrusted to their care— $100, $81.50, $160 and $50 were amounts picked at random from the Hopewell records. The only instance found of any money going awry was this notation in 1817:

> Note Gave David Hart an order on Bullock and Peters to Draw $100 the 25th March last the said David Hart Received from them as per his Receipt $49—and brought or gave up but 40 dollars when he came home.[32]

The incident was closed by charging Hart's account for the missing nine dollars. Hart continued to work at the Furnace for many years.

[27] SM 65, January 3, 1855.
[28] For example see SM 12, p. 82.
[29] SM 59, p. 9; SM 12, p. 140.
[30] SM 15, pp. 35–36.
[31] HV 8220729.
[32] SM 7, August 26, 1817, n. p.

The life of Hopewell Furnace depended upon transportation, and transportation depended upon a supply of animals to pull the wagons. Naturally, then, much attention was given to the problem of obtaining good animals. Purchases of both work and riding horses were frequently entered in the Furnace records, and the prices proved that the Furnace wanted horses in their prime. Sometimes a man wrote to offer horses he had for sale; this letter was an example:

> . . . I understand that Mr. Brooke wishes to purchase a good family Horse, I have two for sale, and will give him the choise a black and a bay both young and well broke to either the saddle or harnes, both handsome and gay and the price low.[33]

But voluntary overtures did not meet the need for animals, and the next year a customer wrote that he regretted that his stoves had not been delivered because the Furnace was short of teams.[34] Twenty years later the Furnace found it necessary to pay a commission to a man who undertook to buy horses.[35]

Horses were bought from employees, neighboring farmers and distant markets. The management seemed to favor purchases when the animals were from four to seven years of age, but even at this last age the price was declining by $10 or $20 from the peak.[36] Almost never did they sell a horse in its prime. There were many recorded sales of old horses or blind horses, but the only example seen of the sale of a superior animal was "a yellow horse" sold in 1851 for $140.00—a very good price.[37] When horses died their hides were sold to the leather dealer, and on one occasion the Furnace paid 25¢ to have a horse killed.[38]

Horse trading was another source for Furnace animals. In almost every transaction the Furnace paid "boot money," an

[33] HV 8240914A.
[34] HV 8250815.
[35] SM 31, p. 14.
[36] For examples see SM 28, p. 124 and SM 31, p. 11.
[37] SM 31, p. 146.
[38] SM 21, p. 93.

indication that the manager was trying to upgrade his teams.[39] A guarantee of soundness was a part of some deals, and in 1844 the Furnace demanded the refunding of $50 "boot money" when the "Horse was not sound and Returned."[40] The purchase of stud horses in 1803, 1817 and 1818 proved that the Furnace was breeding some of its own animals.[41]

Horses were the beasts most used to pull the wagons to and from the Furnace, but oxen and mules had their place at the Furnace also. One pair of oxen was purchased in 1802 at a price of $93.45.[42] Perhaps William Welsh had charge of this yoke, because he appears on the record as a "Bool driver."[43] Oxen again appeared on the inventory of purchases in 1830, 1848 and 1849.[44]

The later managers, beginning with Dr. Clingan, preferred mules; or perhaps they were easier to find than horses. In 1848 a mule was bought for use "at the mineholes,"[45] and mules were frequently mentioned after this date. One six-mule team was purchased in 1850 for $810 plus $83.75 paid for mule harness and the cost of delivering the team to the Furnace.[46] Harker Long bought and sold many mules during his term as manager.[47] He said that in 1864 Dr. Clingan had paid $2700 for nine unbroken mules, which was a quite high price; but of course the Civil War was influencing the market. Long said that six mules were used for heavy hauling and were hitched in three pairs known as the tongue, middle and lead teams. The teamster had a saddle on the left-rear animal; but when the load was heavy, he walked beside this mule and controlled the team with a single "jerk line" attached to the bridle of the left mule of the lead team.[48]

[39] Examples may be found at SM 28, pp. 126, 135, 138.
[40] SM 28, p. 138.
[41] SM 1, p. 25 and SM 8, pp. 144, 156.
[42] SM 1, p. 1.
[43] Ibid., p. 28.
[44] SM 14, p. 86 and SM 31, pp. 104, 130.
[45] SM 31, p. 61.
[46] Ibid., pp. 128, 129.
[47] See HV 8810311.
[48] H. A. Long Interviews, passim.

Charcoal Wagon of Late Period

Rear of Charcoal Wagon Showing Rings Used to Draw Bottom Boards
in Unloading

The usual hitch for horses had apparently been four horses, as several references were found to pay based on a four-horse wagon load.[49] There was another kind of hauling, however, which required a quite different hitch. Wood was hauled from the cutting tract to the hearth on a sled drawn by a single horse, mule or ox.[50]

Several different kinds of wagons were used for the hauling done by the Furnace. Among those mentioned were "Broad wheel," "Narrow wheel," "high wagon," "dearbourne wagon," "one horse wagon" and "road wagon." Charcoal wagons were built in several different sizes varying in capacity from one hundred to three hundred bushels. They had high sides and were built with bottom boards which would pull out for quick unloading. The lead team was unhitched, brought to the rear of the wagon and used to pull out the bottom boards.[51] To load the charcoal a plank was placed with one end against iron bars along the side of the wagon and the other end on the ground. The teamster, carrying baskets of charcoal on his head or shoulders, walked up the plank and filled his wagon bed. A short plank projecting from the left side of the wagon was called the "lazy board" because the driver sometimes rode on it instead of walking. In front of the bed was a tool box in which were kept the supplies necessary to make emergency repairs—and, according to report, a quart of whiskey was some times concealed among the tools.[52]

Not all of the wheeled vehicles at the Furnace were of the commercial variety. The manager had his carriage for travel by himself and his family. A space was reserved for carriages between the mows on the second floor of the barn until Dr. Clingan built a carriage shed.[53] Carriage operation had some aspects which resembled modern family transportation—a

[49] HV 8340122A.
[50] Kemper, "The Making of Charcoal," *op. cit.*, n. p.
[51] *Ibid.*
[52] John Sparr Interview, October 18, 1940.
[53] Nathan Care, Junior, Interview, February 13, 1941.

Receipt of Tax Paid on Matthew Brooke's Carriage

license fee was required, and repairs and remodelling were needed. In 1817 the tax on a chaise was $2 per year.[54] Clement Brooke received the following bill for work on his carriage a few years later:

Varnishing Body and Carage	$ 5.00
Lether work	2.00
Hedlining	7.00
Carpet and Shaft	1.75
New Front Bow	1.25
Molding on Top	1.25
Stufing Cushings	.75
	$19.00[55]

[54] *Brooke Family Papers,* Tax receipt, February 1, 1817.
[55] HV 8290827B.

Accessories included a whip @ $1.25.[56] The cost of a carriage could have cut deeply into a family income, judging from the $356 which Clement Brooke paid for one in 1829.[57] This was more than half of his salary as furnace manager, but he had other sources of income.

While transportation in and out of Hopewell was dependent upon teams for the entire history of the Furnace operations, the development of water travel and the railroad had an influence on the distance the wagons needed to travel and upon the direction of commerce. Markets for Furnace products were changed as new transportation connections became available.

The nearness to the Schuylkill River was an inducement to try cheap water transportation to the towns down the river. Even before Hopewell was built, Bird iron had gone down the river; for example, Samuel High transported three tons of pig iron from Reading *in a canoe*.[58] In 1773 Mark Bird was appointed one of twelve commissioners instructed by act of the Pennsylvania Assembly to investigate means "for making the River Schuylkill navigable."[59]

Early in the nineteenth century there were many tons of iron carried for Buckley and Brooke on a boat operated by Mordicai Millard. He hauled bar iron, stoves and hollow ware to Sweedsford, Phoenixville and Valley Forge.[60] The risks involved in river travel were demonstrated by an incident in 1803 of the stranding of a boat carrying 1800 pounds of Hopewell hollow ware destined for Philadelphia. The boat ran aground near Pottsgrove where a man named "Shance" rescued the iron and undertook to sell it for Buckley and Brooke. He had sold part of it but still had some on hand when he died. Thomas Brooke made a trip to Pottsgrove to

[56] SM 31, p. 68.
[57] *Cash Book* for 1828–1830, May 27, 1829, n. p.
[58] *Montgomery Manuscripts,* Book I, p. 106. William Bird Ledger.
[59] *Pennsylvania Gazette,* April 28, 1773. William Bird had served on a similar commission in 1760.
[60] SM 2, pp. 131, 199, 320; HV 8221100.

reclaim what pieces remained.[61] James Rogers was hauling flour for Mathew Brooke on a river boat in 1817.[62] Wages paid to Birdsboro Forge employees for "Boading to Philadelphia" in 1822 were $7.50 to Rogers for steering and $5.50 to each of four other men listed as "a hand."[63]

The Delaware River also was used for the shipment of goods, especially to dealers in Wilmington. Instructions were written to Hopewell by Delaware merchants to deliver iron or stoves to sloops leaving regularly from Philadelphia. Thomas Garrett operated his own boat, the *Sloop Mary Ann,* to haul his purchases from Philadelphia to his Wilmington store.[64]

But later transportation for Hopewell products had its principal expansion with the opening of the Schuylkill Canal. A charter was issued to the Schuylkill Navigation Company on March 15, 1815, with permission to issue 10,000 shares of stock at $50 per share. Work was begun in 1816; a short section was opened during 1818, and traffic was moving from Reading to Philadelphia by 1825. Eventually the canal was extended west to Mount Carbon. Dividends on stock were first paid in 1829 and increased during the next decade to reach a peak of 19 per cent in 1839. The best year for tolls was 1841 when well over a half-million dollars was collected, but the next year the tolls were cut almost in half because the Reading Railroad was taking business from the canal.[65]

Apparently Hopewell Furnace partners were interested in the canal quite early, for Mathew Brooke was assessed $5 per share for his 20 shares of Schuylkill Navigation Company stock in 1817.[66] The switch from wagons to canal boats is shown by

[61] SM 2, p. 104.
[62] HV 8170501A.
[63] *Birdsborough Forge Book, 1821–1823,* p. 20.
[64] HV 8260315A.
[65] James W. Livingood, "The Heyday of the Schuylkill Navigation Company," *The Historical Review of Berks County,* IV, 1 (October 1938), p. 11–14.
Robert McCullough and Walter Leuba, *The Pennsylvania Main Line Canal* (Martinsburg, Pennsylvania: Morrisons Cove Herald, 1962), pp. 11–12.
[66] HV 8170912.

the following tally for stoves shipped by wagon and by water over a period of five years after the canal opened:

	May 1826– May 1827	May– December 1827	May– December 1828	1830
Wagon	1451	326	326	683
Canal	1090	1488	2128	3007[67]

By 1836 most of the finished goods from the Furnace was moving on the canal with the major part of it going to customers in Philadelphia, New York, Boston and Portsmouth.[68] Robert Cunningham of New York wrote to request that all of his stoves be sent by canal, because they "come so much quicker and I believe safer . . ."[69] Probably the New York shipments were also using the New Brunswick Canal across New Jersey.[70]

But the canals created some problems too. A customer requested the Furnace to rush to him all the stoves possible "before navigation closes" for the winter.[71] Another wrote, ". . . Send me a load By waggon as I understand the canal is frozen and the Canal Boats not able to descend the River."[72] The canal boats caused delays because they were not always ready to take on freight immediately, resulting in this instruction from John J. Hess of Philadelphia:

> . . . I have received the Castings in the Waggons as soon as those arrived by the Canal now I wish you not to delay in waiting for the Boats but to prokure Waggons and furnish me with Castings as fast as you possibly can. . . .[73]

Another merchant offered to pay the difference in cost between the canal and a wagon to insure quicker delivery.[74]

Another modification in the transportation of stoves came

[67] SM 14 and SM 50, *passim.*
[68] SM 51, pp. 1–37. This was a Canal Book kept at the Furnace.
[69] HV 8361001A.
[70] HV 8360910B.
[71] HV 8321112.
[72] HV 8311206.
[73] HV 8311104.
[74] HV 8311109A.

with the opening of sections of the Reading Railroad to Philadelphia. The change in the relative importance of three methods of hauling was shown in the shipments of stoves for three years: .

	1839	1840	1841
Wagon	268	77	54
Canal	3669	3512	1675
Railroad	41	852	1804[75]

The canal assumed a new importance to the Furnace, however, after it no longer carried stoves to the city markets. Coal fields with access to the canals were shipping fuel to the Furnace in sufficient quantity to warrant the erection of a coal house at the canal in 1847.[76] This coal house may have been in Lebanon County. Canal tolls of $205.45 and boat fees of $264 were paid on eleven boat loads of coal delivered during that year from Big Dam on the Union Canal in Lebanon County.[77] Charcoal was shipped by canal in 1851.[78] When the anthracite furnace was operating at Monocacy, at least a part of its iron ore came by canal as indicated in this memorandum by Dr. Clingan:

> George Hoofman has undertaken to boat the Cornwall ore from Lebanon to our furnace at $1.48 per ton—he paying toll on said ore—and he is also to unload the boat or pay any hands that we may give him to help. The hands get at Birdsboro 15 cents per hour for helping.

Whole Cost of Cornwall Ore at the Furnace :
Ore mined at the hill and put in the Cars	$1.25
Delivered from the hill to Lebanon	.50
Freight and Toll on canal	1.48
	$3.23[79]

[75] SM 39, *passim*.
[76] SM 31, p. 44.
[77] SM 32, p. 31.
[78] SM 32, p. 119.
[79] *Kemper Manuscripts*, C. M. Clingan Pocket Note Book. This note was undated. The nearest date to it was July 2, 1857.

A comparison of costs from Philadelphia to Hopewell showed that a wagon load of supplies weighing about three thousand pounds had cost $7.50 in the 1830's. But in 1851 "merchandize" from Philadelphia was billed, for canal charges, at the rate of 12¢ per hundredweight with an additional charge of $1 per ton for hauling from the canal to the furnace.[80] Thus freighting costs via the canal totalled $5.10 for a load, representing a 32 per cent saving from the expense for wagoning. As late as 1860 the furnace sent 130 tons of pig iron on the canal and paid a toll of $52 on the shipment.[81]

Railroading in the Schuylkill Valley had a beginning late in 1837 when a section of the track out of Reading was opened to travel. James Morris recorded in his diary on December 6, 1837, "The first cars started on the Reading and Philadephia at Reading."[82] Several years later its trains had reached Philadelphia. Freight charges were a little higher than those on the canal: in 1851 a wagon load of storegoods from Philadelphia to Douglassville cost $3.75 by rail or $3.60 by water.[83] But the trains were much faster than the boats. The railroad also attracted passenger business from the village at a rate of $3.50 "from the City to Douglassville up and down."[84]

Changes in transportation brought alterations in the market for Hopewell Furnace products. It is possible to trace this effect by checking the locations of customers and the sources of Furnace supplies over the years of our principal interest. In the period 1802–1808 shipments and purchases involved customers at Red Lion, Strasburg, Reading, West Chester, Lancaster, Birdsboro, Conestoga, Philadelphia, Bulls Mill, Warwick, New Holland, Pine Grove Forge, Spring Forge and

[80] SM 32, p. 116.
[81] SM 65, October 15, 1860, n. p.
[82] *Morris Diary, op. cit.*, p. 34.
[83] SM 31, p. 150.
[84] SM 31, p. 49. The date for this rate was 1848.

Coventry. These places were generally local or near the east-west turnpike.[85]

Ten years later the market to the west was still of great importance, and a York dealer was given an exclusive marketing agency for as many Hopewell stoves as he could sell.[86] Other towns to the west mentioned in this period are Marietta, Morgantown, Harrisburg, Lancaster, Middletown, Pequea, Columbia, Lititz, Leacock, Elizabethtown and Ephrata. Wilmington and Baltimore were of interest to the south.[87] In the 1820's the bulk of sales shifted to the east, with Philadephia the major center. More distant markets were opened in 1821 when John W. Jenkins of Hudson, New York ordered plow castings.[88]

After the canal had been opened a few years, there was relatively little concern with sales in the towns to the west. Almost all shipments of molded articles were to or through Philadelphia while pig iron was sold to local forges. Although Lancaster, Columbia and Ephrata were still receiving some stoves, goods were no longer moving to the west in their former quantity. For the period from 1837 to 1845 68 dealers in Hopewell stoves were recorded in the Blast Book. Of these Philadelphia addresses were given for 48. There were four for whom no addresses were given; and, therefore, they may have been in the city. An additional nine were located in towns where transshipment from Philadelphia was probable. Pig iron was still being sold to nearby forges.[89]

How were these customers contacted to place orders? The chief responsibility for sales rested upon the manager, members of the partnership and the clerk. Much of the extensive travel for which the Furnace paid expenses must have been for calling upon new and old customers. In 1816 the Furnace

[85] SM 2 and SM 3, *passim.*
[86] *Hopewell Papers,* undated but apparently about 1817, agreement with George Small and Morris of York, Pennsylvania.
[87] SM 6 and SM 9, *passim.*
[88] HV 8210308A.
[89] SM 39, *passim.*

paid $17.75 for advertising furnace castings in two news-papers,[90] the only recorded instance of advertising of products by Hopewell Furnace. In a four-year period after this date there were scattered references to eight individuals or com-panies which were selling Hopewell stoves on a commission basis.[91] A customer mentioned a call by one of the Buckley boys as the reason for placing an order.[92] Several dealers ordered stoves because they had heard about Hopewell products and service from another merchant.[93]

Abundant evidence survives, however, to prove that not all the buyers were happy all of the time with either product or service. Complaints about slow delivery predominated, especially as there was a certain season when stoves sold well. John Getz of Lancaster seems to have been a little bitter when he wrote:

> I received your stoves but it is 9 or 10 Days after the time so . . . that people that I had engaged stoves to had to supply themselves elseware on act of the whether setting in so cold and the town being over stocked with Phila stoves It will be hard for m[e to] sell them now but whatever I do not I shall consider to your disadvantage . . .[94]

Other customers complained that stove parts were missing or broken in transit, parts were poorly cast or did not fit properly, or the holes were not large enough for the bolts. Hopewell iron was said to have been too hard to drill; so the merchants wanted the molders to be instructed to mold properly. None of these complaints seemed to have been serious enough to cause dealers to cancel orders, although they sometimes threatened to do so. The letter usually concluded with a plea to send more stoves and soon.[95] One buyer of

[90] SM 7, July 6, 1816, n. p. Bills paid but newspapers not named.
[91] SM 8, p. 52; SM 9, pp. 62, 134, 135, 153; HV 8200902A.
[92] HV 8160907.
[93] For example see HV 8160926.
[94] HV 8161112.
[95] Many such letters were found. Examples are HV 8310806A and HV 8330501A.

plow parts complained that Hopewell was making mold boards which were too heavy by as much as 25 per cent. This was a serious matter because moldings were sold by the ton, and the heavier the piece the fewer there would have been per ton.[96] Another complaint was of articles lost or stolen in transit. A pig iron buyer wrote:

> . . . if I buy some again, I will take it away at once, as you sent it over, for I believe that some is carried off, if it lays there at the tavern, the last load we brought away fell short 130 lbs, it laid there about a week before I could get it hauled.[97]

No doubt the manager made some of his calls to try to answer the complaints and find out about the kinds of moldings which were selling well or badly. The alert Furnace manager had to be aware of many trends in product sales. He needed to be prepared to take advantages of new changes and new markets opened by new means of transportation. In the first half of the nineteenth century, the Hopewell managers must have used the changing conditions to their advantage, for the furnace owner who failed to keep his lines of transportation open and at reasonable cost did not stay in business long. Iron-making was highly competitive.

[96] HV 8200225.
[97] *Kemper Manuscripts,* David G. Hertzog to Clingan and Buckley, 1865.

Part Five

The Vocational Village

11 The Worker and His Job

THE OPERATION OF A FURNACE REQUIRED MANY HANDS TRAINED to do a variety of tasks. Some were highly skilled and some were easily learned. Some provided full-time employment and some were seasonal. Some paid a high wage and some were marginal. In an effort to discover the employment needs and labor use at Hopewell Furnace, the author made a study of all classes of employees during five periods of two blasts each between 1805 and 1853. Thirty-three different job classifications were identified in work records kept by the clerks. Not all of these were used in any one of the blast periods, and four of them appeared only once. There may have been other kinds of jobs concealed in such generalizations as "sundries" and "labour."

In Appendix B two tables summarize some of the results of this labor study. The first one shows the number of different persons who were employed at each of the jobs, and the second one shows the approximate man-days of work for which wages were paid for each kind of employment. It is apparent that the most men and the most days were devoted to cutting wood, making charcoal, mining, operating the furnace and driving the teams. Many other jobs were incidental to the production of iron but of importance in maintenance or in

229

caring for the needs of the other workers and their families. The total number of employees varied from 170 in the 1818–1820 period to 246 in the 1835–1837 blasts. Man-days expended had their extremes in the same two periods and ranged from 28,368 to 49,086.

A comparison of the two tables shows clearly that not all the workers could have been full-time employees. For example in 1851–1853 the average woodcutter had about one hundred days of work in twenty-seven months. The reason for this was that almost all wood was cut during the winter months, and the man working with his axe during the cold weather may have been a farmer the rest of the year or a worker at some other job for the Furnace. The tables on the next page show the extent of part-time employment. If we assume that $100 per year represented a minimum wage for full-time employment, most of the employees worked part-time. The second table shows that a fair percentage of the workers did find employment at more than one task at the Furnace, proving that this number did not work all the time at any one job. There were many specialists, however; and the percentage of these was highest in the years when the Furnace was at its productive peak. These data probably show that valuable employees were retained by giving them whatever jobs were available while the furnace was not in blast.

Wage Distribution :
Number of Workers Who Earned Specified Amounts of Wages in the Blast Periods Indicated

Wages Paid	1805–1807	1818–1820	1825–1827	1835–1837	1851–1853
Less than $1.00	10	5	6	3	1
$1.00 to $9.99	34	33	38	47	52
$10.00 to $24.99	34	29	44	49	56
$25.00 to $49.99	27	21	28	34	38

$50.00 to $99.99	17	24	19	30	17
$100.00 to $149.99	15	13	15	18	14
$150.00 to $199.99	11	11	6	10	10
$200.00 to $299.99	14	12	16	15	11
$300.00 to $399.99	14	6	9	8	11
$400.00 to $499.99	2	6	6	4	4
$500.00 to $999.99	2	7	17	22	3
$1000.00 and over	2	3	4	6	8
Unknown	4	2	5	0	0
Total	186	170	213	246	225

Job Specialization :
Number of Persons Paid for One or More Than One Job in the Blast Periods Indicated

	1805– 1807	1818– 1820	1825– 1827	1835– 1837	1851– 1853
One Job	127	120	153	189	158
Two Jobs	34	34	30	37	41
Three Jobs	14	13	18	13	9
Four Jobs	7	2	9	4	11
Five Jobs	3	1	3	2	5
Six Jobs	1	0	0	1	1

In previous chapters the duties and responsibilities of manager, clerk, molders and teamsters have been examined. Similar attention is deserved by those who worked at the furnace and those who were responsible for keeping the furnace men supplied with raw materials.

The success of the operation of the furnace was dependent upon the knowledge and skill of the founder. The manager was expected to know how a furnace was run and to be able

to solve difficult problems, but the founder was on hand for
the hour-by-hour supervision of operations. It was he who
would have been responsible for preventing too many crises
from arising; a good founder left the manager more freedom
to attend to the other duties of his office. He needed skills
which it was believed could be learned only by working at
a furnace. E. S. Cook wrote:

> . . . no one was competent to manage the practical end
> of blast furnace work unless he was "born in a tuyere arch."
> This expression was meant to imply that the mysteries could
> only be solved and handled by a man starting as a laborer
> and working up through the various positions pertaining to
> the stock-house and cast-house—first helper, keeper, and
> finally founder—involving an experience of five or ten years
> or more. The founders were men separated by the forces of
> natural selection from their fellow workmen, possessing more
> than ordinary natural intelligence and good judgment, quick
> to meet emergencies, of some mechanical skill and close ob-
> servers of blast furnace phenomena.[1]

Success in furnace operation was not assured, however, even
when the founder had had that kind of background. The
human factors were also important, according to John Lewis
Barde in a letter to his manager at Hopewell Furnace in the
1790's:

> . . . I must . . . give you a Caution that is Thomas
> Hogsett has never pushed her to what she could or has been
> pushed before he is in general over cautious of loading her
> . . . I give you this hint that he may know it. He ought
> to average at least 20 [tons] per week when everything is in
> order . . . what has been done should be done again and if
> one's method through obstinacy or other wise will not do I
> would not be unwilling to try another.[2]

[1] E. S. Cook, "Management of Blast Furnaces—Transition from 'Rule
of Thumb' to Application of Scientific Methods," *Schools of Mines
Quarterly*, XIX, 3 (April 1898), pp. 227–248.
[2] *Daniel Miller Papers*, J. L. B. to M. Brooke, Jr. Undated. Microfilm
at Hopewell Village Library.

Trade secrets were valuable possessions of the founder which were kept hidden from visitors and even from fellow employees. Methods of making good iron and economical furnace management were passed from father to son. "Technology was more in the heads and hands of skilled iron-workers than in technical works in print."[3] The Care family showed this consanguineous influence by providing founders for about sixty-five years of Hopewell operation.

The founder had many things to watch if his job was done well. He adjusted the blast to the condition of the burden in the furnace, prepared trenches for the sows, set the molds and decided when the furnace was ready to tap.[4] He looked through a space between the nozzles of the bellows to judge the state of the smelting from the color of the molten mass. He wanted bright drops of iron and slag to show a good separation of the two. Another method to observe the iron was to insert a long iron implement called a "ringer" and examine the iron and slag which clung to it when it was withdrawn. He had to recognize signs of danger such as the building of a "scaffold" against the inside of the stack.[5] The founder assumed the duty of tapping the furnace to release the slag and iron; casting was usually at six o'clock in the morning and the same time in the evening so that each twelve hour tour would have the iron from a cast.[6]

The founder watched the flame and gases emerging from the stack, as they could tell him much about the state of the interior. According to Overman:

A heavy, dark top flame indicates that the furnace is cold, and that the burden is too heavy. A bright smoky flame, which throws off white fumes, indicates a too liquid cinder; that too much limestone is present; or that the burden is too light. . . . An almost invisible, lively flame at the top is significant of a

[3] Hartley, *op. cit.,* p. 12.
[4] *Ibid.,* p. 150.
[5] H. R. Schubert, *History of the British Iron and Steel Industry* (London: Routledge and Kegan Paul, 1957), p. 238.
[6] Overman, *op. cit.,* p. 201.

healthy state of the furnace. . . . Where the flame wavers, that is, where it is sometimes large and sometimes small, there is, without doubt, scaffolding in the lining.[7]

Frederick Meck was the Hopewell founder for about five years before the shutdown in 1808. Judging from the number of lawsuits in which he engaged, he was a controversial figure. He was deeply in debt to the Furnace, leaving an indebtedness of £133 19s. 9½d. when he departed at the end of 1808.[8] When the furnace reopened in 1816, John Painter was the founder at a wage of $62.50 per month.[9] Although the Painters were among the most permanent and most numerous residents of Hopewell Village, and this John Painter was long associated with the Furnace, he must have had a short tenure as founder, for on January 1, 1819, Thomas Care was paid "for blowing the furnace."[10] Care continued in this position until December 19, 1835, when he was succeeded by his son Henry.[11] Fifteen years later Nathan Care was the founder, continuing in that position until the end of iron-production in 1883. Apparently he also served for a time as manager.[12] Both Henry and Nathan had had experience as keepers and molders in preparation for the job of founder.

The founder was one of the highest-paid men in the Village in keeping with his responsibilities. In about nineteen years at this position Thomas Care averaged more than $1,000 per year income from the Furnace.[13] Not all of that was pay for blowing the furnace, however, as he was also listed as a molder. Pay for the founder was sometimes based on the output of the furnace during the blast; for example, in 1831 Care was paid $982.12 calculated at $2 per ton of molders' iron, 5s. per ton for pig iron and 50¢ per ton for gate metal.[14] He

[7] *Ibid.,* p. 205.
[8] SM 5, p. 101.
[9] SM 7, January 17, 1817, n. p.
[10] SM 6, p. 75.
[11] SM 21, pp. 161, 206; SM 19, pp. 264, 460.
[12] SM 32, p. 120.
[13] See Appendix B.
[14] SM 15, p. 53.

Molding Pig Iron with Cross Section View of Blast Furnace in
Operation

paid some wages to other furnace workers on a basis which is
not clear from the records, for the Furnace paid some of these
wages too. In 1825 Thomas Care paid the keeper; and in
1876 Nathan Care paid a keeper, two fillers and a man who
put in the ore.[15]

One keeper and one filler were employed on each twelve
hour tour with a gutterman to assist on the daylight one. The
latter wheeled all the cinder to the slag heap from both tap-
pings of the furnace but was able to do it all in the twelve
hours he worked.[16] Some of the time there was also a workman,
or more than one, who was hired for "putting in the ore,"
"putting in the night stock" or "stocking coal." Fillers in 1858

[15] SM 12, p. 32 and SM 61, p. 16.
[16] Long, *Historical Sketch, op. cit.,* p. 19.

were responsible for "puting up their night stock;"[17] so there was not always a separate person hired to do this work.

The keeper was assistant to the founder and would have been expected to operate the furnace when the founder was not present, especially during the night tour. The founder was usually not far away and was called when any emergency arose. In the early days of Hopewell operation the filler needed to be a highly skilled man. His "practiced eye" was the only means of determining the correct amount of the ingredients of the charge which went into the furnace.[18] Scales were installed in the bridgehouse in 1847 to assure more exact loading of the furnace, and then less skill was required on the part of the fillers. Filling must have been a fairly hazardous job with its many opportunities for accidents or burns. It would have been somewhat unpleasant in cold weather to move rhythmically from the open-sided bridge to the heat of the stack. Fillers had a larger amount of absenteeism than other workers, and often it was noted that they were sick or hurt.[19] Wages for a filler were usually above those for common labor but not as high as those for the most skilled jobs.

The ore was brought from the banks to the bridgehouse in wheelbarrows during the day for the use of the workers on the day turn and enough stocked ahead to last through the night.[20] Many references were also made to "putting in the night stock" and "stocking coal," showing that other ingredients beside the ore were placed on the bridge or in the bridgehouse for the use of the night workers. Charcoal was brought from the coal house in baskets or in "coal barrows."[21] Many wheelbarrows were mentioned among the purchases at the furnace.[22]

Usually Hopewell Furnace did only rough casting of stove

[17] SM 35, p. 135.
[18] Miller, op. cit., p. 104.
[19] For example see SM 46, pp. 66–68.
[20] Martha Furnace Diary, op. cit., August 9, 1811 and SM 44, December 15, 1807, n. p.
[21] HVX 8000320.
[22] See for example SM 15, p. 38.

Interior of Hopewell Blacksmith Shop

plates with the merchant assuming the responsibility for finishing and assembling. At one period from 1817 to 1819 the Furnace experimented with hiring its own stove finishers. First Anthony Stewart and then Charles Smith of Philadelphia were hired to assemble stoves and put the hinges and latches on the doors.[23] It is not clear whether the Furnace was wholesaling finished stoves at this time or just preparing stoves for the retail trade at the Furnace store.

Another necessary skilled worker at Hopewell throughout its history was the blacksmith. The blacksmith shop apparently dated from the early years of Furnace operation, possibly as early as 1775.[24] This shop was a social center for the men and

[23] SM 8, p. 148; SM 6, p. 144; SM 9, pp. 114, 115, 176.
[24] J. C. Fisher Motz, "Field Notes—Archeological Investigation of Black Smith Shop" (unpublished study, 1940), p. 5. Hopewell Village Library.

boys of the village. Here the blacksmith made wagon-wheel tires and farm, mine and furnace tools; repaired machinery for the Furnace and neighboring farmers; shod horses, mules and oxen; made hardware items such as hinges, latches, bolts, locks and lock plates; sharpened harrow teeth, coulters and hoes; steeled axes; made his own tools and, when nothing else was to be done, made horseshoe nails out of old horseshoes.[25] Cold feet was one of the discomforts of the smith, partially relieved by placing planks and boards on the dirt floor in front of the forge and anvil, where he spent most of his time.[26]

The Furnace depended upon a regular supply of its raw materials from the woodcutters, colliers and miners who worked in the forest, often several miles from the stack and store. Many of these men lived near their work and were seldom seen at the furnace. Others lived nearby and went out to their cutting, pit or minehole each morning.

The most numerous of all the Hopewell employees were the woodcutters. In the blast periods of 1851–1853 there were 225 persons who were paid wages for all kinds of work, and of these 116 were paid for cutting cordwood.[27] Many choppers were men who added a little to their regular income by cutting a few cords of wood during the winter months. Several cut only 12 cords and earned less than $4. At the other extreme Fred Lindeman earned $504.22 for 325½ cords, Jonah Knauer realized $784 from 560 cords, and Edward C. Gault was paid $882.60 for 1993½ cords.[28] Wages varied from 25¢ per cord for cutting on Brushy Hill near the furnace to 35¢ for some locations on Bear Hill. The pay scale was based on distance from the furnace and condition of the timber tract, with higher pay on rocky slopes or where the timber was scattered.[29] If the cutter worked on woodlots he owned, he was paid

[25] SM 4, *passim;* C. W. Straley Interview, August 14, 1940.
[26] *Ibid.*
[27] See Appendix B.
[28] SM 32, *passim.*
[29] See for example SM 4, p. 89.

about one dollar per cord for the wood plus the price for the cutting. He could also earn an additional amount if he had a team and hauled the wood to the pit where a collier was to make charcoal. Some of the pay Edward C. Gault earned was for "wood in the rank," hauled to the coaling pit at $1.50 per cord. Other pay for "delivering in the ring" was as high as $1.75 per cord.[30]

How much wood could be cut in a day? James Morris reported, "John Diehm sawed, split and piled up a cord of hickory wood today in 3 hours . . ."[31] But this was a feat about which Diehm was boasting in the Morgantown store. The average was probably near two cord per day.[32] Note that Diehm was using a saw. Hopewell cutters apparently were axe men; seldom was there any mention of saws among their purchases. Each man was responsible for purchasing his own axe and keeping it sharpened; occasionally he had to take it to the blacksmith to have a thin strip of steel welded to the edge—"steeling the axe."[33]

Since the worker was paid by the cord, he cut his pieces in four foot lengths to facilitate measuring of a cord pile which was 4 feet by 4 feet by 8 feet. He ranked his own wood and was credited for it after the rank was measured. Some workers tried to deceive the measurement by piling wood over rocks or stumps, piling loosely or cutting billets too short. Such practices could reduce the wood by 30 per cent of volume if not detected.[34] Numerous references to dockage against cutters was evidence that the manager was watching for such tactics and found them at least a part of the time.[35] A man could also lose credit for wood he had cut for reasons which were not necessarily his fault. In 1830 David Hoffman lost $7\frac{1}{2}$ cords of wood "Being Burnt by D.

[30] SM 32, *passim.*
[31] *Morris Diary, op. cit.,* p. 2, January 10, 1837.
[32] Overman, *op. cit.,* p. 84.
[33] Schubert, *op. cit.,* p. 322.
[34] Overman, *op. cit.,* p. 84.
[35] Many references to dockage in SM 1 and SM 46.

Evans tenants,"[36] and Thomas Kurt lost much of his winter's labor in 1802 when 422 cords of his wood burned.[37]

When a woodcutter was working at a distance from home, he sometimes built a shelter near his work and stayed there for a week. Food was taken to him from his home with the boys of the family providing the delivery service.[38]

The Furnace cut about 4,000 cords per year from its own land and bought another 3,000 from woodland owners within a radius of four to five miles from the furnace, according to H. A. Long who was familiar with the last years of Furnace operation.[39] Clement B. Grubb reported in 1839 that Mount Hope Furnace used 4.66 cords of wood to produce the charcoal needed for making one ton of pig iron.[40] An acre of woodland produced from 30 to 40 cords, depending upon the quality of the timber.[41]

The experts were not in agreement about what kind of wood made the best charcoal. Elm and hickory each had its supporters. White oak, black oak, Chestnut, ash, pine and beech were considered acceptable. In America first-growth timber was considered best for coaling,[42] while the English ironmasters preferred charcoal from young trees.[43] Hopewell avoided participation in any such arguments by cutting a tract clean and using all the live wood growing there, then permitting that area to resprout and grow for thirty years before it was recut.[44]

The collier was a very important workman, controlling to some degree the quality and quantity of the furnace product. The ironmaster required a strong, compact, heavy charcoal:

[36] SM 14, p. 78.
[37] SM 1, p. 5.
[38] Thomas Hoffman Interview, November 22, 1940.
[39] H. A. Long Interview, August 13, 1936.
[40] *Mount Hope Letters,* Clement B. Grubb to Edward B. Grubb, November 7, 1839.
[41] Overman, *op. cit.,* p. 85.
[42] *Allens Appeal Record, op.* cit., pp. 182–184.
[43] Schubert, *op. cit.,* p. 222.
[44] H. A. Long Interviews, *passim.*

Collier's Hut in the Woods

Charcoal Making: Building the Chimney

If the charring is pushed too fast, or if, from the kindling of the wood, it is too lively, the coal will be small, light, and the yield will be meagre. If on the Contrary, charring proceeds slowly, the Coal will be light and friable; though the yield, if the cover has been kept tight, will be good.[45]

Charcoal was made by the destructive distillation of wood. By burning a part of the wood, enough heat was produced to expel the tar, "pyroligneous acid" and moisture, leaving the charred remains of the rest of the wood. Charcoal from the common woods varied in weight from 9.8 pounds per bushel for white pine to 18.95 pounds per bushel for sugar maple.[46]

The master collier and his helpers lived in rude huts in the woods while the coaling was going on. Wood was piled in mounds, covered with leaves and dirt and then set afire in the center. Care and skill were needed by a good collier:

> From the time the pit was first "fired" until the very last piece of charcoal was hauled away by the teamster with his large swaying wagon, . . . the pit had to be constantly tended and watched. A master collier and one or two helpers "coaled" together, working as many as eight or nine pits at a time.[47]

> Each hearth was located about the distance of a city block from one another throughout the various charcoal tracts, and the collier's hut was placed, therefore, as conveniently as possible to the group of pits then being coaled.[48]

About twenty-five to fifty cords of wood were used by Hopewell colliers in each pit measuring 30 to 40 feet in diameter.[49] A pit of this size needed from ten days to two weeks to "come to post," and as much as sixteen days was not unusual.[50]

[45] Overman, *op. cit.*, p. 115.
[46] Charles Herman Fulton, *Principles of Metallurgy* (New York: McGraw-Hill Book Company, 1910), pp. 352–353).
[47] Margaret Piersol, whose family were Hopewell colliers, said three men worked three pits at a time.
[48] Kemper, "The Making of Charcoal," *op. cit.*, n. p.
[49] *Ibid.*
[50] Fred W. Shearer, "A Bygone Industry" *Service Letter, The Pennsylvania Department of Forests and Waters,* 7, 11 (March 12, 1936), pp. 1–3.

Charcoal Making: Setting Cordwood Against the Chimney

Charcoal Making: Putting on the Second Tier of Cordwood

Charcoal Making: Cordwood in Place

Charcoal Making: Covering Cordwood with Lapwood, Dirt and Leaves

During this time the pit must never be neglected; so the collier had no work-day or work-week. He was on constant duty, eating and sleeping when the condition of the work permitted him to do so.

Coaling was not done in the winter in the Hopewell area, because "wind, rain, fog, temperature, etc., had a marked effect on the rate of burning."[51] A heavy snow could have flooded the pit area, and excessive moisture made the charcoal unfit to use in the furnace.[52] The end of the coaling season came at different times: Martha Furnace reported the convocation at " the finishing jug" on January 24, 1811; Mount Hope on December 25, 1839, and Hopewell on November 12, 1842.[53]

A good collier was one who could get the highest yield of good-quality charcoal from the wood he used. A good yield was 35 to 40 bushels of charcoal per cord of wood.[54] In 1825 the clerk noted that the wood coaled by Henry Houck "averaged 39 bu. to the cord and some over." Daniel Frye, another Hopewell master collier, averaged 38 bushels per cord during the same year.[55] The conditions for the coaling had been set down in an agreement signed with Frye:

> Agreed with Daniel Frye February 28th 1824 to coal all the wood cut at Hopewell mineholes and the wood bought of Isaac Whitaker and the wood cut on Nathaniel Kerbys land at Thirty Cents per Cord and the waggons to be heaped from end to end and not more than three Baskets brands to each load, the Coal to be drawed a sufficient time before the waggons come so that there be no fire in the Coal, he is to make as much yield out of this wood as David Hoffman will make out of the same number cords. . . .[56]

David Hoffman was apparently considered a good collier, as he was being used for a standard; but Hoffman was work-

[51] *Ibid.*
[52] *Allens Appeal Record, op. cit.,* p. 78.
[53] *Martha Furnace Diary, op. cit.;* HV 8391225B and HV 8421112.
[54] *Allens Appeal Record, op. cit.,* p. 19.
[55] SM 12, pp. 103–105.
[56] SM 46, for date given.

Charcoal Making: Lighting the Pile

Charcoal Making: Collier Working on Top of the Burning Pile

Charcoal Making: Uncovering the Finished Product

ing on a different kind of contract. In 1825 he bought 2,048 cords of wood from the furnace for $682.67 and coaled it at a rate of $2.25 per load. He obtained 642 loads, paid five men a total of $396.70½ wages, and received $1,421.43½ from the Furnace for his charcoal. His wages and profits for the season were $342.06.[57]

The collier was charged for Furnace wood which he permitted to burn through his neglect. In 1822 a fire consumed 108 cords of the wood assigned to David Hoffman.[58] Neglect of the coaling pit could cause too much burning and a low yield of

[57] SM 12, p. 105.
[58] SM 46, pp. 6–19.

Charcoal Making: Raking Charcoal from the Pile

charcoal. Another kind of fire which was especially costly was one on a wagon load of coal on its way from the pit to the furnace. A wagon might have been lost as well as several hundred bushels of good furnace fuel. In 1802 and 1803 the clerk noted fires in wagons driven by Samuel York and J. Simmons as well as two other fires in which the colliers rather than the drivers were named. In two of these four fires the driver was able to save a part of the load, possibly by pulling the bottom boards and scattering the coal on the road. The collier was fined for loading the wagons before the fire was out of the charcoal.[59] Two others kinds of dockage were made from the colliers' pay : when loads were too small and when there were too many uncharred faggots.[60]

Harmony did not always prevail around the coaling pits. Many of the colliers were Irish of both Catholic and Protestant faiths, resulting in "frequent reenactments of the Battle of Boyne in the woods" of Berks County.[61]

Another necessity for the successful operation of an iron furnace was a dependable supply of high-grade iron ore located within reasonable hauling distance from the furnace site. Competition would ruin a company which had to pay more than $7 or $8 at the Furnace for sufficient ore to make one ton of iron.[62]

Hopewell was fortunate in having access to three good ore fields within about five miles of the furnace. Early mining was open pit and bell pit mining with limits upon the depths to which digging could safely go. Ore near the surface was therefore a necessity. Daniel Udree tried a shaft at Oley Furnace before 1800 but found it was too expensive and too dangerous to operate.[63] The usual mining consisted of one man in the pit digging loose the ore and placing it in a bucket or basket and

[59] SM 1, April 24, 1802; May 18, 1803; July 1, 1803; October 24, 1803; n. p.
[60] SM 1 and SM 46, *passim.*
[61] *Reading Eagle,* April 8, 1917.
[62] Overman, *op. cit.,* p. 51.
[63] Handwork, *op. cit.,* p. 123.

Restored Hopewell Coal House and Cooling Shed

another man on the surface drawing up the loaded container on a rope. In the 1780's one such pair of workers supplied the needs of Hopewell Furnace.[64] In the early 1800's seven men were paid for full-time work, and several others apparently were doing some part-time mining.[65] By 1819 there were eight regular miners..[66] Seven years later the Furnace was no longer paying wages to miners but instead bought ore by the load from those who were doing the mining,[67] and from this developed the mining partnerships which hired their own

[64] Bining, *Iron Manufacture in Pennsylvania in the 18th Century, op. cit.*, p. 71.
[65] SM 3 and SM 4, *passim.*
[66] SM 6 and SM 9, *passim.*
[67] SM 59, *passim.*

Washing Iron Ore at Hopewell Mine

workers and delivered ore to the Furnace for a contracted price.[68] Still another system was used in the 1850's when eight or more men were paid wages by the furnace, but a separate bookkeeping account was maintained for the "Mine Holes." Mining expenses including wages were debited and the value of the ore delivered was credited to this account.[69] Miners' wages were relatively high, placing them in the category of skilled workers.

After the ore was on the surface, it was cleaned of its extraneous dirt by washing in a sluice. The miners were docked for dirt in the ore delivered at the furnace.[70] Washing

[68] SM 19 and SM 21, *passim.*
[69] SM 38 and SM 32, *passim.*
[70] SM 46, p. 254.

the ore sometimes created problems with the neighbors, as this letter shows:

> Martha McCormick complains and says that the water running from where the hands are washing mine flows over her meadow lot below and is doing great damage to it, she is willing the water may run through her meadow provided they clean the ditch and keep it from running over and spoiling the meadow, She also says Geo. Simmers is willing to help clean the ditch and Peter Moyers swears he will not put a shovel to it, you will be so obliging to give them some directions about it. . . .[71]

Another extra job was necessary in preparing the ore for furnace use in the 1830's. This was known as "roasting" or "burning mine" and consisted of heating the ore in ovens, piles or pits to remove volatile matter, especially sulphur, before the ore went into the furnace.[72] In the two blasts of 1835–1837 the Furnace paid four men a total of $125.03 for this work at a rate of $7 to $10 per month.[73] Further evidence that mining was becoming more complex at this time was found in payments for "90 yards tunneling at the old mineholes" and for "Sinking Shafts."[74]

The Furnace must have bought at least part of the equipment the miners used, for Peter Moyers and William Clark were reimbursed for tools they had purchased in 1829.[75] Special and heavy equipment was also purchased by the Furnace. In 1806 a "new Screw pump for Hopewell Furnace mineholes" cost £60.[76] In 1849 six "oil cloth coats for miners" were purchased at $1.75 each.[77]

This last purchase was one evidence that a new kind of mining was beginning about this time. There were many references in the journal for this year to timbering, drifting and

[71] HV 8290422, Evan Evans to Charles Brooke.
[72] Overman, op. cit., pp. 39–48.
[73] SM 19 and SM 21, passim.
[74] SM 15, p. 32.
[75] SM 14, p. 50.
[76] SM 4, p. 110.
[77] SM 31, p. 96.

tunneling at the old Hopewell Mine; and also in this year an
engine house was built,[78] evidence that mechanical power was
being used. Drift cars and mules were purchased for the mines
in 1848. Tin lamps were used in 1850, and "coal for Engine"
indicates the use of steam power.[79] A derrick, two coal buckets
and two upright posts on the list of purchases in 1857 point to
power lifting of the ore. Powder and safety fuses were purchased in that year also.[80]

The need for more ore was shown by a number of payments
for "searching for ore" or discovering new ore beds in the mine
fields. At least one man was paid for trying to find a new area
for mine operations "on Bear Hill."[81]

Rivalry among the miners for the best veins of ore resulted
in many fights in the mine fields. When one group tried to get
into a good vein another pair was already working, the owners
would settle the dispute by drawing lines for each pair of
miners.[82]

The skilled workers have been considered in the preceding
pages. Relatively little could be discovered about the unskilled
labor, even though in every period of the labor study made
there were numerous payments "for labour." There were also
workers who appeared in the time books regularly as
"labourers" whose wages were considerably below those of the
skilled classifications. But sometimes the clerk used this term to
generalize for a variety of jobs done, and the wages paid
indicate a more highly skilled task had been performed. It
seems apparent that the Furnace needed and used some men
at unskilled jobs with enough regularity to keep several
workers for such assignment. There were also specialized
workers who came to the Furnace to perform their tasks as
needed. Among these were the weaver, the tailor, the shoemaker, the cabinetmaker, the carpenter, the mason, the

[78] SM 31, p. 87
[79] SM 31, pp. 61, 125, 128.
[80] SM 65, May 16, 1857 and July 24, 1857, n.p.
[81] SM 31, p. 97.
[82] *Allens Appeal Record, op. cit.,* p. 178.

plasterer, the chimney sweep, the tinsmith, the wheelwright and others. Occasionally some of these workers were employed full-time, but usually they were hired when needed or made periodic visits to the furnace.

The operation of a charcoal furnace involved the labor of many people possessing many kinds of skills and earning a wide range of wages. Some were required for full-time employment; others were used during certain seasons or when special kinds of jobs needed to be done. The furnace manager had important responsibilities as a personnel director of his labor force as will appear in the next chapter.

12 The Worker and His Boss

THE WORKER AT A CHARCOAL IRON FURNACE HAD A VERY
personal relationship with his employer. The isolated location
and the relatively small size of the community made it possible
for the ironmaster to know each worker, his wife and children.
Family problems and needs were common knowledge and
received the sympathetic attention of most of the owners of
furnaces. "The living conditions on the iron plantation were
good, fair, or bad, according to the character of the ironmaster."[1] But there was also a matter of self-interest involved.
Good iron workers were not always easy to find, and good
labor-management relations made it possible to retain workers
or find replacements more readily.

There were rarely evidences of labor discontent which
resulted in strikes or other concerted action of workers. Employers handled their labor problems on an individual basis,
except in a few instances when concerted action by employers
on matters of setting wages or blacklisting an employee were
worked on the basis of family interrelationships and friendships.
A considerable uniformity of wages and working conditions
existed among the furnaces of Eastern Pennsylvania in the
first half of the nineteenth century. Harold F. Williamson

[1] Handwork, *op. cit.,* p. 127.

believed that there was little consciousness of "management" as a separate job in the first half of the nineteenth century. There was no "managerial hierarchy" in the mill or foundry.[2]

The ironmaster performed a variety of services for his workers of both a business and a welfare nature. Mixed motives may have induced his doing so, ranging from self-interest in keeping an employee to a genuine sympathy for community needs. Perhaps foremost among the reasons was the almost total absence of commercial establishments which could have provided the people of the Furnace community with goods and services. Working conditions on the iron plantations would have horrified a present-day labor union leader or social worker. But little question was raised about them in the period before the Civil War. They were not worse than those found in other lines of employment and were better than in many factories.

Sullivan was unable to find any strikes among furnace workers in the years 1800–1840.[3] He contended that there was no protest or organized discontent among the wage earners largely because of the nature of the relationship between the owner and his employees.[4] England, on the other hand, had a number of strikes at the furnaces and mines. Several at the Dowlais mine were so serious that troops were called to quell the riots.[5]

Hopewell and its neighboring furnaces were neither as peaceful in labor relations as Sullivan believed nor as violent as their English contemporaries. Changewater Furnace had a dining-room riot in 1803 when James Gold objected to the kind of food being served.[6] More organized labor trouble developed in August of the same year. The clerk reported:

[2] Williamson, *op. cit.*, p. 310.
[3] Sullivan, *op. cit.*, pp. 221–230.
[4] *Ibid.*, p. 62.
[5] Madeleine Elsas (Editor), *Iron in the Making, Dowlais Iron Company Letters, 1782–1860* (London: Glamorgan County Council, 1960), pp. 33–64.
[6] *Changewater Account Book*, p. 39.

A number of Men came to work at the Laid-out Road from Mill to Forge with J*no* Todd (Township Orator) at their head, actuated by his presence and plenty of our whiskey became Revolut[ionary] and Determined not to work upon said Road . . . In the Evening most of them u[nable] to stand.[7]

Hopewell had a strike at the Jones Mine in 1838 when William McIlwain wrote to Clement Brooke that, "A part of our hands turned out last friday for higher wages etc and it is agreed [sic] proposed by a part of the Company to have a special meeting next Monday."[8] Unionization of iron workers began with a molders' union formed in Philadelphia in 1855 with some men bearing names familiar at Hopewell among the early pioneers: Edward Parlaman, David Thomas and Edward Buckley.[9] At least sixty years earlier the ironmasters had organized a kind of loose association which could act on affairs of mutual interest. Berks County ironmasters held a meeting in 1794 to discuss their position on the tariff.[10] Several letters in the Hopewell collection of manuscripts show that there was an expected cooperation among the employers. A letter in 1821 had a hint of blacklisting:

If you have any influence with Wm Long Esq. be so good as to prevent the employment of John Gordon and Sons at the Canall if you can—this in Confidence— . . .[11]

In 1838 Clement Brooke asked Robert L. Potts to discharge employees for unsatisfactory work:

. . . we think it now Proper to Give you this notice that unless those Persons you have engaged to Wash Mine by the Ton do not deliver ore Clear of Sand . . . that we will not Receive Any ore from them washed after this date and will

[7] *Ibid.* p, p. 40.
[8] HV 8380621.
[9] Barford, *op. cit.,* pp. 10–11.
[10] Bining, *The Iron Manufacture in Pennsylvania in the 18th Century, op. cit.,* p. 145.
[11] HV 8210519A. Signature partly destroyed, but apparently Lewis Evans to Clement Brooke.

not be Accountable for Any Part of their Labour and as far as this place is interested we demand of you to discharge them.[12]

The clearest case of proposed collusion was contained in a letter written to Hopewell in the depression year of 1842 :

... owing to the low price for Iron and no prospects of iron getting much better for some time we consider it to our advantage and to sustain our selves in our business to reduce the rates of our workingmen the 1st day of next month which we have notified them to that effect—and want your opinion as well as Whites [probably William R. at Warwick] on the subject—which you will please give ... all the iron works that are of any standing are agoing to do so. And the sooner this is done with, us all will be the better if we intend going on to make iron at the presence prices—moulding $8 per ton keeping $18 per month fillers $18 all other hands at $15 and $16 and board themselves—Carters at $9 single—married $16—the Coleman works Cornwall are agoing to stop for the purpose of reducing the rates—they think it cannot be done without stopping for one month—but we think we can reduce the rates without stopping; and if not—will not stop moulding more than one week or two—for several of our moulders are in debt and they must go on; others perhaps will strike for a few days—but owing to the large quantities of Protested paper we have received from customers—(stove men) we think it not advisable to make all castings—on account of the cost being more than pigs—and if some of our moulders does strike it will be no disappointment to us—Grubbs intend stoping 2 of their furnaces we have received letters from their hands for employment as it is generally understood that Hopewell and Warwick will also follow us in Lancaster County and if that be the case all will and can be done without any difficulty— and we hope you will notify your moulders at once—for now is the time when stove men will not pay and the great risk in sending stoves to men that have not paid for last years stoves; David Care we suppose will endeavour to get all the information he can about what stand you are going to take at Hopewell—give him no satisfaction except you are a agoing to lower rates and stop—and that Rock will do the same—we have

[12] HV 8380815.

told our moulders that Hopewell and Warwick will or had done so and we must follow—keep Dave in the dark—so as he will bring gloomy noose home.[13]

Two months before that letter was written the Phoenix Iron Company of Phoenixville had informed its workers that their wages would be reduced by 20 per cent, and Joanna Furnace cut the wages of all of its "monthly hands" by $1 per month.[14] Another wage reduction came after the Civil War as announced in a curious news item which is quoted here in full :

Protecting Labor—We learn that the wages of the hands employed at the Hopewell mines and Furnace, Berks County, have been reduced to one dollar a day.[15]

The work-day and the work-week were long and varied with different kinds of jobs. Once started, the furnace and the coaling pits could not be stopped day or night or for weekends. They required constant attendance. The usual organization at the furnace was to have two groups of workers who each worked a 12-hour shift, changing at six in the morning and six in the evening.[16] William Darling of Joanna Furnace replied to a United States Treasury questionnaire in 1832 that he employed 95 men who worked all the year on a 10-hour day.[17] He did not explain how his furnace was supervised during the remaining hours.

For some Hopewell workers the day was more than twelve hours long. When a teamster drove a charcoal wagon from Birdsboro to the Furnace, he left at two o'clock in the morning and returned after his children were in bed.[18] In 1825 George

[13] HV 8420610, Brooke Coheen and Company at Rock Furnace to Clement Brooke.
[14] *Village Record,* West Chester, Pennsylvania, April 12, 1842, and *Joanna Furnace Time Book,* 1842–1843, n.p. Hopewell Village Library.
[15] *Jeffersonian,* West Chester, Pennsylvania, July 3, 1867.
[16] SM 35, p. 3.
[17] *McLane Report on Manufacture, op. cit.,* p. 227.
[18] Mary L. Cramp Interview, November 6, 1961.

Painter quit work several times at six o'clock and was paid for only three-fourths of a day. However, on another day under similar circumstances he received a full wage for the day.[19] In 1854 James Friar was paid extra for working $15\frac{1}{2}$ hours; and numerous entries were found showing workers paid for $1\frac{1}{4}$, $1\frac{1}{2}$ or even two days for the same date. These extra-length tours were paid at the normal hourly wage.

For most workers, other than employees at the furnace and coaling pits, the work-week was six full days, Monday through Saturday. The time books show that many workers quit early on Saturday and received credit for only half or three-fourths of a day.[20] Maids and housekeepers were employed by the week and would have had some duties on Sunday in serving meals and routine housework.[21] Workers who were employed by the month had their wages calculated on the basis of 26 days in January of 1834 and were credited with one month and one day; but in February there were only 24 working days, and they were paid for just that number.[22] A working month, evidently, was 26 days rather than a calendar month.

Most of the cost of making iron was represented in the wages paid to the workers.[23] The furnace owner kept his wages from varying widely during the period 1800–1850. Earnings were different because of the number of days worked, but the basic wage rate changed little in good times or in depressions. The table on the next page shows the wages paid for sixteen job classifications in five different periods. The greatest fluctuations were in the managerial class of founder, clerk and manager. The range was not as much as may appear on the surface, because the high and low were often indications of pay with or without boarding rather than differences in scale. Extremely low wages, as with the carpenters, were for a son helping his father.

[19] SM 46, pp. 59–60.
[20] For example see SM 1 and SM 35, *passim.*
[21] SM 65, April 2, 1857, n. p.
[22] HV 8340501C and SM 21, p. 154.
[23] Overman, *op. cit.,* p. 49.

Wages Paid for Different Job Classifications
for Five Periods of Two Blasts Each

	1805–1807	1818–1820	1825–1827	1835–1837	1851–1853
Carpenter per day	.73	.75–$1.20	.60–.65	.35–.87½	.31–.65
Clerk per year	$300		$135	250–$300	$150
Collier per month	$8.62–$20.62	$16–$23	$13.50–$18	$13.50–$18	$17.50–$24
Farm Worker per day	.50–.73	.25–.50	.40–.50	.50–$1	.23–.54
Filler per month	$10–$18	$12–$18	$9–$14	$15–$16	$14–$18
Founder per year	$640	$480	$970	$540–$600	$480
Houseworker per week	.67–.80	$1	.80	.50–$1	.75–$1.50
Keeper per month	$20	$12–$20	$17–$20	$18	$18
Laborer per month	$7.50–$10	$6–$13	$8–$13.75	$6–$14	$6–$15
Manager per year	$325	$541	$652	$600	$650
Miner per month	$12–$15	$11–$19.50	$11.33–$21	$9.50–$18	$13–$32
Molder per ton		$12	$8–$10	$6–$10	
Putting in Mine per month		$12	$10	$7–$16	$20–$24
Smith per month	$14–$16	$17	$9–$13	$8–$20	$15
Teamster per month	$10–$14.66	$10–$12	$9–$14	$8–$14	$8–$14
Woodcutter per cord	.35–.45	.35–.40	.25–.30	.27–.40	.20–.35

The ironmasters considered their pay scale sufficient to feed, clothe and lodge a worker and "to enable the prudent to make some savings for sickness, reverses and old age."[24] It was true

[24] *Documents Relating to the Manufacture of Iron in Pennsylvania, op. cit.,* p. 9.

that the money wage did not tell the whole story of workers' income. Employees often were given a house at very low rent, wood, pasture land, vegetables grown on Hopewell farms and other domestic commodities in addition to their wages.[25]

How did Hopewell wages compare with other kinds of workers or with other furnaces at the same time? Workers on the canals were being paid $14–$15 per month "and found" in the 1820's. Some contractors offered as high as a dollar a day on the Pennsylvania Canal in 1837, but work was not very steady.[26] Women textile workers in Pennsylvania in 1829 were paid $1.50 per week for working from sunrise to ten or eleven o'clock at night.[27] Hopewell's wages for maids compared favorably because they also included room and board.

Comparisons with wages paid at other furnaces may be made from the following scales for some of the same years as the table for Hopewell wages:

> *Mount Hope Furnace—1806*
> Carpenter—$16 per month
> Clerk—$158.50 per year
> Farm Worker— .50 per day
> Housework— .85 per week
> Laborer—$7–$9 per month.[28]

> *Dale Forge—1827*
> Carpenter—$14 per month
> Collier—$17 per month
> Farm Worker— .40 per day
> Housework— .75 per day
> Mason— .70 per day.[29]

> *Manada Furnace—1837*
> Carpenter—$1 per day
> Collier—$20 per month
> Farm Worker— .50–62½ per day

[25] Thomas N. Care Interview, February 10, 1941.
[26] Sullivan, *op. cit.*, pp. 29–42.
[27] Barnes, *op. cit.*, p. 289.
[28] *Mount Hope Furnace Journal, 1800–1819, passim.* Microfilm at Hopewell Village Library.
[29] Gemmell, *op. cit.*, pp. 94–95.

Housework— .75 per week
Laborer—$4–$7 per month
Mason—$1–$1.12½ per day
Teamster—$11 per month
Woodcutter— .30–.45 per cord.[30]

Amounts earned by fourteen Hopewell workers over a period of many years as well as the ways they used their income can be seen on the charts in Appendix B.

There never was a payday at Hopewell because the amount earned was simply credited to the worker's account with the Furnace. This credit could be used to make purchases at the store, to pay bills to the Furnace, to pay for purchases made elsewhere or to make payments for goods delivered at their homes. Unlike the situation at many other furnaces, Hopewell workers seemed always to have been able to draw cash against their credit on company books. Cash books and cash pages in the journals show that money was obtained even in years when business was slow. Most payments were made at the store or office, but numerous entries prove that a worker could meet the manager or clerk almost anywhere and get money from his pocket. A list of such honored requests included payments "at his house," "at D. High's," "at Barny Tavern," "in Reading," "in the city,' "at the mineholes," "at the township meeting," "in Birdsborough," "at Mount Airy" (sixteen men were paid here at the same time), "at Beards Tavern," "in the wood cutting," "at his church," "at the election," "at Golden Swan Hotel," "in Potts Grove," "at the canal" and "at court."[31] The greatest demand for cash was at the end of a blast or of the coaling season. At Mount Hope Furnace $1,500 lasted only a few days against the demands for cash by the colliers at the close of their coaling.[32]

A worker was paid for the time he was actually on the job whether he was a day laborer or a salaried employee. If he

---

[30] *Manada Furnace Journal, 1837*, August–December, 1837.
[31] These items were taken from the cash records covering many years.
[32] HV 8391225B.

Labor Record from Hopewell Journal for 1836

missed work for any reason, his pay was docked for the time he was away from the job. There were no paid vacations, no paid holidays and no excused absences.

In 1822 there was a full complement of workers on Independence Day, but the next year none was listed as working on either Christmas or January 1. Workers were not paid for these days either.[33] According to reports of residents of Hopewell Village, the workers and their families were invited to

[33] See SM 46 for appropriate dates.

parties at the Big House on these last two holidays. It is probable that the furnace group had to work to avoid a costly holiday closing of this operation, but this supposition could not be checked because their work was not recorded in the time book.

At the Martha Furnace the molders took an informal vacation when all of them decided to go to the shore for a weekend.[34] Hopewell had a similar incident when some of the molders refused to do their work because they wanted to go hunting. The clerk reported these circumstances:

The Casting of Pigs left out Monday Morning September 5, 1825 before day weighed 626.1.14
Note. The above castings of Pigs was left out owing to Joseph McKewen, George North and Henry Care Neglecting to mold up last Saturday Sept. 3rd 1825 as it was their duty to have moulded up. Thomas Care told them on Saturday to lade immediately after breakfast and they refused. he presed them to lade at 9 oclock and could not get them to do it until 11 oclock. The Iron all that time was running out of the furnace. McKewen and North was out hunting with their guns.
B. The above Casting was the second casting left out from Saturday.[35]

There was no punishment of these three molders for this neglect except the loss of their earnings for that period. All of them remained with the Furnace, and Henry Care eventually became founder.

There were many records of absenteeism from jobs for a variety of reasons such as sickness, doing farm work, attending a vendue, going to visit relatives, going to Philadelphia, attending a funeral or taking a vacation. In 1803 the clerk lost 21 days "when his Brother died" and two other periods of seven days each without any explanation except that he was "at Mr. Vanleers." He lost pay for these days from his

[34] *Martha Furnace Diary, op. cit.,* July 28–August 1, 1809.
[35] SM 46, p. 62.

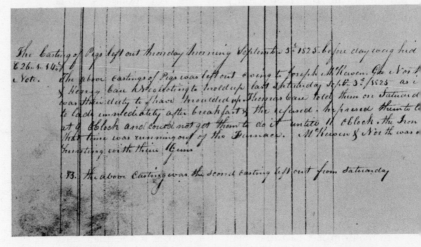

Clerk's Notation of Men Neglecting Work to Go Hunting

annual salary of $300.[36] Drinking was a frequent cause of loss of time; for example, George Harn lost time at the Birdsboro Forge because he was "Drunk frolicken and Idle all this week."[37] The record of time lost was usually accompanied with the name of the person who substituted for the absent worker. Sometimes the turn was shared by two men who each worked one half day. Occasionally a search had to be made to find a man to do the work, and he would not begin until after the tour had started.[38]

Loss of time was not always the only punishment for a man who missed work. Martha Furnace had a collier sign a contract which provided for a fine of $5 for missing one day of work.[39] Fines were also used at Hopewell Furnace, especially when there was a loss in addition to the time not worked. Samuel York had $1 deducted from his earnings "for getting

[36] SM 2, p. 143. There was a Vanleer Tavern.
[37] *Birdsborough Ledger*, 1810, *op. cit.*, p. 7.
[38] For example see SM 35, p. 148.
[39] *Martha Furnace Diary, op. cit.*, October 9, 1809.

intoxesitated with liquer and neglecting hauling 3 loads wash Dird at Joneses."[40] Thomas Johnson lost the same amount "for Neglecting Sending 1 load Coal in—was laying Drunk in ye Cabin."[41] Keeping a team out "all day and part of the night without feed" cost a teamster $2 in 1830.[42] Other kinds of neglect or carelessness which brought fines against Hopewell workers included "neglecting his work and let his pitts burn," wood burned, teams standing idle, failure to bring in loads, failure to load the wagons, small loads, "loosing 2/3 of a load of coal," wood left on the hills which should have been hauled to the coaling areas, coal burned on the road and "Cutting high stumps in the lot of wood cut by him."[43]

Harker Long said that men did not work very hard at Hopewell Village and were never in a hurry but that it was very rare for a man to be discharged for not doing enough.[44] This observation was supported by a search of the Furnace records which showed that many workers quit but few were discharged. Discharging an employee was difficult when he was a friend of a partner, as shown by this letter from Daniel Buckley to Mathew Brooke:

> At your advice and desire I took your friend Mathew Davis into partnership who has during three years acted offen very Improperly, and now at the close seems to shew a very Extraordinary disposition so much so that I fear we shall not part without laying the foundation of much trouble in consequence of your recommendation he came, therefore think you are under some kind or tipe of obligation to get us seperated, I wish you to come over tomorrow and advise what is best to do . . . should you not come I will . . . seize his Property till I get security for the Rent or Paid.
>
> I have at no time been in such a straight if he was not some way a Conection I would think little of putting the Business

[40] SM 44, March 13, 1808, n. p.
[41] SM 2, p. 39.
[42] SM 14, p. 77.
[43] Examples are taken from journals and time books covering the first half of the nineteenth century.
[44] Long, *Historical Sketch, op. cit.,* p. 17.

Perfectly straight and Easey but under the circumstances that are I am lothe your friendship will be considered an obligation.[45]

Another kind of problem which developed between labor and management was the loss or stealing of Furnace property. Tools were stolen in 1816,[46] and a teamster was charged for a log chain he lost in 1852.[47] The most frequent and costly loss, however, was fuel. One man was paid for cutting wood for Hopewell, but later it was discovered that he had hauled 16 cords of it to the canal and sold it in Manayunk.[48] Edward C. Gault, a contract collier, paid $12 in 1851 for charcoal which had been stolen, but there is no certainty whether he was accused of stealing it or having had it stolen from his coaling operation.[49]

The Furnace assessed fines for neglect, but it less frequently gave rewards for diligence. Henry Sheets was paid $9.75 in 1836 "for Sundry work and saving sprouts."[50] No information was given on what was threatening the sprouts or what he did to save them, but he was rewarded with cash for some effort he made. More explicit was this 1847 note, "Furnace Paid for a silver watch and made it a present to Joseph Hart for his perseverance in discovering the new body of mine near old mineholes." The cost of the watch was $14.50.[51]

The Furnace apparently had no rules against a man holding more than one job at the same time. For example in 1803 Edward Hughs received pay for filling, putting up the night stock, putting in the mine, cutting wood and cleaning castings.[52] Possibly some of this work was done by sons who were too young to collect their own wages. David Struck combined woodcutting with shoe making; these could have been seasonal

[45] *Brooke Family Papers,* April 2, 1808.
[46] SM 7, November 17, 1816, n. p.
[47] SM 32, p. 126.
[48] SM 21, p. 170.
[49] SM 32, p. 119.
[50] SM 21, p. 184.
[51] SM 31, p. 26.
[52] SM 2, pp. 173–177.

alternations, however.[53] Perhaps the clearest case of double
jobs was that of Thomas Care who was paid for both molding
and founding over a period of many years.[54] It was not possible
to determine whether his job as founder permitted him sufficient free time to mold some stoves or whether he worked
part of the night tour. His wages were high because of his
dual services.

The association between employer and employee at Hopewell Village showed a considerable character of paternalism
in the many services the management performed for the
workers. One such case was in dealing with suits at law on
behalf of workers. Many references were found to payments
of judgments, costs, fines, debts, bills, interest and constable
charges against Hopewell workers. The Furnace paid for a
pardon for a Negro teamster in 1803,[55] but the record failed to
say for what he was being pardoned. Several times the
Furnace provided bail money.[56] Notes given by workers and
protested by banks were paid by the Furnace and collected
from the worker. In one such case in 1832 the Furnace had
difficulty recovering the amount of such a note.[57] Philip Shafer,
a blacksmith, spent part of 1806 in jail and had his jail costs
of $16.50 paid by Hampton Forge.[58]

On at least two occasions the Furnace resorted to jail to
punish workers. In 1809 the account of George Proudfoot, a
teamster, was charged $1.45 in favor of Mathew Brooke with
this notation "per order in favour Michael Westly for Putting
Proudfoot in Jaol." There was no statement of the charge
preferred, but Proudfoot had owed Hopewell Furnace a debt
with no payment on it for more than three years. If this had
been the reason for the jailing, the results were not favorable;
for his indebtedness was simply increased by the amount of

[53] SM 6, p. 29. This was in 1821.
[54] SM 9, p. 128 was one example.
[55] SM 2, p. 120.
[56] See examples in SM 1, p. 43; SM 4, p. 93.
[57] SM 17, pp. 16, 22.
[58] SM 4, p. 236.

the costs. No payment was made to reduce the debt.[59] In 1816 Samuel Coggins, a Negro servant, was jailed by Mathew Brooke. Again there was no record of the reason, but Coggins was still driving a team for Brooke several years later.[60]

Public sales were popular places to purchase goods and also served as rural social occasions. Men who wanted to make purchases at the vendue sometimes asked for cash, if they could find the boss, or charged the goods to their accounts at the Furnace. The prize example of a public sale transaction must surely have been the purchase of a farm for a worker who did not even know he was bidding. According to a Hopewell tradition, David Shaffer told Clement Brooke he wished he had enough money to buy a farm offered for sale. A few days later Brooke handed Shaffer a deed for the farm. Shaffer protested that he owned no farm. Brooke said he did now, for he had bid in the farm for $1,200 and paid for it out of money Shaffer had standing on the Hopewell books. Shaffer was surprised to discover that he had possessed any such sum of money.[61]

It was an advantage to workers to be able to say that a bill would be paid by Hopewell Furnace. All kinds of persons sold goods and services to employees and were assured that they need only present their bills to the clerk to receive payment. Peddlers and distant merchants; milliners, tailors and shoemakers; doctors and lawyers; carpenters, masons and cabinetmakers all received payments on bills they presented. The tax collector accepted a bulk payment for the money due from a long list of Hopewell employees. Administrators of estates collected the balances due to the deceased at the time of death less bills paid. In some cases the Furnace continued to act as banker for a widow who let her husband's balance stand on the Furnace books.[62] Many workers borrowed money from the

[59] SM 4, p. 253; SM 5, p. 96.
[60] HV 8161128A and HV 8180221.
[61] Albert Painter Interview, January 8, 1959.
[62] For example see *Cash Book* for 1828–1830, *op. cit.*, May 3, 1830.

Furnace when their accounts did not cover needs. For some reason a payment to William Gott in 1826 was recorded as a loan despite the record which showed he had credit on his account for more than the twenty dollar loan.[63] One man rented a stove and paid $2.56 rental, but the clerk did not record the length of time for which it was rented.[64]

The Furnace manager was entrusted with the most delicate missions of social life, although no instance was found to match that of the manager of Martha Furnace who ". . . went with Josh Townsend to settle his business with a lady."[65] In case of illness the mistress of the Big House was the first person called or consulted.[66] On at least two occasions Hopewell Furnace paid the cost of taking an aged resident of the Village to the county poorhouse.[67]

The following letter disclosed that real friendship must have existed between some workers and the owners' families:

> Do you remember the blacksmith, Israel and his wife Julia, they are both here now on a visit, they look very well, Charley and Tom are as fond of them as when they lived here . . .[68]

Labor relations at Hopewell Furnace in the first half of the nineteenth century were relatively stable. Wages changed little but probably represented the basis of as high a scale of living as was available to similar classifications of workmen in other industries and occupations. There were few strikes or walkouts and little evidence of a trend toward labor unionism despite some instances of united action by furnace owners. Workers were kept in line by a system of fines. No evidence was found of any use of corporal punishment, and few workers were discharged for either negligence or dishonesty. Paternalism and self-interest combined to induce the owners to provide a wide variety of services and aids to their workers.

[63] SM 12, p. 130 and SM 11, p. 315.
[64] SM 12, p. 48.
[65] *Martha Furnace Diary, op. cit.,* June 19, 1809, n. p.
[66] Kemper, *American Charcoal Making, op. cit.,* p. 5.
[67] SM 28, pp. 99, 166.
[68] *Brooke Family Papers,* Ann Brooke to George W. Brooke, August 3, 1831.

13 Labor Recruitment, Training and Tenure

THE SUPPLY OF TRAINED, SKILLED FURNACE WORKERS WAS inadequate to meet the demand when the charcoal-iron industry was prosperous. Even common laborers were not always easy to find in the comparative isolation of the furnace sites. Good relations between workers and boss resulted from the difficulty in replacing the dissatisfied workers who went to another furnace; but, on the other hand, the relative uniformity of wages among the furnaces served as a check on much labor migration. Turnover was greatest in the lowest paid and least skilled jobs and rather light in the highly skilled tasks. This must certainly have reflected the attention the manager gave to keeping his founder, miners, molders and colliers contented in their work. When a furnace closed its operations, the workers usually found employment with other ironmasters.

Hopewell Furnace recruited its workers in many places and used many means to induce persons to take employment. This area of Berks and Chester Counties had been a center of ironmaking for more than half a century before Hopewell was built; so many of the families living nearby were in possession of the required skills. Local recruitment provided many of the men needed. This source of labor supply was continually

272

cultivated throughout the history of Hopewell Furnace by giving employment to the children of workers and neighboring farmers. Apprentices, indentured servants and probably slaves appeared among the laborers; on-the-job training passed on skills to the new generations maturing in the village. But recruitment programs of several kinds were used to attract workers from greater distances. The large number of Negroes who appeared on the Hopewell books showed that black laborers formed an important element in the work force.[1]

The similarity between European and American methods of furnace and coaling procedures was noted by many writers. The reason was fairly clear : American iron was first produced by men who brought their skills across the Atlantic. England made an effort to guard its industrial secrets by the passage of an Act of Parliament in 1765 to prohibit the emigration of skilled workmen.[2] Regardless of the effectiveness of the enforcement of this law, it did not serve its purpose of preventing competition for English iron-making. For one reason it came too late. America already had a number of ironmasters who had come here from the British Isles and also from several countries on the continent. Places of origin of some Eastern Pennsylvania Furnace men before 1800 were :

England :	Thomas Rutter, Samuel Nutt, William Branson, John Ross, William Bird, Mathew Brooke.
Wales :	Thomas Potts, James Morgan, James Old.
Germany :	Henry William Stiegel, John Lester, Gerrard Etter.
Hanover :	Valentine Eckert.
Alsace :	George Anshertz.
Scotland :	William Keith, Samuel McCall, James Wilson.
Ireland :	Robert Grace, Robert Coleman, George Taylor.
France :	William Dewees, Daniel Udree.[3]

---

[1] The Negro workers will be given special attention in Chapter 15.
[2] Williamson, *op. cit.*, p. 50.
[3] Most of these were identified by Bining, *Pennsylvania Iron Manufacture in the 18th Century, op. cit.*, p. 131.

Union Township was settled by Swedes, English, Welsh, Palatine Germans, New Englanders, New Yorkers, Jerseyites, Dutch, and French Huguenots.[4] Charles B. Montgomery, Berks County historian, checked the family names in the early Hopewell record books and identified the following by point of European origin:

Swedes: Likens, Boon, Jones, Hulings.
Welsh: Morgan, Cadwalader, Reese, Jones, Roberts, Hughs, Edwards.
Germans: Rhoades, Colver, Redcay, Custar.
Scotch-Irish: Richards, Campbell, Murphy, Robison, Armstrong.[5]

The census of the United States began in 1850 to list the place of birth of each person. A check of this census report for Berks and Chester Counties showed that most of the Hopewell people reported that they had been born in Pennsylvania. Among those of foreign birth the Irish and Germans were numerous; and England, Wales, France and Scotland were listed as the birthplaces of one or more.[6] It is possible that at least a part of these immigrants came to the Furnace for employment because they were familiar with the processes of smelting.

Another possible source of foreign workers at the Furnace was soldiers who decided not to return to their homelands at the end of the Revolutionary War. On April 29, 1779, the Continental Congress passed a resolution offering free land and farm animals to any foreign soldiers who deserted from the British Army. One paragraph in the resolution was aimed particularly at skilled industrial workers:

Such of you as are skilled in manufactures, over and above these lands and other articles, will find riches in prosecuting

[4] *Montgomery Manuscripts,* Origin of Union Township.
[5] *Hopewell Letters,* Charles B. Montgomery to Lemuel Garrison, December 18, 1940.
[6] *Census of 1850* for Berks and Chester Counties, Pennsylvania.

your occupations, the necessities of life being very cheap in proportion to the price of manufactures, and the demand for them is so great, that every mechanic will find full employment. . . .[7]

It is not known now whether any foreign troops came to Hopewell in response to this invitation, but it is certain that two former British soldiers came to the Furnace. John Lewis Barde, who leased the furnace from James Wilson in 1794, was a British officer stationed in Florida before he came north to engage in the iron business.[8] Joseph Whitaker deserted from the British Army some time prior to 1781 and took over a tract of land about a mile from Hopewell. For a half century he appeared on the Hopewell books as a weaver, and several of his sons were employed at the Furnace.[9]

Hopewell Furnace counted upon permanent residents of the village to furnish a considerable share of its work force. Many families provided laborers for several generations; sons grew up to follow their fathers as Furnace employees. The Union Township tax returns for 1779 included the names of many men, and one woman, whose families would be associated with the Furnace for much of its history: Edward Dehaven, Evan Evans, John Gray, Thomas Hughs, Edward Hughs, Geo. Kirst, Stanley Kirby, Cath. Kramp, Evan Lewis, Joseph Millard, Mordecai Millard, Thomas Millard, James Roberts, John Sands, John Umstead, Peter Wampser, William Wampser, William Williams and Martin Wirt.[10] The Hopewell Journal for 1784–1792 contained many more names of families which remained for a long period in the village: John Hart, David Mee, John Rice, William Roads, John Painter, Nicholas Hunter, Ezekiel Thomas, Abram Sink, William Philips, Jacob Meese, Thomas Cuthbert, David Jenkins, Thomas Simes, Peter Moyer, Adam Kephart, John Haws,

[7] *Journals of the Continental Congress*, X, p. 408.
[8] *Brooke Family Papers*, Genealogical Data.
[9] Dennis C. Kurjack, "Joseph Whitaker of Hopewell Furnace," *The Historical Review of Berks County*, XIV, 3 (April 1949), pp. 66–73.
[10] *Berks County Tax Record for 1779*, Union Township, pp. 80–81.

William Merwin, Jacob Yocum and Charles Cramp were some of them.[11]

The Furnace also drew the sons of families living a short distance outside the village area. For example Micajah, Henry, Jessie and William Posey came from the Brandywine region of Chester County. Micajah began work at Hopewell at the age of fifteen, became a molder in 1831 and continued for the most prosperous period of stove-making until 1841. He married a daughter of a Hopewell woodcutter.[12]

Many a Hopewell father brought his son or sons to assist him at his job and thus introduced them to Furnace employment. In 1803 Edward Hughs paid his son David to assist at "Washing mine," and David remained as a long-time worker.[13] Three years later Edward Hughs was being paid for several sons' work, including Isaac as the gutterman.[14] In 1866 Nathan Care signed a contract for himself and his son John to provide the services of both founder and keeper.[15] There were many similar references to a son's doing work and his wages being paid to his father before the son was old enough to collect his own wages.

Another source of workers was the employees of other furnaces. The similarity of names in the records available for other furnaces revealed many who apparently left to come to Hopewell. The original staff for Hopewell must have been drawn largely from Warwick Furnace, for the Warwick ledger in the three years before Hopewell was built contained the names of at least 19 men who were a part of the Hopewell work force in the oldest records extant.[16] The Changewater Furnace account books for 1802 and 1803 listed as employees the following men who shortly after became Hopewell skilled

---

[11] SM 41, pp. 1–4.
[12] *Posey Family History* (unpublished typescript). Hopewell Village Library.
[13] SM 2, p. 143.
[14] SM 44, December 17, 1806, n. p.
[15] SM 60, April 17, 1866. Recorded on front cover of book.
[16] *Warwick Furnace Ledger*, 1767–1770. Historical Society of Pennsylvania.

workers: Frederick Meck, founder; Samuel Meck, keeper; Samuel and Peter Cox, teamsters; James Benson, miner; David Hart, filler; Philip Shafer, Senior and Philip Shafer, Junior, blacksmiths; Adam Johnston, keeper and miner. In 1821 Hopewell hired James T. Johnson after he had worked as molder and flask maker "at the Valley Works."[17] The Joanna Furnace records show that many workers moved back and forth between these two neighboring furnaces. A none too exhaustive survey of the Joanna journals and ledgers for the period 1810–1812 revealed 107 names that were the same as those of people who either had formerly worked at Hopewell or would later be employed there.[18] Of course one reason for so great a number was that Hopewell had ceased operation in 1808. This circumstance also accounted for the appearance in the *Martha Furnace Diary* of Hopewell names in 1808–1810. Philip Shafer, Peter Cox, James Hughs and William Williams were working at this New Jersey furnace during some part of those years.[19] Mary Ann Forge in York County was employing at least seven men with Hopewell names in this period.[20] Three other men left Hopewell Village to go to Orwigsburg in 1809 to help to build a new furnace.[21] Another major migration of workers from Hopewell took place in the 1840's when stove-making was ended, and at least half of the Hopewell molders went to Black Rock Furnace in Lancaster County.[22]

Not all of the workers were free to seek employment elsewhere if conditions did not suit them. It is not certain that slave labor was used at Hopewell, although the fact that Mark Bird owned slaves made it highly probable that some worked there in its early history.[23] But if doubt remains about the use

[17] SM 6, inside front cover, also August 8 and 20, 1816.
[18] *Joanna Furnace Journals* for 1810, 1811 and *Ledgers* for 1811, 1812, *op. cit.*
[19] *Martha Furnace Diary, op. cit., passim.*
[20] *Mary Ann Forge Ledger, 1810–1811, op. cit., passim.*
[21] SM 67, *passim.*
[22] *Black Rock Furnace Ledger,* 1845–1851. Hopewell Village Library.
[23] The account of Negroes at Hopewell is discussed in Chapter 15.

of slaves, there is none about the employment of indentured and apprenticed workers.

In 1773 Mark Bird offered a reward of three pounds for the return of a Dutch servant by the name of Christian Metz who was described as a miller by trade and "a good Scholar in the German language."[24] A few years later Hopewell Furnace paid fourteen pounds and eight shillings for "indenture payments for time of servitude" to each of the following: Patrick Fee, Joseph Somerset, Arthur Money, Edward Riley and Michael Riley.[25] No indication was given as to how or why these men had entered into "servitude;" but the indenture agreement of Jacob Hampf on May 16, 1804, gave these circumstances:

> This Indenture witnesseth, That Jacob Hampf of his own free Will hath bound himself Servant to Mathew Brooke, for the Consideration of Seventy Dollars paid Captn John Green for his Passage from Hamberg . . . during the full Term of Three Years . . . and the said Mathew Brooke . . . during the said Term shall find and provide for the said Servant sufficient Meat, Drink, Apparel, Washing and Lodging and at the Expiration of his Term, the said servant shall have two complete Suits of Cloaths one whereof to be New.[26]

Two of the Hopewell partners were concerned with the problem of how best to use another servant. One wrote:

> I also [wish] to see you on the Subject of my Black fellow Tobe as Mathew Davis [Hopewell manager] wishes him not to work for him and I am unwilling to Dispose of his time he is a stout good workman and only wants steady Employ.[27]

Indentures were still a problem in 1816 when the furnace paid William Duane of the *Country Aurora* $2 for advertising a reward of $30 for the return of a runaway servant.[28] In

[24] *Pennsylvania Gazette*, April 21, 1773.
[25] SM 41, p. 84. This payment was in 1784.
[26] *Brooke Family Papers*, indenture Hampf to Brooke.
[27] HV 8060405, Daniel Buckley to Mathew Brooke.
[28] HV 8160304A. It is possible that this runaway servant incident was associated with the jailing of Sampson Coggins mentioned in Chapter 12.

1818 payment was made for two pairs of shoes soled "for Sampson and Jack."[29] "Sampson" was quite probably the Negro teamster Sampson Coggins. "Jack" was James Jack who received some schooling at Furnace expense and so probably was an apprentice boy.

The use of indentured labor received a sharp setback in Pennsylvania in 1833 when the General Assembly enacted a law against imprisonment for debt. Evidence of involuntary servitude could still be found for a number of years longer, however.[30] The use of apprentice children would also continue for many years. The census of 1860 showed that a number of skilled craftsmen in Union Township had one or more apprentices listed as members of their households. George Montan, wheelwright, had a boy of 17; Levi Keller, blacksmith, two of 20 and 19; Charles Klink, shoemaker, two of 19 and 16; Jacob Hense, carpenter, two of 19 and 19; Samuel Boyer, one of 15; Franklin James, miller, one of 22.[31]

Boys apparently learned most of the jobs at the Furnace by observation, by instruction from their father or another relative, or simply by taking a job and learning while they worked. Two exceptions were noted of examples of more formal instruction for a job. Lewis Evans received $5 from Samuel Templin for "Teaching Jas. Roberts Bookeeping."[32] But the only job at the Furnace for which there was a fairly regular system of vocational training was molding. Boys were not apprenticed to the ironmaster to learn this skill but, instead, paid a journeyman molder to teach them. The boys were paid for any molding they did at the same rate as the adult molders, but they gave a percentage of their earnings to their teachers. In 1819 William Thomas had two pupils. Ezekiel Thomas earned $219.75 and paid one half of it to William. William Rickets also paid William Thomas half of his income of $155.26. Rickets had been a woodcutter but

---

[29] HV 8180302.
[30] Sullivan, *op. cit.*, p. 211 (footnote).
[31] Apprenticeship at Hopewell will be considered in Chapter 17.
[32] *Lewis Evans Journal, op. cit.*, September 16, 1819, p. 122.

became a Hopewell molder after this instruction, as did Ezekiel Thomas. John Sheeler collected $76.20 for teaching the molders' skills to Joseph McKewen, another woodcutter who became a Hopewell molder.[33] Samuel Williams, a teamster, paid William Rickets $84.23½ out of molding earnings of $182.19½ in 1832. Probably this payment was for teaching molding to a ward, for Williams collected the molder's earnings of Joseph Elliott from 1832 to the beginning of 1837.[34]

Workmen sometimes were recommended to the Furnace by letter of application or reference. A few such letters have survived. J. Hamill applied for the job of manager in 1801 in this manner:

> Being informed by Mr. Fincher that you will want some person at Hopewell next Spring to manage if you do and your brother should leave there if you and I could agree I would have no objection to go there. . . .[35]

He did not get the job, nor did Justin Smith who offered to "do writing" or any other of the clerk's duties.[36]

A letter might have come from a person who could recommend the worker. William Linderman was recommended for a job as collier by a relative who wrote that "he is a sober and industerous man."[37] Impediments were sometimes placed in the way of employing men as indicated in this caution that "if his Intended *Lady* is satisfied perhaps you may get him" to work.[38]

On at least two occasions Furnace employees were paid for bringing girls to work as maids at the Big House. The record is not clear, however, whether the payment was for expenses or a reward for helping to recruit a new employee.[39] But near

[33] SM 9, p. 126; SM 6, pp. 37, 98, 127, 128.
[34] SM 19, p. 268; SM 21 ,pp. 158, 190, 205.
[35] *Brooke Family Papers*, J. Hamill to Mathew Brooke, February 10, 1810.
[36] *Ibid.*, Justin Smith to Mathew Brooke, January 13, 1810.
[37] HV 8321216, F. Linderman to Clement Brooke.
[38] HV 8120301, Daniel Buckley to Mathew Brooke.
[39] SM 2, p. 101; SM 31, p. 123.

the middle of the century the services of an employment agency were used to find maids. There were several fees of 25¢ to $1 paid to the Intelligence Office in Philadelphia for securing girls to work at Hopewell. Railroad fare for their passage to Douglassville was an additional expense. Once Mrs. Clingan went to Philadelphia to bring her new maid back, and on another occasion her sister Mrs. William R. White put the girl on the coach and paid her fare.[40]

Workers were given some inducements to take employment at the Furnace; the most common ones found were advancements to pay debts and provide housing for the new employee. Samuel Steel offered his services on the condition that the company would "let him have twenty-five dollars to pay some debts."[41] The employer sometimes lost on this kind of a deal. In 1847 the Furnace advanced Julia Garey $5 for housework she promised to do, but she did not do the work and returned only $1 of the advancement.[42] Daniel Buckley wrote to Mathew Brooke about the necessity to provide a workman with a house as a condition of employment:

> John Funk, the father of Abraham who you have agreed with, has an Inclination to moove into your part of the country, if he can be provided with a house. Should it be convenient for you to let him have one, you will find him and his family Industrious sober and Honest people, and if it was in my power to furnish him with a house that would suit him I would be much Pleased if he would remain in this part of the Country.[43]

The Furnace often gave assistance to the new employee by providing a wagon to move his household goods. Usually the cost was charged to the worker's account, but there were cases in which moving costs were paid by the Furnace as a condition of employment.[44] The usual charges were $2 to $4 for

[40] SM 31, pp. 91, 122, 139, 147, 156.
[41] HV 8400227, Charles Brooke, Junior, to Clement Brooke.
[42] SM 31, p. 46.
[43] HV 8201230A.
[44] Examples are SM 32, pp. 26, 40 and SM 7, April 5, 1817, n. p.

moving from a nearby community. But in 1849 the Furnace must have been recruiting workers at a distance; for William Ellet was paid $25 "to bring his Family," and James Walls drew $50.50 cash for the same reason.[45]

A final kind of attraction for workers to take employment at a furnace was the opportunity which existed there for an ambitious man to rise in power and riches. Many ironmasters began as common laborers at a furnace.[46] Harker Long came to Hopewell as a messenger and office boy and remained to become Furnace manager.[47] Thomas Foster came as teacher and became the company clerk.[48] John Benson began as a miner, advanced to clerk at Hopewell and left in 1835 to become manager of the Oak Grove Furnace in Perry County at a salary of $1200 per year.[49] Two of Joseph Whitaker's sons began to work as laborers at Hopewell and went on to found the Wheeling Steel Company and earn large fortunes.[50]

Clement Brooke gave encouragement and help to at least one of his employees to leave for a better job, as this letter of recommendation proves:

> The Bearer of this is John Care who has Moulded at this place and done other work at the Furnace from his Boy hood up to the Present time he is Anxious to be imployed by you as Founder at the Furnace you intend Building in Maryland the ensuing Summer. his father Thomas Care has Blowed Hopewell for the last twenty years lately his son Henry has taken his place, I can Safely Recomend John as Capable of Blowing Furnace — is otherwise Sober Moral and upright in his Conduct in Case you and him agree his Father Says he would be willing to assist his Son at your Furnace as long as his Services Should be thought Necessary.[51]

For all the advantages of furnace employment it still re-

[45] SM 31, p. 104.
[46] Bining, "Iron Plantations," op. cit., p. 20.
[47] Reading Eagle, February 11, 1917.
[48] HV 8361207A.
[49] HV 8351216.
[50] Kurjack, "Joseph Whitaker," op. cit.
[51] HV 8360000B.

mained true that life in the isolated villages was not very lively, the work was hard, and the hours were long. It was difficult to secure workers and often more difficult to retain them, especially those in the lower-paid categories. House-maids, guttermen and fillers were hard to keep, and turnover was especially high in these jobs. Many different people worked as woodcutters, also, but these were largely local and part-time workers. The city girls who came to work at the Big House in the Clingan era were of especially short tenure. They probably found the forest setting too different from their city ways.

But judging from the following note, incentive pay was used successfully to hold employees:

> Hired this day Henry Henry to do our smithing for one year from the time he is free we are to give him $19.00 per month and if he does his work well we are to give him a pair of coarse boots.[52]

The next year the contract was renewed, and the boots were to be given with no condition imposed.[53] He must have done his work well.

[52] *Kemper Manuscripts,* Charles M. Clingan Pocket Note Book, *op. cit.,* March 13, 1858, n. p.

[53] *Ibid.,* February 18, 1859.

Part Six

The Social Village

14 The Worker and His Associates

THE ECONOMIC CENTER FOR THE COMMUNITY DEPENDING UPON Hopewell Furnace for its industrial income was the company office and store. No similar social center existed for the families of the scattered Hopewell employees. Their associations tended to converge in several rather distinct social groups.

The residents near the furnace did much of their buying at the company store, attended the Bethesda Baptist Church, sent their children to the tutors engaged by the ironmaster and later to the Hopewell schoolhouse, and looked to Birdsboro and Douglassville for their wider community associations. The Pine Swamp dwellers and miners at the Warwick Mines traded at the stores in Warwick, attended the St. Mary's Episcopal Church and sent their children to Lewis Evans' school. The Jones Mine families went to Morgantown to trade at the Morris and Morgan stores; to attend the Episcopal, Methodist or Presbyterian churches; and to enroll their children in the village school. Another group of workers gravitated toward Geigertown. The colored residents of this area built an African Methodist Church, about three miles from the furnace, in 1856.

Community orientation was not this simple, however, for

there were many exceptions. Some Furnace-area people preferred an Episcopal service to the Baptist and, therefore, held membership in a church in Warwick or Douglassville. The Furnace store did not carry sufficient stock to supply all needs, and orders were sent to other stores. Credit established at the company store and ore wagons making regular trips between the furnace and mines made it convenient for mine families to buy goods at Hopewell. Pine Swamp boys crossed the mountain to court girls who lived near the furnace. Workers became acquainted on their jobs, and it was natural for some of their families to form friendships. Members of the same families lived and worked in each of the centers and visited in each others' homes. Then the annual Christmas and New Year's Day parties at the Big House brought together all of the families of employees.[1]

In a sense, then, the Hopewell community had several centers of social life within the general area encompassed by the Furnace business activities. Intermarriage among the families created many family ties in the village. There were both close friendships and animosities. The necessities of rural life developed many interrelationships among the workers and their families: They helped each other in time of need, cooperated on large projects, provided for the necessities of life, sold each other goods and services, occasionally stole from each other, got into fights, took their differences to court and gave aid and comfort to the sick and bereaved.

Hopewell Furnace provided no retirement plan, no health or accident insurance and no unemployment compensation for its workers. These hazards of life were the responsibility of the individual and his family, but in some cases the community or neighborhood provided a kind of welfare program for the unfortunate residents. One rather common means of giving aid was to pass around a "subscription paper" upon which those who desired to do so could pledge to contribute a specified sum to the person whose name appeared at the

[1] These interrelationships will be discussed in subsequent chapters.

top. This paper was then sent to the clerk who debited the accounts of all the donors and credited the account of the recipient. The amounts were not large, and the number of signers indicated that only close friends or immediate neighbors were solicited. Clement Brooke was always among those who gave during his time as manager, but he did not contribute noticeably larger amounts than some of his employees. On several such collections he gave $1, the same amount as one or more of the others.[2] In 1848 he gave $5 on one such collection.[3] John Church contributed one dollar out of his clerk's pay to a collection for James McCormick in 1845; but he was matched by James Mock, and Enoch Squibb gave half as much.[4]

Another kind of help came in the form of mutual aid to a fellow. For example in 1805 Peter Cox and John Boyers each took off one half day, and lost their pay for that time, to go "to John Hart's choping in the Afternoon." Cox was also credited, along with his son Samuel, for helping with "Richards moving" in the same year—an act of charity which cost each of them a day's pay.[5] Such assistance was not altogether in the spirit of altruism, however; for these events were made social occasions, and whiskey was supplied to all who came.

Widows were often left with little or no inheritance from their husbands to provide for themselves and their children. The Furnace record books contain many entries of goods delivered to a widow and paid for by someone else. The clerk did not usually distinguish between gifts and payments for goods or services; so it is not possible to know whether these were examples of welfare or of business transactions. The Furnace made payment in 1806 for goods ordered from Samuel Laverty and Company for "Widow Kephart."[6] In 1819 John

[2] For example see SM 10, p. 30.
[3] SM 31, p. 69.
[4] SM 28, p. 153.
[5] SM 1, pp. 73, 74, 76.
[6] SM 4, p. 114.

Anderson paid for "one quarter of flour for Widow Adams,"[7]
and Founder Thomas Care gave a verbal order at the store
for "the Widow Roger" to receive the following goods:

10 yards Calico	@	2/6
15 yards Cotton Plaid	@	2/6
2 lb Coffee	@	.37
2 lb Sugar	@	.18
Total		$9.43[8]

Funeral expenses were another form of welfare contribution.
Clement Brooke paid the carpenter $8 "for Mrs. Hudson
coffin." Before her death he had bought some coffee for her.[9]

Partnerships of several kinds existed among the workers.
David Hughs and George Painter made a joint purchase of a
barrel of mackerel at $7.50 and divided the fish between
them.[10] They saved a little money over the cost of each buying
what he needed separately. In 1817 David Hughs, Samuel
Richard and Montgomery Hughs operated an equal partnership known as David Hughs and Company to carry on coaling
operations for the Furnace. In January of that year each was
paid $279.48 as his share of what had been earned.[11] Two
decades later Jacob and Peter Hartenstine were listed as partners, but the nature of their enterprise was not given.[12]

Because no one was paid wages and the clerk or manager
was not always available to make a cash payment against credit
on the company books, employees sometimes found themselves
in need of coins or currency; so they borrowed from a friend
or acquaintance. Most of these transactions doubtless took
place with no notice in the business records, but there were
times when the repayment involved a journal entry. George
Painter took a note from Jacob Wolf when he lent him
£5 9s. in 1809. Both of them had been casual workers for

---

[7] SM 9, p. 144.
[8] *Ibid.*, p. 172.
[9] SM 17, p. 9; SM 9, p. 81.
[10] SM 14, p. 60. This was in 1829.
[11] SM 7, January 18, 1817, n. p.
[12] SM 21, p. 164.

the Furnace.[13] In 1827 Joseph McKewen received $2 from the wages of David Hart to repay a loan which had run for some time without payment.[14] John Sheeler repaid a loan of 25¢ made by his son William from Thomas Forster.[15]

Private homes served the purposes now assumed by some commercial establishments or institutions, as can be seen by the following bill paid by Isaac Hughes to David Hughes:

1 Year, 8 mo. 12 days washing and mending	@ .75	15.33
8 „ 29 „ boarding	@ $5.00	44.82
For making 4 shirts	@ .25	1.00
„ „ 4 pairs pantaloons	@ .25	1.00
„ „ 1 jacket		.25
„ footing 2 pairs stockings		.50
„ soaling 1 pair shoes		.50
„ Attendance when laying sick at my house		5.00[16]

Protecting the interests of orphans in their inheritance was another kind of service performed by neighbors. The same Isaac Hughes mentioned above had received money the previous year from George Lloyd, administrator of the estate of Mary Hughes. Lloyd had had a trustee appointed for Isaac at a legal cost of $28.50. Two payments in cash to the heir amounted to $185.00.[17] The settlement of an estate sometimes involved holding a public sale of the assets of the deceased, and the Furnace records became involved by paying for purchases by workers or by the Furnace.[18]

The Hopewell community provided many services for its residents by means of work performed for one another. A wide variety of skilled workmen were available in the neighborhood of whom some worked for the Furnace, and some were occupied full time at their trades. The journal for a few

[13] SM 4, pp. 245, 249, 253.
[14] SM 59, p. 24.
[15] SM 28, p. 84. The date was in 1842.
[16] SM 12, p. 146. This was paid in 1826.
[17] SM 12, p. 86.
[18] For example see SM 28, p. 93.

months in 1830 showed that the following men received pay for the vocation indicated : William McKinty, tailor; Robert Gilmore, weaver; Abraham Dehaven, furniture maker; David Rogers, shoemaker; John Seabold, tailor; Henry Shick, weaver; Henry McKinty, tailor; Joseph Whitaker, weaver; Thomas Kirkpatrick, furniture maker; Thomas Lambert, shoemaker; Jacob Hartenstine, shoemaker; James Everhart, tanner; Samuel Haws, tailor; David Smith, shoemaker; Henry Landis, weaver; Andrew McMichael, shoemaker; George Goheen, shoemaker; Christian Rice, weaver; George Wert, tailor; Samuel Whitman, shoemaker; William Patton, wagon-maker; Jesse Kineday, shoemaker and Thomas Lloyd, shoe-maker.[19] It is evident that shoemakers, tailors and weavers were in demand in this period when relatively little ready-made clothing was available. Secondhand clothing was some-times sold in private transactions between villagers.[20]

A man with a horse and plow could earn some money in the spring by plowing the garden plots of his neighbors. In 1849 Isaac Cadwalader and Sam Wamsher were both plowing gardens and were paid for each plot from 50¢ to $2.50.[21] Gardens also entered into the relationships among families when excess products were sold to neighbors. Potatoes, cab-bage, turnips and beets were mentioned among such sales.[22] Orchards, too, produced a surplus of apples and cider to be sold.[23]

As the following note to the clerk demonstrated, trust of one neighbor for another existed to a remarkable degree :

> Please to Let John Himes have goods to any Amount that May Suit him and return to me the Amount. Thos. Lloyd.[24]

There were many similar notes preserved in the store records

[19] From SM 19, *passim.*
[20] SM 14, p. 64 and SM 21, p. 168.
[21] SM 31, p. 99 and SM 32, p. 60.
[22] SM 21, p. 137; SM 21, p. 2.
[23] SM 14, p. 53.
[24] *Hopewell Papers,* uncatalogued, May 22, 1824.

with the exception that most of them specified a limit to the guarantee extended.

It was not unusual that among so many people the spirit of honesty and amity would not always prevail. A charge of $8.55 was made against the account of David Hart with this explanation, "for ½ ton hay fed of William Thomas. W. Thomas got ½ ton of our hay that was at John Richards in Lieu of his ½ ton fed by you."[25] Most disputes among people of the village were doubtless settled by those involved or by the mediation of the ironmaster, but sometimes they went to law. Three kinds of lawsuits predominated among those recorded in the Furnace books as involving workers. Storekeepers brought suit to secure payment of overdue bills.[26] Worker sued worker in numerous actions of which the only cause recorded in the journals was for debt and costs.[27] Among the suits for which no reason was given doubtlessly some were for damages or trespass. Other frequent suits resulted from charges brought by constables—possibly the aftermath of fights or violations of the law.[28]

One of the greatest needs for social interdependence was the care of the ill, the injured and the dead. No reference to hospital care was found in the Hopewell Furnace records. Each family had most of the responsibility for providing for the incapacitated and incompetent, but the community assumed a share of the work when there was no family to provide the sick room care. John Roberts died in 1843 at the age of 86 or 87 years after his last days had been eased by neighborhood attention, given under difficult circumstances. James Morris reported :

His habits and manner of living, which were filthy in the extreme, precluded that attendance upon his last days and hours, which would otherwise have been given. Nevertheless,

[25] SM 7, November 1, 1817, n. p.
[26] Examples are SM 4, p. 92 and SM 7, November 25, 1817, n. p.
[27] See SM 28, p. 82; SM 9, p. 15; SM 4, pp. 59, 125; SM 44, August 9, 1806, n. p.
[28] SM 44, August 9, 1806, n. p. and SM 10, pp. 38, 40, 41, 46.

he was not left to suffer alone and unaided and unattended. The neighborhood, amongst whom Miss Ann Clymer was the most kind and attentive, rendered every assistance that could, under the circumstances, be given.[29]

Those who could afford to pay for help did not depend entirely on charitable impulses but still drew upon the community for the assistance they needed, as can be seen in this letter:

> I am concerned about Mother I could wish you to have every attention paid her and if her feet have got no better you must procure some person to wait on her perhaps one of Brother Thomas' Daughters could be had. Anne Davis is of the same oppinion. Say she should not be left alone. No expence should be sparred.[30]

In the absence of expert medical diagnosis the determination of the nature of illnesses was lacking in thorough credibility. The lay opinions of the community, however, listed a wide variety of ailments. The yellow fever epidemic of 1798 may not have reached so far west as Hopewell, but it did hit customers of the Furnace products. A letter from Wilmington, Delaware asked that no more iron be sent and requested an extension of time on payments because:

> . . . our little place exhibits a melancholy appearance the yellow fever or some fever which brings great mortality sweeping away our citizens—it appears likely 8 or 10 are or will be buried this day . . . the Tobacconists we believe are all gone as are great part of the inhabitants—and it is likely three or four days will have the place almost desolate . . .[31]

Children's diseases were accepted with a degree of fatalism which in the following instance seems almost callous:

[29] *Morris Diary, op. cit.,* II, p. 74.
[30] *Brooke Family Papers,* George Brooke to Mathew Brooke, no date except 1805.
[31] *Ibid.,* Ferris and Gilpin to Mathew Brooke, September 20, 1798.

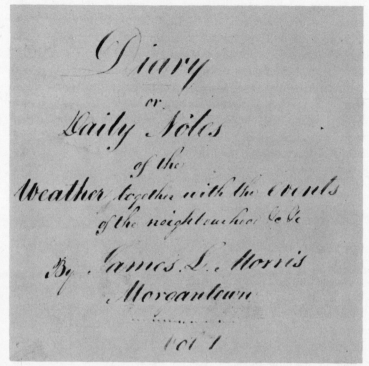

Title Page of the Diary of James Morris, Storekeeper in Morgantown

The dysentery has been prevailing, to some extent, throughout the neighborhood for a few weeks past, but as it has confined itself to children it has as yet excited little alarm. Two children have died of it within the week.[32]

As the writer was a sensitive man with children of his own, he was probably only reflecting the general reaction to childhood diseases. Fatalities among children were noted from typhus, scarlet fever, measles, and "putrid sore throat." Other common childhood diseases were rash, "Bilious pleurisy," whooping cough and "cholera infantum."[33]

[32] *Morris Diary, op. cit.*, September 30, 1843, p. 69.
[33] *Ibid., passim.*

Among adults many suffered from some of the same sicknesses as the children, but other illnesses recorded were "bilious typhoid," influenza, "consumption or bleeding at the lungs," "bowel complaints," "violent pains in the stomach," "sick with a Bile" and lockjaw.[34]

Preventive measures which were taken indicated common fear of smallpox, hydrophobia and malaria. In 1838 James Morris wrote that he had had his son William vaccinated with cow pox.[35] Mad dogs were feared and destroyed, if possible. For example note this case :

> A great hubbub raised in town yesterday by the appearance and transit through of a mad dog. A great crowd armed with bludgeons etc. followed him, but he was protected by his drunken master. . . .[36]

On another occasion five or six dogs were shot because they had been bitten by a dog suspected of being mad.[37]

According to local tradition, malaria was brought to Berks County by the Irish workers on the Schuylkill Canal, and Mathew Brooke was one of its victims. Support for the presence of malaria in the period of canal building was found in the large number of sales at the Hopewell store in 1825–1826 of quinine pills, "Peruvian bark," "yellow bark" and "barks."[38]

Accidents were the causes of disabilities and deaths of many Furnace workers. The Changewater Furnace books listed time lost by laborers for such reasons as "foot cut," "finger cut," "sore foot," "kicked by horse," "Burnt his shoulder badly" and "Fell against wagon and hurt shoulder." One man was killed when the bank wall collapsed and fell on him.[39] Fillers suffered many burns and injuries to hands, feet

[34] *Ibid.;* SM 46, p. 38.
[35] *Morris Diary, op. cit.,* p. 53.
[36] *Ibid.,* p. 71.
[37] *Ibid.,* p. 47.
[38] SM 12, pp. 17, 89, 93, *Hopewell Papers,* Receipt from Joseph Reakert, date destroyed except 1825.
[39] *Changewater Furnace Time Book, op. cit.,* pp. 2–46.

and backs. Broken bones and cuts caused loss of time.[40] Harriet Finger died when her clothing caught fire and "burned off her back."[41]

Travel accidents also caused injury and death to some men of the village. Clement Brooke had expenses of $63 to pay doctor bills and tavern expenses "when laying at Reading Hurt by the upsetting of the Stage some time ago."[42] Samuel Yocum was killed by being "Crushed to death between two cars on the railroad," and Robert Wynn "drowned in the Canal."[43]

The census records showed that many persons suffering from mental diseases were kept in their homes. In 1860 one household in Caernarvon Township was listed as consisting of :

Margaret Wilson	age 49	Housekeeper[44]
Ann Irions	age 73	Insane
Jane Irions	age 47	Idiot
Samuel Irions	age 42	Idiot

Medical help was available to the people of the community from doctors in the nearby towns who were consulted in their offices or who would come to the homes. Like so many other people who worked for the villagers, the doctor received his pay from the Furnace. Occasionally he would take part of his fee in storegoods or iron instead of cash. Perhaps the Hopewell people got more medical service than was customary among rural people because the doctor was more sure of payment, and collection was easy. The Furnace books show many instances of doctors having been paid sizeable sums which were taken from the accounts of workers. The doctor often treated a number of patients on the same trip to the

[40] *Birdsborough Forge Time Book, op. cit.,* pp. 27, 33.
[41] *Morris Diary, op. cit.,* II, p. 12.
[42] *Hopewell Papers.* Memorandum of Expenses. Undated but probably in the 1840's.
[43] St. Gabriel's Episcopal Church, record of burials, March 28, 1847, and November 8, 1861. Berks County Historical Society.
[44] *United States Census of 1860,* Berks County, p. 152.

Furnace. The doctor sometimes performed services that were not medical in nature, as demonstrated by Doctor Isaac L. Vansant who delivered an order of store goods when he came to a woodcutter's home.[45]

Dr. Vansant was not the only doctor listed as receiving payments in 1817 and 1818, and in subsequent years the names of many doctors were listed on the Furnace books: Doctor Jacob Leaser in 1818 and 1819, Doctor James B. Chevington and "Doctor Mitchner" in 1819–1842, "Doctor Evans" in 1821, Doctor Robert May in 1826–1851, Doctor William Happersett in 1826–1829, Doctor David E. Gordon in 1838, Doctor H. Weiman in 1841–1847, "Doctor Meredith" in 1847, "Doctor Jones" in 1848-1849, "Doctor Gross" in 1847 and Doctor Levi Rooke in 1849-1851.[46] The fee most frequently paid was $2, but there were some for $1 and many for higher amounts. The clerk often noted that the payment was for "medicine and attendance."[47] A member of the Clement Brooke family must have undergone surgery in the 1830's, for a receipt from Doctor Joseph Parrish of Philadelphia acknowledged payment of $35 "for Medical and Surgical Services to this date."[48] The only instance found of a payment for nursing service was $2 "paid a Nurse" by John Hoofman in 1850.[49]

Probably the doctor was called only when serious illness was suspected. Patent medicines and home remedies were used for lesser ailments. In addition to malaria cures and many entries for undifferentiated "medicine," the store carried or ordered from Philadelphia many patent medicines and cures for a variety of ills: Epsom salts, calomel, worm oil and worm syrup, "physicks" and "pukes," quick silver and brimstone, "worm tea," paregoric, castor oil, "Ear Oil and

[45] SM 9, p. 44.
[46] From the Journals of the dates listed. Some first names were not given by the clerks.
[47] For example see SM 21, p. 97.
[48] HV 8350110.
[49] SM 31, p. 126.

syringe," "embrocation lotion," eye salve, salve, "bolsom of wild cherry," vermifuge for worms, "worm medicine," "assofoldida" and carminative for gas pains.[50]

The villagers seemed to have been much troubled by worms. A bottle obtained in an archeological dig at the site of the Big House privy had this legend: "Bumstead's Worm Syrup— . —One Bottle has killed 100 worms— . —Children cry for more— . —Just Try It— . —Philada."[51]

The Eli Keen Store at Warwick sold Indian Vegetable Pills, essence of Peppermint, camphor, Swains Vermifuge, saleratus, Scots Pills and tooth powder.[52] Another neighboring storekeeper wrote of the changing demands of his customers for medicines:

> Purchased some "Wright Indian Vegetable Pills," have been keeping them for sale this Year past. They have nearly superseded "Brandreth's," which were all the rage a few years since. Before them I sold the "Dutch," "Keyser," or "Blood Pills,"—they succeeded the "Lees Antibilious" and years ago the "Scots" or "Andderson's" were almost the only ones in use.[53]

Jeremiah Dougherty, Elizabeth Mervine, Henry Care, Levi Care and Clement Brooke bought eye glasses at a cost which increased from 50¢ in 1816 to $3.50 in 1825.[54] Mrs. Mervine was a seamstress for many Hopewell families, and Clement Brooke and Henry Care subscribed to newspapers; so it is possible that these people used their eyes in ways which required the aid of lenses. Samuel Williams and Samuel Witman apparently suffered from hernias as they purchased trusses at prices ranging from 75¢ to $2.50.[55]

[50] From the Journals for many years of store operation.
[51] Leland J. Abel, "Excavation of a Privy at the Ironmaster's House, Hopewell Village, 1962" (unpublished manuscript, 1962). Hopewell Village Library.
[52] Eli Keen Store Book, op. cit., 1844–1845.
[53] Morris Diary, op. cit., p. 210. This was in 1842.
[54] SM 8, p. 52; SM 12, p. 45; SM 28, p. 80; SM 31, pp. 54, 66.
[55] Cash Book for 1828–1830, op. cit., March 8, 1830, n. p.; SM 31, pp. 16, 112.

Doctors had their problems of diagnosis and treatment in an age when diagnostic aids were few and laboratories non-existent. A trip to the seashore, perhaps to Cape May, was considered a possible cure; but it did not always bring results.[56] If the doctor knew the cause of a sickness he was treating, he often failed to enlighten the family. Daniel Buckley showed his anxiety in the following letter :

> Sally still continues confined to her room is some better and other times worse but I think gets weaker. I am much at a loss to know whether she will recover or not as the season is now so Inclement that she cannot be Expected to leave the room, and it [is] the doctors particular directions that [she] use no Exercise whatever, and be most particular in her diet, which we find Extremely difficult, what she may take that does not make her worse.[57]

On the other hand some persons untrained in medicine were quite sure of the cure for other people's illnesses. Daniel Buckley wrote to Mathew Brooke, ". . . you ought to take physick as I am told you have a head ach, it proceeds from a disordered stomach. . . . "[58] Castor oil was regarded as a cure for many of life's troubles, and wild turnips were also used by Hopewell people as a cathartic. An area near the lake was known as the "turnip patch" because this herb grew there in such profusion.[59]

Hex doctors or powwow cures also were available in the community. A farmer claimed to be able to stop hemorrhage from a wound by smearing three wooden wedges with the blood and then driving the wedges into some place where they would remain dry. He also claimed to be able to stop bleeding "by saying some words," and did not even need "to see the person or animal bleeding."[60]

[56] *Brooke Family Papers,* Daniel Buckley to Clement Brooke, August 24, 1821.
[57] HV 8201230. Daniel Buckley to Mathew Brooke.
[58] HV 8080223.
[59] Interview with Albert Painter, January 16, 1956.
[60] *Morris Diary, op. cit.,* II, p. 169.

Ann F. Brooke included some health hints in her letters to her brother George while he was attending West Chester Academy in 1832–1833 :

> I am glad you go to the gymnasium it will be such good exercise for your limbs . . . do . . . not eat much meat — it makes you dull — only take a little ham to strengthen you.[61]

> . . . do not eat much fruit before going to bathe, I believe you often get fruit on your way to the creek, you had better eat it after bathing — the cholera is expected again this summer by almost every one — you particularly ought to avoid the hot sun and eating immoderately of any thing which disagrees with you — you know — in warm weather you are subject to spells of choleramorbus.[62]

> It is well you had your teeth examined by the dentist . . . all you have to do to preserve them is to brush them every morning with water, use no tooth powder.[63]

Sanitation was probably not regarded as a major problem for the Furnace, but there were some provisions made. Homemade soap was boiled for the Furnace[64] and perhaps was used at the catch basin where running water gave the workmen a chance to wash their hands on the way to the dining room in the basement of the mansion.[65] Since Alexander McCarraher was paid $3 for "mason work at Bath house,"[66] it is apparent that provision was made for bathing somewhere in the Furnace area. Close by the office-store was a privy used by the workers in and near the Furnace.[67] Control of pests was attempted by the use of rat poison, roach poison, fly poison and mouse traps.[68]

[61] *Brooke Family Papers,* April 15, 1833.
[62] *Ibid.,* May 1833.
[63] *Ibid.,* February 29, 1832.
[64] SM 28, p. 148.
[65] Interview with Mrs. Sally Boone, March 22, 1941.
[66] SM 21, p. 35.
[67] Earl J. Heydinger, "Orientation Report for Archeology in Lower Working Level at Hopewell Village NHS" (unpublished report, 1962). Hopewell Village Library.
[68] SM 28, p. 124; SM 31, p. 115; SM 65, August 14, 1858, n. p.

Some of the men at the Furnace evidently were vain or interested in good grooming; for in the bottles recovered from the mansion privy were several marked "Batchelor's Liquid Hair Dye No. 1," "Boyle's Electric Hair Dye, Boston, No. 2" and "Bear's Oil."[69]

The final service rendered to its members by any community was to provide a decent burial. The workers at Hopewell were usually laid to rest in a plain wooden box made by the carpenter or cabinetmaker. The normal expenses were $2 for digging the grave and $8 to $10 for a coffin. For a child these prices were 75¢ and $2 respectively. The costs were usually paid from the estate of the deceased or by a member of the family,[70] but in at least one instance the Furnace paid for the coffin of the wife of one of the workmen.[71]

In a few cases the records show a more elaborate preparation for burial. Patrick Clemens sent an order to the store saying:

> . . . please to Let the Bearer have the things [several words unreadable] musling for winding Sheet and Shraud two pound of Cofy two pound Shuger one yard of Black Crape one pair Black Stockings one paire of Black Gloves.[72]

A funeral director's charges were included for the funeral of Samuel Downing in 1821 when these expenses were incurred:

> . . . Clothes for Saml Downing Jr minor to attend his
> fathers funeral $18.79
> For the Coffin, David Finger   12.00
> For digging the grave, John Gordon   1.50
> For the funeral, Robt. Laverty   30.00[73]

Deaths in the wealthy Clingan family brought greater expenses. The funeral of Sarah Clingan, mother of Ironmaster

---

[69] Abel, *op. cit.*
[70] SM 31, pp. 8, 37, 55; SM 28, pp. 42, 72, 179; SM 65, p. 5.
[71] SM 2, p. 28. This was in 1802.
[72] HV 8260910.
[73] *Lewis Evans Ledger, op. cit.*, p. 173.

Charles M. Clingan, cost $229.75. This charge included $108 for the casket and furnishings; and the remainder was for attendants, grave digger, carriers, hire of hearse and carriages, flowers, ribbon for the door and use of the ice cooler. Later other payments were made, including $150 for a grave stone and $25 to the minister.[74] For Dr. Clingan, himself, the funeral cost $422.12, including $125 for 25 carriages and $226.40 for the coffin and case.[75]

Hopewell Village found many ways and reasons for co-operation among its residents. Like most rural communities of the nineteenth century, it would have had difficulty surviving without much mutual interaction within its group.

[74] HV 8720109 and HV 8750208A.
[75] HV 8750510.

15 The Colored Population

NEGRO WORKERS WERE A PART OF HOPEWELL VILLAGE during the entire history of the Furnace operation. A survey of the records provided a list of 107 Negroes employed by the Furnace, but this number was not necessarily complete. The clerk noted beside some names in his ledgers the words "colored man," "negro," "black man" or "a man of color." From other sources some persons were known to have been Negroes, but not all of these were identified as such in the ledgers. For example Ben Hill was placed on the list because his estate was assigned to Wilkinson Hill who was colored. Since Ben was not designated as Negro by the clerk, possibly others were similarly missed. Some persons were listed because they were called by such names at "Negro Bendigo," "Black Frank," "Black Boy," "Black Cook" or "Little Negro." Duplication was possible because some of these later acquired last names, as "Black Bill" and "Black William" became William Jacobs. These repetitions were eliminated when it was definite that the same person was intended, but both names were included when doubt remained. Whatever the exact total should be, Negroes formed a respectable proportion of the entire work force.

Hopewell Furnace was in no way unique in its employment of Negroes, for the iron industry used many colored workers in both the North and the South. Slave-owners of the South sometimes collected wages of $200 per year for permitting an ironmaster to use a slave.[1] A British traveler in 1796 reported that "all the furnaces and forges in Maryland were worked by blacks."[2] Israel Acrelius observed many Negro slaves working at the Pennsylvania furnaces during his travels in the 1750's. He thought they were better treated here than anywhere else in America.[3]

Cornwall Furnace had about 24 slaves when Pennsylvania abolished slavery in 1780. Some of these were house servants; but others were listed as furnace men, wood cutters and colliers.[4] At the same time George Ege owned 10 slaves at Charming Forge.[5]

No positive proof was found that slaves were used at Hopewell, but the records were clear that Mark Bird possessed slaves during the time he was the owner of the Furnace. When slaves were registered according to the Pennsylvania act of emancipation, Mark Bird was the largest slave-owner in Berks County. He listed 10 adult males, 4 adult females, 3 boys and 1 girl.[6] Several times he advertised for runaway slaves. Cuff Dix, a skilled hammerman, escaped in 1774 and again in 1775; in the latter year he was apprehended in Delaware but disappeared from the New Castle jail before he could be returned to Bird.[7] Another escapee was a man of accomplishments, judging from the description given in the advertisement in which a $200 reward was offered for the return of :

[1] Cheesman A. Herrick, *History of Commerce and Industry* (New York: The Macmillan Company, 1918), p. 492.

[2] Victor A. Clark, *History of Manufactures in the United States,* 1607–1860 (Volume I; New York: Peter Smith, 1949), p. 399.

[3] *Allen's Appeal Record, op. cit.,* p. 131.

[4] Hiram H. Shenk, *A History of the Lebanon Valley in Pennsylvania* (Harrisburg: The National Historical Association, 1930), p. 298.

[5] Montgomery, *History of Berks County, op. cit.,* p. 93.

[6] Paul N. Shaeffer, "Slavery in Berks County," *The Historical Review of Berks County,* VI, 4 (July 1941), p. 112.

[7] *Pennsylvania Gazette,* December 7, 1774, June 7, 1775, October 11, 1775, October 16, 1775. The name "Cuff" was used for slaves who were troublemakers.

. . . A Negroe man named Jack, about 30 years of age . . . he plays on the violin and other instruments of music, speaks the English and French languages . . . he is a cunning designing fellow, and it is likely he may forge a pass, and travel the country as a freeman.[8]

As shown by a bill of sale, at least one of Mark Bird's slaves was sold in his bankruptcy on July 9, 1787:

Know all men by these Presents that I Peter Filbert, Esquire Sheriff of Berks County. In consideration of the sum of thirty-three pounds in [one word unreadable] to me in hand paid by William Hays . . . Have sold . . . unto the said William Hays: A certain female negro slave named Matty. Aged nine years, or thereabouts; late the property of Mark Bird, Esq., seized and taken in execution by me at the suit of John Bishop. . . .[9]

Hays wrote in his will that Mattie was to be freed when she was twenty-two years old, but she was only sixteen when he died. Her remaining time was sold to James Biddle of Philadelphia for $60.[10]

Slavery declined rapidly in Berks County after 1780. The Census of 1800 showed only 19 slaves in the county, and of these only one was in Union Township where Hopewell Furnace was located.[11] At the same time East Nantmeal Township, nearest area of Chester County, had no slaves.[12] Caernarvon Township in Berks County listed 3 slaves and West Nantmeal in Chester County 2 in the Census of 1820.[13]

The wooded area of Southeastern Pennsylvania gained a reputation as a refuge for slaves escaping from the South. George Washington wrote to a friend on November 20, 1786, that it was almost impossible to recover a Negro who made his way to this area because there were so many people who

[8] *Ibid.*, November 24, 1779.
[9] *Louis Richards Collection,* Berks County Historical Society.
[10] *Ibid.*
[11] *United States Census for 1800.* Berks County, p. 694.
[12] *Ibid.*, Chester County.
[13] *Census of 1820.*

would "facilitate the escape."[14] Elizabeth Pownall Scarlett gave shelter to escaping slaves at her home "The Forest" near Scarlett's Mill, a short distance from Hopewell, from 1826 to 1839. After her death her son Joseph and son-in-law Thomas Lewis continued the work for several more years.[15]

Hopewell's neighbor, Joanna Furnace, was reported to have given shelter and work to escaping slaves. The forested hills and the remote huts of the colliers and wood cutters made ideal hiding places until the search ended and it was safe to move on north. While they were hiding, the Negroes could earn their food and some money.[16]

Were the Negroes who worked at Hopewell escaped slaves? Many of them were residents of the area over a long period of time, and several generations of some families worked at the Furnace. These may have been the descendants of slaves freed by Pennsylvania law. On the other hand there were circumstances which indicate that Negroes from the South worked here. Most of the 107 names collected from the Hopewell books appeared very briefly, often only one entry, to suggest the possibility of persons passing through. The census for the townships near the Furnace showed a small Negro population for every counting from 1800 to 1870, and those mentioned by names as fairly permanent residents seldom matched the names on the Furnace books. The totals of non-whites in Union Township for 1810 was 4, for 1820—7, for 1830—39, for 1840—8, for 1850—31, for 1860—62, for 1870—40.[17] The fluctuation and increase in the later years disclosed that Negroes were coming into the area at the time of abolition agitation.

In 1850 the census began to report the place of birth of all

[14] Wayne Homan, "The Underground Railroad," *The Historical Review of Berks County*, XXIII, 4 (Fall 1958), p. 112.

[15] John E. Eshelman, "Berks County's Station on The Underground Railroad," *The Historical Review of Berks County*, VI, 4 (July 1941) p. 107–109.

[16] Wayne Homan, "Pennsylvania Heritage, Our Refuge for Runaway Slaves," *Sunday Today, The Philadelphia Inquirer*, September 24, 1961, p. 26.

[17] Census Reports for the years given.

persons and listed all Furnace-area Negroes as born in
Pennsylvania except one in Delaware, a slave area, and two
"unknown."[18] The next census recorded no Union Township
colored persons as having been born out of Pennsylvania.[19] In
1870 it was reported that Samuel Curtis, Robert Miller and
James Miller had been born in Virginia and Isaac Cole and
Charles Ruth in Maryland.[20] Of these Isaac Cole had stated
in 1860 that Pennsylvania was his place of birth.

The Hopewell books and papers were unrevealing about the
source of its colored laborers. The only indication of anti-
slavery feeling by the management was the discovery among
the Furnace papers of a pamphlet with the names of Ironmaster Clement Brooke and Clerk John Church on the flyleaf.
The contents and viewpoint were revealed in this brief
quotation :

> Let then every Christian minister, and every religious associ-
> ation, and each individual member of a religious society
> endeavor to eradicate the stain of slavery from our land, by
> the effectual operation of the lenient principles of Christianity
> . . . let the fiat of universal emancipation be issued from
> every Conference, Synod, and General Assembly throughout
> the Country. . . ."[21]

But Abolition sentiment was not universal in Berks County.
James Morris noted that a Presbyterian minister named
McKim had delivered Abolition addresses at the Harmony
Meeting House on March 11 and 13, 1837. Morris was not
converted to the cause of abolition. He wrote :

> A mission truly for the Rev'd gentleman — though not of
> peace and charity, I take it — or at least the Abolition course
> pursued by J. Q. Adams in the H. R. at Washington did not

---

[18] *Census of 1850*, Berks County.
[19] *Census of 1860*, Berks County.
[20] *Census of 1870*, Berks County.
[21] The pamphlet was by Evan Lewis under the title *An Address to
Christians* [some destroyed] *inations* [some destroyed] *of Admitting Slave-
holders to Communion and Church Membership* (Philadelphia : S. C.
Atkinson, 1831), p. 19.

appear to produce peace but its contrary and whatever charity abolition may bear for the blacks—which even admits of strong doubts—it is surely not charity to the Southerners to force them into measures repugnant to them and their idea— of worse than evil tendency—or measures fraught with evil not only to the South, but to the whole Union.

The next day the lecturer came to Morgantown and brought this comment from the diarist: "The house was full. This is the first lecture delivered in this place on this subject—may it be the last."[22] In 1844 he reported, ". . . there is not a single abolition vote in the District" for James G. Birney for president.[23]

Mathew Brooke used several Negro boys as indentured servants. In 1812 he obtained from Reubin Moore of Philadelphia the remaining seven years of the indenture of John Petres, a Negro boy. Seven years earlier Moore had paid $20 to Marian Dick, "negress and next friend of John Peter."[24] In 1816 Brooke inserted this advertisement in four issues of a Reading newspaper:

> For Sale, The unexpired time of a Negroe Man, he has upwards of seven years to serve—he has been brought up to farming business, is a good carter and is a serviceable hand at all sort of labor. . . .[25]

The early Hopewell records contained a number of workers who used no family names, as in the *Day Book* for 1784–1792 appeared Negro Robin, Negro Cruse, Negro Moriah, Black Majer, Peter Negroe and Negro Samuel. These people were apparently free laborers, however, as they had their own accounts, were paid their own wages and made purchases at the Furnace store. Other Negroes received full names in the

[22] *Morris Diary, op. cit.,* II, pp. 9–10.
[23] *Ibid.,* p. 166.
[24] *Brooke Family Papers,* Indenture, June 9, 1812.
[25] *Berks and Schuylkill Journal,* December 21, 1816, and the three following issues.

same book, as witness James Hooper, Sam Kellar, Anthony Lewis, John Sebass, Isaac Williams and Charles Cox;[26] but most of these were long time employees. James Hooper appeared in the Furnace records as late as 1822.[27]

It is apparent that not all the Negroes were completely free agents, for in 1806 John Hulbey received the wages earned by Negro Levi.[28] Several workers in this period were at the Furnace for a brief time and then disappeared. "Black Frank" worked for 15 days in the autumn of 1802 and was not heard from again.[29] "Black Dine" came on June 22, 1803, and on July 14 "went away" after collecting her wages "as made 3 weeks and 2 day @ 6/ per week."[30] In 1809 "Black Luce" served as maid for 10 weeks.[31]

The company valued its colored workers and gave encouragement to them to come to work. In 1810 James Carmich was lent the following articles to set up housekeeping: "1 bed 2 blankets 1 rug 1 iron pot 2 tins 2 spoons 1 pewter plate 1 erthen dish 2 knives Ironbale Bucket 1 bred Basket."[32] Judging from the purchase of a "a Silver Broach" by Peter Major,[33] life for some colored workers was above the subsistence level. Another Negro paid cash for a large ten-plate stove. The price was identical to that paid by a white customer on the same day and only a few shillings higher than dealers were charged for wholesale quantities of stoves.[34] Homes in the Furnace area were rented to colored families—evidence that segregation in housing was not practiced.[35] Two of these families scandalized the village, however, in the 1870's when Sam England and

[26] SM 41, *passim.*
[27] SM 5, p. 19.
[28] SM 4, p. 129.
[29] SM 1, October 1, November 2, 1802, n. p.
[30] SM 1, pp. 31, 33; SM 2, p. 207.
[31] SM 5, p. 123.
[32] *Birdsborough Store Journal,* 1810, *op. cit.,* p. 8.
[33] SM 41, p. 8.
[34] SM 4, p. 247.
[35] HV 8320203C and Interview with Reginald Smith, March 16, 1941.

George Toogood traded wives without the aid of the law or the clergy.[36]

In the first half of the nineteenth century the colored people of the area participated in the religious activities of several of the Episcopal churches. Between 1808 and 1822 the records of the St. Mary's Episcopal Church at Warwick included the baptisms of the following Negroes: Hester, "a black Woman;" Quash, Kuba, Benjamin and John, "black people;" Draper,[37] "a black man;" Elizabeth Morgan, "a colored woman;" Dorethea, "a black woman;" "Hannah, Wife of Quash (colored)" and "Andrew, (colored) born December 23, 1820, son of Phillis." Quash and Catherine were recorded as communicants in 1814. The marriage register for 1812 listed Stephen Brown to Hester Charms and Quash to Catherine and for 1816 Joseph Cagers to Susan Robeson.[38] Most of these people had no family names given; although if the "Hesters" were the same person, she acquired a second name between her baptism and her marriage. The St. Gabriel's Episcopal Church at Douglassville listed three Ford and two Dunlap children baptized on October 8, 1830, and four colored men buried in their churchyard from 1818 to 1850.[39]

The demise of Negro James Green at Hopewell in 1834 was attended by the same kind of care as for a white person. He had received the medical services of Doctor Robert May, and his account was debited $9.65½ for a coffin and the digging of his grave.[40] These were nearly normal costs for any adult.

An increase in the colored population in the townships near the Furnace about the middle of the century probably accounted for the building of a Negro church about three miles from the Furnace. Near the peak of the roof a stone was set upon which was carved this inscription :

[36] Interview with Hunter Care, January 26, 1941.
[37] There was a Draper Nixon at Hopewell.
[38] *St. Mary's Episcopal Church Records, op. cit.,* pp. 166, 170, 186, 188, 203.
[39] *St. Gabriel's Episcopal Church Records, op. cit.,* pp. 191, 305, 309, 317.
[40] SM 21, p. 97.

THE
A M E
MOUNT FRISBY
CHURCH
FOUNDED IN
AD 1856[41]

Wayne Homan said this church was founded by escaped
slaves and was also known as the Six Penny Colored Church
and the Mt. Zion Church.[42] An area map drawn in 1860
showed this church and nine homes surrounding it which were
identified as the residences of P. Jones, J. Watson, J. Nixon,
C. Butler, I. Dehart, D. R. Wamsher, S. Wamsher, I. Coal,
Bodley and G. Woolf.[43] The census of 1860 identified Peter
Jones, John Watson, Jehu Nixon, Charles Butler, Catherine
Bodly and Isaac Coal as heads of Negro households in Union
Township. A John Dehart was registered as living with
Charles Butler; so the Deharts may have been colored.[44] The
other three families were presumably white, but a Negro
colony centered around the new church.

The Mount Frisby Church was still being used for religious
services as late as 1886.[45] A picture taken in 1936 shows an
entrance on the north side covered with a shed roof. There
were no windows in this end, but a tablet of some kind was
set into the wall.[46] This wall has since been removed to make
a garage of the other three sides. The present remains of the
old church are of a building 24 feet by 30 feet. There are two
windows on the east, two more and evidence of an old door
on the south, and one window and evidence of another on
the west. The remaining walls are of brown field stone. A hole,
apparently for a stove pipe, had gone through the wall; but

[41] Reading obtained from a pencil rubbing taken in December 1962
by Earl Heydinger and the author.
[42] Homan, "The Underground Railroad," *op. cit.,* p. 114.
[43] D. J. Lake and N. S. Beers, "Map of Vicinity of Philadelphia and
Reading," Based on Actual Surveys, Philadelphia, 1860.
[44] *Census of 1860,* Berks County, pp. 887 ff.
[45] Montgomery, *History of Berks County, op. cit.,* p. 1187.
[46] Photo Collection at Hopewell Village.

no chimney remains. South of the building is a cemetery where among the graves are those of James Jackson and Isaac Cole, veterans of the Union Army.[47]

In 1888 the Bethesda Baptist Church, near the Furnace, accepted for baptism and membership five "colored Brethren" and two months later dismissed them to form a new Baptist congregation at Sancanock in Chester County.[48]

Work was not very steady for some of the Negro workers. The following time report showed an employment record which would have applied also to other short-term workers. James Thomas began work as a laborer on Friday, August 22, 1823, and was credited with one-half day. He appeared on the time sheets for every working day through September 23, but on the next day he was on the job only one-half day and none on any of the next four work days. On September 30 he worked three-fourths of a day and continued in full employment until the first Saturday in November. The next week he worked six full days, but on Monday, November 10, he was absent. The clerk noted, "James Thomas was drunk." He managed a half-day on Tuesday and then eleven full days in succession. He missed five days at the end of November, and worked five and one-half in the first week of December. On Saturday, December 6, he got a hat and $7.93 in cash and then disappeared from the record. He had earned a total of $23.79 in a little more than three months.[49]

Examples such as James Thomas' irregular employment and the large number of Negroes who came to Hopewell and left after working for only a few weeks could have meant that the work pattern of "last hired and first fired" applied to colored employees at the Furnace. But in contrast to these transient laborers there were other Negroes who held highly skilled jobs, who were trusted with large sums of money, who worked for long periods of time, who secured the status

[47] Information from observation on a visit in December 1962.
[48] *Bethesda Church Minute Book,* September 30, 1888, and November 25, 1888, n. p. Hopewell Village Library.
[49] SM 46, pp. 36, 37, 38, 39, 40; SM 11, p. 213.

symbols of modest affluence, and who were the recipients of neighborly charity from their white colleagues. The following examples were selected to illustrate these points.

Joab Lee was a skilled worker and a respected member of the Furnace family from 1806 to 1809. His wages as filler were 135s. per month—among the highest paid to any of the employees—and he boarded with the white Furnace men at the Big House. He hired white men to work for him when he took time off. His purchases of bulk feed indicate that he owned some kind of livestock. When he left the village in 1809, he borrowed $50 from Buckley and Brooke[50] and found immediate employment at Joanna Furnace.[51]

The Negro longest in the employment of the Furnace was William Jacobs with a record of sixty years in Hopewell Village. In his later years he was unable to work and received care from another elderly man who had been assigned the task by the Furnace management. Jacobs claimed that in his boyhood he had attended school in "Lloyd's Baptist Church" (Bethesda).[52]

Several Negro teamsters for the furnace were at times entrusted with large sums of money. In 1818 Robert Coleman acknowledged receipt of $497.75 "per Negro Peter" (probably Peter Jones) and $500 delivered by "Negro Sampson" (Coggins).[53] Edward Ford owned his own team and was paid by the Furnace for hauling goods to and from Philadelphia.[54]

Another Negro who worked for the Furnace for a long period of time was Wilkinson Hill, a laborer on monthly salary from 1827 to at least 1846.[55] He rented a house in the Village from John Care at $12 per year. The rental agreement provided for Care to furnish rails to fence the lot and "to put

---

[50] SM 4, pp. 74, 194; 205; SM 5, p. 60; SM 44, November 20, 1806, n. p.
[51] *Joanna Furnace Journal, op. cit., passim.*
[52] Long, *Historical Sketch, op. cit.,* pp. 10–11.
[53] HV 8180501 and HV 8181208.
[54] SM 8, p. 56. This was in 1816.
[55] SMR 19, p. 2; SM 28, pp. 108, 122, 136.

on a new upper floor and a new six Light window sash and glass." Hill agreed to give a week of labor to the building of a chimney for which Care would provide the materials.[56] In 1843 Hill paid $20 in cash for a cow.[57] Possibly he had some education, for in 1844 he paid postage on letters "sent to his Brother." At least two of his children were educated in the subscription school.[58]

Wilkinson Hill apparently was related to several other Hopewell employees who bore that family name. Benjamin Hill was apprenticed to the Furnace, or to Clement Brooke, in the late 1820's and early 1830's. Educated in the Village school at Furnace expense from 1830 to 1834,[59] he worked for two years as hostler for $6 per month until a general wage increase in 1836 raised his pay to $7. When he died in 1841, his balance on the Furnace books, the sum of twenty dollars, was paid to Wilkinson Hill.[60] In 1850 Charles Clingan employed Eliza Hill, a thirty-three-year-old Negress, as a maid in the Big House at $1.25 per week.[61]

Moses Morton came to the Furnace in 1829, worked as a laborer at $8 per month and later put up the night stock at $12,[62] on which he supported a wife, two boys and two girls. The children were all under ten years of age in 1830.[63] The next year he bought a cow for $14 and pastured her on Samuel Lloyd's land at 18¢ per week.[64] He bought goods at the store and even hired the Village seamstress to do some sewing for the family.[65] There was every appearance of normal life for the Morton family until the middle of April, 1832, when the

[56] HV 8320203C.

[57] SM 28, p. 104.

[58] *Ibid.*, pp. 61, 128, 134.

[59] *Cash Book* for 1828–1830, January 25, 1830, n. p.; SM 15, p. 39; SM 21, pp. 32, 101.

[60] SM 21, *passim.*

[61] *Census of 1850,* Berks County, pp. 569 ff. and SM 32, p. 96.

[62] SM 14, p. 95. His wage was the same as that paid to white workers who did the same work.

[63] *Census of 1830,* Berks County, pp. 515–521.

[64] SM 15, p. 64; SM 21, p. 31.

[65] SM 14, pp. 68, 74, 76.

worst tragedy in Hopewell history befell them. This account appeared in a Norristown newspaper:

> A most distressing accident happened near Hopewell Furnace, Berks County, the week before last, which adds another to the many warnings to mothers already published. A home occupied by a colored man in the service of Mr. Brooks of Hopewell, was destroyed by fire, together with three of his children. It appears that the mother, having occasion to visit some neighbor, locked up the children in the house, and when she returned the house was a pile of ruins, and her children victims of the devouring elements. The cries of the children were heard soon after the mother had left home, but nothing unusual was to be seen about the house, the flames having not yet burnt out, their cries were unheeded.[66]

The newspaper account did not mention Moses Morton by name, but events at the furnace in the next few weeks identified him with the tragedy. The community rallied to his support with "a subscription paper" which raised $18.75. Clement Brooke gave $2 and 12 others gave $1 each—most of the molders and the clerk were in this group. Polly Kid, a maid, gave half of her week's salary of $1; and another maid gave 25¢. In all, 26 persons made contributions.[67] On May 19 Morton sold his cow to David Smith for $12, paid his bill at the Furnace store and disappeared from the Furnace accounts.[68]

Negro workers were an important part of the labor force at Hopewell Furnace; and while they never reached any managerial positions, they were used in skilled jobs and sometimes attained a measure of prosperity. The records, understandably, contain no reference to the hiring of escaping slaves; but the census records on place of birth and the large number of nameless Negroes who appeared briefly on the Furnace books suggest that a traveler from the South might have found aid at the Furnace. Negro families lived in amity among their

[66] *Norristown* (Pennsylvania) *Free Press,* April 25, 1832.
[67] SM 21, p. 33.
[68] SM 21, pp. 31, 32; SM 19, p. 245.

white neighbors, attended the churches of the area, went to school with the white children and received the same wages as white workers engaged in the same jobs. But most of the colored workers were kept in the least skilled and lowest paid jobs, and many of their families apprenticed their children for years of service. The community response to the Morton fire showed that misfortune elicited compassion regardless of the color of the victims.

16   The Women

THERE WAS A SAYING THAT HOPEWELL "WAS HEAVEN FOR horses but hell for women" because horses were given the best of care, and the women had to look out for themselves.[1] The historians of the iron plantations have had little to say about the place of women and have dismissed the subject with such statements as, "Women had little or no part in the production of iron,"[2] or, "Women in Berks County did not work in mine, forge or furnaces." They were credited with doing house and farm work and little else.[3]

The women of Hopewell Village concentrated largely upon the traditional women's jobs of the care of the home and the rearing of children, and many of them worked on the farm. But they also entered into the economic life of the community in an amazing number of ways, not all of which were in keeping with the tradition of retiring home-bodies of the nineteenth century.

Women of the Village found a number of ways to add to the family income without going from their homes to work. Men without homes needed food and were willing to pay for the

[1] Reginald and Emlen Smith Interview, August 4, 1940.
[2] Bining, *Pennsylvania Iron Manufacture in the 18th Century, op. cit.*, p. 115.
[3] Handwork, *op. cit.*, p. 127.

318

privilege of eating where a housewife was preparing meals for her own family. Eight cents per meal did not add up to riches, but it helped to put meat on the table for the family.[4] Homes with spinning wheels afforded the wife a chance at income through the sale of thread. She sometimes used her needle at "footing a stocking."[5] Foods were prepared to sell, such as butter, pickles and baked goods.[6] Home-dipped candles and home-boiled soap found a market along with eggs and chickens from the family coop.[7]

Men's clothing needed a woman's care, providing a source of income for a large number of Village women who were paid for washing and mending. Rebecca Richard furnished this service for a number of the single men in 1816 and received her pay in the form of storegoods charged to the accounts of the men for whom she had worked. Since she was also good with the needle, she made clothing for William Thomas and was paid 33¢ by Clement Brooke "for Making Eliza a frock."[8] William Jacobs, Negro, had his washing done by Rebecca Williams, who had been a maid at the mansion before she married Samuel Williams.[9] The Furnace paid many women and girls for laundering at the Big House. A Yankee inventor came into the area in 1843 demonstrating a washing machine which he guaranteed to get the clothes clean without injuring the garments,[10] but no record was found to indicate that any Hopewell housewives invested in this labor-saving device.

The majority of women supporting themselves or adding to family income did not do their work at home. Instead, they found a variety of jobs they could perform throughout the community, even though most still sought the traditional women's jobs. The only occupation on a professional level was

[4] See SM 32, p. 104.
[5] SM 17, p. 10.
[6] SM 7, June 4 and November 4, 1817; SM 28, pp. 68, 77.
[7] SM 7, November 7, 1817; SM 31, pp. 51, 89, 127.
[8] SM 7, November 8, 1816.
[9] SM 17, p. 6; SM 31, pp. 39, 83.
[10] *Morris Diary, op. cit.,* II, p. 85.

teaching. There were several women teachers in the Hopewell public schools, but just one among the private tutors[11] More women worked as maids, cooks or seamstresses than at any other occupation except housewife.

The operation of the mansion for the ironmaster's family, the clerk, guests and downstairs boarders required a staff of maids, cooks and housekeepers. In the early part of the nineteenth century the girls who worked at the Big House were evidently drawn from the locality as their names were of familiar Village families — Painter, Griffith, Wynn, Williams, Sheeler, North, Rhoads and Ford. Mary Youst, Rebecca Elliot and Eliza Cook married Furnace men[12] Older women, both married and widowed, worked at these jobs, too.[13] Some like Polly Kid worked for a long period of time as maids.[14] But by the middle of the century a fast turnover of employees was indicated by the numerous journal entries for girls hired and quitting, and the names were seldom those of Furnace families. Mrs. Clingan brought some of her maids from Philadelphia; and the names Murray, Brady and Lafsley suggest that some were Irish immigrants.[15]

Wages were never very high for housework, ranging from 50¢ to $1.50 for a seven-day week. But most of the maids' needs were supplied, and wages were sometimes not touched for several years. Some of the maids bought goods at the store and found themselves in debt. For example Mary Youst owed money to the Furnace and to John Sheeler in 1818. She evened her store account with her maid's wages and possibly her debt to Sheeler by marrying him.[16] Purchases at the store were most often shoes, clothing accessories, cloth and food. In 1819 Clement Brooke executed an order in Phila-

[11] The censuses of 1850, 1860 and 1870 contained many listings of women as "teacher in the Common School."
[12] *St. Mary's Church Records.*
[13] SM 1, p. 81.
[14] SM 28, p. 14.
[15] SM 31, p. 134; SM 32, pp. 54, 66.
[16] SM 6, p. 36 and *St. Mary's Church Record,* p. 190.

delphia to purchase "a silk shall" for $5 and have a bonnet repaired @ $1.25 for Caty Wynn.[17] Wages sometimes increased as the services of the worker improved, as verified by the record of Susan Munshower whose compensation rose from 50¢ per week in 1847 to three times that in 1851.[18] House-cleaning was more highly paid than normal housework. Susan Griffith received $1 for three days of cleaning in 1830 when the normal wage for maids was that amount per week[19]

The scarcity of good maids brought an exasperated comment from the Morgantown diarist:

> Was out nearly all day in search of that tease and torment of married life or housekeeping—that necessary evil—a maid of all work and without success.

> Of all the ills of married life this one thing of maidhunting and maidkeeping is the worst.

> Husbands may expect to hear a continual tale from their wives of faults and shortcomings . . . until his soul is fairly sickened at the sins of the maid-kind.[20]

When women looked for sources of income, another normal feminine pursuit was sewing, for which there was a considerable demand at Hopewell Furnace. Married women did most of the sewing for their families, but there were men without wives and special sewing jobs which demanded the services of an expert seamstress. Many instances appear in the Furnace records of women who did sewing for the Furnace or for employees on a casual basis, and other examples of those who made it a regular business. Margaret Benson was paid a weekly wage for sewing and "making carpet and quilting for the furnace" over a period of six years. However, she did not have steady work and earned additional income by selling butter and dried peaches.[21] In 1829 Margaret Cook was

[17] SM 9, p. 167.
[18] SM 32, pp. 33, 100, 106.
[19] SM 15, p. 14.
[20] *Morris Diary, op. cit.,* p. 233.
[21] SM 12, p. 137; SM 17, pp. 19, 22, 24.

sewing for a group of Furnace men. Four of them paid for her boarding over a period of time during which she ate $11.50 worth of food. The time was not given, but this charge for boarding would have covered meals for several months. She continued to earn money with her needles for the next four years.[22] Widow Elizabeth Merwine rented a house from Clement Brooke and sewed for the Furnace and individuals in the 1820's and 1830's. She was apparently skilled in all kinds of sewing and tailoring.[23] Eliza Hudson had a specialty of making stockings to sell in wholesale lots to the Furnace store.[24] The store sold large quantities of cloth of many varieties, buttons, trimmings, needles, pins, thimbles, scissors, dye and patterns to the amateur and professional seamstresses of the community.

These normal female occupations did not fill all the needs of women to add to the family incomes in Hopewell Village. Contrary to the common view of their limited opportunities for employment in the iron plantations, there were women who found jobs in many of the areas of vocational activity of farm, furnace and forest.

Recruiting women and children was the normal method of securing most of the seasonal workers needed on the farms. Harvest time required many extra hands, but even some of the regular needs were filled by the women and children. A search of the farm time books for 1811–1814 revealed these different tasks being done by them: hoeing corn, binding grain, hauling grain, pulling flax, shearing sheep, harvesting oats, mowing, haymaking, picking apples, sorting apples, dressing corn, spreading flax, picking potatoes, planting corn, loading dung, reaping, cradling, killing caterpillars, cutting buckwheat, cutting apples, pulling corn and pulling turnips. Women were used on all of these except mowing and loading dung where boys were employed. In later years women were

[22] *Cash Book* for 1828–1830, July 17, 1829, and February 2, 1830; SM 12, p. 4; SM 17, pp. 13, 34, 39.
[23] SM 59, pp. 2, 15; SM 14, pp. 44, 46.
[24] SM 28, p. 78.

also employed at whitewashing fences and buildings, milking, butchering, rendering lard, raking oats, setting up cornfodder and picking stones. The pay for this work was most commonly 25¢ per day with a top of 30¢ in 1816.[25]

Less common than farm work for women were jobs about the furnace, at the mines or in the wood lots; but women worked in all of these places. Two widows, Margaret Painter and Elizabeth Mervine, were paid for "cleaning castings" in 1831 and 1832. This was heavy work tipping the stove plates and other cast items to remove the molders' sand clinging to the surface. The compensation was 75¢ per ton paid by the molder.[26] In this same period of Furnace history Mary Beavens, Elizabeth Mauger and Eliza Painter were paid for ore mined; and Henry Painter collected for more than 13 loads of "mine" sent to the Furnace by his daughter.[27] Over a period of more than thirty years six women were credited with cutting wood for the furnace, and in 1829 Eve Jones was paid for hauling wood "bought of her in 1827."[28] Elizabeth Mock earned over $90 in two years cutting wood and spent all of that plus an additional $28.19 at the Furnace store.[29] Elizabeth Hughs was paid for cutting 41 cords in 1836 which would represent about twenty days of work for a good male chopper.[30]

It is possible that all of this heavy work was done by teenage sons whose wages were collected by widowed mothers. But the clerks were usually quite careful to record the information that the work was done by someone other than the person who received the wages. Since no such record was found in the instances given, it is presumed that the work was done by the women.

Among Hopewell Village women there were some who

[25] SM 7, September 3, 1816, n. p.
[26] SM 15, pp. 23, 24, 52; SM 21, pp. 11, 12, 32.
[27] SM 14, p. 27; *Cash Book* for 1828–1830, July 11, 1829, and October 17, 1829, n. p.; SM 21, p. 164.
[28] SM 14, p. 145.
[29] SM 6, p. 84.
[30] SM 21, p. 182.

conducted their own businesses. Operating a farm and handling the details of the sale of crops was fairly common for Village women. Indian corn, feathers, cows, pork, pigs, potatoes, veal and grain were among the wares sold to the Furnace by women farmers. In a number of instances the purveyors were listed as widows, indicating that they were carrying on the work after their husbands had died.[31] Stoves with a price of more than $20 each were sold to several women with payments made in cash or services.[32] Barbara Thomas, Elizabeth Lloyd and Phoebe Shaner owned woodland and sold "wood leave" or cord wood to the Furnace.[33]

Even the iron business itself was not beyond the competence of nineteenth century women. "Widow" Lynch, Rebecca Lukens and Rachel L. Smith were regular buyers of Hopewell furnace castings. The size of their orders implied a considerable retail business. Mrs. Smith sold Hopewell products on commission from her Philadelphia store.[34] Sarah Loeser bought pig iron in 1825 to process at Dale Forge which she was operating.[35] Sarah Gilmore was listed as a merchant in Caernarvon Township of Berks County, and the census of 1850 placed a valuation of $28,000 on her real estate. Eliza Mast at the age of 34 owned real estate worth $20,000 according to the same source. Two other women of some means were Margaret Amon and Rebecca Wynn, each of whom held Furnace notes amounting to more than $800.[36]

When a woman had a husband, he could collect her wages. Numerous notations in the records show that husbands received pay for sewing, washing, farm work, spinning and butter-making. Men also were credited with work done by their mothers, and Hugh Welsh was compensated for spinning

---

[31] For example see SM 5, p. 38.
[32] SM 6, p. 168; SM 10, p. 33.
[33] SM 14, pp. 28, 55; SM 31, p. 60; SM 32, p. 120.
[34] SM 19, pp. 107, 126; SM 6, p. 166; SM 15, p. 35; SM 21, pp. 14, 17, 26, 35, 40.
[35] HV 8250501A.
[36] SM 9, p. 135; SM 12, p. 25; SM 10, pp. 17, 25, 28.

done by his mother-in-law.[37] But on the other hand wives
bought at the Village store or even ordered goods from more
distant merchants and charged the amounts to their husbands' accounts. It was also possible for a wife to secure cash
against the credit balance of a husband as many, many entries
in the cash books attested. Acording to one such entry Mrs.
Charles Smith was paid $10 in Philadelphia. Smith at that
time in 1818 was working at Hopewell as a stove finisher, and
apparently the Furnace was advancing his wife money for
living expenses in the city.[38] Women were also paid considerable sums for work done by their children.[39]

Not all women paid their bills or had a man who could
be held accountable for what they spent. In 1818 Hannah
Whitaker owed a debt to Buckley and Brooke of $14.25. She
managed to pay only $1 of it in the next thirteen years, and
the remainder was written off as a bad debt.[40]

One of the most frequent ways in which women were
recorded in the Furnace books was as the recipients of payments from men. Usually no reason was given for the payment, but often it can be surmised that it was for sewing
or washing. More difficult to account for was such a blanket
endorsement as this one :

> Sir please to let Mary Simins have what goods She wants
> at this time and charg it to my Acc Please to Send abill and
> ablig yours and
> April 15, 1823   John McGowan[41]

Possibly the lady was a housekeeper for McGowan and was
trusted to buy only what was needed. But more intriguing
was an item in the *Lewis Evans Journal* which gave a long
list of articles as an "acct of Goods gave delivered [Note the
word "gave" was crossed out] Hetty Filman."Among the com-

---

[37] SM 4, p. 39.
[38] SM 10, p. 19.
[39] SM 41, p. 110; SM 6, p. 254; SM 11, p. 92; SM 14, p. 50.
[40] SM 6, p. 9; SM 11, p. 5; SM 54, p. 3.
[41] Hopewell Papers at Berks County Historical Society.

modities were: "Bed and bedding, rose Blanketts, bed quilt $7.50, looking glass, Coverlid $5.00, ½ doz. chairs, queens ware" and 2 cows at $13 each. At the end was this note, "The above amt. of goods is carried to page 151 in the day book under conditions there stated." Unfortunately the day book is not available to check the conditions. No record of payment was noted in the journal.[42] Apparently someone was setting up housekeeping at well above the subsistence level, but who was paying the bill and why?

In many respects other than economic the women of Hopewell Village showed interests like those of any other community or in any other time. They were interested in clothes, shopping, men and marriage. They gossiped and visited. Most were reasonably moral, and some were not.

Ready-made dresses and coats were not kept in stock at the store. There was no record of purchases of lingerie. The store carried the raw materials, and most women must have made their own. Some dresses were made by the seamstresses at rates ranging from 50¢ to 62¢ for labor.[43] The materials would have been extra. Although the store sold a wide variety of kinds of cloth, the girls did not always find what they wanted and placed orders in Morgantown, Reading or Philadelphia.[44] The store journals recorded kinds of cloth and sometimes colors but seldom any information about designs. But for 1844 in Morgantown James Morris reported, "The fashionable apparel for both men and women is now very gay—even gaudy. Stripes and plaids of worsted material, . . . of the most brilliant colours are much worn by the ladies."[45]

The articles of clothing most frequently bought were shoes and hats. Shoes were sold at the store and also custom-made by the shoemakers. Most women's shoes or slippers sold for about $1.25 to $1.50 per pair, but some were bought as low as one dollar and as high as $2.12½. The latter price was paid

[42] *Lewis Evans Journal, op. cit.,* May 10, 1822–February 11, 1825, p. 32.
[43] SM 10, p. 18; SM 31, p. 52; SM 13, p. 107.
[44] For example see SM 9, p. 45; SM 10, p. 66.
[45] *Morris Diary, op. cit.,* II, p. 168.

in 1820 by Rebecca Elliot for a pair she bought in Reading while she was working as a maid at $1 per week.[46] "Bonnetts" were rather expensive with prices ranging from $1 to a sum of $10 which George Kephart paid Mrs. Clingan "for a Bonnett and to go to Reading."[47] Normally travel expenses to Reading were not more than $1. In general the single girls paid more for their bonnets than did the married women. Rebecca Elliot put more than a month's salary into her $4.50 hat in 1819.[48] Perhaps she wore it and her Reading shoes the next winter when she married Samuel Williams. Hats, judging from the frequency with which they were repaired, must have been meant to last more than one season.

Shawls were in fashion for much of the nineteenth century and were available in a wide range of materials at many prices. Polly Kid paid $2.25 for a silk hood in 1832.[49] Gloves, "mits," stockings and umbrellas were purchased; but there were few references to ornamentation except side combs. However, Blacksmith David Jenkins spent 10¢ for "beeds" in 1827.[50] Whatever cosmetics and grooming materials that were used must have been produced at home as none were seen among purchases except "A Bottle Hare Tonick" for which Ann Church paid 50¢[51]

Possibly because they were not tied to a very rigid time schedule, the women did much of the marketing at the Village store. Those who came from some distance often had lists for a number of men or families and charged the items to the persons for whom they were shopping. The miners regularly sent one of the women to make their purchases.[52] Mrs. Clingan made frequent trips to Reading or Philadelphia; and on many occasions she took money entrusted to her to buy articles of

[46] SM 10, p. 54; SM 31, p. 10; SM 4, p. 134; SM 9, p. 129.
[47] SM 31, p. 104.
[48] SM 10, p. 41.
[49] SM 17, p. 25.
[50] SM 13, p. 98.
[51] SM 28, p. 20.
[52] SM 9, pp. 26, 29, 34, 42, 52, 53.

clothing for women of the community, especially the maids.[53]

Women were honored by being selected to preside at the ceremony of putting fire in the furnace for the beginning of a new blast. Most frequently, however, this privilege was reserved for the wife of the ironmaster and, therefore, did not become the basis for a popularity contest among the Village belles.[54]

Young women's interests as revealed in their letters to each other were of clothes, travel, parties, visits, family health and gossip about their friends. Matchmaking was a favorite topic of speculation.[55] Sarah Brooke asked her brother:

> Have you heard any talk of our Cousin Clements [possibly C. B. Buckley] going to be married? report says he is engaged to Miss Sarah Penrose . . . one of those young ladies who spent a day at Hibernia last Summer. . . . She is very pretty and quite young, not more than half his age, the old capitain is doing very well for himself, I hope he will not get disappointed this time, if he does I think he will take it hard; . . . he is now in the city and appears to be very attentive to her.[56]

But girls were not the only ones who were interested in gossip or in trying to get each other married, since a male letter reported that John Birkenbine ". . . is . . . flying around with the girls at a great rate. . . ." and that "Jane Barde has got a Beau already he had her out Sleighing yesterday."[57] The most avowed matchmaker was also a man who wrote to a bachelor friend:

> . . . I have often enquired after thee and from all Information I could get concured in pronouncing they determination to gog on through time with the title of batchelor. I know not what charms that name can produce to thee but I can

[53] SM 31, *passim*.

[54] SM 6, pp. 5, 6, 7.

[55] See *Sharpe-Marshall Letters* and *Brooke Family Papers*.

[56] *Brooke Family Papers*, Sarah Brooke to Edward Brooke, May 16, 1833.

[57] *Ibid.*, John Springer to Edward Brooke, January 11, 1833.

say since I have tryed both that I greatly prefer the Married state and I believe if thee would condescend to honour us with a visit thee would be convinced that my Ideas are no delusion for besides an agreable wife I have a lovely Daughter turned of 2 years old . . . I saw Dan*l* Buckley at Phila. about two years ago and he promised me to Inform thee of a Charming young Lady living in our Neighbourhood of about 3000 pound portion and such natural perfections that I believed that all that was wanting was thy seeing her to be in love with her—but I kept her as long as I could for thee she was married about two weeks since but . . . we have several others of euquel Charms if not quite as much money.[58]

What did a young Hopewell lass want out of life? One of them gave her ambitions under the title "What are your most anxious wishes:"

1. To be independent	13. To be virtuous
2. To be admired	14. To meet the esteem of all
3. To receive and offer	15. To get a convert
4. To be joined in matrimony	16. To be always visiting
	17. To keep a carriage
6. To set the fashions	18. To have patience
7. To be happy	19. To do as you should
8. To go to Europe	20. To be as you should
9. To see the one you love	21. To be alone
10. Reign in all things	22. To inherit a title
11. To be an ornament in society	23. To be in love
12. To be envied	24. To be wealthy[59]

It was perhaps not significant that virtue came far behind admiration, or that it made the list ahead of the possession of a carriage or a title. A proposal and marriage came early.

Courting on horseback, with the girls riding sidesaddles, was a common practice among the young people at Hopewell.[60] Winning the ironmaster's daughter required something more formal, including a very flowery request of her parents.

---

[58] *Ibid.,* Israel Lancaster to Mathew Brooke, Junior, March 18, 1806.
[59] *Hopewell Papers,* undated and unsigned. Found among school sums and penmanship practices.
[60] Albert Lloyd Interview, September 1962.

Charles M. Clingan wrote this letter to Mr. and Mrs. Clement Brooke :

> Dear Sir and Madam;
>   The object of this communication, in propriety should have been made long ago.
>   But as I hoped, the nature and intentions of my visiting your family were neither unknown nor misunderstood; the immediate necessity of the avowal and request I am about to make did not appear to me necessary.
>   In soliciting to become a member of your Family, I have nothing to urge why you should grant the favour; but the kindness and attention you have both invariably treated me with, and the firm attachment I have for your daughter.
>   To support my claims I can neither urge the influence of family conexions, nor the aid of wealth; in lieu of which all I offer is the steady exertion to acquire and support a character which gives me a pasport into good society, and a Profession which I purport to follow, with Industry and attention . . .
>   I now with the permission of your daughter, and under the influence, of the serious importance of the step, request that you will give me the pleasure, of admitting me into your family, by permitting her to unite her destiny with mine.
> . . . .[61]

June was not the month of brides at Hopewell Village. Of 118 marriages involving Hopewell family names taken from the St. Mary's Episcopal Church records from 1808 to 1846, only four took place in June. January was most popular with nineteen, closely followed by December with eighteen. Christmas season, even Christmas Day, was the time for many weddings. July was least popular with two weddings, and August was next with three.[62] Although most Hopewell girls married men from the immediate neighborhood, there were examples of weddings involving men from Philadelphia and one from as far away as Erie, Pennsylvania.[63]

Weddings were high social occasions in the Furnace com-

[61] HV 8420930.
[62] *St. Mary's Episcopal Church Records, passim.*
[63] *Ibid.*

munity. In 1803 Matthew Dunkings and Christian Heverly "went to the weding the Evening before and were Sick the next Day."[64] Early in the century it was customary for wedding parties among the Amish to last for several days for everyone invited. By the 1840's this practice was largely abandoned; but an Amish wedding was still "quite a party" with "the young Homish folks . . . invited by the dozens," and "cakes and wine were provided in abundance."[65] Guests at rural weddings reacted differently to the solemn occasion. Some ". . . had a great time ended of kissing the Bride and . . . taking gates of the hinges and throwing them in the woods and some . . . quarreling."[66] The married couples and the wedding attendants were each expected to give a large party for the newlyweds. For one marriage in Morgantown on January 13, 1842, there had been four parties given for the couple within the next nine days.[67]

Childbirth was seldom attended by the doctor in the iron plantations. The women of the community looked after one another and did what was necessary for mother, child and family. For special needs the midwife or "granny" was on hand. Births were happy events with the proud father standing treat for drinks for all his friends.[68]

Not all marriages of the nineteenth century were endlessly happy or free from discord. Men got drunk and abused their wives and children.[69] One "put his wife out of doors and told her to seek Lodgings."[70] Another man hanged himself, and ". . . Some of the neighbors say he could not live agreeable with his wife."[71] According to report even the ironmaster's family had domestic difficulties. On one occasion Dr. Clingan had apparently been abusing a mule and was reprimanded by

[64] SM 1, p. 23.
[65] *Morris Diary, op. cit.*, II, p. 73.
[66] *Martha Furnace Diary, op .cit.*, July 30, 1814.
[67] *Morris Diary, op. cit.*, p. 179–180.
[68] *Martha Furnace Diary, op. cit., passim.*
[69] *Ibid., July* 5–6, 1813.
[70] *Ibid.*, January 29, 1811.
[71] HV 8400306A.

Mrs. Clingan, who reminded him that her money had bought the mule. The doctor's reported reply was, "Well, damn it, your money bought me, too."[72]

Chastity for the unmarried and fidelity to the marriage bed were not universal practices although the iron community may have been neither better nor worse than other groups of people in this respect. Hopewell history did not contain very many instances of illicit activities, but there were some. The Reverend Mister Levi Bull of St. Mary's Episcopal Church did not record that a child baptized was a bastard, as the rector of St. Gabriel's Church did. Mr. Bull just enrolled the mother's name without the usual entry of a father or the identification of widows.[73] The Pennsylvania General Assembly passed an act in 1828 to legitimize Marie Eve Snyder as the daughter of Daniel Udree and to give her rights of inheritance in his property.[74]

Although the following reference is no longer clear, it is apparent that even the highest Furnace families were not immune from the tongues of gossips:

> Mrs. Cabeen on Tuesday last made you an uncle by presenting me with a fine daughter, which I think will be apt to put the noses of the Cats out of Joint completely.[75]

Many of the old residents of Hopewell Village recalled Dr. Clingan as having been "extremely popular among the female sex throughout the section."[76] He was quite handsome, was reported to have had affairs with several village women[77] and was suspected of being the father of two of the children of a Mrs. Strock who lived across French Creek from the mansion. A Hopewell story related that the doctor was dumped from a foot log into the creek while returning at night from

[72] Morris Lyman Care Interview, February 6, 1941.
[73] *St. Mary's Church Record*, pp. 165–184.
[74] *Pamphlet Laws of Pennsylvania*, P. L. 1828, p. 28.
[75] HV 8420610, Rob B. Cabeen to Clement Brooke.
[76] Morris Lyman Care Interview, February 6, 1941.
[77] Albert Painter Interview, December 12, 1947.

a visit to Mrs. Strock. Lief Houck and several other furnace workers were supposed to have been responsible for the "ducking."[78]

Hopewell had its "bad girls" of whom Mary Ann Marks and Sally Hampton had the most lasting notoriety for ill-repute.[79] Sally worked in the woods cutting timber with the men, sharing their hard work and difficulties. Some aspersions were cast that difficulties were not the only things she shared with the men. She was reputed to have had several children by both white and Negro fathers.[80] Sally's conduct became a matter of record in an agreement between the Furnace management and John Hampton for the rental of a house in 1881. The clerk recorded:

> Agreed . . . that he could have the house formerly occupied by the family . . . The understanding is that they must keep a decent and respectable house. If Sarah's conduct is as it used to be, it will be sufficient at any time to remove them. Must not abuse or disturb any of their neighbors.[81]

Life was difficult and often lonesome for the women who lived in the remote homes on the wooded hillsides of Hopewell Village. Beside the normal activities of home and family care, many of them found ways to add to the family income through jobs requiring normal feminine skills and also from tasks usually reserved for the men. But on the whole they worked hard, lived fairly orderly lives and retained quite normal interest.

[78] Reginald Smith Interview, August 24, 1941.
[79] Mary Krewson Interview, June 29, 1941.
[80] Hunter Care Interview, January 26, 1941.
[81] SM 34, p. 232.

17   The Children

ACCORDING TO A RESPECTED AUTHORITY ON IRON-MAKING IN the eighteenth century, "Child labor found small place in iron manufacture."[1] The situation must have changed by the nineteenth century, or Hopewell was an exception; for many children were employed, and they were found in almost every type and kind of occupation around the Furnace except administrative positions. Many bound or apprenticed children lived and worked at Hopewell Furnace, but also many parents put their children to work and collected their wages.

In 1824 the General Assembly of Pennsylvania placed upon the Directors of the Poor for Berks County the responsibility:

> . . . to bind out as apprentices to any art, mystery or occupation, so that such apprenticeship may expire, if males, at or before the age of 21 years; if females, at or before the age of eighteen years, such poor children as shall come under their notice, or as may now be bound apprentices by the overseers of the poor, but no such apprentices shall be bound to any person or persons whose religious persuasion shall be different from that which the parents of such apprentices may have last professed, or to persons that are not of good repute, if others of good repute and of the same persuasion may or can be found. . . .[2]

[1] Bining, *Pennsylvania Iron Manufacture in the 18th Century, op. cit.*, p. 111.
[2] *Pamphlet Laws of Pennsylvania*, P. L. 1824, p. 201.

This law must have legitimized a practice which had long been followed or clarified the responsibilities of the stated officials in the matter, because indentured or apprenticed children were working at Hopewell Furnace at a much earlier date. Clement Brooke had at least two children bound to him in 1816 and then hired their services to the Furnace. On two dates he received payment, the first "for $6\frac{1}{2}$ months work done from the first of april last to the 17th of Octor by his Black Boy James @ $9 per month," and the second for $31.29 as wages for 39 weeks of work "by Mary."[3] The year after the new law was passed, the Furnace paid a shoemaker $9 "for making and mending shoes for Bound girls and Boy."[4] The number of girls was not given, but the size of the bill indicated several as shoes at this time were about $1.50 per pair. The expense for mending was not specified. In 1830 Clement Brooke had in his household four female Negroes, one under ten years of age, another under 24, and two between that age and 36.[5] Five years later Brooke paid a tailor $4.50 for "Making Suit for Black Boy."[6]

Children could be had from the county poorhouse for apprenticing at a quite young age—one girl was taken at the age of 8 to become a house servant.[7] But some agreements for even younger children were made directly with the parents. David Johnston must have been less than five when his mother placed him with the Brooke family in this agreement:

This Indenture witnesseth that David Johnston of the Township of Union in the County of Berks Son of Sarah Johnston by and with the Consent of his Mother . . . both put himself and by These Presents doth voluntary and of his own free will and accord put himself Apprentice to Clement and Maria Brooke their heirs and Asignes of the Same Place to learn his art Trade and mystery; and after the manner of an apprentice to Serve them from the day

[3] SM 7, December 23, 1816, and February 24, 1817, n. p.
[4] SM 12, p. 103.
[5] *Census of 1830,* Berks County, pp. 515–521.
[6] HV 8350407A.
[7] *Morris Diary, op. cit.,* II, p. 146.

of the date hereof; for and during the full end and term of
Sixteen years and one month Next ensuing. During all which
term the apprentice his said Master faithfully shall serve, his
Secrets keep; his lawfull commands every where gladly obey.
He shall do no damage to his said master nor see it done by
others; without letting or giving notice thereof to his said
master. He shall not waste his said Masters goods nor lend
them unlawfully to any. With his own goods nor the goods of
them; without license from his said Master he shall neither
buy nor sell. He shall not Absent himself day nor night from
his said Masters Service; without Leave, nor haunt ale-houses,
Taverns; or Play houses; but in all things behave himself as a
faithfull, Apprentice ought to do; during the said Term. And
the said Master Shall use the utmost of his Endeavours to
teach, or cause to be taught or instructed; the said apprentice
in the trade or mystery of husbandry and procure for him
sufficient meat; and drink; apparel; Lodging and washing,
fitting for an apprentice, during the said term of sixteen
years and one month and give him within the said term one
years Schooling. And when he is free to give him one suit of
Cloths to be Entirely new and all his old cloths. . . .[8]

Thomas Lloyd took Mary Young when she was only six to
live at his farm until she was eighteen years of age. During
her apprenticeship she was to receive eighteen months of
schooling "one half of which after she attains the age of
fourteen years." Mary was to be given religious instruction
and to be confirmed by a minister "of her own choosing." At
the end of her service she was to receive the usual two
changes of clothing, and Lloyd also promised to give her "a
bed and bed Stead worth seventy dollars, and a Chest or
Spining wheel whichever She may Choose."[9]

The tax records in the years before the public school system
was founded contained the names of "poor children" who
were eligible for aid in schooling. In Union Township the
number was 14 in 1829, 16 in 1830, 18 in 1831, 13 in 1833,
20 in 1834 and 19 in 1835. The ages ranged from 5 to 11,

[8] HV 8300212A.
[9] *Brooke Family Papers,* Indenture of Poor Girl, 1846.

inclusive.[10] These names were not of bound children whose education was provided by their masters but of the children of parents who could not afford to educate them.

The records show that the Furnace met its obligations to educate its bound children. Tutor Andrew Collins was paid by the company for teaching "A. Church, Benj. Hill and D. Johnston in 1834."[11] Ann Church, who lived at the mansion, was a niece of Mrs. Brooke; D. Johnston was apparently the apprentice whose terms of service were related above; and Ben Hill was a Negro apprentice and later a hostler for several years. All three of these names appeared in other years for schooling; Ben Hill attended school during parts of six years. There were also memoranda of clothing provided for these children.[12]

If Mary Monshour was at all typical, bound girls must have had time to give to plans for their lives after they reached freedom age. She apparently attracted the attention of Blacksmith Samuel Henderson while she was an apprentice at the Big House and married him when she gained her freedom. Mary was the daughter of Jacob Monshour who cut wood for the Furnace. In 1846 the Furnace bought for her a pair of shoes costing $1; and the next year paid for her a $15 doctor bill, 75¢ for repairing a bonnet and $2.09½ which she owed a peddler.[13] During this time Henderson was paying for boarding and to have his washing done—signs of bachelorhood. On March 22, 1848, Mary collected $20 for her "Freedom Money," and a month later the Furnace paid $13.80 "per Mary Munshour freedom Clothes in Philadelphia." On the same day Samuel Henderson "Paid for Sundries in Philadelphia got by Mary Munshour" to the amount of $10.65. Henderson began paying bills for storegoods on January 1, 1849, and the following year he was a householder providing

[10] *Berks County Tax Records,* Union Township.
[11] SM 21, p. 101.
[12] For example see SM 21, p. 32.
[13] SM 31, pp. 12, 29, 33, 41, 54, 58.

boarding for his brother George.[14] All of this seems to add up to romance and marriage; which is further confirmed by the census of 1850 which included a Furnace household of Samuel Henderson, age 26, occupation smith; Mary, age 19, and William, age 2.[15] The ages of mother and son possibly disclose that Mary had gained her freedom before she was eighteen and William had been born early.

Furnace employees, other than the manager, had apprentice children who were employed by the company. Edward Hughes collected wages for James Lacey over a considerable period of time, and Esabella Ewens had an income from the work of Esram Haselip.[16] Perhaps the outstanding success story of a "poor child" at Hopewell was that of Joseph Elliot. He was included among the pauper children in the tax records of 1823 when his age was given as seven years.[17] In 1832 at the age of sixteen he was a molder; but his wages were being paid to Samuel Williams, teamster.[18] Williams paid for a coat "for J. Elliot" in 1837,[19] and in May of that year the boy came of age and began to draw his own wages.[20] In 1840 he was married and the father of a little girl under five years of age.[21]

Why did Samuel Williams collect wages earned by Elliot? Williams had worked at the Furnace in 1802 when his father died while Samuel was a minor. The boy began boarding at the mansion two days after his father's death;[22] he even collected the wages of his younger brother Jesse.[23] He was, therefore, a man of maturity when he married Rebecca Elliot on January 1, 1820.[24] Rebecca had been a maid for Clement

[14] SM 32, pp. 64, 93.
[15] *Census of 1850*, Berks County, p. 569.
[16] SM 9, pp. 137, 152.
[17] *Berks County Tax Records*, Union Township, 1823.
[18] SM 21, p. 190.
[19] *Ibid.*, p. 193.
[20] SM 19, p. 184.
[21] *Census of 1840*, Berks County, p. 397.
[22] SM 1, p. 15.
[23] SM 2, p. 177.
[24] *St. Mary's Episcopal Church Records, op. cit.*

Brooke before the marriage. Joseph Elliot must have been a relative of hers, perhaps a brother or son. Elliot worked as a molder at Hopewell Furnace until molding ended and afterwards continued to reside in the village. In 1846 he had a child in the Hopewell school.[25]

Children of Hopewell Village were to be found working at almost every kind of job the company offered. The Furnace, itself, provided work for many boys before they reached their majorities. The job of gutterman was handled regularly by a boy. From Samuel Williams in 1802 to Robert Wampsher in 1851 many boys did this work and had their wages paid to parents or guardians.[26] Isaac and John Hughes were the guttermen from 1817 to 1825 with their wages going to Edward Hughes and Mary Hughes.[27] The next most frequent Furnace jobs done by minors were putting in the mine and stocking coal. Frederick Meck, David Hart and John Painter provided sons who did this work from 1808 to 1831.[28] Samuel McCollister, minor, was entrusted with substitute work as filler in 1803,[29] and several boys earned money cleaning castings for the molders.[30] The height of success for a family was to have a son who could become a molder and earn the high wages paid to these skilled workers. Thomas Care trained several of his sons for this work and at one time was collecting molding pay, based on production, for sons David and Thomas in addition to his own salary as founder and molder. His income was high at that time.[31] John Care, John Painter, Joseph Hart and Joseph Elliot also began molding before they were old enough to collect their own wages.[32]

Providing iron ore for the furnace also furnished work for

[25] SM 31, p. 20.
[26] SM 2, November 2, 1802, n. p.; SM 32, p. 120.
[27] SM 6, p. 254; SM 11, p. 92; SM 7, January 31, 1817, n.p.; SM 9, p. 137.
[28] SM 4, p. 249; SM 5, p. 101; SM 9, p. 142; SM 15, p. 50.
[29] SM 1, p. 217.
[30] SM 9, p. 129; SM 8, pp. 63, 66.
[31] SM 12, p. 144.
[32] SM 59, p. 12; SM 21, pp. 69, 70, 88; SM 12, p. 108; SM 14, p. 59.

many boys and young men, with several instances where a father and son formed a mining team. Jonathan McKewen and Thomas Ray both appeared in the time record as miners in 1818. But their wages were added to those of their fathers who were miners also.[33] William Philips was paid for his own work at raising ore and also for the same work done by his son Nugent in 1818 and 1819. In 1817, however, Nugent Philips' wages had been credited to the account of William Adams with no reason recorded. Two years later Adams was paid for mine work by his son William.[34] Robert Gilmore had several boys working at mining and loading ore into the wagons in 1816–1819.[35] Esram Haselip worked for William Adams and Company, mining contractors, from 1818 to 1820 as the bound boy of Esabella Ewens. He must have been a good workman because his employment was steady, and his wage of 75¢ per day was higher than that of several of the adults working "at the mineholes." Haselip apparently became of age about April 10, 1820, when the clerk opened an account in his name into which wages were credited until the end of 1821.[36] Some boys earned the same wages as their fathers for mining; others were paid less—possibly these latter ones were learning the business.[37]

The work of a collier would seem to have been another good opportunity for a father-son partnership, but little evidence was found that such was the case. Henry Houck was a master collier and received wages for coaling done by his son Samuel. However, Samuel worked with Daniel Frey's coaling team and not with his father.[38] Jacob Cramp, David Ireson, Henry Wampser and Jacob Woolf's son worked at the colliers' pits before they were old enough to collect their wages; and Edward Hughes was paid $19 per month in 1818

[33] SM 9, p. 121; SM 6, p. 13.
[34] SM 9, pp. 124, 142, 151, 192; SM 8, p. 138.
[35] SM 7, December 24, 1816, n. p.; SM 9, p. 135.
[36] SM 9, pp. 120, 140, 151, 152; SM 4, pp. 265, 357.
[37] SM 32, pp. 109, 113.
[38] SM 21, p. 5; SMR 19, p. 13.

for coaling by his bound boy James Lacey. Lacey's rate was a
little under the $23 per month paid some other colliers.[39]

Several of the skilled crafts were open to boys as workers
or apprentices. When Henry Frye quit as blacksmith in 1807,
his partner Philip Shafer brought Philip, Junior, to the shop.
The son began work at 60s. per month, compared with his
father's 110s. The boy must have proved a good worker,
however, as his wage jumped to 97½s. after only four months
of employment.[40] The next year Shafer began to use another
son, Abraham, at a starting wage of 45s. per month. Within
the year he, too, earned a pay boost to 83½s.[41]

In the last half of the nineteenth century the Hopewell
Village blacksmith shop employed several apprentices. In
1855 Henry Henry began a training period of three years
during which he was to recieve $25 worth of "cloaths" each
year and a freedom suit at the end of his term.[42] The same
conditions were offered to Davis Painter six years later.[43]
Henry Care was promised more in 1862. He was to receive,
in addition, a pair of boots; and the Furnace was to pay
Nathan Care $75 per year to board his son.[44] Lincoln Pals-
grove said he began to work at the blacksmith shop with his
father at a very young age. He remembered making frequent
trips to check the sundial in front of the shop to find how
much longer the work day would last.[45]

Several father-son carpenter teams appeared in the Hopewell Furnace records. Jacob Keim, John Crosby and George
Painter each collected wages for himself and a son. Keim
was paid $1.25 per day and his son only 50¢.[46] But at about
the same time John Sands earned at the very good rate of

[39] SM 2, pp. 53, 63; SM 4, p. 208; SM 14, p. 50; SM 9, p. 113.
[40] SM 4, pp. 167, 193.
[41] Ibid., pp. 221, 235, 244.
[42] SM 35, p. 56.
[43] Kemper Manuscripts, C. M. Clingan Pocket Note Book, May 21,
1861.
[44] Ibid., June 27, 1862.
[45] J. Lincoln Palsgrove Interview, October 13, 1940.
[46] SM 9, p. 125.

$1 per day which was paid to his father.[47] George Painter
collected wages in 1835 for both himself and David and then
asked the clerk to credit $119 to David's account.[48] Joseph
Thomas was paid 4½s. per day for mending flasks "by his
Prentise."[49]

According to an old resident, about 1821 a 16-year-old
boy named Wortz came to Hopewell as an apprentice wheelwright under Master Henry Houck. They made ox yokes,
plow beams, wagon wheels and wagon tongues. After Houck
died, Wortz stayed on as Hopewell's last resident wheelwright.[50]

The less skilled tasks in the community naturally offered
opportunity for boys, and even girls, to earn some money
for their families. Cutting wood was probably available to
older boys most of the time because of the constant demand
and also because the pay was on a piecework basis. There
were a number of specific references to wood cut by boys[51]
and possibly others where payment was made for wood without a concern for which member of the family did the work.
Boys also found a source of income in picking pieces of iron
from the slag heaps. The Furnace paid 1¢ per pound for this
iron in the 1870's.[52]

Both boys and girls worked on the farms when there was
a need for extra help, especially at reaping and harvesting.
Day-rate pay for farm work held steady at 25¢ during the
first half of the nineteenth century; but compensation for
some farm jobs was on a piecework basis—for example,
picking up potatoes. In almost all cases earnings were
credited to the parents, but an exception was made in 1806

[47] SM 7, July 25, 1817, n. p.
[48] SM 21, p. 160.
[49] SM 44, June 15, 1805, n. p.
[50] Reginald Smith Interview, March 16, 1941. There was no record of
such an employee in 1825 although John Wert and Peter Wert were
teamsters. Henry Houck was a collier at that time.
[51] Some examples are SM 1, pp. 238, 267; SM 59, p. 18; SM 15, p. 27;
SM 31, p. 29.
[52] Thomas Hoffman Interview, November 22, 1940.

when the clerk noted that cash payments had been made to "Cramp Girls" and "Hughes boys" for making hay. "John Harts Daug" also received cash for eggs which she sold to the Furnace.[53] On another occasion James Simmons was paid for haymaking done by his daughter, and two days later the daughter drew the same amount in cash from her father's account.[54]

Girls had fewer choices of kinds of work available to them than did the boys. Aside from farm work the girls were most frequently employed as maids and housekeepers. References to "Little Negro" and "Little dutch girl" indicated that they began service at the mansion at a young age.[55] In 1784 Mary Paine, seamstress, was collecting the wages for two daughters who were working as housekeepers.[56] "A Boadley girl" went to Philadelphia to do housework in 1830.[57] Since some of the Boadleys were Negroes, this girl may have been colored.

Much of the work done by children was not specifically identified as to the kind of job. The only reference found in many cases was the clerk's statement in the books that an adult was receiving payment "for work done" by a son, daughter or ward. Sometimes, but not always, the name of the child was included. Another source of income for a few fathers was a payment to sons for attending "the Batallion."[58]

Having a child working for the Furnace and collecting his pay was not all profit for a parent, however; for there were expenses which had to be met. Clothing represented the greatest cash outlay. Hats, trousers, jackets and shirts were sometimes purchased; and shoes were the cause of regular cash expenditures. In addition to shoes bought at the company store, several shoemakers made regular calls at the Fur-

[53] SM 4, pp. 88, 93.
[54] SM 1, p. 198.
[55] SM 35, pp. 66, 70.
[56] SM 41, p. 110.
[57] *Brooke Family Papers,* Probably Sarah Brooke to Edward Brooke, December 5, 1830.
[58] SM 10, p. 33. The reference was to militia duty.

nace and took orders. Jacob Hartenstine submitted an accounting for three years work done for Clement Brooke showing shoes bought or repaired at Brooke's expense in that time: "For Margaret 7 pairs, Miss Ann 1, Mr. Brooke 2, Charoline 10, Mariah 8, Church 8, Ben 5, Charles 7, Adoline 3, Eliza 4, Clement 3 and Mrs. Brooke 2." These people include members of the family and also children working at the Big House[59]

Grown children entered the record in relation to parents in a number of ways. So long as they were unmarried, they continued to live at home and paid for boarding, washing and sewing.[60] Joseph Hart employed his father to clean castings as additional income. David Hart had a large family and probably needed the extra money he could earn in this way.[61] David Hart, Junior, settled the account at the store after his father's death by a payment of $76.36½.[62] Daniel Buckley sent his daughter Mary to the Furnace to collect cash in the amount of $1,060 owed to him, a small fortune by 1827 values.[63]

Children were prohibited from playing in the area around the cast house because of the danger of burns from the hot metal. They were not welcome anywhere that their presence would interfere with the work being done. But the attraction of the glowing stream of molten iron drawn from the furnace and flowing into the sand beds was too great for the children. When no one noticed, they would at least find a vantage point near a window to watch the casting. The ore roaster was also out of bounds to children when the fire was burning. Accidents were frequent around a furnace, and many children were injured in falls on the flight of stone steps near the office.[64]

[59] HV 8290228.
[60] SM 14, pp. 38, 69; SM 21, pp. 160, 161.
[61] SM 14, pp. 61, 78, 79.
[62] SM 38, p. 95.
[63] SM 59, p. 7.
[64] Samuel March Interview, January 22, 1941.

Lincoln Palsgrove recalled a gang fight between the boys who lived near the furnace and those who lived at the Pine Swamp. Fighting erupted in the area near the furnace over the attention paid to Hopewell girls by the boys from across the mountain.[65]

Some of the Furnace books had blank pages after the accounts ended, and the school children used these pages to practice their school sums and penmanship. On several pages the signatures of a long list of children appeared. Most of them were Cares, but scattered among them were several Coles. Since the Cares were white and the Coles were black, it would appear that integrated play was practiced in the Village.[66]

The Hopewell records show that the children worked from an early age and made a contribution to the family income. Boys were employed at most of the jobs at the furnace, and many girls found employment on the farms and in the homes. Orphans and the children in poorer families were sometimes bound or apprenticed under formal contracts which specified the conditions of their service and the obligations of the guardians. Except in the wealthier families the carefree period of childhood was of short duration, although many of the young people did not work full-time until their late teens.

[65] J. Lincoln Palsgrove Interview, October 13, 1940.
[66] SM 5.

18   Education

HAVING THE FURNACE OWNER LIVING IN CLOSE PROXIMITY TO his workers and remote from others of his class was an aid to the promotion of education among the children of the Hopewell community. The Brookes and Buckleys had children of their own to educate; so they found a teacher and permitted the other families to share the cost by paying tuition for sending their children. The Furnace was too far from other furnaces or from the towns to send the children to a central school or for a school to operate for ironmasters' children alone. The Hopewell Village child attended the one of several schools which was closest to his home. A school was located each year near the furnace with others at Warwick, Morgantown and the Jones Mine.

Until 1836 teaching was on a subscription or tuition basis. After that a public school for Union Township was located at the Furnace, although for some time longer a subscription school was conducted during the summer months. Ordinarily the instruction did not go beyond the elementary grades. The ironmasters sent their children to boarding school for secondary education, and most other children did not go any further with formal schooling. There were, however, other means to improve the mind for older children and adults such as newspapers, magazines, books and lectures.

346

The school at the Furnace had a number of men and at least one woman teacher from the beginning of the nineteenth century until the establishment of the public school. The earliest one was John Mullan (or McMullen) who gave Clement Brooke some of the last formal education he was to receive.[1] James Sands and Abraham Corb taught Hopewell children in the period from 1804 until the Furnace ceased operation in 1808. The number of pupils was not large, and they were for the most part from the families of higher incomes. Matthew Davis, manager; the two blacksmith Shafers; Edward Hughes, filler and job contractor; and Hugh Welsh, teamster, each sent one or more children.[2] Corb allowed his pay for 1808 to stand on the books until 1822 when it was transferred to Hampton Forge.[3] Perhaps he had taught at the Forge in the meanwhile.

William Brown, Robert Rankin, Ralph McClintock and William McGillivoray were paid for tuition in the period from 1817 to 1820.[4] McGillivoray was listed as a resident of East Nantmeal and was paid only by Clement Brooke; so he may not have been teaching at the Furnace. Lewis Evans taught the children of the Warwick area in the same period.[5] Rankin earned $57.82 in tuition for two quarters in 1819. Of this he drew $45.60½ in cash when he left in 1820.[6] Two payments for Rankin's tuition were made to Merchant R. Laverty of Morgantown and apparently were for storegoods.[7]

In the next fifteen years the following four masters and one mistress presided over the school sessions of the Hopewell subscription school: Christian Halderman, Andrew Collins, Thomas Foster, Robert D. Powell and Susan Brown. Collins was a minister who opened a school at least as early as 1825

[1] SM 2, p. 5.
[2] SM 1, p. 320; SM 4, p. 235; SM 5, p. 70; SM 67, May 6, 1807, n. p.
[3] SM 5, p. 70.
[4] SM 6, pp. 190, 216; SM 10, p. 18; HV 8170800; HV 8180710.
[5] Lewis Evans Journal, op. cit., pp. 30, 164.
[6] SM 6, p. 190.
[7] SM 10, p. 61.

when he proposed teaching in a house which, he was notified, was too far from the Furnace and in too bad condition for winter classes. He was informed that he might hold summer school there, however.[8] He was still teaching at Hopewell as late as 1837,[9] but there were several others who taught one or more terms during this period.

Teaching was not a full-time occupation for some of these men. Collins performed religious duties and Foster did a variety of jobs about the Furnace and became the clerk in 1836.[10]

While the higher-income families predominated among the pupils in this era, there were children from every economic level in the school. Many more of the children were receiving an education, including some who were apprenticed to the Furnace and the children of Wilkinson Hill, a Negro laborer.

The cost of sending a child to the subscription school was based on days of attendance with a flat rate for the quarter for those who attended regularly. In 1830 Foster assessed $1.75 per pupil per quarter, and Collins was charging the same the following year. The latter collected $2\frac{1}{2}$¢ per day for a pupil who did not attend the entire quarter.[11] Clement Brooke paid full tuition for four unnamed children, and the Furnace paid "for E. North and B. Hill" at these rates.[12] Gilmore and Miss Brown received several payments of $3.00; so perhaps this was their fee per quarter.[13] It is possible that summer school had a different rate, for in 1833 Collins received payments ranging from 25¢ to $1.75 with only two being the same amount at 1.62\frac{1}{2}$.[14] Or maybe the quarterly payment was the same, but pupils were more difficult to hold

[8] *Hopewell Papers,* Note to Revd Andrew Collins, unsigned and undated but notes on reverse of the paper were dated October 22, 1825.

[9] SM 21, p. 201.

[10] SM 15, p. 39; SM 21, p. 200. His name was also spelled Forster.

[11] SM 15, pp. 39, 61.

[12] *Cash Books* for 1828–1830, *op. cit.,* January 25, 1830, n. p.

[13] SM 59, p. 20; SM 14, p. 45.

[14] SM 21, p. 75.

to regular attendance when the weather was pleasant. By 1835 the tuition was raised to 3¢ per day.[15]

Subscription teaching continued at Hopewell after a public school had been established near the Furnace. In one quarter of 1840–1841 Daniel Jones had 21 pupils in attendance, including 4 Negroes. The tuition had dropped to $1.15 per quarter.[16] Another woman teacher must have served in 1846, for several persons made payments to "the School Mrs."[17]

Agreements with the teacher sometimes took the form of a contract, as this one in 1830 with Thomas Foster:

> We the subscribers do hereby Engage Thomas Foster to teach an English School Viz Spelling, Reading, Writing and Arithmetic for the term of three months to Commence on the first day of Dec 1830 for which we do agree to pay him one Dollar and Seventy five cts per quarter for Each Scholar Including firewood the School to be taught in the house lately occupied by Peter Wert.[18]

Although most of the education at the local school was on the lower level of elementary courses, there was at least one effort to teach some secondary subjects. Note in the following contract that prices were considerably higher for these classes, but the results were guaranteed:

> We the undersigned promise to pay Robert D. Powell for the tuition of our children the following prices, viz for instruction in the Latin Language five dollars per quarter, for English Grammar, Geography, or any of the higher branches of an english education three dollars per quarter, and for Reading writing and arithmetic two dollars and twenty five cents per quarter—with this understanding that if any subscriber should be dissatisfied to the price, at the expiration of one month he shall have the prevelege of withdrawing his subscription. The quarter shall consist of thirteen weeks. Those

[15] SM 21, pp. 124, 135.
[16] SM 28, pp. 61, 62.
[17] SM 31, pp. 19, 20.
[18] *Hopewell Papers,* Copy of agreement with Thomas Foster, uncatalogued.

who subscribe for a quarter and should exceed that time will be charged in the ratio as above stated—those who do not subscribe for a quarter, and should send by the day will be charged 4 cents per day.[19]

Under the public school system the county superintendent of schools made an effort to maintain standards for the teachers under him by means of examinations in the subjects to be taught. The following letter shows the struggle he faced :

Have raised the standard and Warwick must come up to a higher mark in qualification or lose the state appropriation. They are disposed to employ teachers of too low qualification. This year I rejected 2 Employed last year, who made no improvement whatever. I will do this in an emergency : If the School Board of Warwick are disposed to employ you, they must request me to endorse your Certificate or Examine. This must be done in writing and signed by at least 3 Members of the S. B. They had better have 4.

I cannot promise you a certificate, if Examined, for my standard has been raised and as you barely received one before, and have been off for one year, the probabilities are you cannot reach it. But, if you are conscious of having improved since then in any of the branches, I would try to secure better marks. . . .[20]

Sending a child to school involved expenses other than tuition. Writing materials were costly as "1 led Pencell" sold at the Hopewell store in 1817 for $12\frac{1}{2}$¢, one-half-day's pay for work on the farm.[21] Quills cost $\frac{1}{2}$¢ each, ink powder $12\frac{1}{2}$¢ per packet [22] and paper 1¢ per sheet. The children often used pages spoiled by the clerk for their arithmetic and penmanship practices. Spelling, grammar and arithmetic books were purchased by parents from the Hopewell store, from stores in Reading or West Chester, from the teacher or from another

[19] *Ibid.*, Contract between Parents and Teacher. Undated but Powell taught at Hopewell in 1835–1836. See SM 21, p. 165.
[20] HV 8750731. HFP on letterhead of Superintendent of Common Schools of Chester County to "Friend Long." This may have been Harker Long, sometime manager of Hopewell Furnace.
[21] SM 8, p. 79.
[22] *Ibid.*, p. 136; SM 40, p. 234.

parent. "Lewis' Arithmetic" sold for $37\frac{1}{2}$¢ and "Kirkham's Grammer" at $87\frac{1}{2}$¢. Spelling books cost 25¢ new and 11¢ on the secondhand market.[23] Mathematics students sometimes compiled a kind of textbook of their own by copying rules and problems on folded ledger paper and working out the solutions on the bottom of the sheets.[24]

Pupils came from all classes of Hopewell society, from apprentices who were sent to fulfill the requirements of their apprenticeship agreement and poor children who received some help from the township to the children of the ironmaster's family. They began at less than five years of age[25] and continued as long as the parents could afford to send them or until they were old enough for jobs. Apparently by 1830 most of the Hopewell people were able to sign their own names. In that year a subscription for the Bethesda Baptist Church contained 32 signatures. The handwriting differed for each name and was clearly not all done by the same person.[26] On the other hand the official collector of militia fines for Union Township in 1820 signed his receipts with "his mark" and had them witnessed. He was not a Furnace employee, however.[27]

The public school system brought a new kind of financing of education for Union Township. School taxes were collected in 1844 in the amount of $53.45 for the Furnace property. The clerk also paid the collector for the individual tax of 23 workers in amounts ranging from 10¢ to $2.70.[28] State appropriations now provided another source of educational income. Union Township forfeited its state allotment in 1835, because it had no public school in operation. It began collecting its appropriation in 1836 and continued regularly thereafter. For

[23] SM 9, pp. 181–183; SM 10, pp. 37, 38; SM 28, p. 16; *Cash Book* for 1828–1830, November 10, 1829, and January 8, 1830, n. p.
[24] *Hopewell Papers, Stokes Collection.*
[25] *Mount Hope Journal, 1800–1819,* memorandum page.
[26] HV 8300111.
[27] HV 8200609A.
[28] SM 28, pp. 130, 131.

1839 the amount was $155.38.[29] Caernarvon Township received $189 for 1838.[30]

The early school sessions were held in vacant houses in the Village, in the "boarding house" and at the Bethesda Baptist Church, which was located about three-fourths of a mile from the Furnace.[31] In 1836 the company paid to have a schoolhouse built near the center of furnace operations. Thomas Knaur received $34.80 for the mason work and an additional $1 for building a chimney at the new school. The Union Township School District reimbursed Clement Brooke and Company the sum of $425 "for building a new schoolhouse etc." An additional payment of $20.25 was made for "3 Tons of Stone coal del. to schoolhouse."[32] There were later payments for both coal and wood used for fuel.[33]

From the descriptions given by old Hopewell residents this building was 28 feet by 35 feet, one story, built of stone with a shingle roof. The single door opened inward to a partitioned entry extending the length of the building and used to store wood and supplies. The building was heated by a stove placed in the center of the room. A "disciplinary bench" was placed between the teacher's desk and the stove. The desks and backless benches occupied by the pupils were ordered along three sides. The pupils sat with their faces to the wall and their backs to the teacher. Boys sat on the north side, girls on the south and the excess of each on the west. The teacher's desk was on a raised platform on the east side of the room. Books and papers had to be kept on the tops of the study tables because there were no drawers or under-desk compartments.[34]

There must have been an earlier movement to build a

[29] *Berks and Schuylkill Journal,* January 20, 1838.
[30] *Morris Diary, op. cit.,* p. 53.
[31] Long, *Historical Sketch, op. cit.,* p. 10.
[32] SM 21, pp. 194, 195.
[33] SM 28, p. 120; SM 32, p. 39.
[34] Sally Boone Interview, March 22, 1941; and Katherine Rhoads and Rose Sands Interview, March 4, 1941. Mrs. Rhoads taught at Hopewell in 1871.

school at Hopewell, for in 1832 David Shaffer paid his tuition
for two children and gave an additional 25¢ as "so much
paid subscription to school house."[35] Another building, constructed about 1870 a half mile from the furnace along the
road to the Jones mine, served the educational needs of Hopewell children until after the Furnace closed in 1883.[36]

The public school law received criticism from the Village
people, with particular opposition to the system of State
appropriations from one writer who declared :

> It is time that this humbuggery on the part of the state in
> the matter of common school appropriations should cease. Let
> the people in each school district elect directors as they now
> do and let these directors have power . . . to raise by tax-
> ation, a sum sufficient to keep the schools of the district open
> as they now are. . . . In any case the state should cease
> her appropriations for educational purposes, even if the whole
> common school system should fall to the ground. She ought
> to be honest before being liberal.[37]

Mrs. Catherine Rhoads, who taught at Hopewell in 1871,
said she had 25 pupils ranging in age from 6 to 20. The
school term at this time was six months, and in addition a
summer subscription school of two months was held. Although
most parents paid for the summer school, Dr. Clingan paid
for some whose parents could not afford it. Mrs. Rhoads was
of the opinion that summer school was scheduled whenever
Dr. Clingan was annoyed by the number of children playing
around the Furnace. He would say, "There are too damn
many youngsters about; we'd better open a summer school."[38]

In its earliest period the free school had a five-month term
beginning in August and was sometimes followed by a subscription term in the spring.[39] The schoolmaster summoned the
pupils for each session by the ringing of a small hand bell.

[35] SM 21, p. 32.
[36] H. A. Long Interview, August 13, 1936.
[37] *Morris Diary, op. cit.,* II, p. 103. Written in 1844.
[38] Catherine Rhoads Interview, May 13, 1941.
[39] *Morris Diary, op. cit.,* pp. 84, 115.

Hopewell Schoolhouse Built About 1870

1870 Schoolhouse, Side View

On the last day of school teacher and pupils brought lunches and walked to a grove on the northwest slope of Mount Pleasant for a picnic.[40]

Conduct of pupils was not always exemplary. Ann Church wrote on her penmanship practice sheet, "Nathan Care is a very bad Boy he . . . has threatened the girls very bad."[41] Later the bigger boys persuaded a pupil to start a fight with a woman teacher, but she won and administered a good whipping.[42] Lincoln Palsgrove recalled a quick exit through a window to escape a switching.[43] Physical punishment was evidently severe at the boarding schools, also. Ann Brooke wrote to her brother Edward :

> I heard in the city of Mr. Fuller having chastised George in the most brutal manner . . . I heard that for some slight provocation (throwing a chesnut shell) Mr. Fuller had whiped and then *kicked* George, such treatment as that no man shall ever inflict on a brother of mine while he is at school. . . .[44]

The ironmaster's children, and occasionally others, went to boarding school after attending the Hopewell school. George Brooke progressed from Mr. Buck's School in Lititz to Mr. Fuller's in West Chester and finished with Samuel Gummere in Burlington, New Jersey.[45] The girls studied at Mr. Price's School in West Chester and then went to Mr. Hamilton's in Philadelphia and possibly to Bristol College or Mr. Gummere's, both in Burlington.[46]

Tuition in the boarding schools was $30 to $40 per quarter in the 1830's. Master Gummere announced that for 1835 he

[40] Sally Boone Interview, March 22, 1941.

[41] *Hopewell Papers,* Penmanship practice sheets. The date March 25, 1831, appeared.

[42] Charles Sheridan Painter Interview, April 12, 1958. The teacher was the Mrs. Rhoades previously mentioned.

[43] J. Lincoln Palsgrove Interview, November 26, 1948.

[44] *Brooke Family Papers,* probably March, 1832, as George entered Mr. Fuller's School at West Chester in 1831.

[45] *Ibid.,* September 3, 1831; HV 8351228B.

[46] SM 12, p. 107; HV 8320420; *Hopewell Papers, Stokes Collection,* Elizabeth Barde to Sarah A. Brooke, February 12, 1837; HV 8351228B.

was raising his fee from $35 to $40 per quarter; but he also stated that he was striking out the charge formerly made for fuel, candles, pens, ink and slate pencils.[47] Other expenses added considerably to the cost of education. In 1825 Clement Brooke paid one bill of $388.21 "for schooling received in City."[48] Caroline and Marie Brooke had a total of $5 for spending money for a quarter at West Chester, but they were not intrusted with this sum at one time. It was left with Philip Price to be advanced to them.[49] The kinds of expenses a child at school incurred are shown in the following accounting for Caroline and Maria for 1831 and 1832 at the Price School:

For Stationery etc . .   for 2 qrs. Viz
Blank Books 89 Knife 37½ India Rubber 12½   1.39
Woodbridge's Geog. and Atlas 1.00
    Willard's Geog. and At. 50   1.50
Lead Pencils 49 Paper 51 B. Bks 2 17   3.17
Ruler 6¼ Slate 25 Knives 50¼ Paper 76   1.63¼
Willard's Atlas 37½ Quills etc for each 1 qr 1.00   1.37½
Paper 94 2 Gummere's Geog 50 Gramr 37½   1.81½
India Rubber 6 Pencil 4 Blank bks 1.153/4   1.25¾
1 Sheet of Transparent ppr. 50 ppr 12½   .62½
Wafers 6¼ Arith 25 Quills etc 1.00   1.31½
Board and Tuition of each 1 qr.   60.00
1 Course of Lessons in Painting   5.00

Extras Furnished
Cash for glass etc 93¾ Cutting hair and tooth
    brush 25   1.18¾
1 Pr of Booties 1.44 lacings 8 Hooks 6 Tape 5   1.63
Comb 20 Mending shoes 25 Trunk 1.12½   1.57½
Shoes for M. 1.12½ Comb, Brush Cup and Soap
    for C. 62½   1.75
Cup and Comb for M. 31¼ Boots for do. 1.37½   1.68¾
Medicine $1.00 Shoes for Caroline 1.37½ 2 Bags 37½ 2.75
Vaccination (for 2) 50 Filing teeth 50 Carmine 25   1.25
Medical Attendance of Marie 5.25   5.25
Carmine 43¼ Lacings 8 2 prs. of Gloves 1.50   2.01¾

[47] HV 8351228B.
[48] SM 12, p. 44.
[49] SM 15, p. 24.

Bristol Board 40 Postage 1.75 Mending Shoes 12½   2.27½
Show 40 Pins 10 Print Box 3.00 Buttons 10   3.60
Allowance of .25 per wk for C and M 24 Wks   6.00
Repairing Clothes 1.14 Cash 23½ Ribband 1.06   2.43½
                                                    _____
                              Total Amount $112.49[50]

The expenses of a young man at boarding school are disclosed in this accounting for John Church:

TO 1 Olneys Gography and Atlas $1.00 1 Slate .25 1
      Arith .31¼
    1 Gummals Surveying $1.62½ Box Instruments $5.25
    1 Blank Book .81¼ 1 Bonnycastle Mensuration .87½
    18½ weeks Board and Tuition @ $30 per 12 weeks
    Light $1.15½ Medicine .12½
    8 sheets paper .08 Quills .10 Ink .12½ Pencils .02
    Hickman and Mercers shoe acct. $2.12½
                                          $60.10½[51]

Boarding schools had their financial problems and sometimes were forced to close. Elizabeth Barde wrote in 1837:

> . . . I suppose you have heard long ere this that Bristol
> Colege was very much involved in debt; for the last two weeks
> the studants had but one meal a day, the butchers and baker
> were not willing to trust and of course they were obliged to
> eat food of the coarest kind . . . College closes Wednesday
> and if they can collect funds sufficiently to go on they will
> commence again. . . .[52]

In addition to the common school subjects young ladies
learned dancing, riding, French and Latin.[53] Young gentlemen
learned natural philosophy, Latin, French, Greek and survey-
ing.[54] Apparently both boys and girls found difficulty in keep-

[50] HV 8320420.
[51] HV 8340109A.
[52] *Hopewell Papers, Stokes* Collection, Elizabeth Barde to Sarah R.
Brooke, February 12, 1837.
[53] *Brooke Family* Papers, Sarah Brooke to Edward Brooke, January 14,
1835; Ann F. Brooke to George W. Brooke, April 15, 1833.
[54] *Ibid.,* G. B. R. to Edward Brooke, January 28, 1833.

ing their minds on their work. A young man announced he was ". . . banishing from my mind the gravity of . . . hard study, the girls, and a thousand other ills that flesh is heir to. . . ."[55] A young lady complained of Professor Cleveland's long lessons. But she spent "very little time in committing them to memory."[56]

George Brooke gave some impressions of his school at Burlington in the following letter to his brother:

> We have but 16 or 18 schollars, 5 of which are old ones and 4 preachers or rather learners to be preachers. One of the latter is 41 years old another about 30 and the remainder over 21. We have a Chapter of the Bible read and a prayer every morning before school commences besides grace said before every meal. . . . The man I spoke of as being 41 years old rents a little house by our dwelling house, to live in; he cooks for himself and makes his own bed and does everything for himself but washing. He lives on bread and milk and studies in his own room but recites in the school house. . . .[57]

Any consideration of education in the Village would be incomplete without some attention to the reading matter available and non-institutional means of education. The wide interests of the ironmaster and a part of the workers was reflected in the number and variety of newspapers which came to the Furnace in the nineteenth century. The market for Furnace products created an interest in events in nearby communities and the large cities.

Berks County news was obtained from the *Berks and Schuylkill Journal* for which a subscription appeared as a Furnace expense as early as 1816 and as late as 1859. This newspaper was a weekly published in Reading and sold at $2 per year for most of the span of time mentioned.[58] Interest in the Lancaster area market accounted for subscriptions over many

[55] *Ibid.*
[56] *Ibid.*, Sarah to Edward Brooke, January 14, 1835.
[57] *Ibid.*, G. W. Brooke to Edward Brooke, May 8, 1834.
[58] HV 8160806A; SM 65, January 29, 1859, n. p.

years to the *Lancaster Journal* at as much as $5 per year.[59] The Furnace paid $12.25 "for newspapers at Harrisburg," but the clerk did not name the publications.[60]

Politics as well as business entered into Clement Brooke's interest in the *Chester County Whig* in 1834 when he ordered subscriptions for himself, John Care and James Roberts. He added, "Probably I may get more Subscribers in the Course of this Month." He obtained at least one more, for later in the year David Care was listed with this group.[61] Chester County news was also secured from the *Village Record* of West Chester and possibly from the *Chronicle of the Times*—no place of publication was given for this newspaper.[62]

City newspapers were common at the Furnace with chief emphasis on the Philadelphia publications. In 1809 Mathew Brooke subscribed to William Duane's *Aurora*. He received the country edition which was published three times per week at $5 per year. The city editions appeared daily at $9. The *Aurora* was continued for a number of years among Furnace expenses.[63] Many names of newspapers appeared only once; or possibly the same newspaper was intended by similar but not identical names, for example: *Pennsylvania Enquirer, Inquirer and Gazette, United States Gazette, United States Post, United States Saturday Post and Chronicle* and *Saturday Chronicle*. The Furnace had subscribed for many years to the *National Gazette* and continued through several mergers in the 1840 which brought the *Pennsylvania Inquirer* and *United States Gazette* into the same publication. In 1859 this combination became *The Philadelphia Inquirer*.[64] The *New York Ledger* and a newspaper called the *Repertory* of unknown origin also were among the publications read at Hope-

[59] HV 8190501A.
[60] SM 28, p. 84.
[61] HV 8340422A and HV 8341213E.
[62] SM 65, April 2, 1857, n. p.; SM 17, p. 8.
[63] *Brooke Family Papers*, Bill from William Duane, February 1, 1809, and HV 8181020A.
[64] *The Philadelphia Inquirer*, Supplement, September 16, 1962; HV 8350107A; HV 8390103A; HV 8400103B.

well.[65] Special interests and vocational concern accounted for subscriptions to *The Episcopal Recorder, The Temperance Advocate, The Tariffite and Guard* and *The Miners Journal.*

In addition to the ironmaster there were workers who had their own subscriptions to newspapers. Specific mention was made of subscription or postage charges for newspapers bought by John Lloyd, J. B. Wickel, Hashabiah Clemens, John Wamsher, John Richards, Henry Care, Joseph Hart, David Smith and Thomas Care. These included not only a founder and several molders but also a shoemaker, a farm worker and two woodcutters.

For the magazine readers the *Saturday Evening Post* came to the Furnace during a number of years. The price was $2 per year in the 1840's but dropped to $1 in the 1850's.[66] Magazine tie-in sales evidently were not unknown early in the nineteenth century when this offer appeared:

> For $10 sent postage free to C. Alexander, Athenian Building, Franklin Place, Phila., he furnishes 5 Copies of the Weekly Messenger and 5 of the Silk Growers and Farmers Manual and a premium Copy of the Popular Magazine or 1000 Nights Entertainment.[67]

Books were present in the homes of quite a few Hopewell families. On several occasions the Furnace purchased a number of books, but there was no indication whether they were for sale or as managerial reading matter.[68] For several years the Furnace also paid a $5 subscription to "the Select Circulating Library,"[69] and in 1847 bought a map of the United States for $6.[70] Many purchases of books were probably school texts for the use of children in the family, but the house-to-house book salesman made visits to the Village to sell books

[65] SM 12, p. 95; SM 65, February 19, 1859, n. p.
[66] SM 31, pp. 4, 108, 137; SM 65, January 9, 1855, n. p.
[67] *Morris Diary, op. cit.,* p. 67.
[68] SM 21, p. 151; SM 28, pp. 59, 136, 142.
[69] SM 17, p. 31; HV 8350106B.
[70] SM 31, p. 45.

for more general reading. In 1833 seven of the molders paid $2.75 each for copies of *The Family Encyclopaedia*.[71] In the next decade Isaac Eaby sold books to eight village families at prices ranging from 25¢ to $2.[72] The almanac was stocked annually at the Furnace store.

Traveling lecturers brought a different kind of educational opportunity to the people of the Village in the middle decades of the nineteenth century. A handbill announcing a series of lectures by Alex. A. Young was circulated at Hopewell to ascertain interest and promote ticket sales. According to the handbill, the speaker proposed to deliver:

> A course of Lectures, on Ancient and Modern History, Geography, and miscellaneous subjects of Natural Philosophy, etc.
> The main object of these Lectures being, to cultivate the understanding, by rendering the exercises both interesting and instructive, he will make it his principal aim, to deliver his illustrations, in an easy and familiar style. . . .[73]

The weekly series cost $1, or $1.50 for a "gentleman and lady." Children under twelve years of age could hear all addresses for 50¢. Admission for a single lecture was 25¢ for adults and half that amount for children. Twelve Hopewell men signed the handbill to signify an interest; but, when it came to making payment, eight lost their enthusiasm. However, seven adults and three children paid $10.50 for twelve admissions. Benjamin Hill, Negro hostler, paid $2 from his weekly pay of six dollars.[74]

The handbill did not say where the lectures were to be held, but the next January this man gave his talks at Morgantown. The response of one customer was not effusive:

[71] SM 17, p. 47.
[72] SM 31, p. 17.
[73] *Hopewell Papers.* Handbill of Lectures by Alex. A. Young, probably 1836.
[74] *Ibid.*

attended a lecture by Alex. E. Young on ancient history, illustrated by the magic lanthorn. He exhibited Adam and Eve leaving the garden, the building of the Tower of Babel, Moses striking the Rock, the Feast of Balshazaar, the gathering of the Manna, etc. — Lecture poor.[75]

Other lectures in the series considered Egypt, Carthage and "Phrenology with a mapped head."[76] The evident versatility of the speaker, however, did not prevent him from certain indiscretions. The sheriff came looking for him to answer charges that he had used "some hard names as scoundrel, villian, swindler" in reference to General George M. Keim, the "Democratic-Van Buren-Loco Foco-Radical-Hard Money Candidate" for Congress.[77]

Morgantown was also treated, over a period of several years, to lectures on astronomy, phrenology by another expert on "the science of bumps on the craniums" and education. The last was a free address by "a Mr. Warren," who was seeking scholars for an academy which he had recently opened in Strasburg.[78]

An interest in science led James Morris to visit Reading to see "an electro-magnetic machine exhibiting at the public buildings."[79] He also experimented personally in science by spending a day making a camera obscura and "succeeded tolerably well."[80]

The people of Hopewell Village showed an interest in education for their children in their support of subscription schools until the public school act encouraged the building of a school at the Furnace. Even after this a subscription school found support for at least summer terms. In the early Furnace history education was largely for the children of the better-paid employees, but by the 1820's the children of the

[75] *Morris Diary, op. cit.,* p. 3.
[76] *Ibid.,* pp. 5, 10.
[77] *Ibid.,* pp. 12, 44.
[78] *Ibid.,* I, p. 100; II, pp. 26, 116.
[79] *Ibid.,* p. 52.
[80] *Ibid.,* p. 222.

lower-paid workers also were receiving some instruction. Many people of the Village kept informed by reading newspapers, books and magazines and by attending public lectures and exhibits.

19   Religion

ACCORDING TO TRADITION THE IRON COMMUNITIES WERE rough and irreligious. George Whitefield, the celebrated Methodist evangelist, was reported to have been saved from bodily harm at Coventry Forge only by the intervention of Rebecca Grace, wife of ironmaster Robert Grace.[1] Support for a claim of lack of religious zeal at Hopewell Furnace was found on a Berks County map for 1820 which showed no church in Union Township, location of the Furnace.[2] But an examination of Hopewell records showed much religious activity among its people from ironmaster to laborer.

In 1806 young Clement Brooke made a contribution of £7½ for "the Subscription Money in Behalf of the New Church."[3] No identification of the church was given, but it was probably the St. Mary's Episcopal Church at Warwick. In the same year Daniel Buckley wrote to Mathew Brooke that he would like to see him about a business matter to be settled with the firm of Laverty and Jenkins. He suggested:

> I will be at the meeting . . . at Warwick mine holes, about

[1] MacElree, *op. cit.*, pp. 510–511. Doubt about this incident, however, arises from the failure of Whitefield to mention Coventry in his journal.
[2] "Map of Berks County in 1820," Berks County Historical Society, F10HC.
[3] SM 44, November 20, 1806, n. p.

Noon to lay the foundation of the New Church . . . Mr. Laverty will be there and perhaps Mr. Jenkins also.[4]

Clement Brooke later made contributions of money to assist a church in Morgantown and one in Potts Grove.[5] In 1833 he received a letter thanking him for a gift of a stove for a church in Junerville.[6]

The interest of the ironmaster in churches was a pattern followed also by many of the workers. The Bethesda Baptist Church, also known as Lloyd's Church, was located about three-fourths of a mile from the Furnace and was supported by Hopewell Village people. The African Methodist Episcopal Mount Frisby Church was about three miles away. Many villagers also attended St. Mary's Episcopal Church at Warwick, the Evangelical Association Church along the road from the Furnace to Warwick, St. Gabriel's Episcopal Church in Douglasville, St. Thomas' Episcopal Church or the Methodist and Presbyterian Churches in Morgantown, and the Plow Lutheran Church in Robeson Township.

An early interest in regular religious instruction in Berks County was shown in a letter signed by a number of settlers, including William Bird, and sent in 1760 "To the Venerable Society for Propagating the Gospel in Foreign Parts." The Society in London was requested to send a missionary to reside in Reading, and the signers promised to pay him £60 in Pennsylvania money above whatever the Society allowed him. The petitioners regretted that the children were not being instructed in the Episcopal faith and lamented that "various sorts of Sectaries, and which is still worse the Roman Cathalic priests are making converts among us."[7]

The absence of a church at the Furnace compound did not mean that religious services were not held there. The

---

[4] HV 8060404.
[5] SM 12, p. 60; *Cash Book* for 1828–1830, August 13, 1829, n. p.
[6] HV 8331119.
[7] Quoted in William DuHamel, "Historical Sketch of Willam Bird, Founder of Birdsboro, Pa." (Unpublished typescript, 1928), Hopewell Village Library.

Reverend Mister Levi Bull, who served the St. Mary's Church for about half of the nineteenth century, recorded in his diaries a number of times that he had preached at Hopewell. He mentioned services in the private homes of the Buckleys, Bensons and Wynns and at the "Union S. H.," which indicated meetings were held in the East Nantmeal schoolhouse. In the period from 1838 to 1847 he listed services at Hopewell with regularity in the winter months during some of these years. He seemed to think that the Psalms were the most valuable sources of texts for sermons to the Furnace-area residents. He also held services at the Hopewell Mineholes.[8]

St. Gabriel's Episcopal Church at Douglasville was the earliest regular center for the worship of Furnace people. The building had been used first by a Swedish Lutheran congregation, but it became Episcopal in 1753.[9] William Bird's marriage to Brigitte Hulings was published there in 1735, and also his widow's remarriage to John Patton in 1762.[10] William was one of the first two trustees chosen for the St. Gabriel's congregation, and his son Mark served several terms as vestryman in the 1760's.[11] Maria Church, who became Mrs. Clement Brooke, was confirmed in this church two years before her marriage in 1808.[12] Mathew Brooke took Elizabeth Barde as his bride there some five years before he received the sacrament of adult baptism in 1815.[13]

Many other Hopewell families were among the communicants and officers of St. Gabriel's Church in the nineteenth century. Prominent among them were Umstead, Kirlin, Jones, Sands, Trago, Millard, Yocom, Bannan, McKinty, Donehower, Bunn, Wamsher, Dehaven, Chestnutwood, Pierce and Evans. The Reverend Mister Levi Bull served as rector of this church, as well as St. Mary's and St. Thomas', until about

[8] *Levi Bull Diaries, passim* pages, Chester County Historical Society.
[9] Montgomery, *History of Berks County, op. cit.,* p. 949.
[10] *St. Gabriel's Church Records,* Berks County Historical Society, pp. 65, 70.
[11] *Ibid.,* pp. 62, 103.
[12] *Ibid.,* p. 113.
[13] *Ibid.,* pp. 275, 343.

1830 when "Rev. Mentzer" began his pastorate at Douglasville.[14]

Levi Bull was a celebrated minister who made Warwick the center of his activities for more than fifty years. He covered a large parish and was frequently invited to preach at more distant churches. He was the son of Colonel Thomas Bull of Revolutionary War fame and a celebrated ironmaster.[15] Levi was a businessman as well as preacher; he must have needed the additional income to support his household of 19 persons in 1830.[16] At St. Mary's many Hopewell families were communicants: Ubel, Goheen, Chestnutwood, Painter, Richards, Mervine, Danahower, Yocum, Templin, Kaler, Filman, Pawling, Millard, Thomas, Bingaman, Hare, Dampman, Mengel, Lloyd, Mee, Care, Sheeler, Landis, Palsgrove, Wamsher, Dehaven, Hartenstine, Gilmore, Kephart and North were among them. Both the Mathew and Clement Brookes families were members there.[17] Clement Brooke was baptized in 1813 as were his six children over the years from 1809 to 1825.[18]

In 1843 St. Mary's church was closed in order that a new building could be erected on the same site. During the construction Mr. Bull served full time at Morgantown at a salary of $200 per year. Since this was an increase over the amount St. Thomas' had been paying, the congregation found it necessary to raise the pew rents by 40 per cent to 50 per cent.[19] The cornerstone of the new Warwick church was laid before a large crowd on June 14, 1843; and the building was consecrated the following December 22.[20]

The St. Thomas' Episcopal Church was opened at Morgantown in 1825. Support for the religious program was obtained

[14] *Ibid.*, pp. 6, 397.
[15] *Reading Eagle*, February 18, 1917.
[16] *Census of 1830*, Chester County, East Nantmeal Township, p. 198 ff.
[17] *St. Mary's Episcopal Church Records*, Berks County Historical Society.
[18] *Ibid.*, pp. 167–179.
[19] *Morris Diary, op. cit.*, II, p. 30.
[20] *Ibid.*, pp. 59–60.

Bethesda Baptist Church and Churchyard

by renting the pews at annual fees ranging from $3 to $8. Some pews were shared by two families who divided the expenses. Hopewell names among the first pew renters were Henry Mengel, Robert Laverty, Jacob Kurtz, Daniel Ubil and Edward Goheen. All paid $6 rental except Merchant Laverty who paid a dollar more.[21] Women were much more numerous than men in the early work of this church. The membership roll for 1828 included 85 women, 41 men and 5 names which could not be identified by sex.[22]

The Plow Lutheran Church in Robeson Township was founded in 1810 when a lottery was held to raise money to build a church and school. Five thousand tickets were sold

[21] *St. Thomas Episcopal Church Records*, Berks County Historical Society, p. 114.
[22] *Ibid.*, p. 120.

at $3 each. Everyone with a ticket was to receive a prize
ranging from a top of $600 to a low of $2. There were 4,723
of the latter amount. Twenty per cent was deducted from
each prize for the church-school fund. Many ticket-holders
did not draw their prizes but gave the entire amount to the
church. Hopewell names among the communicants at Plow
Church included : Segfred, Fries, Ammon, Westley, Wirt,
Donahauer, Wamsher, Mengel, Ehrgood, Kramp, Roads,
Handwart, Handwork, Hartenstine, Hottenstein and Pals-
grof.[23]

The church most closely identified with the Furnace was
the Bethesda Baptist Church, located in Chester County but
less than a mile from the Big House. Tradition claims this
area as a place of worship as early as 1780, and on a collar-
beam in the attic of the present building someone wrote with
charcoal, "Built 1782 By T. Lloyd." In 1962 the earliest
readable date on a tombstone in the cemetery was May 10,
1807, but several crude stones were undated and could have
been earlier. The will of Thomas Lloyd, dated July 27, 1819,
contained this provision :

> . . . I do . . . convey all that certain lot of three quarters
> of an acre of land whereon the meeting house and grave yards
> stands on my land for the use it was intended.[24]

The Lloyd family identified this lot as the one on which the
Bethesda Church was located. Transfer of title to the land
appears not to have been made, however, as this ground
was mentioned in several subsequent transfers of the Lloyd
titles. It was always stated that this lot was to be reserved
for church use.[25]

From the evidence presented above it is apparent that a
building which had been used for worship services stood at

<hr>

[23] History of Plow Church, Robeson Township, Berks County, Pennsylvania (unpublished typescript, 1874), Berks County Historical Society.
[24] *Hopewell Papers,* Will of Thomas Lloyd, H–18 General.
[25] Russell A. Apple, "Bethesda Baptist Church Lot of ¾ Acre" (unpublished typescript, 1956), Hopewell Village Library.

that place prior to 1819. But the formal organization of the Baptist congregation took place on December 8, 1827. Simeon Seigfried, Senior, assisted with the organization and served for some years as the pastor.[26] Another early minister was Andrew Collins who also acted as schoolmaster for Hopewell children and taught classes at the church.[27] The 1827 founding date was confirmed by a service held in the church on December 8, 1877, to mark the fiftieth anniversary of the congregation.[28] Baptisms were held in the nearby stream, which gave it the name Baptizing Creek.[29]

In 1848 when a fund was solicited by David Lloyd to do some work at the graveyard, $22 was collected from Hopewell families.[30] A charter of incorporation was issued to the Bethesda Baptist Church on August 20, 1888, with the name of H. A. Long appearing as one of the ten petitioners.[31] As of 1963 services are still being held in this church with The Reverend Mister J. W. Sandiford as the minister. Like at least one of his predecessors he is a schoolteacher.

Support for services at the Bethesda Church was by pledges from its members rather than the more aristocratic pew rental. In 1830 the list of subscribers included 32 names, almost all of them Hopewell employees:

Thomas Lloyd	$ 8.00	William Hartman	$ 3.00
David High	8.00	Thomas S. Sharp	4.00
Nathaniel Sands	6.00	George Painter	2.00
George Lloyd	3.00	David High	1.00
David Lloyd	3.00	John Sheeler	3.00
Martin Richards	2.00	Susana Beavens	1.50
David Smith	2.50	Jonah John	2.00
Levi Bolls	2.00	John Hartenstine	1.00
David Smith	2.50	Samuel Richards	1.00
Sarah Matthias	2.00	Jacob Hartenstine	1.00

[26] *Daily Local News,* West Chester, Pennsylvania, August 24, 1929.
[27] *Bethesda Minute Book, op. cit.,* p. 6.
[28] *Ibid.*
[29] H. A. Long Interview, August 13, 1936.
[30] SM 31, pp. 72, 77, 81.
[31] *Bethesda Minute Book, op. cit.*

John Sands	2.00	John Richards	1.00
E. R. Sands	2.00	Henry Hartenstine	1.00
Samuel Hill	2.00	Andrew Keene	1.00
Samuel Lloyd	3.00	Frederick Miers	1.00
Isaac Kaplin	3.00	Lewis Evans	2.00
Nathaniel Kirby	3.00	Margaret Cook	1.00[32]

Activity at the church fluctuated, probably with the vigor of the pastors. In some years there were a number of accessions and then long periods when there were none.[33] The arrival of John J. Eberle as pastor in 1864 began a period of cleansing of the church roll and a check on the conduct of members. A committee of five men was appointed to call on "Delinquent Members," and 22 persons were named as worthy of the attention of the committee. The checkers reported back that two of those listed had joined another church. The remainder wanted to be continued on the Bethesda roll, but Henry Hartenstine "gave a very poor excuse for himself."[34]

At the same time a committee consisting of Sisters Parlaman and Smith was directed to call upon Sister Hannah Pearson and instruct her to be present at the next church meeting where her case would be considered. On February 4, 1865, the clerk recorded that "Sister H. Pearson Case was to lie over till the next meeting." But the wayward member never was able to answer whatever charges were made against her. Death came before trial.[35]

According to the minutes, Clerk Edward Parlaman resigned in 1865 and asked for his church letter:

> On account of Misconduct in the Church on the part of some evil disposed persons, he believing it his duty with others to prosecute the offenders, there being a difference of opinion in regards to it, in not taking legal process — he felt it his duty to offer his resignation and ask for his Letter. . . .

[32] *Brooke Family Papers,* List of subscribers to support Baptist Services at Bethesda Meeting House, January 11, 1830.
[33] *Bethesda Minute Book, op. cit.*
[34] *Ibid.,* December 10 and 31, 1864.
[35] *Ibid.*

He was persuaded to remain with the promise that "hereafter any violation of good order in the Church should be dealt with According to Law."[36]

This high resolve prompted action against additional members in the following year when the records stated :

> Moved . . . that John H. Miller be Excluded from the Church after hearing testamony of Several witteness and considerable talk he was Excluded for Neglecting the Church and drunkeness. Brother Eberle was appointed a committee to wait on John Houck, Hannah Houck his wife, Julia Keims to Say to them that the church has brought a charge against them of profanity and unless they doe appear at Church and give an Account of themselves they will be excluded.

These cases ended with the report that the accused persons had joined another church.[37]

Religion entered the Hopewell Furnace account books most frequently when the clerk made a payment of a pledge or pew rent for one of the employees. Many such payments were made to St. Mary's Church. Clement Brooke paid $5.33 in each of several years.[38] Jacob Mock had a better seat at an annual rent of $6,[39] but Henry Care could have listened to the same sermons from his $1.10 seat.[40] James Morris gave $5 for a pew which he shared with Samuel Jones in the Morgantown church.[41]

At a fashionable church in the city the cost of pew rental ran considerably higher. The estate of Charles M. Clingan in 1875 paid $51 for six months rent on "Pew Number 45" at the Church of the Holy Trinity in Philadelphia.[42] However, pew rights in this church were valuable assets. In the appraisement of the Clingan estate the pew right was valued at $900;

[36] *Ibid.*, February 4, 1865.
[37] *Ibid.*, March 18, 1866.
[38] SM 12, p. 131; SM 17, p. 17.
[39] SM 31, p. 9.
[40] SM 28, p. 98.
[41] *Morris Diary, op. cit.*, p. 12.
[42] HV 8750401B.

and, proving that this was not assessed too high, it sold soon afterwards for $1200.[43]

Men were expected to dress properly when they attended church services in the first half of the nineteenth century. But sometimes meteorological conditions dictated that less attention be paid to decorum than to comfort. In the intense heat of summer, coats and stocks were discarded.[44]

Judging from this Hopewell letter, the ministers' sermons had their critics:

> . . . this morning we attended church—the Rev gave us one of his *declamatory* sermons—addressed particularly to Parents—his style of preaching does not suit me—tho it may be the best adapted for the majority of his audience—there's nothing soothing or composing in his manner or language— mildness and persuasion forms the smallest part of his discourse. . . .[45]

Funerals were social occasions for the gathering of many people. James Morris noted that:

> The burial of Christian Hertzler at 10 A.M. was very numerously attended.
>
> As usual, with the Germans especially, a general and pressing invitation was given out for *all* to stay and dine. The number that set down to dinner is differently estimated at from 150 to 200.
>
> The preparations for this meal had been immense. Two whole quarters of beef had been provided, some 30 odd fowls and other things in proportion.[46]

Funeral plans were sometimes subject to change because of weather conditions. Henry A. Muhlenberg of Reading died on August 11, 1844, while he was campaigning for governor of Pennsylvania. The funeral was set for August 14, but "owing to Mr. Muhlenberg's retaining his freshness of appear-

---

[43] HV 8750508; HV 8751207.
[44] *Morris Diary, op. cit.*, p. 157.
[45] *Hopewell Papers, Stokes Collection*, Anna [no last name given] to Ann T. Brooke, February 16. No year given but probably 1835.
[46] *Morris Diary, op. cit.*, p. 229.

ance, the family on yesterday postponed his burial until today."[47]

In addition to the regular church services on Sundays, the people of Hopewell Village also attended prayer meetings, camp meetings and "protracted meetings." Prayer meetings were held either on weekdays or Sundays and were not always in the church.[48] Camp meetings were a popular summer activity and attracted a varied gathering of Furnace people. Clement Brooke attended in 1820 and May Hoyle, a maid, in 1849.[49] Miners, molders, founders, blacksmiths, keepers, teamsters and ordinary laborers drew cash in amounts from 22¢ to $10 to take with them when they went to the camp meeting.[50]

James Morris reported a Baptist protracted meeting in his diary:

August 9, 1844 Friday
This afternoon the Baptists commenced holding a protracted meeting out at the Rock School House near Jones' Mine holes. They have prepared a stand and seats and a large congregation. Very few attended this afternoon. . . .

August 11, 1844 Sunday
A large congregation assembled in the woods. Revd. Mr. Nichols preached. . . .

August 18, 1844 Sunday
The Baptist meeting is still going on in Col. Jacob's woods. There were 5 persons baptized in the pool at the mine holes. A great number of people were present—some 2000 perhaps. . . .

August 25, 1844 Sunday
The Baptists immersed 6 or 7 men and women at the mine holes this forenoon. . . .

September 1, 1844 Sunday
The Baptists are still holding their protracted meeting in the woods by day and in the neighboring houses by night. . . .

[47] *Ibid.*, II, p. 148. August 15, 1844.
[48] *Ibid.*, II, p. 8.
[49] SM 10, p. 61; SM 31, August 6–16, 1849, n. p.
[50] Examples are SM 31, p. 153; SM 10, p. 39.

Revd. Mr. Bull [Episcopalian] took occasion this afternoon to preach a sermon on Baptism, in which he advocated infant baptism and sprinkling. . . .

September 4, 1844 Wednesday

The Baptists, whose meeting still continues, baptized nine persons this afternoon at Jones' Mine holes. They likewise organized a Society and have made some arrangements towards building a Church on land of David Potts, who has given them a free grant of ¾ of an acre, near the mine holes. The Society has 23 names on its lists.[51]

The Episcopalians of the Village area held their Associations and the Methodists their Quarterly Meetings "to make new converts" and "to rally the spirits of the old ones." Ministers combined their efforts, and people attended from distant towns at these fall or winter gatherings which lasted ten days to two weeks.[52]

Sunday School picnics were the high points of summer religious activity. July 3, 1841, was an especially lively day in and around Morgantown. According to one observer :

A celebration of the various Presbyterian and Episcopal Sunday Schools within some miles around takes place today at Waynesburg. The Episcopal S. School of this place [Morgantown] attends there. The Methodist Schools of the Circuit meet also today at Springfield for the same purpose.

From 8 to 10 o'clock A.M. the town was quite thronged with neatly dressed children with their teachers. A procession of the Episcopal School was got up. Several banners were aloft by the children bearing appropriate mottoes. A hymn was sung and the young folks with their teachers and parents shortly after moved off in wagons, dearborns, carriages, etc. to the number of about sixty.

The Methodist S. School got up no procession, being few in numbers, but moved off towards Springfield in a two horse wagon, dearborn, etc. Cakes in profusion were carried along with each party.[53]

[51] *Morris Diary, op. cit.,* II. Items taken from dates given.
[52] *Morris Diary, op. cit.,* pp. 240, 241, 248, 249; *Brooke Family Papers,* Ann to George W, September 3, 1831.
[53] *Morris Diary, op. cit.,* p. 155.

The Methodists must have picked up considerable strength in the next two years, for in 1843 they were reported to have had more than 2,000 in attendance at their Sunday School "Celebration" at the foot of Welsh Mountain.[54] The Episcopalian children carried a banner that year which read, "Morgantown Sunday School," on one side and on the other, "We have seen thy star and have come to worship thee." Cakes for the occasion consumed 150 pounds of flour. It was a successful affair except "that a couple of drunken men knocked up a fight towards evening."[55]

Religious reading matter at the furnace included family Bibles and regular issues of the *Episcopal Recorder*. Thomas Lloyd paid $5.00 for a Bible in 1819,[56] and a number of families had Bibles costing from $2.50 to $3.00 each.[57] Clement Brooke possessed a "Quarto Bible No. 4" for which he paid $2.25 in 1843.[58] Thomas Lloyd and John Painter bought testaments at 30¢ and 37½¢ each.[59]

The religious ferment in the nation in the 1840's brought some agitation to the people of Hopewell Village. A Mormon preacher was locked out of the Morgantown schoolhouse when he proposed preaching there in 1842. A "considerable congregation" had come to hear him.[60] A few months later two itinerant ministers of the Church of God were permitted to use the schoolhouse to proclaim the necessity of immersion to salvation and the damnation of all Mormons.[61] The Methodists were greatly alarmed in 1843 by a report that the Roman Catholics were collecting arms to massacre Protestants. This was a time when anti-Catholic feeling was strong in Philadelphia and elsewhere in the East.[62]

[54] *Ibid.*, II, p. 58.
[55] *Ibid.*, II, pp. 65, 66.
[56] SM 10, p. 38.
[57] SM 31, pp. 10, 12, 20.
[58] HV 8430503C.
[59] SM 6, p. 226; *Cash Book* for 1828–1830, March 3, 1830, n. p.
[60] *Morris Diary, op. cit.*, p. 181.
[61] *Ibid.*, p. 208.
[62] *Ibid.*, II, p. 26.

William Miller's Adventist movement won some Village people to watch for the end of the world. The Millerite newspaper, *Midnight Cry,* was read in the area; but interest declined after the foretold date passed without heavenly visitation.[63]

Some people in the Hopewell area still held a belief in witchcraft as late as the middle of the nineteenth century. Educated people, however, did not believe or were "ashamed to say so" if they did. Witchcraft was credited with being the cause of the following series of events in 1842 :

> The dinner pot of a family which had been used a couple of days before, was found to contain three small balls of silvery lustre. These balls were a token of witchcraft, especially as some of the family had been very restless at night and unable to sleep. It was plain that they were bewitched, so the balls were taken and according to the regular method in such cases, were fired from a gun into a tree—a white oak and shortly after a woman in the immediate neighborhood complained sadly of a sore leg. The case was now plainer than ever. It was undoubtedly one of witchcraft and the woman with the sore leg was the witch that had bewitched the family and that was shot by the silver bullets. So the witches are not all dead yet.[64]

David Mast, Junior, shocked the community in 1839 by hauling his grain from the fields on Sunday. Farmers did not work in the fields on the Lord's Day.[65] But, of course, everyone was aware that furnace workers and colliers kept their fires burning seven days a week.

Religious holidays were observed or ignored according to the strength of traditions, superstitions clinging to the day or nationalities. The Germans, in general, were holding onto the old traditions more firmly than others; and they were most likely to associate weather conditions with certain days. The

---

[63] *Ibid.,* II, pp. 1, 11. This was in 1843 and 1844.
[64] *Ibid.,* p. 225. Morris was relating this with tongue in cheek. He was not a believer.
[65] *Ibid.,* p. 82.

new year was welcomed by "watch meetings" in most
churches.[66] Sunshine on Candlemas Day caused the ground-
hog to see its shadow and was believed to frighten it into
returning to its burrow for forty days more of cold weather.[67]
Whitsun Monday was a day for Amish visiting dressed in
their best clothes, but rain on Whit Sunday meant seven wet
Sundays in succession.[68] To the Germans, also, July second was
the day "Mary goes over the mountain;" and whatever
weather prevailed on that day would continue for the next
six weeks.[69] The Irish took time from work to celebrate "Sent
Pattrick Day" and honor their homeland.[70] By the 1830's few
except the Amish considered Good Friday a holy day, but
some "Germans and Catholics observed Easter Monday."[71]
Many farm children hid eggs for a month or more before
Easter and brought them to the house on Good Friday to be
boiled and colored.[72]

Thanksgiving Day received political as well as religious
sanction on December 21, 1843, when Governor David R.
Porter proclaimed its observance for Pennsylvania. Most of
the people of the Hopewell community seemed uncertain
about the proper commemoration of the new holiday. Church
services were held with few worshipers attending. Both of the
stores in Morgantown were officially closed for the day but
sold goods to people who came and asked at the door.[73]

Christmas was the most generally observed of the religious
days; but, it was said, "Some few keep it strict as a *holy* day
while with the vast majority it is only kept for pleasure, visiting feasting, etc."[74] Religious service, held on Christmas and
sometimes the day after, was like the Sabbath service but dealt

[66] *Ibid.*, II, p. 90.
[67] *Ibid.*, p. 97.
[68] *Ibid.*, pp. 202, 203.
[69] *Ibid.*, p. 81.
[70] *Changewater Account Books, op. cit.*, II, p. 4.
[71] *Morris Diary, op. cit.*, pp. 11, 12, 104.
[72] *Lewis Rishards Scrapbook, op. cit.*, Vol. D., p. 340.
[73] *Morris Diary, op. cit.*, II, p. 88.
[74] *Ibid.*, p. 250.

with the birth of Christ. Christmas night was spent quietly at home, and the next day was used for visiting among the country people.

"Belsnickling" was practiced in Berks County, with people dressing in grotesque uniforms and frightful masks to visit the homes. They carried switches to hit the children who stooped to pick up nuts dropped on the floor.

Children received as gifts molasses and sugar cakes molded into horses, riders, hearts, birds and other shapes. Few gifts were given, and stores were seldom decorated or stocked with special Christmas goods. A large family did not spend more than $2 for Christmas. But still a belief in Saint Nicholas or Santa Claus persisted among the children.[75] Sales at the Hopewell store did not show any large increase in the weeks before Christmas except for some luxury foods such as sugar, tea, coffee, oysters and cranberries.

Irreligious persons, doubtless, were numbered among the people of Hopewell Village; but religion played an important part in the lives of many families in the community. Perhaps the religious interest of the ironmasters set the pattern for the community.

[75] *Lewis Richards Scrapbook, op. cit.*, Vol. 9, p. 245. This description of Christmas was for about 1835 and came from the recollections of an old minister after fifty years.

20 Amusements and Recreation

"SOCIAL LIFE [AT THE FURNACES] CONSISTED OF SUCH AFFAIRS as corn huskings, barn dances, quilting and apple-butter bees and . . . visits to fairs."[1] Thus did one writer describe the amusements and recreation of the people of the iron plantations. This picture of rural, and essentially frontier, social life was similarly presented in several other articles on the iron furnaces.[2] Hopewell Village had all of the activities named above, but the lives of the workers and their families were enriched with a much greater variety of amusements. And the ironmasters' families drew upon the resources of the outside world for a more sophisticated social fare. Philadelphia, New York and even more distant places were available to amuse or divert those who could afford to travel.

Organized sports played little part in the lives of the children of the village, although they may have been familiar with town ball, predecessor of baseball. Small children found much to attract their attention in the working world of the furnace community. They liked to play on the high cinder piles[3] and found the casting house fascinating. When the molders caught

[1] Victoria Lyles, "Forges and Furnaces of York County," *Papers of the Historical Society of York County*, New Series, No. 4, n. d.
[2] Gemmell, *op. cit.*, p. 88; Handwork, *op. cit.*, p. 125.
[3] Sally Boone Interview, March 22, 1941.

a child, they put him in the tub of water used to cool the tools after the furnace was tapped—to the huge delight of everyone concerned.[4] In warm weather the waters of French Creek and the Furnace pond were available for swimming or bathing.[5] Spelling bees filled a need for competition in the schools. Sometimes teams from one school competed against the representatives of a neighboring school.[6]

"Frolicking" was a common amusement for the Furnace men. Frequently these were combinations of work and amusement as when Joseph Ogal entertained at a "Chopping Frolick" during the winter of 1803.[7] Frolics sometimes lasted for days. John Cummings at Martha Furnace, beginning one on July 31, 1808, did not return to the furnace until August 5; and even then he was "not yet able to work."[8] The frolics usually lasted as long as the whiskey held out, for it was the practice to treat all who came to work.[9] But some change in this custom was apparently taking place in the 1840's when James Morris reported :

> John Gillespie was engaged with a number of hands this afternoon, in raising "old Johnny's House" from one story to two, by means of logs. No liquor—and as a consequence very little noise, no drunkenness and no wounds or accidents. Twenty years ago—aye even ten—and such a thing as a "raising" without liquor, would have been a perfect anomaly. I even doubt whether *any* persons would have touched a timber. Now *very few* indeed expect or think of any drink being offered on such occasions.[10]

Apparently many furnace men were gamblers, for instances of card-playing were mentioned throughout the nineteenth century. Matthew Davis, Hopewell manager, purchased cards

---

[4] *Ibid.*, February 25, 1941.
[5] *Brooke Family Letters,* Ann Brooke to George W. Brooke, May 1833.
[6] *Reading Eagle,* February 4, 1917.
[7] SM 1, p. 23.
[8] *Martha Furnace Diary, op. cit.,* see dates mentioned.
[9] *Changewater Account Books, op. cit.,* III, pp. 14, 19, 35.
[10] *Morris Diary, op. cit.,* II, p. 105.

in 1803.[11] Near the end of the century the workmen gathered to play poker in the evening, at Boone's Store—"Hopewell's den of iniquity."[12] At neighboring Changewater Furnace Henry Conner was fined one half day's pay for "playing cards with Jane Stratten." The clerk failed to note whether the objection was to the cards, to Miss Stratten's company, or to playing during working hours.[13] The latter reason was probably the correct one, because there were other references to gambling with no penalty. Quarts of whiskey were often the forfeit of the loser at card games, "drawing cuts" or "tossing."[14] A few Furnace employees bet on horse races.[15]

A more respectable form of gambling was the purchase of lottery tickets, the sale of which was a recognized means of raising money for a church, a school or a public work. The Hopewell record books contained many references to accounts debited for the amount of a lottery ticket, especially in the period from 1825 to 1827. Clement Brooke invested $63.50 in a lottery in 1826 which also was patronized by Clerk James Benson, Founder Thomas Care and two molders.[16] Tickets in this same lottery were shared by some who could not afford a whole ticket or who did not want to risk so much. Seven men were each charged $1 for one-fourth of a ticket.[17] Henry Care purchased one and sold one-third of it to Joseph McKewen and the same to John Care.[18]

Since Furnace people were outdoor folk, it was natural that much of their amusement came from outdoor activities. In the winter skating and sleighing were popular sports. Matthew Davis hired "Kerby's four horse slay" in January 1804 and took all of the hands for a ride.[19] But many individuals owned

---

[11] SM 2, p. 152.
[12] Reginald and Emlen Smith Interview, August 4, 1940.
[13] *Changewater Furnace Account Books, op. cit.,* II, p. 39.
[14] *Ibid.,* pp. 23, 24, 33.
[15] *Ibid.,* pp. 4, 60.
[16] SM 12, p. 107.
[17] *Ibid.,* p. 122.
[18] SM 59, p. 22.
[19] SM 2, p. 297.

one- or two-horse sleighs; so, when snow was on the roads, there was "a perpetual jingle of bells all day."[20] Not everyone, however, was enthusiastic about the sport. A few disliked the resulting "blue noses and cold fingers,"[21] and Sarah Brooke pitied the horses which, she said, were "completely worn down" from pulling the sleighs.[22]

Men and boys of the Village enjoyed hunting and fishing. Trout were taken from the streams with a seine, and eels were found in the pool under the Warwick Road bridge.[23] When mill ponds were drained, people gathered to catch the fish stranded in the low water.[24] Many Furnace men owned guns for hunting foxes, rabbits, "pheasants," partridges, wild geese and deer. But hunting was curtailed somewhat in 1844 when the Pennsylvania General Assembly adopted a law prohibiting the shooting of "pheasants" from January 1 to August 1.[25]

A flock of wild geese landed on the mill pond at Morgantown on April 4, 1838; and an army of hunters surrounded the pond. The slaughter continued until dark and was resumed at daylight the next morning. Not one member of that flock escaped. One observer remarked, "They were strangers and the sportsmen took 'em in. They'll learn better next time they come along here. . . ."[26]

Hunting dogs were purchased by the Furnace and by the ironmasters; for example, Charles Clingan paid $10 "for a pup" in 1863.[27] Possibly this animal was a foxhound, for fox

[20] *Morris Diary, op. cit.,* p. 42.

[21] *Ibid.,* p. 43.

[22] *Brooke Family Letters,* Sarah Brooke to Edward Brooke, January 14, 1835.

[23] Reginald Smith Interview, August 24, 1941; David Boone Interview, March 22, 1941.

[24] *Morris Diary, op. cit.,* p. 24.

[25] *Ibid.,* II, p. 177. Morris probably meant grouse when he used the word pheasant.

[26] *Ibid.,* p. 49. Morris was a lover of wild life and something of an amateur naturalist.

[27] SM 69, p. 9; *Kemper Manuscripts,* C. M. Clingan Pocket Note Book, *op. cit.,* n. p.

hunting was popular in the village in the nineteenth century. Even as late as the 1880's John Care was noted for possessing the best foxhounds in the area.[28] James Morris described a fox hunt in 1843 :

> The letting of a "bag fox" . . . was made the occasion of a great gathering of men, horses and hounds, much to the profit of the landlord at whose tavern the fox was let off. Then followed the confusion of starting—the neighing of horses, the yelping of hounds, the cheering of hunters and then the pell mell hurry of the chase—the hounds are on the track and give "mouth"—horsemen hurry off by the roads while numerous footmen pursue the route the fox has taken.[29]

The wooded hillsides provided an opportunity to combine pleasure and profit in the gathering of wild fruits. Native black mulberries came into season about the middle of June. Early the next month the red sour cherries, esteemed for pies, attracted "parties of from two up to a half dozen, going out, armed with baskets, kettles, buckets, etc."[30] Later in July, blackberries enticed those pickers who were convinced the fruit was worth the annoyance from the bite of ticks.[31] Chestnuts drew the Furnace people into the woods in the autumn when the prickly burs opened to drop their fruit.[32]

For those who could afford a trip to the shore Cape May, New Jersey was a popular summer resort. A memorandum found among the Hopewell Papers, in Clement Brooke's handwriting, listed these expenses :

At Cape May	$82.50
Passage	36.00
Stage Fair and expenses	3.00
Porters at different times	1.50
Expenses at Cape for wriding, etc.	6.00[33]

[28] John Henry Interview, January 23, 1941.
[29] *Morris Diary, op. cit.,* II, p. 85.
[30] *Ibid.,* II, pp. 51, 133.
[31] *Ibid.,* p. 218.
[32] *Brooke Family Letters,* Ann to Edward, October 15, 1828.
[33] *Hopewell Papers,* uncatalogued and undated but apparently the 1830's.

Elizabeth Brooke received an invitation to join a group of relatives going to Cape May in July, 1845. She was advised to bring a riding habit, as "a ride upon the Beach with an agreeable Companion is esteemed Bliss by the young ladies."[34]

Quilting bees for the women were sometimes combined with harvesting or "raisings" for the men, and the mixed parties produced "great hilarity."[35] Among the Hopewell Village people another very popular heterosexual affair was the "apple-butter boiling."[36] A kind of social calendar was established in the autumn, because several boilings were scheduled each week over a period of six or eight weeks. The young men came to "see home" the girls after the kettles were emptied, and the elders enjoyed a chance to visit and gossip.

Three to 5 barrels of cider were used with 12 to 15 bushels of apples pared and sliced into "schnitz." Cooking was done over an outdoor fire or in a summer kitchen. The container—often several were used—was a huge copper kettle, owned by the family or rented at 25¢ per day.

Activity began for the host family at about 3.00 A. M., and the finished butter was in crocks by midnight. The cider was boiled for an hour before dawn when the first pailful of 'schnitz" was added. From this time on the stirring with a long-handled wooden paddle was never stopped for fear that the butter would burn on the bottom of the kettle and spoil the flavor—possibly, also, ruin the kettle. As the volume of liquid in the kettle was reduced by evaporation, more cider, more 'schnitz," sugar and spices were added.

Father and mother may have taken a nap during the morning when the larger children were on hand to keep the stirring going. Perhaps a few neighbors dropped in during the day for a glass of cider. There was never a limit to the amount of cider they could have, but in return for the hospitality they would customarily stir for fifteen or twenty minutes.

[34] *Hopewell Papers, Elizabeth Brooke Letters,* M. G. B. to Elizabeth Brooke, July 7, 1845. Hopewell Village Library.
[35] *Martha Furnace Diary, op. cit.,* July 6, 1811, n. p.
[36] For examples see SM 35, pp. 134, 135, 136.

The real fun began about six o'clock in the evening when the neighbors started to arrive. They came and went until midnight, with the largest influx between eight and nine o'clock. No one was specifically invited; everyone was welcome. Each guest was expected to stir the apple butter for a few minutes. If a young man and a young lady grasped the wooden handle together, it was a public announcement of their engagement; so a close watch was kept on that handle.

Outdoor games were played during the evening, but all activity ceased when the time came to unhook the kettles. The contents were cooled a little and then dipped into crocks. Everyone tested the taste quality by scraping a little from the kettle with his fingers. Sometimes the young people ended with their faces well smeared with apple butter. The whole crowd left together with the young men escorting the young ladies along the dark roads and paths through the woods.[37]

A few holidays or special days provided amusement for the Hopewell community. In the early part of the nineteenth century New Year's Eve was the occasion for calls upon the scattered homes by groups of the young men. James Morris remembered the custom and left this description:

> . . . a troop of 30, 40 or even 50 jovial young fellows would join in a band, equipped with powder, wadding and shooting irons and after having appointed a captain to guide and direct them and a musician to blow music out of a conch shell or on some particular occasions, scrape it out of an old Cremona—the line of march would be taken up for the nearest farm house, where a salute would be given, executed with a grand running fire precision, followed by a most hearty "wish you a happy New Year" from the throats and open mouths of the grand troupe. . . .
>
> After all this the party is invited into the house where all manner of good cheer is set before them. . . . Full justice having been rendered to the collation, . . . the party takes its leave, to make another call at the next neighbors where the same [procedure] is repeated, to be again renewed until every

[37] This account was based upon *Lewis Richards Scrapbooks, op. cit.,* Vol. H, p. 93.

farm house shall have received a call and greeting, thus often-times consuming the whole night. . . .[38]

This custom had about died out by 1843 when Morris was writing. One reason was that careless shooting by revelers who had enjoyed too many "collations" had resulted in the wounding and even death of several men.[39] On New Year's Day the children received cakes, sweetmeats and toys as presents.[40]

The day to express patriotism was July 4. One village resident observed :

> This day as usual will be celebrated by all sorts of societies —military, political, temperance, literary, benevolent and Sunday School—in all sorts of ways—too many in a way to beget drunken men and drunken habits and too many in a manner to beget evil feelings and animosities. Nevertheless, it is a good thing to celebrate, in a becoming way the Declaration of our Independence. . . .[41]

But Independence Day in Philadelphia was not very enjoyable for Polly Grubb in 1833 when she was attending school there. She wrote :

> The 4th of July passed a little duller than any I ever remember spending, almost all the gentlemen had gone to public dinners, and the ladies were too much occupied with their own concerns to attend to my amusement : we had no precession, but a few companies were out; it is said there was a grand music at the Adelphi in 5 street, but I did not hear it. . . .[42]

October 31 was a night for mischief for the boys of the Hopewell area. One report stated :

[38] *Morris Diary, op. cit.,* p. 252.
[39] *Ibid.,* II, p. 181.
[40] *Ibid.,* p. 176.
[41] *Ibid.,* p. 211.
[42] *Hopewell Papers, Stokes Collection,* Polly Grubb to Ann F. Brooke, July 6, 1833.

. . . it was . . . the rule on this night [for] our boys to steal folks cabbage and then thump their doors with it, while children of larger growth would remove and change gates —fence up roads—post up plows and harrows . . . on stacks, etc.[43]

Dances were held at the Big House on Christmas and New Year's Day, and the entire Village was invited. Of course some men had to work at the furnace on these days, but perhaps they came to the party after their tour was over. Lincoln Palsgrove claimed to have been the best jig dancer at Hopewell in his youth. He also recalled that his mother "used to dance on a pewter plate." A Negro shoemaker and a Negro woodcutter played their fiddles for the dances.[44] Henry F. Care may have been another fiddler for these occasions; for in 1929 he was one of the featured performers at the Chester-Lancaster Old Fiddlers Association reunion where he played tunes from his younger days, such as "Bummers' Reel," "Devils Dream," "Turkey in the Straw," and "Fishers Hornpipe."[45]

Fairs of several kinds were popular in the first half of the nineteenth century. The semi-annual fairs in nearby boroughs drew the Furnace families until drinking and gambling caused many towns to abandon them—York, Lancaster and Harrisburg in 1816. Mechanical and agricultural fairs generally replaced the borough fairs.[46] Some Hopewell people were probably in Reading on June 5, 1806, when, according to Bennett Nolan, this scene would have greeted them :

The square was lined with booths and festooned with bunting. Around the central court-house and under the arcades of the brick marketplace which flanked it, swirled an eddying throng of merrymakers. Venders cried their wares; jugglers and sword-swallowers amused the spectators. The taverns were doing a thriving business and some tipsy revelers had hoisted

[43] *Morris Diary, op. cit.,* p. 32.
[44] J. Lincoln Palsgrove Interview, October 13, 1940, and Hunter Care Interview, January 20, 1941.
[45] *Reading Eagle,* August 14, 1929.
[46] Bining, "Iron Plantations," *op. cit.,* pp. 12–13.

a wagon upon the roof of the markethouse for the discomfiture of the village constable.[47]

In that same year bachelor Clement Brooke drew $1 in cash "when he went to the "water millen" fair."[48] And Helen Brooke visited her relatives, the William R. Whites, in Philadelphia in 1864 to attend a fair in the city.[49]

Since leisure time was not a plentiful commodity in the Hopewell community, it is not surprising that hobbies received little mention. The storekeeper in Morgantown was a coin collector who noted that he had "put away . . . a collection of cents beginning at 1793 and from thence to 1841 inclusive excepting only those of 1804 and 1815."[50] A modern numismatist would value that collection, and he would know that few cents were made in 1804 and none in 1815.

Traveling entertainers were welcomed on their infrequent visits to the Furnace. "Mr. Skelline" gave a demonstration "on ventriloquism and vocal illusion" and was so popular he returned for a repeat performance.[51] The organ grinder played his tunes and asked for a donation at each house as he walked through the Village.[52] A more elaborate show was provided in 1837 with the arrival of a "Cosmorama" on wheels. A room, built on a wagon thirty feet long and seven or eight wide, contained pictures of "battles, harbours, towns, etc." Sixty to 70 people could get into it at the same time.[53] Animal shows were fairly common; but they always attracted attention, whether the *pièce de résistance* was "the learned Goat" or "the Exhibition of Wild Beasts."[54] An especially large ani-

[47] J. Bennett Nolan, *Play at Reading Town* (Reading, Pennsylvania: The Feroe Press, 1935), n. p., identified as Plate IV.

[48] SM 44, August 26, 1806, n. p.

[49] HV 8640621. William R. White to C. M. Clingan.

[50] *Morris Diary, op. cit.,* p. 223.

[51] *Ibid.,* II, pp. 73, 83. The year was 1843.

[52] *Ibid.,* p. 20 .

[53] *Ibid.,* p. 28.

[54] *Martha Furnace Diary, op. cit.,* October 11, 1809; *Morris Diary, op. cit.,* II, p. 42.

mal show was in the area in 1844 and passed through Morgantown on November 7. A resident of the town reported :

> The town was thrown into a great stir and commotion this forenoon by the passage through it of a caravan of animals. First came four enormous elephants with their keepers on horseback. The appearance of these, coming on us by surprize, completely aroused the attention of the goodly citizens . . . and caused them to throng men, women and children to the upper end of town. The elephants were next followed by a train of some 20 or more wagons ,containing the lions, etc. of the exhibition, Behind these came a camel and two shetland ponies. There were about 70 horses. They came from Reading and were going to Waynesburg for their next show.[55]

Balloon ascensions drew Furnace people to Reading in 1835 and again in 1838.[56] But in 1841 the people at the Jones Mine had a balloon land among them. An observer wrote :

> A great stir was made at about $4\frac{1}{2}$ o'clock P.M. by the sight of a balloon to the N. East. It remained but a very little time in sight and then disappeared as though it had descended. In the evening we learned that the balloon had descended at Jones' mine holes and that Wise the aeronaut had landed in safety having left Danville in Columbia County some $2\frac{1}{2}$ hours previous.[57]

Two occasions of civic significance which never failed to attract Hopewell Village people were election day and militia training day. Elections, combining civic duty with a holiday, were the cause of much absenteeism from jobs for part or all of the day. Many workers asked for cash to spend "at the election," because the voting place was usually a tavern.[58] Battalion Day for militia drills was observed in Pennsylvania from soon after the Revolution until the Civil War. Berks

---

[55] *Ibid.*, pp. 167–168.
[56] *Ibid.*, p. 65; *Lewis Evans Ledger, op. cit.*, p. 211.
[57] *Morris Diary, op. cit.*, p. 152. This was probably John Wise.
[58] Examples are to be found in SM 67, October 13, 1807; October 11, 1808; SM 7, October 15, 1817; SM 10, p. 53; SM 17, p. 24; SM 31, pp. 74, 157; SM 35, pp. 19–20; SM 65, p. 3.

County had six battalions, each of which held its own review days. But Battalion Day was much more than a military parade. Personal grudges were settled in bare-fisted fights; dances were held in the tavern; tables were set up in the streets to sell cakes, confections and mead. Dancing began after dinner and lasted until late at night. One man in a set paid the fiddler and another bought the drinks, whiskey at 3¢ with a free cigar for the men and cream beer for the women.

The militia were supposed to drill about two hours before dinner and the same in the afternoon;[59] but, judging from the following description, the military aspect of Battalion Day was of questionable quality:

> Today our Battalion of Militia trains at the White Bear [Tavern], which will be made the occasion of a vast meeting of half uniformed officers without science or knowledge of what they pretend to teach—of citizen soldiers whose arms and accoutrements consist of a cornstalk perhaps, or at farthest nothing more dangerous than an umbrella or a goodly cudgel and whose knowledge of the art of war is equivalent to the "little end of nothing whittled down." These with a numerous band of lookers on in the shape of young boys . . . of cripples—of old men "out of the muster rolls" years agone— old women and. young ones—married and single—with and without babies—black, blue and brown, "from snowy white to sooty"—comely and plain, trigged out in finery—some neat and others tawdry, ill-looking and well-looking—well behaved and ill behaved. These with a sprinkling of old huckster women, drunken men, fiddlers, dancers, fights and squabbles make up the grand rare show of a training in Battalion.[60]

Officers were generally disobeyed or even made to appear ridiculous by the privates who were more interested in the drinking, dancing, fighting and gambling.[61]

Many Furnace people attended the annual Battalion Days and drew cash to finance the fun. In 1801 the following

[59] *Lewis Richards Scrapbooks, op. cit.,* Vol. H, p. 63.
[60] *Morris Diary, op. cit.,* p. 200. The year was 1842.
[61] *Ibid.,* p. 147.

Hopewell men were on the muster roll of Captain Will Witman when the call was issued for a training day at the White Horse Tavern on May 2: Mathew Brooke, Samuel Umstead, Matthew Davis, Thomas Kerby, James Sands, Peter Huttenstein and Amos Lewis.[62] Men were paid to attend the muster and fined for failure to report. The number of fines collected from Hopewell employees indicated that there was less enthusiasm for Battalion Day among those with military duties than among the revelers.[63]

Visiting among friends and relatives occupied much of the time of the ironmasters' families. The big mansions were filled with visitors who came and stayed for days and then moved on to another house. Ann Brooke wrote, "You will go to Hopewell I expect and to Birdsborough during your vacation perhaps to Lititz with Elizabeth Mary. . . ."[64] The group often was quite large: "Uncle Charles and Cousin Brooke Buckley are here . . . We expect Aunt Tacy and Aunt Anna and Aunt Sarah and her 2 children up tomorrow."[65]

The young ladies planned parties and dances for their visitors. Ann instructed her brother, "When you come here . . . bring your new black clothes . . . [Sarah] is quite *fidgety* for fear the boys will not bring their *Sunday Clothes*."[66] But they spent much time on the move, as Ann later reported:

> . . . Cousin Eliza Buckley was here [Morgantown] the week before last and I went with her to Hopewell and spent a few days there. I had not been home more than a day or two when Sarah and Louisa Anderson came up in the stage to Morgantown we sent the barouche over for them and the next day Ann C. Brooke and Charles came for us in their handsome new carriage so we all accompanied them home and staid there [Hopewell] a week, we went to Birdsborough

[62] *Brooke Family Papers*, Muster Roll.
[63] For examples see SM 10, pp. 16, 20; HV 8200609A; SM 12, p. 72; HV 8271004A; SM 28, pp. 18, 59, 155.
[64] *Brooke Family Papers*, Ann to Edward, July, 1829.
[65] *Hopewell Papers*, Unsigned and undated, possibly Ann Brooke to Elizabeth Brooke about 1830.
[66] *Brooke Family Papers*, Ann to Edward, July 1829.

and staid over night, from there we returned home. . . . I have just received a letter from Louisa Anderson in which she says she and Ann are going with Cousin Clemment to Mauchunk next Thursday and I must go to Hopewell tomorrow to go with [them].[67]

Ann Brooke seems to have felt there was a kind of obligation upon the ironmaster's family to create diversion for the people of the neighborhood when she wrote to her cousin:

Well Sally the time is rapidly progressing when I shall expect your Ladyship here — then I shall insist upon the Grubbs coming over and invite Mrs. Jenny Hopkins — Ann Hopkins — and have a little turn out — something of the kind is necessary to set them a going in this neighborhood.[68]

The ironmasters' families also spent time traveling. In 1834 Sarah and George Brooke went to Niagara Falls,[69] and the young people often visited Philadelphia and New York. Life in the cities must have been gay for the children of wealthy iron families. From January to June of 1840 Ann C. Brooke was advanced $6,961.78 in cash for her stay in Philadelphia.[70] It was a good investment, however; for in June she married William R. White, a promising young Philadelphia banker.

Sally Brooke wrote to her cousin Elizabeth Brooke about her trip to New York in 1844 with three other girls and Edward Brooke. They stayed at the Astor House and found the food prepared by the new French chef not to their liking. They toured the town "in a cab" but missed "the Croton Water Works and the Theological Seminary" which Sally had especially wanted to see. Edward promised to take them to the opera but failed to do so. However, they had a good time at the weekly dance sponsored by the hotel for its guests

[67] Brooke Family Papers, Ann to Edward, August 4, 1829.

[68] Hopewell Papers, Stokes Collection, Ann Brooke to Sarah R. Brooke. Dated May 3, no year but probably in the 1830's.

[69] Brooke Family Letters, G. W. Brooke to Edward Brooke, May 8, 1834.

[70] Kemper Manuscripts, Memorandum of Cash paid by Clement Brooke for Ann C. Brooke, January–June, 1840.

where they danced until midnight with partners they had never seen before. The girls shopped for clothes and found the dresses were gayer than those offered by the stores in Philadelphia.[71]

Despite all the apparent activity the following letter shows that there were dull moments in the mansions:

> . . . I wish you to bring me Irving's Alhambra — Swallow Barn — or any new publication, you can get in West Chester — I am dreadfully at a loss for something to read our old books I have read—and reread some of them—they are getting stale to me, and require a *tale* to freshen them up.[72]

Cultural opportunities or interests were limited among these people in the first half of the nineteenth century. Ann Brooke attended a performance of *Hamlet* in 1832, and Elizabeth Brooke heard Jenny Lind sing in Philadelphia in 1850.[73] George Brooke played the flute and possessed a collection of music for that instrument.[74] For the workmen's families the winter singing school filled a cultural void.[75]

Long working hours left little time for recreation among the Hopewell villagers, but they found a surprisingly large number of opportunities for entertainment and social and cultural enrichment.

[71] *Hopewell Papers,* Cousin Sallie to Elizabeth Brooke, April 24, 1844.
[72] *Brooke Family Papers,* Ann to Edward, probably 1829 but no date given except July.
[73] *Ibid.,* Ann to George W., February 29, 1832; *Hopewell Papers,* Fanny Crutcher to Elizabeth Brooke, January 19, 1851.
[74] *Ibid.,* R. D. Powell to Clement Brooke, undated but probably 1835.
[75] *Morris Diary, op. cit.,* pp. 35, 172, 182; *Lewis Evans Ledger,* p. 179.

2 I Hopewell and the Outside World

HOPEWELL FURNACE WAS IN A WOODED REGION OF HILLS AND narrow valleys, distant from cities and not located on any of the main routes of transportation. Was it therefore an isolated and self-contained community? Earlier chapters have demonstrated the influence of changing transportation upon the Furnace market and the dependence upon the surrounding cities and towns for supplies and cultural outlets. In the following pages the Village will be considered as a part of the economic, political and social growth of the wider community of nineteenth century America. How did it reach into Hopewell Village? What reaction did it evoke from the people?

Since Hopewell was an industrial unit with a product to sell to an outside market, it was naturally linked with the state of business in general. Iron sold well on a lively market and poorly on a dull market. The ironmaster had to consider the probable demands for his pig iron and cast items when he was writing contracts to make charcoal or when he was setting a selling price to his customers for future deliveries. Errors in predicting the influence of business cycles caused many bankruptcies. The iron manufacturer needed large financial resources to see him through an unprofitable season. As Victor S. Clark wrote, "The dependence of the iron industry upon special skills and an organized personnel, and therefore upon continuous operation, was greater than that of most other manufactures."[1]

The iron industry, suffering from foreign competition since the end of the Napoleonic wars, began a decline in 1816. By 1819 the Pittsburgh iron works were shut down, a condition which lasted until 1821. Then a slow recovery began and continued until 1826 when Pittsburgh iron production had returned to the 1815 level.[2]

Hopewell encountered less difficulty from the national depression which began in 1819 than did the Pittsburgh furnaces, but there were anxious moments for the partners in 1820 and 1821. Daniel Buckley wrote on May 23, 1820:

> . . . I have not been able to sell any iron of Consequence in Lancaster or Columbia . . . at Columbia business is so Dull that no . . . man seems Inclined to take Iron only for Lumber which would not suit us to Deal for. . . .[3]

Customers were reluctant to place orders. One wrote, "The Iron appears to be of a good quality but would not wish you to send any more at this time. . . ."[4] Another said, "I have been in Philadelphia . . . and I found that Iron was much more duller sale then wen you ware in town. . . . I think you must com down with your Pigs according to Market. . . ."[5]

Even when iron was sold, collections were difficult: ". . . you state in your letter," wrote Lewis Morgan, "that you stand in grait need of money . . . [I shall] youse every exertion in my power to accomodant [sic] you with some against Saterday two weeks. . . ."[6] Two other merchants were apolo-

---

[1] Clark, *op. cit.*, p. 384.
[2] Richard C. Wade, *The Urban Frontier: The Rise of Western Cities, 1790–1830* (Cambridge: Harvard University Press, 1959), p. 168.
[3] *Hopewell Papers*, uncatalogued. Daniel Buckley to Clement Brooke.
[4] HV 8201024, H. F. Slaymaker to D. Buckley and Company.
[5] HV 8201215, J. S. Spang to Daniel Buckley and Company.
[6] HV 8201221, Lewis Morgan to Mathew Brooke.

getic: "It is almost more then I can ask but I must beg a little time yet. . . ."[7] and, ". . . I have been Last week down in Maryland after money but find it is not to be had. . . ."[8] Respected customers found it impossible to continue in business, and Hopewell learned that some who owed the Furnace money were being subjected to sheriff's sales "unexpectedly to almost everybody. . . ."[9]

Hopewell apparently made most of its iron into pigs in the emergency.[10] Stoves were in little demand; some customers expressed the belief that "they will come Lower" in price.[11] The income of the molders was much below normal for the blast of 1820, and William Ricketts was employed at coaling instead of molding. But in the next blast Ricketts was again molding, and three other molders more than doubled their incomes over the previous year.[12]

Even in the midst of the depression Hopewell's credit was considered the equivalent of cash by people in the neighborhood. A weaver informed a customer, "You may call for your Blanketing any time. Please to Bring the cash or an order from Hopewell we dont Intend weaving any more on Trust. . . ."[13]

Business improved by the spring of 1822. Two customers wrote that they wished to order stoves as word had reached them that Hopewell Furnace would be back in production about March 1, 1822.[14] Stove prices moved up during the year from $65.00 per ton to $75.00.[15] Stove dealers, wrote Daniel Buckley, "seem to want castings much," and one offered to

[7] HV 8201031A, William Hamill to Mathew Brooke.
[8] HV 8201030, William Walker to D. Buckley and Company.
[9] HV 8211024B.
[10] HV 8210409C.
[11] HV 8210409A.
[12] SM 6, *passim.*
[13] HV 8201228.
[14] HV 8220221A; HV 8220308A. These letters indicate the furnace had been shut down. They may have meant merely the normal period of repairs between blasts. If there had been any cessation because of business condition, it must have been quite short.
[15] HV 8220508A; HV 8221010B.

pay cash for quick delivery.[16] Men who had wanted no stoves the previous year were now complaining that they were not having their orders filled fast enough.[17] William Walker in Wilmington feared he had been forgotten because he had received no stoves for so long, and he hoped he would be sent a wagon load before the end of the blast.[18]

The backlog of orders seemingly had been filled by the autumn of 1824, when a Philadelphia dealer wrote on September 30:

> You will please be careful not to send us any more stoves this season we have so many on hand and the sales appear so dull that we are afraid we shall not be able to get them off.[19]

After 1824 business in general improved throughout the country.[20] Hopewell Furnaces benefited from the enlarged demand for iron and cast products and entered into a period of about fifteen years of the greatest prosperity it ever knew.

Two factors combined to bring an end to the "boom" times of the 1830's: The Jacksonian money supply and the increases in productive capacity in the iron industry. Since these two did not coincide, there was a short recession in 1837 followed by a brief revival and then a prolonged depression.[21] Hopewell had its most productive blast in 1836-1837, but already there were signs of coming trouble. One of the largest buyers of Hopewell stoves wrote in 1836, ". . . the price appears so high we shall not want so many castings as we should if they came at a lower rate. . . ."[22] The same customer said he was finding payments difficult because of the money shortage:

[16] HV 82201010B; HV 8221022A.
[17] HV 8221106; HV 8221108.
[18] HV 8221125.
[19] HV 8240930.
[20] Sullivan, *op. cit.*, pp. 51–57.
[21] Douglas C. North, *The Economic Growth of the United States* (Englewood Cliffs: Prentice Hall, Inc., 1961), p. 13.
[22] HV 8361212A. G. P. Willard Company of Portsmouth, New Hampshire.

Such is the unprecedented scarcity of money and the facilities of raising it being entirely cut off, we have thought best to say that we do not wish you to draw on us for any part of your a/c. it has always before afforded us pleasure and have a source of pride that we could anticipate all our demands before they become due but from a man of 20 to 30,000 dollars the best of paper which before has always commanded cash at our Bank; we are unable to raise one dollar. . . .[23]

By the late Spring of 1837 the depression was becoming severe. James Morris had much to say of business conditions in his diary entries for these months:

April 28. A universal complaint of a scarcity of money — many failures. . . .

May 9. One nowadays hears of nothing else but hard-times, failures, scarcity of money and what is worse bread-stuffs. The ironmasters are beginning to feel the pressure. Pig-iron has fell from $50 to $20[24] per ton — for Casting there is no sale — some of the forges have stopped and several of the furnaces intend discharging their moulders. . . .

May 12. Report that Reading banks had suspended species payment. . . .

May 17. It is rumored that the shin plasters — ie — small notes . . . are about to be inflicted upon us.[25]

Three days after this rumor on fractional currency, Morris reported seeing the first one—a ten cent note of the city of Philadelphia. They were promptly named "Hickory leaves" by the Whigs, a designation "much disliked by the Jackson men."[26]

[23] HV 8361128.
[24] This was certainly an exaggeration, at least in so far as Hopewell is concerned. But the price did fall below $30 per ton for pig iron. Stove casting dropped in price from $110 per ton in 1837 to $60 in 1844. HV 8440605.
[25] Morris Diary, op. cit., pp. 15–18.
[26] Ibid., p. 25.

Letters from customers show that Hopewell was having trouble making collections for its iron in 1839. One said :

> Frequent and continued disappointment in the receipt of money funds from the South, long since due us, and the necessity of taking up lately large amts of the protested paper of correspondents, will make it impossible for me to meat our note to you. . . .[27]

Another apologized :

> I am very sorry to inform you that I cannot let you have that money according to promise I have Been out trying to Collect it for you and I could not get a cent. . . .[28]

Business conditions were still bad in 1842 when a Philadelphia dealer wrote, ". . . Times are no better, rather worse, Girard Bank is broke, One other is Strongly suspected of going next."[29] Discounts were charged on paper money. Store keepers refused to take it on "book accounts" and would not give coins in change.[30] However, by May 1843 paper money had recovered most of its value with discounts as low as 5 per cent and even less.[31] Pig iron prices rose to $28 per ton. By 1844 Clement Brooke was offering Hopewell pig iron at $30 per ton. "We have a quantity . . . on hand at Present," he wrote on June 17. "Not selling any for sometime owing to no regular price being established," he added.[32] Casting of stoves ended at Hopewell before the close of the year.

The depression hastened the adoption of such new technical improvements in iron-manufacturing as the hot-blast and the anthracite furnaces. From 1839 to 1850 there were 27 sheriff's sales of the 60 cold-blast charcoal furnaces in Eastern

[27] HV 8391113. From New Castle, Delaware.
[28] HV 8391102. From New Holland, Pennsylvania.
[29] *Hopewell Papers,* Uncatalogued, James H. Deas to Clement Brooke and Company.
[30] *Morris Diary, op. cit.,* p. 189.
[31] *Ibid.,* II, p. 37.
[32] HV 8440617A.

Pennsylvania. Of these 27 only seven were in blast in 1850. Thirteen of those which had not been sold were also out of blast.[33] Hopewell Furnace was one which survived and continued to produce iron for many more years although business conditions troubled the management again in 1854, 1857 and on several occasions in the 1870's.[34] While Hopewell Furnace managed to survive the serious depressions of the first half of the nineteenth century and for thirty-three years longer, its production and profits were seriously curtailed. The Depression of 1837 was undoubtedly influential in the decision of the partners to discontinue stove-casting.

Defending the American market for their products, according to William Sullivan, made the ironmasters of Pennsylvania "The most zealous partisans of the protective tariff."[35] The first session of Congress placed a tariff on slit and rolled iron, iron castings, nails and unwrought steel.[36] Further provisions for protection against imports of iron were made in the revenue acts of 1791, 1792 and 1794.[37] The tariff acts of the first half of the nineteenth century also retained provisions for protecting the iron manufacture. In 1816 a duty on cast iron was set at 20 per cent *ad valorum,* and this was changed in 1818 to 50¢ per hundredweight. The latter rate was raised to $62\frac{1}{2}$¢ in 1828. The tariff of 1832 put a 50¢ rate on each hundredweight of pig iron, changed to $9 per ton in 1842 and set at 30 per cent *ad valorum* in the Walker Tariff of 1846.[38] The ironmasters blamed the depression of 1819 on the inadequacies of the tariff of 1816, but they considered the

---

[33] *Documents Relating to the Manufacture of Iron in Pennsylvania, op. cit.,* "Table on Cold Blast Charcoal Furnaces."

[34] HV 8541216; *Kemper Manuscripts,* protest of note September 26, 1857; *Ibid.,* Edward S. Buckley to Harker A. Long, November 17, 1876.

[35] Sullivan, *op. cit.,* p. 9.

[36] Harold F. Williamson, *The Growth of the American Economy* (New York: Prentice-Hall, 1946), p. 229.

[37] Barnes, *op. cit.,* p. 155.

[38] Harry Scrivenor, *History of the Iron Trade from the Earliest Records to the Present Time* (London: Longman, Brown, Green, and Longmans, 1854), pp. 210, 223, 236, 238.

Tariff of 1828 "a triumph of protection."[39] The reduction in rates under the Walker Tariff permitted the English to flood the American market with iron which they could not sell on the European market. But the settlement of California and the restoration of the English market on the continent revived the prosperity of the American furnaces.[40]

The ironmasters' convention of 1850 noted that in the previous year 20 per cent of the iron used in the United States was imported.[41] They did not mention, however, the rise in exports of American iron which increased from 85,000 tons in 1839 to over 500,000 tons in 1852.[42] The convention went on record as approving the following resolution:

> Resolved, That a crisis has arisen in the iron business which calls for the immediate revision of the revenue laws, so far as that article is concerned, and that the number of establishments which have already been forced to suspend by the influx of foreign iron, proves that without such a change, the business cannot permanently sustain itself in its rightful position, as a great branch of our national industry.[43]

Charles M. Clingan represented Hopewell at the Philadelphia convention where the above resolution was adopted. He did not oppose the action. But the manager at Hopewell probably would have been in agreement with the views expressed in 1832 by William Darling, manager of Joanna Furnace. In reply to a Congressional inquiry on the need for a tariff on iron, he wrote:

> I am satisfied that furnaces would not be materially injured; but, of the twenty-seven forges, nearly two thirds of them would be compelled to stop [if protection were removed]; and, when you take into consideration the thousands of men,

[39] Arthur Cecil Bining, "The Rise of Iron Manufacturing in Western Pennsylvania," Reprint from *The Western Pennsylvania Historical Magazine*, 16, 4 (November 1933), pp. 235–256.

[40] *Ibid.*

[41] *Documents Relating to the Manufacture of Iron, op. cit.*, p. 2.

[42] Scrivenor, *op. cit.*, p. 318.

[43] *Documents Relating to the Manufacture of Iron, op. cit.*, p. 19.

women, and children, who derive their support from these works, it is obvious that such an event would produce great distress. As far as I am interested in iron works, I feel but little interest in the fate of the tariff; but as a matter which is to affect so large a portion of my fellow-citizens, I feel a deep interest in it.[44]

As Mr. Darling pointed out, the furnaces had less foreign competition for their pig iron and rough castings than had the forges for their more expensive bar iron and finished products.

The influence of tariffs upon the iron industry naturally led to participation in politics by the ironmasters. Among Hopewell owners Mark Bird, James Wilson and James Old combined furnace management with public office; and Daniel Buckley served two terms as the Lancaster County representative to the Pennsylvania legislature before he became a Hopewell partner.[45] After 1800 the managers were not public office holders, except for Charles M. Clingan's service on the Union Township School Board.[46] But politics was a matter of great interest to the people of Hopewell Village in the nineteenth century.

In the midst of the financial problems which troubled him in 1807, Mathew Brooke was urged to take a greater part in the politics of the day. A Berks County political leader wrote:

> We all know Sir that you are a firm and stedfast Repub —but we must sensure you for being so inactive these fiew years past, there is now a glorious field for triumph Open, the Quids and Federalists are now divided, we have no longer to fear their United force, if we will but exert ourselves. . . .[47]

The specific reason for this letter was a campaign for the election of another ironmaker, Colonel Daniel Udree, to the office of Brigadier General.

[44] *McLane Report on Manufacture, op. cit.,* p. 227.
[45] *Reading Eagle,* February 4, 1917.
[46] HV 8590318.
[47] *Brooke Family Papers,* Gabl Heister to Mathew Brooke, August 27, 1807.

Buckley-Brooke correspondence sometimes revealed a depth of political feeling on one side or the other. In 1823 Clement A. Buckley wrote to Clement Brooke from Brooke Forge in Lancaster County:

> We have had a complete triumph over the Shultsites in our township, after the greatest exertions made by his friends we have a majority of 48 votes. . . . If you know anything about the results in your adjacent townships let me know. The demos are most sanguine of success.[48]

A stove dealer included in an order for stoves a wrong guess about the outcome of the election of 1828, "What do you think of the Election now Adams will Be Presadent."[49] Berks County, however, voted 4,583 for Jackson and 894 for Adams.[50] George W. Buckley was pessimistic about the outcome of the election for governor in 1829:

> Lanc[aster] Co. gave Ritner a majority of 1600 votes—But tis my Opinion that the wolves will be hard on the sheep in the end.[51]

The Anti-Masonic movement reached into the Hopewell community. Clement Brooke was a member of the lodge at Morgantown, but he withdrew because of the political furor against the Masonic Order.[52] His political leadership in the area was attested by a letter containing political "tickets" which he was asked to distribute among his "neighbors and hands" in 1832.[53]

Another letter to Brooke commented on the national political scene in 1836:

[48] HV 8231015.

[49] HV 8281028A, Ephr Bailey to C. Brooke.

[50] Sullivan, *op. cit.*, p. 231.

[51] *Hopewell Papers*, Uncatalogued, George W. Buckley to Clement Brooke, 1829.

[52] *Ibid.*, H. A. Long to A. Clingan, November 20, 1904.

[53] HV 8321001A, Henry Betz to Clement Brooke.

I regret very much to see that the opposition in Va. have nominated Judge White—I think if they had waited for the action of Pennsylvania upon that subject they would have taken up Harrison—and the Key-Stone State and the Old Dominion shoulder to shoulder would have borne him triumphantly through—But the Va politicians have been so much accustomed to lead that they have not *yet* learned the lesson of following. . . .[54]

Whig sentiment was strong in Morgantown, and James Morris left no doubt about his political beliefs:

Monday next being the day for the Whig Convention of young men of Pennsylvania at Reading, everybody almost is talking of it and talking of going.

Sunday . . . convention delegates are passing through here on their way to Reading in sulkies, gigs, dearborns. . . .

All Morgantown appeared to be astir by 4 o'clock [this] morning getting ready for a start. In company with B. Jones I got off about 5. When we neared Reading the roads were full of people. . . . The Loco foco also had a convention— a County one, and again it was "fair" day. All these produced a jam unexampled in old Reading.

I remained in Reading over last night Attended Convention and listened with pleasure to a speech by Ed. McCoy Morris of Philadelphia and one by Mr. Pennepacker of W. Chester. 1700 delegates are in attendance.[55]

To the diarist political parties were black or white. The Democrats were despicable people—at least when engaged in political activities:

Yesterday was the great Loco foco Porter State Convention at Reading and today some 10 or 12 of the Chester County delegation passed through here . . . with pink banners flying with the inscription "Chester County delegation Porter and Democracy" . . . which inscription ought to have read . . . "Porter and Drunkenness" for to say the truth some of them were not a little the "wus for licker," and looked Loco-foco-ism.[56]

[54] *Hopewell Papers,* Uncatalogued, R. D. Powell to Clement Brooke, no date.
[55] *Morris Diary, op. cit.,* June 2–5, 1838, p. 52.
[56] *Ibid.,* p. 59.

Again in reference to a Democratic convention to pick a slate of officers, he wrote:

> Today . . . the hearts of some hundreds of office hunters, beat high with hope—and fear—for today their destiny will be fixed, and what the leaders say, the Convention will do and what they do, will be agreed to by the "dear people," who follow their "dimmykratik" leaders like a herd of sheep follows the old bell whether of the flock.[57]

The elections of 1840 and 1844 produced much excitement in the Hopewell Village area. A gigantic rally for William Henry Harrison drew many Furnace people to Morgantown on August 17, 1840. Morris, again, was the reporter:

> A Whig meeting had been advertized to be held here today and to be addressed by [John W.] Baer, the celebrated Buckeye Blacksmith. In the morning early David Morgan had the Stars and Stripes flying from his sign post. The Committee of escort had met and gone out to meet Baer and the Reading people and another had gone to meet the Chester County delegation and log cabin. About 10 the people began to come in on foot, on horseback and in vehicles of every description. At 11 o'clock the Reading and Forest folks, under escort came in—there was quite a throng. Shortly after the Chester County delegation, about a mile long, appeared carrying several beautiful banners, being accompanied with a band, a neat Log Cabin, and about a dozen Miner's Carts filled with folks from Jones' Mine holes. There was also a 6 horse wagon along filled with delegates. There was said to be about 650 people in that single arrival. . . .
>
> About 1 o'clock, the people went to Kurtz's Woods where seats and a stand had been prepared . . . and after organizing by appointing John M. Keim of Reading as Chairman . . . Mr. Hazlehurst of Phila. was called and gave us a short speech after which the Buckeye was listened to with great interest and attention for the course of an hour or two. . . .
>
> The number of people present was very differently estimated —some saying 1000, 1500, 2000, 2500 and one man computed them at above 3000. . . .

[57] *Ibid.*, p. 86.

In the evening there was a good deal of drunkenness, Much noise and a little squabbling—not very much blood was shed however.[58]

After all the excitement was over, Morgantown gave Harrison a disappointing majority of only 25 votes when the Whigs had expected as many as 40.[59] Berks County gave its usual two-to-one majority to the Democratic candidate, Martin Van Buren. In most elections Union Township, like Morgantown, supported the Whig candidates. Later this area favored the Republicans.[60] In their politics the area residents were usually found voting the same ticket as the Hopewell ironmasters. Support of the latter for the Whig ticket in 1844 was shown by contributions of $100 each by Clement Brooke, Charles Brooke and M. Brooke Buckley to "the Whig Committee of Philad[a] for Election purposes."[61] The tariff issue was undoubtedly influential in this support of Whig candidates. No record was found to show whether or not the Hopewell ironmasters used pressure to get their workers to vote the "right ticket."

Much excitement again prevailed at Hopewell over this election of 1844. Rallies for Henry Clay were held near the Furnace and at Morgantown, Birdsboro and Mt. Airy.[62] Undoubtedly many Furnace people attended these meetings in their neighborhood. They would have heard Thaddeus Stevens give the main address at Morgantown on September 24.[63] Some of the speeches were in both English and German.[64]

Charles M. Clingan continued the interest in politics which had been shown by his predecessors as Hopewell ironmasters. In 1852 he received an invitation to join a group going to a Whig mass meeting at Pottsville. Two passenger cars were

[58] *Ibid.*, pp. 113–114.
[59] *Ibid.*, p. 122.
[60] *Lewis Richards Scrapbooks,* Volume G, pp. 1–24.
[61] SM 28, p. 136.
[62] *Morris Diary, op. cit., passim* in Volume II.
[63] *Ibid.*, p. 156.
[64] *Ibid.*, p. 157.

reserved by the Reading Railroad to take the delegates and the Birdsboro Band.[65] In the 1860's Clingan had a page in his pocket notebook headed "Political Expenses." He gave no indication about who was running for what office, but the page listed payments in amounts from $1 to $200 and totaled $500.[66] Union township gave a strong vote to A. G. Curtin, the Republican candidate for governor in 1860.[67] The outcome might have been influenced by the presence on the ticket of a neighbor, Ironmaster Levi Smith of Joanna Furnace, who made an unsuccessful campaign for Congress on the Republican slate.

From time to time other matters of national import attracted attention or influenced actions at Hopewell Village. The Brooke family had an interest in the attempts of the United States Government to reach a settlement on the French Spoliation Claims. Clement Brooke wrote to his Congressman about this matter:

> I am informed that there is a bill now before Congress for the settlement of claims held by our citizens for Spoliation committed by the French Government prior to the year 1800 — I have taken the liberty of addressing you on this subject and hope you will be among those favorable to the adjustment of these claims — I have not a large interest myself but several of my relations have, one of whom is a widow now . . . with several children and stands greatly in need of any means she could receive . . . in payment of those claims.[68]

Wars had their influences in two ways upon the iron furnaces: Demand for iron and drain upon manpower. Hopewell Furnace was closed during all of the War of 1812; so there was no prosperity from an increased demand for pig iron. On the contrary Birdsboro Forge, owned by Buckley and Brooke, found itself overstocked with pig iron bought at war prices when the war ended sooner than expected.[69] A number of

[65] HV 8520922.
[66] *Kemper Manuscripts,* C. M. Clingan Pocket Note Book.
[67] *Lewis Richards Scrapbooks,* Volume G, p. 21.
[68] *Hopewell Papers,* Clement Brooke to John Ritter, June 29, 1846.
[69] HV 8150401B.

Hopewell Village men served in the army during this war: Thomas May, John Linderman, Captain Jonathan Jones, Sergeant Thomas Church, Philip Filman, Daniel Stubblebein, Henry Minker, Matthew M. Brooke, Robert May, Samuel Barde, Abraham Seifert and William Dewees.[70]

A gap in the existing Furnace books made it difficult to trace an influence at Hopewell of the Mexican War. But the Civil War revived the prosperity of the company when the price of pig iron rose from its normal $30 to almost $100 per ton. John Rutter Brooke of the Birdsboro branch of the family raised a volunteer company and attained the rank of major general in the Union Army before the end of the war.[71] Henry Houck and Frederick Mosteller also served in the Union Army,[72] and several Hopewell men were among the casualties of the war. Henry F. Care was taken prisoner and held in both the Andersonville and the Libby prisons;[73] Daniel Buckley, Linderman Britton and Henry Wamback died of wounds; and Daniel Hunsberger "Died of disease contracted in the Army."[74]

Hopewell-area people were among those attracted by the cheap land in the West, and some of them became a part of the "westward movement." David Evans moved to Morgan County, Illinois, in 1829 in time to break ground for spring planting.[75] Two families from the Morgantown area, the David Buckwalters and the James Flemings, left for Davenport, Iowa, on June 3, 1840. Buckwalter took with him " a 2 horse wagon complete, bed and all, one or two ploughs, harness of all descriptions, tools of almost every kind, two tables, one bureau, Queensware and a quantity of clothing and clothing stuff." He went by the canal from Columbia.[76]

[70] *Lewis Richards Scrapbooks,* Volume G, pp. 239–240.
[71] Witzel, *op. cit.,* p. 83.
[72] Bethesda Baptist Church Cemetery.
[73] *Reading Eagle,* August 14, 1929.
[74] *St. Gabriel's Church Records, op. cit.,* Record of Burials.
[75] *Brooke Family Letters,* Ann to Edward, April 12, 1829.
[76] *Morris Diary, op. cit.,* p. 106.

A few days earlier neighbors had raised $50 on a subscription for a family moving west; possibly it was one of these two families who received the help.[77] Two years later Benjamin W. Gehman and his wife Elizabeth Morris Gehman started for Ohio. They sent their goods ahead by canal.[78] In 1880 the Bethesda Baptist Church near the Furnace dismissed Brother John Stoneback and Sister Sarah Stoneback to a Baptist church in an unspecified town in Kansas.[79]

One regular source of contact with the outside world for Furnace families was by means of letters, packages and newspapers delivered by the United States mails. It is not clear how mail reached Hopewell. In 1816 the Furnace paid postage of 16¢ for two letters "at the Reading Post Office."[80] Several references indicated that mail was left at the tollgate on the turnpikes to be picked up by the teamsters returning to Hopewell. After 1823 a carrier delivered mail to the Furnace and was paid his total bill quarterly or annually. Perhaps the mailman left letters at the company store and received his pay from the clerk, for many workers' accounts were debited for postage on personal letters. The charge in the first half of the nineteenth century usually ranged from 5¢ to 10¢ per letter. Among those paid for carrying mail to Hopewell were Rees Evans, David Morgan, "Lewis," Abraham Dehaven, "Doctor Ludwig" and "Spatz."[81]

On April 22, 1852, the Furnace purchased "30 Letter Stamps" at 3¢ each,[82] but for several years more they paid "Doctor Ludwig" and L. B. Holloway lump sums for mail service over a period of time.[83] In 1859 Hopewell was listed as a post office.[84]

[77] *Ibid.,* p. 103.
[78] *Ibid.,* p. 224.
[79] *Bethesda Baptist Church Minutebook, op. cit.,* April 11, 1880.
[80] SM 7, November 2, 1816, n. p.
[81] *Passim* in Furnace journals.
[82] SM 32, p. 126.
[83] SM 65, November 5, 1854, January 9, 1855, July 21, 1857, February 19, 1859.
[84] J. P. Lesley, *The Iron Manufacturers Guide to Furnaces, Forges and Rolling Mills of the United States* (New York: John Wiley, 1859), p. 40.

The outside world also came to the Furnace area in the form of business people who had goods or services to sell to the villagers: The tinker, drover, salesman, "foot peddler" and "wagon peddler," shoemaker, tailor, tinsmith, hatter, saddler, chimney sweep, spinner, weaver, clock repairer, gunsmith, candlemaker, basketmaker, pumpmaker, whipmaker, coppersmith, cabinetmaker and fishmonger served many of the people's needs. They brought with them scythes, kettles, worm syrup, brushes, books, pins, needles, tapes, thread, mirrors, cutlery, cigars, chewing tobacco, snuff, paper, hats, coffee mills, fish nets, shovels, baskets, powder, confections, drugs, whetstones, whips, crackers, rope, boots and shoes, axes, cotton yarn, and garden seed. One basketmaker had a small wagon to which he hitched a team of dogs. He thus attracted attention and increased his sale of baskets.[85]

Did the humanitarian and reform movements of the first half of the nineteenth century reach into Hopewell Village for adherents? It has already been noted that there was support for Abolition and public education and opposition to the compulsory military drills. Labor organization and labor reforms made little headway among the Furnace employees. One observer thought there was general opposition to the abolishing of debtor prisons in 1842. He argued:

> Rich and poor are alike loud in their denunciations—the former because it takes off a means of enforcing payments from their debtors and the latter because it takes away their credit.[86]

In the same year the movement against capital punishment was attacked from the Episcopal pulpit by the Reverend Mister Levi Bull.[87]

The reform movement with the greatest support in the Hopewell area, however, was temperance. Perhaps because of

[85] *Morris Diary, op. cit.,* II, pp. 33, 43, 44.
[86] *Ibid.,* pp. 222–223.
[87] *Ibid.,* p. 190.

the danger from accidents, the ironmasters had made early attempts to control the sale of intoxicants near the Pennsylvania furnaces and forges. In 1726 the colonial legislature prohibited the sale of liquor within two miles of a furnace except with the permission of the ironmaster. Ten years later the distance was made three miles.[88] But of course intoxicants were not barred at the company stores, and were sold at most of them. Whiskey was regularly stocked at the Hopewell store in its early history. Seldom were sales of other intoxicants mentioned; but the store purchased, apparently for use in the Big House, brandy, fine wines, beer, rum, "peach whiskey" and cognac.

Whiskey sales appeared in the store journals until November 8, 1816. The last recorded sale on that day was one quart bought by Daniel Buckley "for the molders to make plates."[89] Sales then ceased until 1822. Whiskey was sold to workers as late as 1826,[90] but after this was no longer stocked by the store. Manager Clement Brooke and Clerk John Benson were both regular subscribers to a publication called the *Temperance Advocate*,[91] and Hopewell workers were fined for having whiskey on the job.[92] Someone at Hopewell wrote a letter to the legislature requesting support for a bill relating to "Temperance Taverns." A local judge had recently declared that such taverns were illegal. The writer of the letter thought the legislature should legalize taverns which did not serve intoxicants.[93]

In the community generally the temperance movement made progress. James Morris discontinued at his store the sale of any "ardent spirits but Brandy, which is often wanted for medicinal purposes."[94] Temperance meetings were held under

[88] Bining, "Iron Plantations," *op. cit.,* p. 11.
[89] SM 7, November 8, 1806, n. p.
[90] SM 12, *passim.*
[91] HV 8340414A.
[92] SM 46, October 24, 1822, n. p.
[93] *Hopewell Papers,* Uncatalogued, unsigned and undated but reference to Marion Furnace places it as probably in the 1840's.
[94] *Morris Diary, op. cit.,* p. 30. The date was September 25, 1837.

the auspices of "The Sunday School Beneficial Society Temperence Men" or "The Sons of Temperence."[95] The Methodist Church in Morgantown was the location for many of the rallies held in the 1840's. In 1843 a mass meeting assembled in the woods south of the Jones mine holes about which one participant reported :

> The Morgantown Band went out to play for it. Many people were present and among the rest, the very celebrated "Razor Strop Man" who sold perhaps a hundred of his strops at 25 cents each . . . The speakers were Wm. Darling, Esq., the "Razor Strop Man" and a gentleman from Pottsgrove.[96]

The program of the temperance movement included an attempt to induce people to "sign the pledge" against use of intoxicants and a demand for the closing of "all unlicensed drinking houses, and the bars of all taverns, on the Sabbath."[97] The activity of the societies failed to generate enough support, however. Prohibition was submitted to a popular vote in Pennsylvania in 1854 and lost by 5,178 ballots. Berks County voted against the proposed law.[98]

Hopewell Village obviously was influenced by and participated in many of the same activities as engaged Americans generally. The Village was not isolated from the world of ideas and movements.

---

[95] *Ibid.,* p. 155; *Lewis Richards Scrapbooks,* Volume G, p. 126.
[96] *Morris Diary, op. cit.,* II, p. 63.
[97] *Lewis Richards Scrapbooks,* Volume G, p. 37.
[98] Louis Hartz, *Economic Policy and Democratic Thought: Pennsylvania, 1776–1860* (Cambridge : Harvard University Press, 1948), p. 211.

22   Conclusion

NEEDING IRON FOR WEAPONS, FOR TOOLS AND FOR HOUSEHOLD
utensils and conveniences, colonial Americans defied the
British legal restrictions on the fabrication of iron products in
the colonies.[1] Perhaps because of their long experience in
flouting English laws, the ironmasters were numerous and
active in the fight for independence.

Hopewell Furnace, born during the controversy over the
Townshend taxes, helped to provide the arms and ammunition
for the Continental Army in the Revolutionary War. Mark
Bird, founder of the Furnace, was an early and energetic
worker in the cause of separation from the mother country.

The end of the war in 1783 reduced the demand for iron
and brought the American iron industry into competition with
the British. A business recession in the postwar period forced
bankruptcy upon many ironmasters, including Mark Bird.
During the Federalist period Hopewell Furnace was bought
and sold by a succession of business men and speculators who
tried to make a profit from its operation. In 1800 the Furnace
was purchased by a partnership consisting of members of the
Buckley and Brooke families. After a legal struggle to establish

[1] For a discussion of British restrictions on colonial iron see Arthur
Cecil Bining, *British Regulation of the Colonial Iron Industry* (Philadelphia: University of Pennsylvania Press, 1933).

their land titles, the partnership profited from a long period of prosperity at Hopewell.

Success for the owners of the Furnace was the result of a fortunate combination of circumstances: the effective management of the business by Clement Brooke; the growing demand in America for all kinds of iron products; and the opening near Hopewell of highways, canals and railroads leading to the markets in and beyond Philadelphia. Brooke made a decision in the 1820's to convert most of the iron from the Furnace into stoves. In the next twenty years tens of thousands of Hopewell stoves in more than a hundred patterns were sold to heat homes and public buildings from Baltimore to Portsmouth, New Hampshire.

Except for a brief and costly experiment with an anthracite furnace in the 1850's, Hopewell was always a cold-blast, charcoal furnace. The peculiar needs of this kind of operation created a distinctive community to serve it and to share its periods of prosperity or depression. The making of charcoal consumed the wood grown on thousands of acres of forest land and gave employment to many men who worked at a distance from the furnace. Miners also lived several miles from the furnace stack.

A charcoal furnace was not the center of an urban community. The people who worked for the furnace were living a rural life. Most Hopewell families did some farming. Some of them were primarily farmers, becoming Furnace employees only during the winter months. Therefore, they were never so dependent upon their employer as city industrial workers were. They showed little interest in the labor unions which were struggling for recognition in the cities.

In Hopewell Village the ironmaster and his clerk were the management. From the front door of the mansion the owner could have seen almost all that was transpiring in his little industrial empire. The activity at the furnace and cast house, the wagons coming and going, and even the work on his nearest farm were all under his immediate gaze. Many of his workers lived in houses within sight. Their wives came to the store, only a few steps below the mansion; and their children played around the grounds. Both women and children were also a part of the work force.

The owner was almost solely responsible for the success of his furnace. He provided the working capital, he purchased land and raw materials, he found the market for his products, he set his prices on the basis of competition with rival furnaces, he hired his laborers and tried to keep them content on their jobs.

The relationship between the ironmaster and his workers was much more than that of employer-employee. He operated a store largely for their convenience. He performed many services for them in the distant cities or in nearby towns. He, or his wife, gave medical and legal advice and entertained the Village families in the mansion. From the clerk the manager could obtain a financial statement for any employee, and often he provided advice and help in money matters.

The Hopewell managers, especially Clement Brooke, gave community leadership in religion and education. They hired tutors before 1836 and in that year constructed a building at the furnace to house a public school. They bought books, magazines, newspapers, trade journals and religious publications. They gave employment in their homes and in the furnace operation to large numbers of Negroes, some of whom may have been escaped slaves. The use of intoxicants was discouraged, and the temperance movement received support from the Hopewell management.

The managers displayed patience with their workers for neglect of duty and even dishonesty. The usual form of punishment was a fine assessed against the earnings of the worker. Seldom was an employee discharged. The skilled workers, particularly, formed a stable work force. Wages were competitive with other furnaces and with other jobs and remained remarkably uniform for the same tasks over long periods of time. Fringe benefits sometimes provided low rental in company houses, free moving by Furnace teams, free fuel and a plot of ground for a garden.

By his business acumen Clement Brooke became a man of wealth and influence in the world of industry and politics. He owned several other furnaces and forges as well as stock in railroads, canals and coal mines. The income of his workers did not improve as rapidly as the wealth he gained from the Furnace.

Hopewell families lived in plain but usually substantial houses, furnished them with necessities and some luxuries, ate well and dressed adequately. Most of them stayed out of debt and paid their bills to the Furnace and others. The Village was not a slum area. The people cooperated on jobs which needed the labor of many hands and in support of the sick and unfortunate among their members. There was a high value placed upon the ability to read and write. Parents sent their children to the tutor even when the tuition represented a considerable sacrifice. They also participated extensively in the religious activities of the surrounding communities.

Next to management the skilled workers at the Furnace formed the upper level of Village society. The founder, the keeper and the molders had incomes several times as great as those of the unskilled workers. They were able to afford a higher scale of living and sometimes owned a riding or driving horse. Skilled jobs were often handed down from father to son. But there was no rigid caste system. A boy with skill and industry could learn the mysteries of the molders' trade, and some attained this position before they reached adulthood. Some Hopewell workers left to become managers or even owners of their own iron works.

Negro and white, skilled and unskilled, intermingled in vocations and residences, sent their children to school and attended the parties at the ironmaster's mansion. The iron-master's children usually married within their own class, but woodchoppers' daughters sometimes married molders and blacksmiths.

Hopewell workers had six or seven long workdays per week. They sometimes took time from the job, with or without permission, and seldom suffered any penalty other than loss of wages for the time not worked. They enjoyed no paid vacations or sick leave. But they apparently considered it worth a day's pay to attend a fair, a battalion day, an election, a camp meeting, a political rally, a house raising, an apple-butter boiling or a "frolic."

The character of Hopewell Village began to change before the middle of the nineteenth century. The introduction of hot-blast, coke furnaces reduced the labor cost of producing iron and permitted large concentrations of furnaces in urban centers where transportation facilities were available. The cold-blast, charcoal furnaces could no longer compete. Stove-casting ended at Hopewell in 1844. The expansion of the railroads and the Civil War created a high demand for iron and permitted another forty years of Furnace operation for the production of pig iron. But this was only a reprieve. In 1883 the last blast ended at Hopewell Furnace.

Hopewell Furnace, with its single stack producing a thousand tons of iron annually by the efforts of a hundred or more workers, may appear to have had little in common with today's gigantic iron and steel plants. But only a century and a quarter ago this furnace and several hundred others much like it were the American iron industry.

Glossary

BLAST—The period the furnace was in operation before it closed to rebuild the hearth. IN BLAST was the time the furnace was making iron. *OUT* OF BLAST was any period when the furnace was not operating.

BURNING MINE—Heating the ore to remove impurities, especially sulphur, which would interfere with the production of good iron.

COALING—The destructive distillation of wood to produce charcoal.

COLLIER—The workman who made charcoal.

FILLER—The workman who fed the raw materials into the furnace stack.

FLASKS—Wooden frames used in making cast products. They held the sand into which the molten iron was poured.

FOUNDER—The highly skilled manager of furnace operation. His experience and knowledge were important factors in determining the quality of the iron the furnace produced.

GATEMETAL—Scraps of iron left from the molding process.

419

GUTTERMAN—Unskilled workman at the furnace whose principal duty was to remove the slag, or cinder, to the slag piles.

HOLLOW WARE—Molded cooking utensils such as pots, kettles and skillets.

IRONMASTER—The general manager of the furnace enterprise. He was usually the owner or a partner of the company.

KEEPER—Principal assistant to the founder. Directed the furnace work when the founder was not present.

MINE HOLES—Site of open pit mining for iron ore.

PUTTING IN THE MINE—Wheeling ore from the banks to the bridge house where it would be available to the filler to feed into the furnace.

PUTTING UP THE NIGHT STOCK—Placing in the bridge house the quantities of ore, limestone and charcoal which would be needed to keep the furnace supplied during the night.

STEELING AN AXE—Welding a thin strip of steel to the cutting edge of an iron axe to improve its ability to hold its sharp edge.

TUYERE—The opening into the furnace through which the air blast was carried. The founder used this opening to observe the interior of the furnace to determine how the smelting was proceeding.

WASHING MINE—Removing dirt from the ore by means of a stream of water running through a trough.

Appendix A

Year			
1771	Mark Bird		
1785	John Nixon		
1788	Cadwallader Morris ($\frac{1}{3}$)	James Old ($\frac{2}{3}$)	
1790	Benjamin Morris ($\frac{1}{3}$)	James Old ($\frac{2}{3}$)	
1791	Benjamin Morris		
1793	James Old		
1794	James Wilson		
1796	James Old		
1800	Benjamin Morris		
1800	Daniel Buckley ($\frac{1}{3}$)	Mathew Brooke ($\frac{1}{3}$)	Thomas Brooke ($\frac{1}{3}$)
1824	Daniel Buckley ($\frac{1}{2}$)	Thomas Brooke ($\frac{1}{2}$)	
1827	Daniel Buckley ($\frac{1}{6}$)	Charles Brooke ($\frac{1}{6}$)	
	Clement Buckley ($\frac{1}{6}$)	Clement Brooke ($\frac{1}{6}$)	
	M. Brooke Buckley (($\frac{1}{6}$)	Ann and Tacy Brooke ($\frac{1}{6}$)	
1831	M. Brooke Buckley ($\frac{1}{3}$)	Charles Brooke ($\frac{1}{3}$)	Clement Brooke ($\frac{1}{3}$)
1852	Clement Brooke		
1852	M. Brooke Buckley ($\frac{1}{2}$)	Clement Brooke ($\frac{1}{2}$)	
1856	Edward Buckley ($\frac{1}{2}$)	Clement Brooke ($\frac{1}{2}$)	
1859	Edward Buckley ($\frac{1}{2}$)	Maria Brooke Clingan ($\frac{1}{2}$)	
1895	Charles Clingan ($\frac{1}{6}$)	Maria Brooke Clingan ($\frac{1}{2}$)	
	Louise C. Brooke ($\frac{1}{6}$)		
	Alan Clingan ($\frac{1}{6}$)		

Appendix B

TABLE I

RESIDENTS AT THE IRONMASTER'S MANSION,
CENSUS OF 1850

Name	Age	Occupation
Charles M. Clingan	30	Manufacturer
Maria T. Clingan	29	. .
Clement B. Clingan	7	. .
William W. Clingan	5	. .
Andrew Bust	25	Gardner
Eliza Hill	33	Negro
Sarah Bendigo	28	Mulatto
Susanna Bendigo	5	Mulatto
Anna Maria Wilson	23	Negro
William Jacobs	50	Negro
Anna Keller	22	. .

422

RESIDENTS AT THE IRONMASTER'S MANSION, CENSUS OF 1860

Name	Age	Occupation
Charles Clingan	40	. .
Maria Clingan	39	. .
Clement B. Clingan	16	. .
Charles B. Clingan	9	. .
David D. Clingan	6	. .
Alan H. Clingan	3	. .
John Shafer	36	Clerk
Lidgu Chafer (Female)	22	. .
Rebecca Graham	17	Servant
William Jacobs	55	Negro
Ellen Dickerson	14	Mulatto
Letitia Watson	15	Negro
Samuel Everhart	27	Clerk

TABLE II

HOUSEHOLD ARTICLES PURCHASED BY WORKERS

Date	Article	Price
April 28, 1785	Looking Glass	£1-2/6
December 2, 1802	1 Beadstead	£1-5/0
. .	1 Chest	£1-0/0
. .	1 Doughtrough	10/9
. .	2 Coffins	£4-2/6
February 2, 1803	A Beaurow	£7-10/0
March 3, 1803	Desk	£7-10/0
June 15, 1805	A Beaurow	£5-12/6
April 5, 1805	Bed and Bedding	$9.50
. .	Puter Dish	1.05
. .	6 puter plates	1.10
. .	2 Winsor Chairs	1.20
. .	Bed and bed stead	9.50
. .	4 Winsor Chairs	1.20
. .	Bed and Bedstead	6.10
. .	Large Chest	1.60
May 4, 1807	Clothes Chest	£3-0/0
July 24, 1819	Chest	$3.00
September 28, 1819	A Trunk	4.00
February 22, 1826	A Rug	.50
March 22, 1828	A pair bedsteads	3.50
September 1, 1829	A half doz. chairs	7.25
November 16, 1829	A tub	1.18½
June 1, 1830	A Pair Bedsteads	3.00
. .	Cradle	2.00

April 4, 1832	A Clock	10.00
December 6, 1832	A Shaving Cup	.18½
November 26, 1832	A clock	10.00
February 28, 1833	A Clock	10.00
December 12, 1832	A bureau	20.00
April 30, 1835	1 pair of bedsteads	3.00
. .	„ „	5.00
. .	„ „	3.00
. .	1 Rocking Cradle	2.50
. .	Bedsteads and Breakfast Table	9.50
October 26, 1835	30″ circular stove	9.12½
April 6, 1843	A Coverlet	7.00
February 6, 1849	Carpet	3.03
June 10, 1848	A cupboard	9.50
November 16, 1849	Chairs	10.00
May 5, 1851	Washing Tubs	2.75
April 7, 1857	Comforters and Sheets	5.00

TABLE III

FURNACE PRODUCTION AND LABOR USED IN FIVE SELECTED PERIODS OF TWO BLASTS EACH

	1805– 1807	1818– 1820	1825– 1827	1835– 1837	1851– 1853
Duration of Blasts	2 years	2 years	2 years	2 years 2 mo.	2 years, 3 mo.
Pig Iron (Tons)	448	618	752	355	1,904
Gate Metal (Tons)	...	...	143	315	...
Cast Iron (Tons)	118	123	565	1,144	...
Value of Iron (Approx.)	$20,000	$28,700	$67,700	$126,500	$61,000
Total Persons Employed	186	170	213	246	225
Wages Paid	$19,070	$23,410	$31,020	$43,760	$29,500
Man-days Worked	30,580	28,370	42,860	49,090	41,580

TABLE IV

NUMBER OF PERSONS EMPLOYED IN DIFFERENT JOB CLASSIFICATIONS FOR FIVE PERIODS OF TWO BLASTS EACH

	1805–1807	1818–1820	1825–1827	1835–1837	1851–1853
Banksman	...	...	...	...	2
Burning Mine	...	...	...	4	...
Cabinet Maker	...	...	...	2	...
Carpenter	2	2	3	6	3
Clerk	2	...	1	3	2
Collier	27	21	20	18	14
Commission Sales	...	1	...	...	...
Farm Worker	12	11	21	11	15
Filler	5	3	5	2	6
Founder	1	1	1	2	1
Gardner	...	...	...	2	3
Hostler	...	...	...	2	1
Houseworker	4	6	10	3	16
Keeper	3	4	6	2	3
Laborer	35	19	31	18	27
Maker of Boxes and Baskets	2	6	12	3	...
Manager	1	1	1	2	1
Mason	3	1	4	3	2
Miner	18	23	20	18	35
Misc. Furnace Repair	5	6	5	3	5
Misc. Work by Outsiders	10	10	17	6	7
Misc. Work for Employees	...	...	7	10	...
Molder	6	8	13	19	...
Molder's Helper	1	4	7	10	...
Patternmaker	1	2	2	3	...
Putting in Mine	...	2	3	6	2
Smith	7	1	2	5	1
Stocking Coal	3	3	...	1	3
Teamster for Furnace	11	5	7	9	10
Teamster, Indep.	31	35	49	27	10
Tutor	1	4	2	3	...
Wheelwright	1	3	4	2	1
Woodcutter, Cord.	70	52	60	112	116

| Woodcutter, Posts and Rails | 13 | 4 | 3 | 3 | 21 |
| Total Persons Employed | 186 | 170 | 213 | 246 | 225 |

Table V

MAN-DAYS OF LABOR USED IN DIFFERENT JOB CLASSIFICATIONS FOR FIVE PERIODS OF TWO BLASTS EACH

	1805–1807	1818–1820	1825–1827	1835–1837	1851–1853
Banksman	...	...	...	...	93
Burning Mine	...	...	...	375	...
Cabinet Maker	...	...	...	55	...
Carpenter	28	284	1,033	1,419	397
Clerk	624	...	624	1,300	703
Collier	4,843	4,134	5,300	4,787	4,484
Commission Sales	...	9	...	...	...
Farm Worker	61	112	116	51	1,310
Filler	1,690	787	1,147	1,321	1,337
Founder	624	624	624	762	672
Gardner	...	...	...	371	283
Gutterman	...	453	486	637	524
Hostler	...	...	...	731	62
Houseworker	322	1,281	1,366	2,216	1,967
Keeper	316	737	769	644	679
Laborer	353	1,523	1,994	2,602	1,193
Maker of Boxes and Baskets	299	132	123	237	...
Manager	624	624	624	1,248	1,404
Mason	108	20	681	153	6
Miner	5,035	3,695	4,541	6,528	8,514
Misc. Furnace Repair	184	179	39	148	73
Misc. Work by Outsiders	130	703	393	272	399
Misc. Work for Employees	...	...	72	216	...
Molder	1,687	3,636	3,402	5,797	...
Molder's Helper	3	139	406	663	...
Patternmaker	3	77	71	346	...
Putting in Mine	...	566	1,065	598	668
Smith	870	613	444	1,210	768
Stocking Coal	96	3	...	364	378

Teamster,					
Furnace	1,467	1,552	1,840	1,901	2,281
Teamster,					
Independent	322	936	1,880	2,996	1,490
Tutor	50	300	100	200	...
Wheelwright	205	158	519	185	102
Woodcutter,					
Cordwood	9,973	5,082	13,193	8,698	11,711
Woodcutter,					
Posts, etc.	124	7	8	58	85
Total	30,583	28,368	42,858	49,086	41,581

Note: Fractions of days were rounded.

TABLE VI

SUMMARY OF INCOME AND EXPENDITURES FOR 14 WORKERS, 1818–1842

	John Benson	*Thomas Boyer*	*Thomas Care*
Occupation	Miner–Clerk	Teamster	Founder–Moulder
Years Covered	1818–1830	1818–1836	1818–1841
Total Income	$608.22	$1,193.51	$21,350.93
Cash Drawn	93.63	173.00	6,089.57
Storegoods Bought	130.69	676.91	3,411.51
Storegoods and Cash	...	...	801.62
Furnace Products and Services	5.65	13.81	575.93
Paid to Outsiders	331.39	210.18	9,154.21*
Sundries	89.07	59.19	1,703.28
Unaccounted for	−41.21	+41.21	−384.21

	David Evans	*Robert Gilmore*	*David Hart*
Occupation	Woodcutter	Miner	Teamster
Years Covered	1818–1837	1818–1836	1818–1840
Total Income	$1,252.93	$954.41	$5,690.37
Cash Drawn	926.85	591.98	553.52
Storegoods Bought	304.82	231.45	4,248.05
Storegoods and Cash	5.43	2.30	48.68
Furnace Products and Services	8.70	32.62	203.22
Paid to Outsiders	80.31	113.09	600.30
Sundries	4.43	...	87.39
Unaccounted for	−77.59	−17.03	−50.77

* Includes some labor at the furnace for which the founder paid the wages.

	Henry Houck	George Kephart	Thomas Lloyd
Occupation	Collier	Filler–Keeper	Farmer
Years Covered	1818–1842	1819–1842	1818–1842
Total Income	$3,685.78	$3,483.61	$2,570.89
Cash Drawn	1,947.38	506.69	1,293.41
Storegoods Bought	515.20	2,364.19	726.69
Storegoods and Cash	25.68	51.28	39.79
Furnace Products and Services	19.25	4.27	128.98
Paid to Outsiders	688.16*	378.49	325.87
Sundries	250.61	80.21	126.00
Unaccounted for	+239.50	+98.48	−69.85

	George North	William Pierce	Samuel Williams
Occupation	Moulder	Woodcutter	Teamster
Years Covered	1818–1841	1819–1829	1819–1842
Total Income	$5,303.77	$511.01	$4,696.54
Cash Drawn	693.98	31.82	295.75
Storegoods Bought	3,259.05	268.84	3,254.91
Storegoods and Cash	235.90	...	39.05
Furnace Products and Services	71.88	22.11	2.21
Paid to Outsiders	735.29	24.23	802.34
Sundries	280.63	116.31	266.39
Unaccounted for	+27.02	+47.71	+35.89

	Solomon Williams	Thomas Wynn
Occupation	Woodcutter	Farmer–Miner
Years Covered	1818–1839	1818–1841
Total Income	$344.38	$2,135.44
Cash Drawn	83.42	1,039.87
Storegoods Bought	172.57	45.14
Storegoods and Cash	10.48	...
Furnace Products and Services	9.45	2.25
Paid to Outsiders	29.97	464.62
Sundries	27.90	...
Unaccounted for	+10.59	+593.56

Note: Fractions of a cent were rounded.

Note: The "unaccounted for" item is due in part to the absence of journals for some years.

Appendix C

A RECORD OF THE PURCHASES AT THE HOPEWELL FURNACE
store by 26 customers during the period from December 1831
to February 1833. The information was taken from the Hopewell record book referred to as SM 20. The period used was
one in which the operation of the Furnace was prosperous.
The accounts were for a variety of classifications of wages and
skills. Purchases have been grouped by the kind of goods
bought. Examination of the record book would show the
chronology of the transactions.

JOHN BENSON, CLERK

Cloth	Prices		Quantity	Amount of Purchase
Cord	No Price		None given	$1.00
Calico	$0.21, .25, .30 yard		30 yards	7.53
Buckram	.16	,,	1¼ ,,	.20
Padding	.40	,,	1¼ ,,	.50
"Cloth"	2.37½, 2.40	,,	7 ,,	16.67½
Holland, B	.22	,,	4 ,,	.88
Muslin	.12½, .14, .18½	,,	16 ,,	2.70
Nankeen, Blue	.16½	,,	8 ,,	1.32
			2 pieces	3.00
			Total	$33.80½
Clothing				
Cravat, Jaconete	.30, .40 each		3	1.00
Gloves	.70 pair		1	.70
Handkerchief	.44 each		2	.88
Shoes	1.50 pair		1	1.50
Suspenders	.20 pair		1	.20
			Total	$4.28
Miscellaneous				
Saltpetre	.20 pound		1 lb.	.20
Knives	.20, .40 each		2	.60
Nails	.09 pound		2 lb.	.18
Shoe Polish	.10 box		2	.20
Storegoods to Charity	...		...	34½
			Total	$1.52½

Notions				
Buttons	.06, .12½, .25 doz.	50		1.18½*
Cord	.06 piece	1		.06
Pattern, Vest	.75 each	1		.75
Thread, Silk	.06¼ skein	17		1.05¾
		Total	$3.05¼	
Personal Items				
Tobacco	.03 roll	1		.03
		Total Spent	$42.69¼	

Note: Lived at Big House and bought no food. Family of three in 1830.

* Totals so marked are incorrect, but they are given as the clerk listed them in his records.

CLEMENT BROOKE, MANAGER

Cloth	*Prices*		*Quantity*		*Amount*
Bobinette	$0.70, .80, 1.00	yard	3 15/16	yards	$ 3.25
Buckram	.16	,,	2½	,,	.40
Padding	.30, .40	,,	2¼	,,	.75
Calico	.12½, .13, .15, .18, .20, .22, .25, .27, .31	,,	131	,,	27.76
Cashmere	.30	,,	3¼	,,	.97½
Casinete	1.25	,,	1 lot and 3½	,,	6.03½
Check	.22	,,	1¼	,,	.22*
Cloth, Blue	5.00	,,	3¼	,,	15.00*
Drilling	.20, .22, .25, .50	,,	11⅜	,,	3.33½
Flannel Cotton	.16, .20, .24, .35, .44, .53	,,			
Yellow	.30	,,	22½	,,	7.57
Holland, Brown	.20, .25	,,	2¾	,,	.58½
Jaconete	.35, .62é	,,	1⅛	,,	.68
Lace	.18	,,	2½	,,	.45
Lace Bobinete	.18½, .80	,,	1¾	,,	.78½
Linen, Irish	.58	,,	66	,,	38.28
Marino	.41, .44	,,	26	,,	10.73
Marino, Black	.56	,,	2	,,	1.12
Millinete	No price given		?		?
Millinete and wire	.20	,,	½	,,	.10
Muslin	.12½, .14, .15, .18, .18½, .30 .31, .40, .60, .65, .75	,,			
Black	.10, .14	,,			
Brown	.12½	,,			
Book	.44, .75	,,			
Mull	.60, .67	,,			

Jaconete	.60	,,	117⅞	,,	28.74
Nankeen	.14	,,	1 piece and		
			¾	,,	1.35½
Pittsburgh Cord	.37½	,,	¾	,,	.28
Quilting	.12½, .15, .18é	,,	8¾	,,	1.33é
Satinette	1.40	,,	3¼	,,	4.55
Vesting	1.12	,,	½	,,	.56
Waist Ribbon	.15 each		3	,,	.45

Total $155.29½

Clothing	Prices	Quantity	Amount
Belt	$0.20 each	1	$0.20
Handkerchief	.20, .35, .50, .62½, .87½, 1.00 each	15	8.27
Stockings	.20, .22, .25, .27, .37½, .40, .44, .46 pair	38 pair	14.13é
Suspenders	18½ pair	1	18½

Total $22.79

Miscellaneous

Paper	.20 quire	1½	.30

Notions

Buttons	.20 dozen		
Gilt	.15 ,,		
Bone	.06 ,,		
Small gilt	.18½ ,,		
Pearl	.18 ,,		
Molds	.03 ,,	9 purchases	
Patterns	.25, .65, .75, .87½ each	4	2.52½
Ribbon, Black	.12½ yard		
Green	.04, .10, .12½, .25 yard		
Belt	.12, .20 yard	20½ yards	2.52
Scissors	.18¾ pair	2	.37½
Tape	?	3 pieces	.16
Thread, Silk	.06¼ skein	6 purchases	1.76¾

Total $9.13¾

Personal Items

Comb, Pocket	.12½ each		
Fine toothed			
Side	.05, .25 " each	6	.97½
Soap	.03 cake	2	.06

Total $1.03½
Total Spent $188.54¾

Note: Lived at Big House and bought no food. A household of 15 in 1830.

JOHN CARE, MOULDER

Bulk Items	*Prices*		*Quantity*	*Amount*
Corn, Shelled	$0.56 bushel			
Ear	.37 ,,		3½ bu.	$1.77
Feed	.01 pound or		52 lb. and	
	.60, .62 bushel		8¼ bu.	5.63½
Rye Seed	?		2¾ ,,	?
			Total	$7.40½
Cloth				
Bobinette	1.00	yard	⅝ yards	.62½
Calico	.10, .12½, .15,			
	.16, .17,.18			
	.18½, .20, .21			
	.23, .25	,,	62⅜ ,,	11.47½
Casinette	.56, .67	,,	5¾ ,,	3.43½
Check	.16, .18½, .20,			
	.22	,,	8¼ ,,	1.10*
Drilling	.33	,,	3½ ,,	1.15½
Flannel	.24, .50 .56	,,	10 ,,	3.57
Gingham	.37½	,,	1¼ ,,	.47½
Jaconete	.40, .67	,,	⅝ ,,	.35½
Millinette	.16	,,	½ ,,	.08
Muslin	.10, .12½, .13,			
	.14, .18½	,,		
Plain	.18	,,		
Book	.68	,,		
Cotton	.28, .40	,,	65 ,,	6.76*
Pittsburgh Cord	.22	,,	10 ,,	2.20
Plaid	.18, .18¾	,,	4 ,,	.73½
			Total	$31.96½
Clothing				
Cravat	.62½ each		1	.62½
Gloves, Buckskin	.75 pair		1	.75
Mitts	.50 ,,		1	.50
Handkerchiefs,				
Cotton	.15, .23, .25, .28 each		6	1.31
Silk	1.12½ each		1	1.12½
Hat, Palm leaf	.37 each		1	.37
Fur	3.50 each		1	3.50
Cap—boy's	1.00 each		1	1.00
Shoes	1.25, 1.50 pair		3	4.25
Stockings	.32 pair		1	.32
			Total	$13.75
Food	*Prices*		*Quantity*	*Amount*
Bacon	$0.10 pound		62½ lb.	$6.25
Beef	.05 ,,		9¾ ,,	.49
Cheese	.12½		4⅜ ,,	.54
Coffee	.16, .17 pound		57 ,,	10.53*

Flour	.60 quarter (28 lb.)	4 quarters	2.40
,, , Wheat	.03 pound	11 lb.	.33
Mackeral	5.50 Barrel	2 bbl.	11.00
Molasses	.14, .16 quart	37 qts.	5.47
Pork	.04½ pound	303 lb. (1 Hog)	13.63½
Potatoes	.34, .40, .50 bushel	11¼ bu.	4.47
Salt, Coarse	.03 quart		
Fine	.04 ,, or .85, 1.00 bu.	4¾ ,,	2.17½*
Spices, Pepper	.40 pound	¼ lb.	.10
Saltpeter	.24 ,,	¼ ,,	.06
Sugar	.12½ ,,	70 ,,	8.75
Tea	.31, .31¼, .32 per ¼ lb.	3 ,,	3.42½

Total $69.62½

Miscellaneous

Almanac	.08 each	1	.08
Blacksmith work	...	2 jobs	.40
Hardware, Building	...	7 purchases	.85
File	.10	1	.10
Glass	.05 each	11 panes	.55
Putty	.05 pound	1 lb.	.05
Coffee Mill	1.00 each	1	1.00
Starch	.16 pound	¼ lb.	.04
Nails	.09, .11, .12 pound	26 ,,	4.19*
Nails, Ceiling	.11, .12½ ,,	21 ,,	2.32½
Spikes	.08 pound	4¼ ,,	.34
Jar	.10 each	1	.10
Oil	.12, .12½ quart	3 qt.	.37
Packing Box	.10, .75 each	2	.85
Fish net	1.12½ each	1	1.12½
Horse Collar	2.00 ,,	1	2.00
Fish Barrel	.37½ each	1	.37½
Black Lead	.24 pound	¼ lb.	.06
Paper	.01 sheet	5	.05
Pasteboard	.06 each	1	.06

Total $14.91½

Notions

Braid	.03 yard	5 yd.	.15
Buttons	.06, .19 dozen	20 purchases	.92½
Cotton Balls	.02 each	19	.38
Cord	.04 piece	1 piece	.04
Patterns, vest	0.87½ each	1	0.87½
Pins	.12½ sheet	3 sheets	.37½
Ribbon	.03½, .04, .15 yd.	2¾ yds.	.12
Black	.05, .15 yard	3 ,,	.35
Tape	?	2 pieces	.12¼
Thread, Spool	.03 spool	2	.06
Skein	.01 skein	12	.12
Silk	.06¼ ,,	8	.50
Others	?	?	.51

Total $4.52¾

Personal Items			
Comb, Large	.31 each	1	.31
Pocket	.15	1	.15
Fine Toothed	.15, .17, .25, .31 each	4	.88
Medicine, Magnesia	.18½ ounce	1 oz.	.18½
Castor Oil	.12½ ,,	2 ,,	.25
Razor	.63½ each	1	.63½
Shaving Soap	.05 cake	2 cakes	.10
Tobacco, Rolls	.03 each	46	1.38
Papers	.05, .10	3	.25
Half Pounds	.20, .28 pound	2 ½-lb.	.24
		Total $.4.38	
		Total Spent $146.56¾	

Note: No family record identified in census of 1830.

ALEXANDER CHURCH, MINER

Bulk Items	*Prices*	*Quantity*	*Amount*
Corn, ear	$0.74 bushel	¼ bu.	$0.18½
Feed	.61 ,,	1⅛ bu.	.67
		Total $0.85½	
Cloth			
Calico	.14, .16½, .18, .25 yd.	32½ yards	6.02
Check	.16, .20, .22 ,,	3¾ ,,	.68
Muslin	.10, .12½, .13, .15 ,,	51 ,,	6.44½
Plaid	.12½, .13, .17 ,,	24 ,,	3.12½
Russia Sheeting	.31 ,,	¾ ,,	.22½
		Total $16.49½	
Clothing			
Handkerchief	.16 each	1	.16
Hat, Fur	3.00 ,,	1	3.00
Palm Leaf	.37½ ,,	1	.37½
Mitts, Buckskin	.50	1	.50
Shawl	.25	1	.25
		Total $4.28½	
Food			
Bacon	.10 pound	10 lb.	1.00
Chocolate	.20 ,,	1 ,,	.20
Coffee	.16, .17 pound	35 ,,	6.04
Flour	.60 quarter (28 lbs.)	53 qr.	30.60*
Mackeral	.05 each	6	.30
Molasses	.14, .16 quart	13 quarts	1.97
Pork	.05 pound	230 lb. (1 hog)	11.50
Potatoes	.37, .40 bushel	10 bu.	3.94½
Salt	.04 quart	6½ qt.	.26
Spices, Saltpetre	.48 pound	⅛ lb.	.06
Pepper	.40, .48 pound	⅜ ,,	.32
Sugar	.12½ pound	23 ,,	2.87½
Tea	.31, .31¼ per ¼ pound	2¾ ,,	3.73½
		Total $62.80½	

Miscellaneous			
Glass	.05 each	4 panes	.20
Putty	.10 pound	½ lb.	.05
Knives and Forks	1.00 dozen	1 doz.	1.00
Paper and Tape	.06 lot	1 lot	.06
		Total	$1.31

Notions	*Prices*	*Quantity*	*Amount*
Braid, pins and thread		1 lot	$0.12
Buttons	$0.01 per ¼ dozen	9	.03
Cotton Balls	.02 each	16	.32
Pins, Row	.01 row	1	.01
Sheet	.12 sheet	½	.06
Ribbon, Black	.20 yard	1 yd.	.20
Tape w Paper	.06 lot	1 lot	.06
Tape w Thread	.22¼ lot	1 "	.22¼
Thread, Skein	.01		
Spool	.03	9 purchases	1.08
		Total	$2.10¼

Personal Items			
Comb, Fine Tooth	.12, .12½, .40 each		
Side	.04 pair	6	.97½
Medicine, Salts	.03 ounce	2 oz.	.06
Tobacco	.03 roll	1 roll	.03
Tobacco	.20 pound	3½ lb.	.70
Soap	.10 "	14½ "	1.45
		Total	$3.21½
		Total Spent	$91.06¾

Note: Supporting a household of nine persons in 1830.

PHILIP FILMAN, COMMERCIAL TEAMSTER

Cloth	*Prices*	*Quantity*	*Amount*
Bobinete	$0.87½ yard	1 yd.	$0.87½
Buckram	.16 "	¼ yd.	.04
Calico	.18, .20, .22 yard	21 "	4.27
Casinete	.80, 1.50 "	5¾ "	6.70
Check	.20 "	2½ "	.50
Drill	.37½ "	4½ "	1.68½
Muslin	.12½, .14, .15 "	8 "	1.06
Velvet	.67 "	2¼ "	1.51
Vesting, Silk	1.31 "	1 "	1.31
		Total	$17.95

Clothing			
Gloves, Buckskin	.37½, .75 pair	2	1.12½
Hat, Palm leaf	.37½ each	1	.37½
Cap, boys'	1.00 "	1	1.00
Stockings	.35 pair	1	.35
		Total	$2.85

Food			
Coffee	.16 pound	24 lb.	5.76*
Cheese	.09, .12½ pound	5 "	.53½
Chocolate	.20 "	1 "	.20
Lard	.09 "	1 keg of 53 lb.	4.77
Sugar	.12½ "	9 lb.	1.12½
Tea	.31 per ¼ "	¾ lb.	.93
		Total $13.32	
Miscellaneous			
Blacksmithing	...	1 job	.07
Candlestick	.15	1	.15
Knives and Forks	2.75	½ doz.	1.37½
		Total $1.59½	
Notions			
Buttons and Thread	...	...	.22½
Pattern, Vest	.87½ each	1	.87½
Thread	.03 spool		
Thread Silk	.06¼ "	7	.45½*
		Total $1.55½	
		Total Spent $37.27	

Note: Supporting family of five in 1830.

BARNEY HART, KEEPER

Bulk Items	*Prices*	*Quantity*	*Amount*
Corn, Eear	$0.25, .38 bushel	2½ bu.	$0.81
Feed	.60, 62½ "	3¼ "	2.00
	1.24 per 100 pounds	28 lb.	.31
Wheat	1.10 bushel	2 bu.	2.20
		Total $5.32	
Cloth			
Brown Holland	.25 yard	2 yards	.50
Buckram	.16 "	⅝ "	.10
Padding	.40 "	⅝ "	.25
Calico	.10, .12½, .16, .17, .20 yard	12 "	1.54½
Casinete	.67, 1.06 yard	3¾	3.68
Check	.16, .20, .22 yard	12¾ "	2.32
"Cloth"	4.25 "	2 "	8.50
Drilling	.23 "	3 "	.69
Flannel	.24, .56 "	5¾ "	1.62
Muslin	.09, .10, .13, .14, .15 yard	20 "	2.85½
Pittsburg Cord	.24 "	3 "	.72
Plaid	.18½ "	12 "	2.22
Russia Sheeting	.15, .22 yard	10½ "	2.06½
Ticking	.33 "	2½ "	.82
		Total $27.88½	

Clothing			
Cravat, Jaconete	.44 each	1	.44
Mitts, Buckskin	.50 pair	1	.50
Handkerchief	.25 each	1	.25
Hat	.87½ ”	1	.87½
Shoes	1.25, 1.50 pair	5	6.95
Stockings	.31 pair	1	.31
Suspenders	.15 ”	1	.15
		Total	$9.47½
Food			
Bacon	.08, .10 pound	143 lb.	13.72
Beef	.08 ”	76¼ ”	5.90*
” Side	.04¼ ”	231 ”	10.39½
”	.05 ”	11¼ ”	.56
Cheese	.12 ”	3¾ ”	.47½*
Coffee	.17 ”	44 ”	7.48
Flour	.60 quarter (28 lbs.)	37 qr.	22.20
”	.03 pound	12 lb.	.36
Lard	.10 ”	22⅞ ”	2.28½
Mackerel	7.00 barrel	½ bbl.	3.50
Food—Continued	*Prices*	*Quantity*	*Amount*
Molasses	$0 14, .16 quart	32 qt.	$4.91
Pork, Spare ribs	.03 lb.	28 lb.	.84
” Pickeled	.09 ”	6¼ ”	.56½
” Hog	.04½ ”	250 ”	11.25
Potatoes	.30, .32, .40, 1.00 bu.	12 bu.	4.56½
Rice	.05 pound	1 lb.	.05
Salt	.04 quart	26 qt.	1.04
”	.85, .88, 1.00 bushel	1⅛ bu.	1.05
Spices, Pepper	.40 pound	½ lb.	.20
Sugar	.12½ ”	27 ”	3.37½
Tea	.31 per ¼ pound	2¼ ”	2.48*
		Total	$97.20
Miscellaneous			
Barter, Wool and Pigs	for Storegoods	...	2.25
Charity, Storegoods	...	...	1.87½
Almanac	.08 each	1	.08
Bedcord	.45 ”	1	.45
Broom	.12½ ”	1	.12½
Fish Net	1.12 ”	1	1.12
Knives, Pen	.33 ”	1	.33
” Butcher	.20 ”	1	.20
Oil	.12½ quart	7 qt.	.87½
Pasteboard	.05 each	2	.10
Whetstone	.09	1	.09
Plaister	.74 bushel	¼ bu.	.18½
		Total	$7.68
Notions			
Buttons	.06 dozen		
” Pearl	.01 each		
” Giltcoat	.62½ dozen		
” Giltvest	.20 ”	?	.89½

Cord	.24 yard	1 yd.	.24
Cotton Balls	.02 each	8	.16
Pattern	.45 each	1	.45
Tape	...	4 pieces	.21½
Thread	.01 skein		
,, Silk	.06¼ spool	?	.56
		Total	$2.52

Personal Items	*Prices*	*Quantity*	*Amount*
Comb, Fine toothed	$ .18 each	2	$0.36
Medicine, Salts	.06¼ dose	1	.06¼
Soap	.10 lb.	6¾ lb.	.67
Tobacco, Roll	.03 each	97	
,, Paper	.10 ,,	10	
,, Pound	.20	1	3.94*
		Total	$5.03¼
		Total Spent	$155.11¼

Note: Supporting a family of six in 1830.

DAVID HART, COLLIER

Bulk Items	*Prices*	*Quantity*	*Amount*
Corn	$0.50, .56 bushel	29 bu.	$14.68
,, Ear	.37½ ,,	14 ,,	4.85*
Feed	.60, .62 ,,	7 ,,	4.21
Oats	.37, .40 ,,	2½ ,,	.94*
Plaister	.75 ,,	2 ,,	1.50
Wheat	1.10, .25 ,,	30½ ,,	22.85*
		Total	$49.03

Cloth			
Calico	.12½, .15 yard	3½ yd.	.45
Cashmere	.22½, .37½, 2.87½ yard	10¾ ,,	10.91½
Casinette	.50, .80 ,,	6½ ,,	4.45
Check	.16, .18½, .20, .22 ,,	5⅛ ,,	1.16*
Cord, Velvet	.67 ,,	3½ ,,	2.34½
Flannel, Cotton	.17, .24 ,,	5 ,,	1.13
Muslin	.12 .13½, .14, .15, .22, .22½ ,,	74½ ,,	
,, Domestic	.13 ,,	and	
,, Black	.17 ,,	1 lot	11.42½
Buckram	.16 ,,	⅞ yd.	.14
Padding	.42 ,,	½ ,,	.21
Pittsburgh Cord	.22, .28 ,,	6¾ ,,	1.53
Plaid	.18½ ,,	7 ,,	1.30
Russian Sheeting	.22½ ,,	¾ ,,	.16½
Stripe	.18, .37½ ,,	3 ,,	.93
		Total	$36.15

Clothing	*Prices*	*Quantity*	*Amount*
Cap, Men's	$1.25 each	1	$ 1.25
Mitts, Buckskin	.50 pair	1	.50
Hat, Boys' Wool	.62½ each	1	.62½
" "	.80 "	1	.80
" Fur	3.50 "	1	3.50
Handkerchiefs	.18, .23, .25,.28 , .30,	2 silk	1.55
	.31½, .65, .90 each	6 cotton	1.55½
Shoes	1.25, 1.37½, 1.50 pair	7	9.87½
Stock	.67 each	1	.67
Stockings	.50, .56 pair	2	1.06
Suspenders	.15 "	2	.30
		Total $21.68½	
Food			
Bacon	.10 pound	357½ lb.	35.39½*
Beef	.08 "	9 "	
" Offal	.50 each	1 "	
" Side	.04½ pound	256 "	12.33½
Cheese	.12, .12½ pound	17¼ "	2.12½
Chocolate	.20	1½ "	.30
Coffee	.16, .17 "	72 "	12.21
Fats, Lard and Tallow	.10 "	20¾ "	2.04*
Flour	.50, .60 qtr. (28 lb.)	45 qr.	25.50
" Wheat	.03, .04 pound	17 lb.	.59
Mackerel	5.75, 6.00, 7.00 barrel	2 bbl.	12.25
Molasses	.14, .15 quart	57½ qt.	8.06½
Pork	.03, .05 pound	11¾ lb.	.45
" Hog	.04½ "	196¼ "	8.30
Potatoes	...	...	3.59½
Rice	.05 "	2 "	.10
Salt	.03, .04 quart	?	
	.85, .88 bushel		2.10
Spices, Pepper	.37, .40 pound	1¼ "	.48½
" Alspice	.40 "	¼ "	.10
Storegoods	...	1 lot	.12
Sugar	.12½ "	27 lb.	3.37½
Tea	.31 per ¼ "	3¼ "	4.03
		Total $133.36½	
Miscellaneous			
Blacksmith work	...	7 jobs	1.82
Firewood	.50 load	1	.50
Boiler	.40 each	1	.40
Tools, Collier's			
Hoe	.50 "	1	.50
Pitch fork	.37½ "	1	.37½
File	.12½ "	1	.12½
Curry comb	.27 "	1	.27
Knives, Pen	.18½, .33 each	2	.51½
" Barlow	.12½ "	1	.12½
" Butcher	.20	1	.20
Shoeblacking	.10 box	2	.20
		Total $ 5.03	

Notions

Buttons		.01, .01½ each, .06 dozen		
„	Bone	.00½ each		
„	Pearl	.05, .10, .12½ dozen		
„	Yankee	.12½ „		
„	Gilt vest	.25 „	14 purchases	1.83
Cotton Balls		.02 each	8	.16
Braid		.01, .03 yard	4 yards	.05
Patterns		.45, .87½, 1.00 each	3	2.32½
Pins		.01 row	4 rows	.04
Tape		.01, .02 yard	5 yd., 1 piece	.12
Thread		.01, .01½ skein		
„	Silk	.06¼ „	28 sk., 12 lts.	1.92

Total $ 6.45½

Personal Items

Combs	.08, .12½, .15, .17 ea.	4	.54½*
Soap	.10 pound	4⅝ lb.	.49½*
Tobacco	.03 roll, .20 lb., .10 paper		12.13

Total $13.17
Total Spent $264.88½

Note: A household of seven in 1830.

WILKINSON HILL, NEGRO LABORER

Bulk Items	Prices		Quantity	Amount
Corn	$0.50, .56 bushel		9 bu.	$ 4.56
Feed	.62½ „		1 „	.62½
Oats	.33 „		1 „	.33
Wheat	.56, 1.10 „		2¼ „	2.34

Total $ 7.85½

Cloth	Prices		Quantity	Amount
Calico	.10, .12½, .16, .25, .31	yard	49½ yd.	6.90½
Cap Stuff	.42	„	½ „	.21
Casinette	.45	„	½ „	.22½
Check	.16, .18½	„	6⅜ „	1.18
Flannel	.40	„		
„ Cotton	.12, .18½, .24	„		
„ Red	.33	„	14¾ „	3.52½
Jaconete	.67	„	⅛ „	.08½
Muslin	.10, .12½, .13, .14 yd.		31¼ „	3.58
Pittsburg Cord	.22	„	7 „	1.54
Ticking	.20	„	11½ „	2.30

Total $ 19.55

Clothing

Handkerchief	.12½ each	2	.25
Hat, cotton	.25	1	.25
Mitts, Buckskin	.50 pair	1	.50
		Total $ 1.00	

Food

Bacon	.10 pound	45¾ lb.	4.57½
Beef	.08 ,,	16½ ,,	1.32
,, offal	.04½ ,,	129 ,,	5.80½
	.50 each	1	.50
Cheese	.12 pound	1½ ,,	.18½*
Coffee	.17 ,,	18 ,,	3.06
Fat, lard	.10 ,,	2¾ ,,	.26½*
Flour	.60 quarter (28 lb.)	15 qr.	9.00
Mackerel	.05, .07½ each, 6.75 bbl.	9 and ½ bbl.	3.87½
Molasses	.15, .16 quart	3 qt.	.47
Salt	.03 quart, .21½, .25 peck	2 pk. & 6 qt.	.63½
Spices, Pepper	.40 pound	¼ lb	.10
Sugar	.12½ ,,	52	6.50
Tea	.31, .31¼ per ¼ pd.	½ ,,	.62¼
		Total $ 36.91¼	

Miscellaneous

Sugar Bowl	.18½ each	1	.18½
Dutch Oven w. Lid	.62½ ,,	1	.62½
Starch	.20 pound	¼ lb.	.05
Oil Barrel, empty	.37½ each	1	.37½
Oil	.12½ quart	6 qt.	.75
		Total $ 1.98½	

Notions	*Prices*	*Quantity*	*Amount*
Buttons	$0.10 dozen	6	$0.05
Cotton Balls	.02 each	9	.18
Tape	...	2 pieces	.08
Thread, Patent	.12½ each		
Thread	.03 each, .01 skein	10 purchases	.36
		Total $ .67	

Personal Items

Soap	.10 pound	9½ bl.	.91
Tobacco	.10 paper	4 papers	.40
		Total $ 1.31	
		Total Spent $ 69.28¼	

Note : No report on family identified in census of 1830.

ISAAC HUGHES, GUTTERMAN

Cloth	Prices	Quantity	Amount
Cloth, Blue	$1.00 yard	$\frac{1}{4}$ yard	$0.25
Flannel, Red	.56 ,,		
,, Yellow	.50 ,,	$12\frac{1}{2}$,,	
,, Cotton, Red	.24 ,,		5.44
Linen, Tow	.25 ,,	2 ,,	.50
Muslin	.14 ,,	1 ,,	.14
Pittsburg Cord	.22, .24 yard	6 ,,	1.38
		Total $ 7.71	

Clothing			
Handkerchief	.23 each	1	.23
Hat, Wool	.80 ,,	1	.80
Shoes	1.25 pair	1	1.25
Stockings, Germantown	2.00 ,,	1	2.00
		Total $ 4.28	

Food			
Pork	.04$\frac{1}{2}$ pound	444 lb.	21.05*

Miscellaneous			
Knives, Pen	.16 each		
,, Pocket	.45 ,,	4	.93

Notions			
Thread	.05 hank	3	.15

Personal Items			
Shaving Soap	.05 cake	1	.05
Soap	.10 pound	1$\frac{1}{8}$ lb.	.11$\frac{1}{2}$
		Total $ .16$\frac{1}{2}$	
		Total Spent $ 34.28$\frac{1}{2}$	

Note : Probably lived with relatives.

WILLIAM JACOBS, NEGRO TEAMSTER

Cloth	Prices	Quantity	Amount
Baize	$1.00 yard	$\frac{3}{4}$ yd.	$0.75
Buckram	.16 ,,	$\frac{1}{2}$,,	.08
Padding	.40 ,,	$\frac{1}{4}$,,	.10
Calico	.12$\frac{1}{2}$, .17, .18, .23, .27 yard	23 ,,	4.52$\frac{1}{2}$
Casinette	.70, .80, 1.06 ,, 1.12$\frac{1}{2}$,,	4$\frac{1}{4}$,,	5.87*
Check	.21, .22 ,,	5 ,,	1.06$\frac{1}{2}$
Flannel	.24, .50, .56 ,,	17$\frac{1}{8}$,,	6.82
Jaconete	.40, .67 ,,	1 ,,	.47
Muslin	.12, .12$\frac{1}{2}$, .13, .14 yd.	12$\frac{1}{2}$,,	1.68$\frac{1}{2}$

Pittsburg Cord	.24 yard	8¼ ,,	2.15½*
Tear-not Cloth	1.25 ..	4½ ,,	5.62½
Ticking	.33 ,,	3 ,,	.99
Velvet	.37½ ,,	½ ,,	.18
		Total	$ 30.31½
Clothing			
Gloves	.75 pair	1	.75
Mitts, Buckskin	.45, .50 pair	3	1.45
Hat, Wool	.75 each	1	.75
,, Fur	2.75, 3.50 each	2	6.25
Handkerchief	.12½, .20, .29, .44,	5	1.39
	.65, .99 each	3 silk	2.45
Shoes	1.50, 1.75 pair	2	3.25
Stockings	.37½, .56, 1.00 pair	6	3.87
Suspenders	.37½ pair	1	.37½
		Total	$ 20.53½
Food			
Cheese	.12 pound	2 lb.	.24
Coffee (given to others)	.17 ,,	?	.54½
Molasses	.15 quart	2	.30
Sugar	.12½ pound	2	.25
Tea	.31 per ¼ pound	¼ lb.	.31
		Total	$ 1.64½
Miscellaneous			
Barter	...	1 lot	.37½
Knives, Barlow	.10 each		
Double Bladed	.30 ,,		
Pocket	.45 ,,	3	.95*
Storegoods, Charity	...	...	2.62½
		Total	$ 3.95
Notions			
Braid	.03 yard	4½ yd.	.13
Binding	.03 ,,	3 ,,	.09
Buttons	.04, .06 dozen		
Pearl	.18 ,,		
Gilt	.01 each		
Yankee	.01 ,,	14 purchases	1.33
Cotton Balls	.02 ,,	2	.04
Pattern	.50 ,,	1	.50
Ribbon	.15 yard	¾ yd.	.11¼
Tape	.01½ ..	2 yd. and 2 pieces	.15
Thread, Silk	.06¼ skein	11 sk.	.78*
		Total	$ 3.13½
		Total Spent	$ 59.58

Note: May have lived at Big House. He was listed there in later censuses when each person was named.

POLLY KIDD, HIRED GIRL

Cloth	*Prices*	*Quantity*	*Amount*
Calico	$0.12½, .23 yard	16 yd.	$2.84
Muslin	.20	2 ,,	.40
		Total $ 3.24	
Clothing			
Shawl	.20 each	1	.20
Notions			
Thread, Silk	.06 skein	1 sk.	.06
		Total Spent $ 3.50	

Note: Undoubtedly lived at the Big House.

THOMAS LLOYD, NEIGHBORING FARMER

Cloth	*Prices*	*Quantity*	*Amount*
Bobonete	$1.00 yard	⅝ yd.	$0.62½
Calico	.18½ ,,	1¼ ,,	.23
Cashmere	.22, .23 yard	9 ,,	2.04
Casinete	1.06 ,,	2¾ ,,	2.91½
Check	.20, .22 ,,	2½ ,,	.52
Drilling	.20 ,,	9 ,,	1.80
Jaconete	.75 ,,	⅝ ,,	.46½
Muslin	.12, .13, .14, .15, .18, .22, .24 yard	48 ,,	7.97½
Quilting	.18½ ,,	9 ,,	1.68½*
Velvet	.56 ,,	2¾ ,,	1.54
		Total $ 19.79½	
Clothing			
Gloves	.31 pair	1	.31
Handkerchief	.15, .20 each	3	.50
Hat, Palm leaf	.31, .37½ ,,	2	.68½
		Total $ 1.49½	
Food			
Cheese	.12 pound	2¾ lb.	.33*
Coffee	.17 ,,	34 ,,	5.78
Molasses	.14, .16 quart	29 qt.	4.50
Salt	.04 quart, 1.00 bu.	4 qt., ¾ bu.	.83½*
Spices, Pepper	.37, .40 pound	1½ lb.	.58½
,, Saltpetre	.25 ,,	½ ,,	.12½
Sugar	.12½ ,,	29 ,,	3.62½
Tea	.31 per ¼ pound	¾ ,,	.93¼*
		Total $ 16.71¼	

Miscellaneous	*Prices*	*Quantity*	*Amount*
Black Lead	$0.25 pound	½ lb	$0.12½
Blacksmith Work	...	12 jobs	1.17½
Calf Skins	.10 "	53 lb.	5.30
Glass	.05 pane	6 panes	.30
Putty	.10 pound	½lb.	.05
Knife, Barlow	.10 each	1	.10
" Pen	.16 "	1	.16
Nails	.09 pound	1 "	.09
Oil	.12 quart	½ qt.	.06
Paper	.01 sheet	26 sh.	.26
Plowshares	.37½ each	3	1.12½
		Total	$ 8.67½

Notions			
Buttons, Gilt	.20 dozen		
" Pearl	.01½ each	3 purchases	.49
Braid, Black	.03 yard	2½ yards	.07½
Tape	...	2 pieces	.10
Pins	.12½ sheet	1 sh.	.12½
"	.01 row	2 row	.02
Cotton Balls	.02 each	2	.04
Hooks and Eyes	.12½ box	1 box	.12½
Scissors	.25 pair	2	.50
Thread, Silk	.06¼ skein	6 sk.	.43½*
" Others	...	12 purchases	.80¼
		Total	$ 2.71¼

Personal Items			
Combs, Dressing	.12½ each	1	.12½
" Fine toothed	.06 "	1	.06
Soap	.10 pound	5 lb.	.50
Tobacco, Rolls	.03 each	4	.12
" Pound	.20 pound	6 lb.	1.20
		Total	$ 2.00½
		Total Spent	$ 49.90½

Note: Supporting a household of seven persons in 1830.

MOSES MORTEN, NEGRO LABORER-TEAMSTER

Bulk Items	*Prices*	*Quantity*	*Amount*
Feed	$0.01 pound	10 lb.	$0.10
Wheat	1.10 bushel	1½ bu.	1.65
Corn, Ear	.37 "	½ "	.18½
		Total	$ 1.93½

Cloth	*Prices*	*Quantity*	*Amount*
Calico	$0.18½, .20 yard	20 yd.	$3.85
Check	.18½, .22 "	2⅝ yd.	.48½
Flannel	.33 "	1 "	.33
Jaconete	.40, .67 "	⅞ "	.41½

	Prices	Quantity	Amount
Muslin	.12½, .13, .14, .15 yd.		
” Black	.25 yard	35¼ ”	4.60½
Pittsburg Cord	.22, .24 yard	11 ”	2.48
Ticking	.20 ”	12 ”	2.40
		Total	$ 14.56
Clothing			
Handkerchief	.12½, .37½ each	2	.50
Hat, Wool	.87½ each	1	.87½
Shoes	1.50 pair	2	3.00
Stockings	.37½ ”	1	.37½
		Total	$ 4.75
Food			
Bacon	.10 pound	8¾ lb.	.85*
Cheese	.12½ ”	1½ ”	.18½
Chocolate	.20 ”	½ ”	.10
Coffee	.17 ”	5½ ”	.93½
Flour	.60 quarter (28 lb.)	11½ qr.	6.90
” Wheat	.05 pound	9½ lb.	.47½
Mackerel	.05 each	18	.90
Molasses	.12½, .14 quart	26 qt.	3.42
Pork, Hog	.05 pound	308 lb.	15.40
Potatoes	1.75 row	1½ row	2.62½
Salt	.04, .05 quart	12 qt.	.46*
Spices, Pepper	.40 pound	¼ lb.	.10
” Alspice	.48 pound	⅛ ”	.06
Sugar	.12½ ”	1 ”	.12½
Tea	.31 per ¼ pound	1 ”	1.71¼
Goose	.40 each	1⅜ ”	.40
		Total	$34.64¾
Miscellaneous			
Blanket	3.75 pair	1 pr.	3.75
Comforter	1.44 each	1	1.44
Black Lead	.24 pound	¼ lb.	.06
Oil	.12½ quart	4 qt.	.50
		Total	$ 5.75
Notions	*Prices*	*Quantity*	*Amount*
Buttons w. thread	...	2 lots	$0.32½
Thread	.01 skein	6 sk.	.06
Cotton Balls	.02 each	3	.06
		Total	$ .44½
Personal Items			
Combs	.12½ each	2	.25
Medicine, Salts	.03 ounce	3 oz.	.09
” Caster Oil	.12½ ”	1 ”	12½
Razor	.62½ each	1	.62½
Strop and Box	.45	1	.45
Shaving Brush	.10 ”	1	.10
Soap	.10 pound	4⅝ lb.	.46½

Tobacco, Roll	.03 each	18	.54
,, Paper	.10 each	3	.30
,, Pound	.20 pound	1	.20

Total $ 3.14½
Total Spent $65.23¾

Note: A family of six in 1830.

ELIZABETH MOYERS, HIRED GIRL
(Salary—$.75 per week)

Cloth

Calico	$0.12½, .23, .27, .31, .40 yard	29 yards	$6.54½
Check	.20, .21, .22, .25 yard	7½ ,,	1.61
Chince	.32 yard	8 ,,	2.56
Flannel	.44 ,,	1¼ ,,	.55
Muslin	.12½, .14, .15, .17 ,,	8½ ,,	1.14

Total $12.40½

Clothing

Handkerchief	.30, .44 each	2	.74
Hood, Silk	1.50 ,,	1	1.50
Shoes, Monroes	1.75 pair ,,	1	1.75

Total $ 3.99

Food

Coffee	.17 pound	2 lb. and 1 lot	.46½
Sugar	.12½ ,,	1 ,,	.12½

Total $ .59

Miscellaneous

Pasteboard	$0.06 per sheet	1	$0.06
Storegoods	...	1 lot	.12½

Total $ 0.18½

Notions

Tape, Buttons and Thread	...	1 lot	.10
Buttons	.01 each	6	.06
Braid, Black	.03 yard	1 yard	.03
Tape	.01 ,,	2 ,, and 2 pieces	.18
Braid and Thread	...	1 lot	.07
Cotton Balls	.02 each	3	.06
Hooks and Eyes	.10 box	1 box	.10
Pattern	.25 each	1	.25
Thread	...	6 purchases	.34

Total $ 1.19

Personal Items

Comb, large, Side	.20 pair	1 pair	.20
,,	.12½ each	1	.12½

Total $ 0.32½
Total Spent $18.68½

Note: Undoubtedly lived at the Big House.

FREDERICK PAINTER, BEGINNING MOULDER

Bulk Items	Prices	Quantity	Amount
Wheat	$1.10 bushel	2 bu.	$2.20

Cloth	Prices	Quantity	Amount
Calico	.21 yard	7½ yd.	1.52*
Linen, Tow	.17 ,,	⅝ ,,	.10½
Muslin	.12½, .15 yard	12 ,,	1.75
Sheeting	.31 ,,	7 ,,	2.17
		Total ,,	$ 5.54½

Clothing	Prices	Quantity	Amount
Cravat, Jaconete	$0.62½ each	1	$0.62½
Handkerchief	.15 ,,	1	.15
Shoes	1.50 pair	1	1.50
Stock	.67 each	1	.67
		Total	$ 2.94½

Food		Quantity	Amount
Bacon	.10 pound	108¾ lb	10.87
Chocolate	.20 ,,	2 ,,	.40
Coffee	.17 ,,	1 ,,	.17
Flour	.60 quarter (28 lb.)	1 qr.	.60
Molasses	.14, .16 quart	13 qt.	1.98
Pork, 1 Hog	.04½ pound	256 lb.	11.92½*
Salt	.03 quart, .84 bushel	12 qt.	.33⅓
Tea	.31 per ¼ pound	1 lb.	1.24½*
Sugar	.12½ pound	16 ,,	1.99¾*
Spices, Pepper	.40 pound	¼ ,,	.10
,, Saltpetre	.32 ,,	1 oz.	.02
		Total	$29.61

Notions			
Thread	...	3 lots	.15

Personal Items			
Comb	.31 each	1	.31
Tobacco	.03 roll	39 rolls	
,,	.20 pound	½ lb.	1.30
		Total	$ 1.61
		Total Spent	$42.06

Note: May have been living with parents at this time.

JOHN PAINTER, FILLER

Bulk Items	*Prices*	*Quantity*	*Amount*
Corn, Ear	$0.37, .50 bushel	6¼ bu.	$3.18½*
Feed	.60, .61 "	3 "	1.81½
Mushmeal	.01½ pound	13 lb.	.20
Wheat	1.10 bushel	6 bu.	6.60
		Total	$11.80

Cloth	*Prices*	*Quantity*	*Amount*
Baize, Green	$1.00 yard	½ yd.	$0.50
Calico	.12½, .20, .28		
" Blue	.21 yard	23¾ "	4.38
Casinete	.67, 1.12½, 1.87½ yd.	8¾ "	9.92½
Check	.16, .20 .22 "	5¼ "	1.00½
Flannel, Cotton	.24, .33 "		
" Green	.24 "		
"	.50 "	16⅝ "	5.08¼
Drill	.33, .37½, .50 "		
" Check	.21, .27 "	12 "	4.59
Millente	.15 "	1 "	.15
Muslin	.12, .12½, .13, .14 "		
"	.15, .18, .22 "		
" Domestic	.10 "	73 "	9.93½
Patron	.32 "	1¾ "	.57*
Pittsburg Cord	.24 "	8½ "	2.04
Plaid	.18½ "	12 "	2.24*
Russian Sheeting	.31 "	2½ "	.78
Stripe	.18 "	4 "	.72
Ticking	.33 "	3 "	.99
		Total	$42.90¾

Clothing			
Belt	.27 each	1	.27
Gloves	.37½, .75 pair	2	1.12½
Mitts, Buckskin	.50 "	2	1.00
Handkerchief	.10, .25 each		
" Cotton	.20, .23 "		
" Cravat	.62½ "		
" Silk	.90, 1.66 "	7	3.33
Hat, Fur	2.50 "	1	2.50
" Wool	.75 "	1	.75
"	3.50 "	1	3.50
Shoes	1.50 pair	3	4.50
Stockings	.27, .67 pair		
" Cotton	.27 "	3	1.21
Suspenders	.15 "	2	.30
		Total	$18.48½

Food			
Bacon	.10 pound	374 lb.	37.36¾*
Beef, Side	.04½ "	266 "	11.97
Butter	.13 "	4 " and 1 lot	.53

Cheese	.12½ ,,	19⅛ ,,	2.48
Chocolate	.20 ,,	1 ,,	.20
Coffee	.16, .17 pound	125 ,,	19.49
Fats, Lard	.10 ,,	8 ,,	.80
Flour	.50, .60 quarter	?	48.95
	(28 lb.)		
Mackerel	.05 each, 10.70 barrel	10 and ½ bbl.	5.85
Molasses	.14, .16 quart	125 qt.	18.70
Pork, Spare Ribs	.03 pound	?	.50½
,, Hog	.04½ ,,	506 lb.	22.67
Rice	.05 ,,	3 ,,	.15
Salt	.03, .04 quart	74 qt.	2.44½
Spices, Pepper	.40 pound	1⅛ lb.	.45
,, Allspice	.40 ,,	¼ ,,	.10
,, Irespec	?	?	.05
Sugar	.12½ ,,	49 ,,	6.37½
Tea	.30, .31, .31¼ per ¼ lb.	2⅞ ,,	3.72½
Veal	.04 pound	14 ,,	.56
		Total	$183.36¾

Miscellaneous
Store Goods Bartered for butter — Amount not Recorded

Almanac	.08 each	1	.08
Bedcord	.45 ,,	1	.45
Building Hardware			.04½
,, Glass	.05 pane	1	.05
Knives, Pen	.33		
,, Double Blade	.45 each	3	1.13*
Pasteboard	.06 sheet	1	.06
Starch	.32 pound	½ lb.	.16
		Total	$ 1.97½

Notions

Braid	.03 yard	8½ yards	.25½
Braiding	.01 ,,	5 ,,	.05
Buttons	.01, .01½, .02 each		
,,	.25 dozen		
,, Yankee	.13 ,,	11 purchases	1.14
Cotton Balls	.02 each	24	.48
Pins	.01 row	8 rows	.08
Tape	...	2 pieces	.24
Thread	.01 skein		
,, Silk	.06, .06¼, .06½ skein	?	1.66¼
		Total	$ 3.90¾

Personal Items

Combs, Fine Tooth	.15 each		
,,	.20 ,,		
,, Side	.06 pair	3	.41
Soap	.10 pound	5½ lb.	.55
Tobacco	.03, .05, .10, .20	?	10.86
		Total	$11.82
		Total Spent	$274.26¼

Note: Supporting a household of six in 1830.

MARGARET PAINTER, WIDOW

Bulk Items	*Prices*	*Quantity*	*Amount*
Plaister	$0.75 bushel	1½ bu.	$1.12½
Cloth			
Flannel, Cotton	.16 yard	2⅞ yd.	.49*
Linen, Figured	.75 "	½ "	.37½
Muslin	.14 yard	9 "	1.26
		Total	$ 2.12½
Clothing			
Shawl	.20 each	1	.20
Shoes	1.50 pair	1	1.50
		Total	$ 1.70
Food			
Bacon	.10 pound	13½ lb.	1.32*
Coffee	.17 "	3 "	.51
Molasses	.15 quart	3 qt.	.45
Sugar	.12½ pound	3 lb.	.37½
Tea	.30¼, .31 per ¼ lb.	⅜ "	.46
		Total	$ 3.11½
Miscellaneous			
Knife	.45 each	1	.45
Nails	.09 pound	2 lb.	.18
		Total	$ 0.63
Notions			
Tape	...	1 piece	.06
Thread	.02 skein	6 sk.	.12
"	...	1 lot	.06
		Total	$ 0.24
Personal Items			
Soap	.10 pound	2⅛ lb.	.21½
		Total Spent	$ 9.15

Note: Supporting a household of eight in 1830.

POLLY PARLIMENT, HIRED GIRL

Cloth	*Prices*	*Quantity*	*Amount*
Calico	$0.12½, .20, .28 yard	10½ yd.	$1.60
Check	.18½, .25 "	2¾ "	.43½
Flannel, Yellow	.37½ "	1½ "	.56
Muslin	.13, .50 "	1¼ "	.43¾
		Total	$ 3.03¼
Clothing			
Handkerchief, Crepe	.44 each	2	.88
Stockings, Cotton	.50 pair	1	.50
		Total	$ 1.38

Food			
Chocolate	.20 pound	½ lb.	.10
Coffee	.17 "	3½ "	.59
Cheese	.12½ "	1⅞ "	.23½
Fats, Lard	.10 "	2 "	.20
Potatoes	.40 bushel	1 bu.	.40
Spices, Pepper	.40 pound	⅛ lb.	.05
Sugar	.12½ "	4 "	.49*
Tea	.31 per ¼ pound	½ of ¼ lb.	.15½
		Total	$ 2.22
Notions			
Cotton Ball	.02 each	1	.02
Ribbon	.20 yard	1 yd.	.20
Tape	.01 "	5 " and 1 piece	.09
Thread	...	1 lot	.08
		Total	$ 0.39
Personal Items			
Tobacco, Rolls	.03 each	2	.06
		Total Spent	$ 7.08¼

Note: Probably lived at the Big House.

MICAJAH POSEY, MOULDER

Bulk Items	*Prices*	*Quantity*	*Amount*
Corn, Ear	$0..25 bushel	2 bu.	$0.50
Feed	.60, .62 bushel	1 "	.61
Wheat	1.10 "	10 "	11.00
		Total	$12.11
Cloth			
Calico	.20 yard	7 yd.	1.40
Casinete	.50, 1.50 yard	5¾ "	5.62½
Flannel, White	.17, .18 "	11 "	2.97*
Satinette	.67 "	3¼ "	2.18
		Total	$12.17½
Clothing			
Gloves and Fur Hat	...	...	3.94
Handkerchief, Silk	.87½	1	.87½
" Cotton	.25	1	.25
Stockings	.50 pair	1 pr.	.50
Suspenders	.15 "	1 "	.15
		Total	$ 5.71½
Food			
Bacon	.10 pound	76¾ lb.	7.67¼
Beef	.08, .09 pound	49 "	4.06
Cheese	.12½ "	11⅜ "	1.50½
Chocolate	.20 "	½ "	.10
Coffee	.17 "	23 "	3.91

Fats, Lard	.10 ,,	3⅜ ,,	.33*
Flour	.60 quarter (28 lb.)	15 qr.	9.00
Mackerel, No. 1	7.00 barrel	½ bbl.	3.50
Molasses	.14, .16 quart	38 qt.	5.90
Pork, Chine	.03 pound	6½ lb.	.19
,, Spare Ribs	.03 ,,	22¼ ,,	.66
,, Hog	.04½ ,,	513 ,,	23.08½
,, Pickled	.10 ,,	4 ,,	.40
Potatoes	.30, .37½ bushel	5 bu.	1.80
Salt	.90, 1.00 ,,	¾ ,,	.47½*
Sugar	.12½ pound	65 lb.	8.12½
Spices, Pepper	.40 ,,	½ ,,	.20
,, Saltpetre	.12 ,,	¼ ,,	.03
Tea	.31 per ¼ pound	3⅛ ,,	3.87¼
		Total $74.81½	

Miscellaneous

Almanac	.08 each	1	.08
Blacking	.10 box	1	.10
Black Lead	.25 pound	¼ lb.	.06¼
Glass	.05 pane	2	.10
Knives, Barlow	.12½ each	1	
,, Pocket	.18½ ,,	1	.31
Oil	.12½ quart	2 qt.	.25
Pot, Four-Gallon	1.31 each	1	1.31
Soap	.10 pound	2¼ lb.	.22½
Storegoods	...	2 lots	.80
Tablespoons	1.50 dozen	½ doz.	.75
		Total $ 3.98¾	

Notions

Braid	.03 yard	1 yd.	.03
Buttons	.04, .06 dozen	5 purchases	.08
Scissors	.40 pair	1	.40
Thread, Silk	.06 skein	5 ,,	.45
		Total $ 0.96	

Personal Items

Comb	.37½ each	1	.37½
Medicine, Salts	.03 ounce	3 oz.	.09
,, Castor Oil	.12½ ,,	1	.12½
Razor Strop	.25 each	1	.25
Tobacco, Roll	.03	97	
,, Paper	.05	2	
,, ,,	.10	3	
,, Pound	.20	1	3.51
		Total $ 4.35	
		Total Spent $113.04¾	

Note: No family record identified in census of 1830.

DAVID SHAFFER, COLLIER

Bulk Items	*Prices*	*Quantity*	*Amount*
Buckwheat Meal	$0.03 pound	11¼ lb.	$0.33
Corn, Ear	.56, .37 bushel	1¼ bu.	.65
Feed	.60, .62, .67 ,,	6¼ ,,	3.87
Oats	.40 ,,	½ ,,	.20
Wheat	1.10 ,,	7 ,,	7.70
		Total $12.75	
Cloth			
Calico	.10, .16, .18, .18½ .32 yard	15¼ yd.	2.25
Casinete	1.12½ ,,	½ ,,	.56
Flannel, Cotton	.20, .21 yard		
,, Red	.67 ,,	14½ ,,	4.10½
Muslin	.11, .12½, .13, .14, .15, .18, .25 yard		
,,			
,, Figured Book	.67 ,,		
,, Cotton	.50 ,,	53⅜ yd.	7.29
Pittsburgh Cord	.22 ,,	2 ,,	.44
Russia Sheeting	.22 ,,	2 ,,	.44
Ticking	.20 ,,	2½ ,,	.50
		Total $15.58½	
Clothing			
Buckskin Mitts	.50 pair	2 pr.	1.00
Food			
Bacon	.10 pound	190 lb.	19.00
Beef	.08 ,,	16¼ ,,	1.30
Cheese	.12½ ,,	10¾ ,,	1.34
Chocolate	.20 ,,	1½ ,,	.30
Coffee	.17 ,,	49 ,,	8.55*
Fats, Lard	.10 ,,	21¾ ,,	2.17
Flour, Wheat	.04 ,,	51½ ,,	2.06
,,	.60 quarter (28 lb.)	43 qr.	22.80*
Mackerel, No. 1	8.75 barrel	½ bbl.	4.37½
,, ,, 2	7.00 ,,	½ ,,	3.50
,,	.05 each	6	.30
Molasses	.14, .16 quart	38 qt.	5.66½
Pork, Hog	.04½ pound	210 lb.	9.45
Potatoes	.27½, .40 bushel	1½ bu.	.57½
Salt	.04 quart, 1.00 bushel	4 qt., 2½ bu.	2.22*
Spices, Allspice	.40 pound	¼ lb.	.10
,, Pepper	.40, .44 pound	⅜ ,,	.15½
Sugar	.12½ ,,	13 ,,	1.62½
Tea	.31 per ¼ pound	1½ ,,	1.86
		Total $87.34½	
Miscellaneous			
Barter for sewing	...	1 lot	.44
Bed Cord	.45 each	1	.45

Black Lead	.24 pound	¼ lb.	.06
Glass	.05 pane	5	.60*
Horse Rasp	.40 each	1	.40
Knives	...	5	1.30
Nails and Spikes	.09, .10, .12½ pound	12¾ ,,	1.16
Paper	.01 sheet	2	.02
Storegoods, Charity	...	3 lots	5.02¼
Teaspoons	.40 dozen	½ doz.	.20
		Total $ 9.65½	

Notions	*Prices*	*Quantity*	*Amount*
Braid	$0.03 yard	1½ yd.	$0.04½
Buttons	.03, .06, .12½ dozen		
,, Pearl	.12½ ,,	5 purchases	.48½
Cotton Balls	.02 each	27	.54
Knitting Needle	.01 ,,	4	.04
Pins	.01 row	4 rows	.04
Thread	.01 skein		
,, Patent	no price		
,, Cotton	.06 hank	6 purchases	.37¼
		Total $ 1.52½	

Personal Items			
Comb, Horn	.08½, .12½ each		
,, Fine Tooth	.15, .16 ,,	4	.51½
Medicine, Salts	.04 ounce	1 oz.	.04
Soap	.10 pound	10⅝ lb.	1.06
Tobacco, Pound	.20 ..	11 ,,	
,, Roll	.03 each	5 rolls	2.39*
		Total $ 4.00½	
		Total Spent $131.86½	

Note: No family record identified in census of 1830.

JOHN SHEELER, MOULDER

Bulk Items	*Prices*	*Quantity*	*Amount*
Corn, Ear	$0.37½ Bushel		
,, Shelled	.50 ,,	16 bu.	$7.55
Feed	.37, .50 ,,	1½ ,,	.60
Oats	.40 ,,	6 ,,	2.40
Wheat	1.10 ,,	9 ,,	9.90
		Total $20.45	

Cloth			
Bobinette	no price	4 pieces	.14
Buckram	.16 yard	⅝ yd.	.10
,, Padding	.25 ,,	⅝ ,,	.25*
Calico	.18½, .21, .23, .27,		
	.31 yard	25¼ ,,	6.31½
,, Cap Stuff	.44, .67 yard	1½ ,,	.89
Cashmere	.37½ ,,	7 ,,	2.62½
Check	.18½, .20, .22 yard	8⅞ ,,	1.78

Flannel, Red	.67 yard		
" Yellow	.40 "		
"	.44 "	3¾ yd.	1.86½
Holland, Brown	.22 "	2¼ "	.49½
Jaconete	.40 "	2 "	.80
Muslin	.13, .14, .25 yd.		
" Figured	.44 "		
" Book	.40, .70 "	31¼ "	4.85½
Plaid	.18 "	6 "	1.08
Ticking	.20, .40 "	2 "	.50
		Total	$21.69½
Clothing			
Gloves	.37½ pair	1	.37½
Handkerchief	.20, .23, .37½ each		
" Black Gauze	.44 "		
" Flag Silk	1.12 "	5	2.36½
Hat, Boy's Wool	.62½ "	2	1.25
" Man's	.87½ "	1	.87½
" Palm Leaf	.31 "	1	.31
Stockings	.35 pair	2 pr.	.70
		Total	$ 5.87½
Food			
Cheese	.12½ pound	9¾ lb.	1.19
Chocolate	.20 "	2 "	.40
Coffee	.17 "	34½ "	5.86½
Fats, Lard	.10 "	35⅜ "	3.53½
Flour	.60 quarter (28 lb.)	9 qr.	5.40
" Wheat	.03 pound	17 lb.	.50*
Mackerel, No. 1	7.00 barrel	1 bbl.	7.00
Molasses	.14, .16 quart	41 qt.	6.21
Rice	.05 pound	3 lb.	.15
Salt, Fine	.04 quart		
" Coarse	.03 "	28 qt.	.85½
Spices, Pepper	.40 pound	¼ lb.	.10
" Saltpetre	.20 "	⅝ "	.12½
Sugar	.12½ "	44½ "	5.42½
Tea	.31 per ¼ pound	3 "	3.72
		Total	$40.47½
Miscellaneous			
Almanac	.08 each	1	.08
Blacking	.10 box	1	.10
Blacksmithing	...	12 visits	3.13
Fish Net	2.24 each	½	1.12
Hame Strap	.06 "	1	.06
Kettle, 20 gal.	3.62½ "	1	3.62½
Knives	.12½, .20, .31	3	.63½
Moulds	.06 dozen	1 doz.	.06
Nails	.09 pound	4 lb.	.36
Paper	.01 sheet, .12½ quire	12 sh. and 1½ qr.	.24*
Storegoods, Undesignated		...	.60
Tar	.10 quart	1 qt.	.10
		Total	$10.11

Notions

	Prices	Quantity	Amount
Braid	.01, .03, .12 yard	4¼ yd.	.27½
Buttons, vest	.06, .12 dozen		
„ Bone	.06, .06¾ „		
„ Plain	.12½ „		
„ Coat	.25 „	80 buttons	.74
Cotton Ball	.02 each	3	.06
Pins	.01 row	24 rows, 1 lot	.48
Tape		9 pieces	.44
Thread	01 skein		
„ Silk	.06 „	15 purchases	2.10¼
		Total $ 4.09¾	

Personal Items

Comb, Side	.08 each		
„ Dressing	.12½ „	3	.28½
Soap	.10 pound	9 lb.	.90
Tobacco	.20 „	½ lb.	.10
		Total $ 1.28½	
		Total Spent $103.98¾	

Note: Supporting a family of seven in 1830.

JOHN WERT, DIED APRIL 1832

Bulk Items	Prices	Quantity	Amount
Mushmeal	$0.01 pound	6 lb.	$0.06

Cloth			
Bobonete	.87 yard	½ yd.	.44
Flannel	.30 „	¼ „	.07½
Muslin	.37½ ,,	5 „	1.87½
		Total $ 2.39	

Clothing			
Gloves	.37½ pair	1	0.37½
Handkerchief,			
Blue Silk	.65 each	1	.65
		Total $ 1.02½	

Food			
Coffee	.16, .17 pound	4 lb.	.66
Molasses	.14 quart	7 qt.	.98
Salt	1.50 bushel	¼ bu.	.37½
Sugar	.12½ pound	5 lb.	.62½
Tea	.31 per ¼ pound	¼ „	
		Total $ 2.95	

Personal Items			
Castor Oil	.12½ ounce	1 oz.	.12½
		Total Spent $ 6.55	

Note: A family of three in 1830.

REBECCA WERT, WIDOW OF JOHN

Cloth	Prices	Quantity	Amount
Jaconete	$0.75 yard	⅛ yd.	$0.09½
Food			
Cheese	.12½ pound	3¾ lb.	.46
Chocolate	.20 ,,	½ ,,	.10
Coffee	.17 ,,	17 ,,	2.89
Eggs	.06½ dozen	2 doz.	.12½*
Flour	.60 quarter (28 lb.)	2 qr.	1.20
Mackerel	.05 each	2	.10
Molasses	.14, .15 quart	24 qt.	3.35
Potatoes	1.75 row	1 row	1.75
,,	.40 bushel	1 bu.	.40
Sugar	.12½ pound	9 lb.	1.12½
Tea	.30 per ¼ pound	⅜ ,,	.46
		Total $11.96	

Notions			
Tape and Thread	...	2 lots	.12¼

Personal Items			
Castor Oil	.12¼ ounce	1 oz.	0.12½
Soap	.10 pound	5⅝ lb.	.56
		Total $ 0.68½	
		Total Spent $12.86¼	

Note: This account began after husband's death.

JOSEPH WHITAKER, WOODCUTTER, FARMER AND WEAVER

Clothing	Prices	Quantity	Amount
Handkerchief, Cotton	$0.22 each	1	$0.22
Shoes, Monroes	1.62½ pair	1	1.62½
		Total $ 1.84½	

Food			
Bacon, Pickled	.08 pound	16 lb.	1.28
Flour	.60 quarter (28 lb.)	2 qr.	1.20
Potatoes	.30 bushel	½ bu.	.15
Sugar	.12½ pound	4½ lb.	.56
Tea	.31 per ¼ pound	½ ,,	.62
		Total $ 3.81	

Miscellaneous			
Oil	.12½ quart	1½ qt.	.19½
Personal Items			
Tobacco, Rolls	.03 each	2	.06
,, Paper	.10 ,,	1	.10
		Total $ 0.16	
		Total Spent $ 6.01	

Note: A family of three in 1830.

SAMUEL WILLIAMS, TEAMSTER

Bulk Items	*Prices*	*Quantity*	*Amount*
Buckwheat	$0.50 bushel	2 bu.	$ 1.00
Corn	.50 „	2 „	1.00
„ Ear	.25, .27 bushel	26¼ „	6.68½
Feed		5 „	3.51*
„	1.20 per hundred wt.	1 qr.	.30
Wheat	1.10 bushel	6 bu.	6.60
		Total	$19.09½
Cloth			
Baize, Green	1.00 yard		
„	.10 „	1⅛ yd.	.56
Calico	.20, .23 yard	12 „	2.67
Cashmere	.37½ „	6 „	2.25
Casinete	.62, .67, .80 yard	11½ „	6.61
Check	.16, .22 „	2½ „	.46
Flannel	.21 „		
„ Cotton	.24 „		
„ Green	.24 „	13 „	2.83
Linen, Tow	.17 „	2 „	.51*
Muslin	.10, .11 .12, .12½ .13, .14, .15 yard	74$\frac{15}{16}$ „	9.86
Pittsburg Cord	.22¼, .24 „	3¼ „	.75
Plaid	.15, .18, .18½ „	20¼ „	3.54½
Ticking	.20, .22 „	5 „	1.03
		Total	$31.07½
Clothing			
Handkerchief	.18½, .25, .28 each	3	.71½
Hat, Wool	.80 „	2	1.60
„ Palm Leaf	.37½ „	1	.37½
„ Man's Cap	1.25 „	1	1.25
Mitts, Buckskin	.33, .40 pair		
„	.50 „	3	1.30
Shoes	1.25, 1.50, 1.75 pair	5	7.25
		Total	$12.49
Food			
Bacon	.10 pound	100 lb.	10.00
Beef	.08 „	49⅝ „	3.61*
„ Side	.04½ „	247 „	11.11½
„ Offal	.50 lot	1 lot	.50
Butter	.13 pound	13 lb.	1.70½
Cheese	.12½ „	11⅜ „	1.40½
Chocolate	.20 „	2 „	.40
Coffee	.17 „	62 „	10.87*
Fats, Lard	.10 pound		
„ Tallow	.10 „	13 lb.	1.30½
Flour, Wheat	.04 „	19¼ „	.77
„	.50, .60 quarter (28 lb.)	42½ qr.	23.15

Molasses	.14, .16 quart	70 qt.	10.64
Pork, Spare Ribs	.03 pound	4½ lb.	.13½
„ Hogs	.04½ „	492 „	22.14
Potatoes	1.75 row	2 rows	3.50
„	.40 bushel	1½ bu.	.60
Salt	.03, .04 quart	7 qt.	
	.85, 1.00 bushel	2 bu.	2.24½
Spices, Pepper	.40 pound	1¾ lb.	.70
„ Saltpetre	.20, .25 pound	½ „	.11½
Sugar	.12½ „	15 „	1.87½
Tea	.31, .31¼ per ¼ pound	2¼ „	3.75*
Turkey	.50 each	1	.50
Veal	.03½ pound	25 „	.87½
		Total	$111.90½

Miscellaneous

Broom	.10 each	1	.10
Knives, Pen	.16, .18 each		
„ Barlow	.12½ „		
„ Two Bladed	.40 „	5	.99
Oil	.12½ quart	7 qt.	.87½
Paper	.01 sheet		
Pasteboard	.06 „	3 purchases	.17
Soap	.10 „	4¼ lb.	.41*
Starch	.12 „	½ lb.	.06
Storegoods, Undefined	...	1 lot	1.45
		Total	$ 4.06

Notions

Braid	.01½ yard		
„ Black	.04 „	4 yd.	.06½
Buttons	.04, .06 dozen		
„ Gilt, Vest	.12½ „	6 lots	.59
Cord	...	1 „	.12
Cotton Balls	.02 each	7	.14
Pattern	.25 „	1	.25
Pins	.01 row	1 row	.01
„ Paper	.06 paper	1 paper	.06
Tape	...	8 pieces	.44
Thread	.01 skein, .00½ hank		
„ Silk	.06¼ „	6 purchases	.41½
		Total	$ 2.09

Personal Items

Medicine, Salts	.03, .06½ ounce	?	.15½
Shaving Soap	.05 cake	1	.05
Tobacco	.03 roll, .20 pound	20 rolls, 8½ lb.	2.28
		Total	$ 2.48½
		Total Spent	$183.20

Note: A family of six in 1830.

DAVID WYNN, TEAMSTER

Bulk Items	*Prices*	*Quantity*	*Amount*
Corn, Ear	$0.25 bushel	1 bu.	$0.25
Feed	.60 "	½ "	.30
Oats	.33 "	½ "	.16½
Wheat	1.10 "	4 "	4.40
		Total	$ 5.11½
Cloth			
Calico	.10, .16, .18, .20, .23, .27 yard	24 yd.	4.26½
Cambric	.28 "	½ "	.28*
Cap Stuff	.40 "	¼ "	.10
Casinette	.45, .56, .62½, .67 yard	7 "	4.22½
Check	.16, .20 "	2⅝ "	.46½
Flannel, Red and Cotton	.24 "	7½ "	1.80
Gingham	.27½ "	½ "	.18½
Jaconete	.40, .67, .75 yard	⅞ "	.37½
Muslin	.10, .13, .14, .15 yard	41¼ "	5.45½
Pittsburg Cord	.24 yard	3 "	.72
Ticking	.30 "	9 "	2.70
Velvet Cord	.67 "	3¼ "	2.18*
		Total	$22.75
Clothing			
Gloves	.75 pair	1	.75
Handkerchief	.12½, .23, .37½ .56 each	4	1.29
Hat, Wool	.75 "	1	.75
Shoes	1.50 pair	3	4.50
		Total	$ 7.29
Food			
Bacon	.10 pound	130¾ lb.	14.07½*
Beef	.08 "	18 "	2.15*
" Quarter	.04½ "	138 "	6.21
Cheese	.12½ "	6 "	.73½
Chocolate	.20 "	½ "	.10
Fats, Lard	.10 "	11 "	1.10½
Flour, Wheat	.03 "	9½ "	.29
"	.60 quarter (28 lb.)	27½ qr.	16.50
Mackerel	5.75 barrel	1½ bbl.	8.62½
Molasses	.14, .16 quart	54 qt.	8.17
Pork, Chine and Spare Ribs	.03 pound	20 lb.	.60
" Hog	.04½ "	531 "	23.89
Potatoes	.30, .40 bushel	4 bu.	3.52½*
Salt	.02, .05 quart	4 qt.	
	.84 bushel	1¼ bu.	1.30½

Spices, Pepper	.40 pound	1$\frac{3}{8}$ lb.	.50
,, Allspice	.40 ,,	$\frac{1}{8}$,,	.05
,, Saltpetre	.24 ,,	$\frac{1}{8}$,,	.03
Sugar	.12$\frac{1}{2}$,,	22$\frac{1}{2}$,,	2.68
Tea	.30, .31 per $\frac{1}{4}$ pound	2 ,,	2.76
		Total $93.30	

Miscellaneous

Black Lead	.12 pound	$\frac{1}{4}$ lb.	.03
Oil	.12$\frac{1}{2}$ quart	4 qt.	.62$\frac{1}{2}$*
		Total $ 0.65$\frac{1}{2}$	

Notions

Buttons	.03, .04, .06, .08 dozen	6 purchases	.21$\frac{1}{2}$
Cord	.20 yard	2$\frac{1}{2}$ yd.	.50
Cotton Balls	.02 each	16	.32
Knitting Needle	.01$\frac{1}{2}$,,	1	.01$\frac{1}{2}$
Pins	.01 row	3 rows	.03
Thread	.01, .03, .06$\frac{1}{4}$ skein	12 purchases	.52$\frac{1}{4}$
		Total $ 1.60$\frac{1}{4}$	

Personal Items

Comb	.12$\frac{1}{2}$ each	1	.12$\frac{1}{2}$
Soap	.10 pound	10$\frac{1}{8}$ lb.	1.08$\frac{1}{2}$*
Tobacco, Rolls	.02, .03 each	57	1.54
,, Pound	.20 pound	1 ,,	.20
		Total $ 2.95	
		Total Spent 133.66\frac{1}{4}$	

Note: In 1840 he had six children all except one old enough to have been living in this period. Others may have left home in the decade.

SUMMARY OF STORE PURCHASES BY 26 WORKERS
DECEMBER, 1831–FEBUARY, 1833

	John Benson	*Clement Brook*	*John Care*
Bulk Items	...	...	$ 7.41
Cloth	$33.81	$155.29	31.97
Clothing	4.28	22.79	13.75
Food	...	...	69.63
Miscellaneous	1.53	.30	14.91
Notions	3.05	9.14	4.53
Personal Items	.03	1.03	4.38
Total Spent	42.70	188.55	146.58

	Alexander Church	Philip Filman	Barney Hart
Bulk Items	$ 0.85	...	$ 5.32
Cloth	16.49	$ 17.95	27.89
Clothing	4.29	2.85	9.47
Food	62.81	13.32	97.20
Miscellaneous	1.31	1.59	7.68
Notions	2.10	1.55	2.52
Personal Items	3.21	...	5.03
Total Spent	96.06	37.26	155.11

	David Hart	Wilkinson Hill	Isaac Hughes
Bulk Items	$ 49.03	$ 7.85	...
Cloth	36.15	19.55	$ 7.71
Clothing	21.69	1.00	4.28
Food	133.37	36.91	21.05
Miscellaneous	5.03	1.99	.93
Notions	6.45	.67	.15
Personal Items	13.17	1.31	.17
Total Spent	264.89	69.28	34.29

	William Jacobs	Polly Kidd	Thomas Lloyd
Bulk Items	...	...	...
Cloth	6 30.31	$ 3.24	$ 19.79
Clothing	20.53	.20	1.49
Food	1.65	...	16.71
Miscellaneous	3.95	...	8.67
Notions	3.13	.06	2.71
Personal Items	...	...	2.01
Total Spent	59.57	3.50	49.88

	Moses Morten	Eliz. Moyers	Fred. Painter
Bulk Items	$ 1.93	...	$ 2.20
Cloth	14.57	$12.41	5.55
Clothing	4.75	3.99	2.95
Food	34.65	.59	29.61
Miscellaneous	5.75	.18	...
Notions	.45	1.19	.15
Personal Items	3.15	.33	1.61
Total Spent	65.25	18.69	42.07

	Marg. Painter	John Painter	Polly Parliment
Bulk Items	$ 1.13	$11.80	...
Cloth	2.13	42.91	$ 3.03
Clothing	1.70	18.49	1.38
Food	3.11	183.37	2.22
Miscellaneous	.63	1.97	...
Notions	.24	3.91	.39
Personal Items	.21	11.82	.06
Total Spent	9.15	274.27	7.08

	Mica. Posey	David Shaffer	John Sheeler
Bulk Items	$12.17	$12.75	$20.45
Cloth	12.17	15.59	21.69
Clothing	5.71	1.00	5.87
Food	74.81	87.35	40.47
Miscellaneous	3.99	9.65	10.11
Notion	.96	1.53	4.10
Personal Items	4.35	4.01	1.29
Total Spent	113.06	131.88	103.98

	John Wert	Rebecca Wert	Joseph Whitaker
Bulk Items	$ 0.06	...	...
Cloth	2.39	$ 0.10	...
Clothing	1.03	...	$ 1.85
Food	2.95	11.96	3.81
Miscellaneous	...	...	.20
Notions	...	.12	...
Personal Items	.13	.69	.16
Total Spent	6.56	12.87	6.02

	Samuel Williams	David Wynn
Bulk Items	$ 19.09	$ 5.11
Cloth	31.07	22.75
Clothing	12.49	7.29
Food	111,91	93.30
Miscellaneous	4.06	.65
Notions	2.09	1.60
Personal Items	2.49	2.95
Total Spent	183.20	133.65

Note: Fractions of a cent were rounded. The largest error resulting was $0.02½.

Bibliographic Essay

IN ONE SENSE THERE IS AN EXTENSIVE LITERATURE ON Hopewell Village, but in another sense it is very restricted. Since the remains of the old furnace and surrounding buildings became the property of the National Park Service in 1938, there have been many pamphlets and articles in magazines and newspapers giving the historical background of the present tourist attraction. The bibliography lists some of these. For the most part the material in them appears to have been drawn from two published pamphlets: Harker A. Long's *A Short History of the Hopewell Furnace Estate*[1] or Dennis C. Kurjack's *Hopewell Village National Historical Site*.[2] Long was the last manager of Hopewell Furnace, and Doctor Kurjack was for several years the historian at Hopewell for the National Park Service.

In addition to Kurjack there have been a number of other professional staff members at the Hopewell project who have written historical or archeological articles based upon their research. Most of these, prepared as guides for the restoration work at the Village, are unpublished and exist only at type-

---

[1] Harker A. Long, *A Short History of the Hopewell Furnace Estate* (Reading: Reading Eagle Press, no date given).
[2] Dennis C. Kurjack, *Hopewell Village National Historical Site* (Washington: National Park Service Handbook Series, Number 8, 1950).

465

scripts in the files of the National Park Service. This author is most grateful for having had the opportunity to read them. In none of these papers was any attempt made to write a connected account of the life of the community. The social history has received very little attention.

A somewhat similar condition exists when the literature of the charcoal-iron communities in general is surveyed. The best account of a single furnace is E. N. Hartley's *Ironworks on the Saugus.*[3] Dr. Hartley has directed the restoration of the pioneer iron furnace of Massachusetts. In his book he has a valuable account of the seventeenth century iron industry of the British Colonies in America, but he made no attempt to discuss the life of the workers at Saugus.

No similar booklength account of any Pennsylvania furnace was found. There were regional and statewide studies[4] and a few pamphlet length studies of a single iron works.[5] The story of Pennsylvania's charcoal-iron communities, therefore, remains rather generalized. Arthur Cecil Bining died before he was able to carry his account into the nineteenth century, but his book on the eighteenth century has been most influential since it was published.[6]

Three characteristics of the iron-making villages appear with considerable frequency in the literature written about the charcoal-iron industry: These communities resembled medieval, feudal manors; they were essentially self-sufficient; they resembled Southern tobacco or cotton plantations. Bining

[3] E. N. Hartley, *Ironworks on the Saugus, op. cit.*

[4] For examples see: Committee on Historical Research, *Forges and Furnaces in the Province of Pennsylvania, op. cit.*

Alfred Gemmell, *The Charcoal Iron Industry in the Perkiomen Valley* (Norristown: Hartenstine Printing House, 1949).

[5] Some examples are: *Geigertown* (Reading: Leon D. Evans, 1959). *One Hundred and Twenty-Five Years of Pig Iron Manufacture at Robesonia, Pennsylvania* (Philadelphia: The Robesonia Iron Company, 1918). John C. Wetzel, *200th Anniversary of Birdsboro, Pennsylvania* (Birdsboro: The Executive Committee, 1940). Dean Friday, "Tinton Manor: the Iron Works," *Proceedings of the New Jersey Historical Society,* LXX, 4 (October 1952), p. 250.

[6] Bining, *Pennsylvania Iron Manufacture in the 18th Century, op. cit.*

was one of the first to compare the iron villages with small feudal manors of medieval Europe.[7] Evarts B. Greene called the iron plantation "a quasifeudal community."[8] Each of the above writers had reference to the eighteenth century; but Dean Freiday said that through the first half of the nineteenth century, also, the iron communities were "semi-feudal" in organization, labor relations and economics. He said that they were isolated and self-contained establishments.[9]

Alvin P. Stauffer and Charles W. Porter spoke of "a compact semifeudal industrial village,"[10] and Kurjack said Hopewell was "feudalike."[11] Jackson Kemper went all the way and called it "a little feudal village."[12]

The idea of a feudal community was coupled with isolation and self-sufficiency by these and other writers. Bining used this idea also when he wrote that the furnaces "made up an almost self-sufficient community."[13] Frederick K. Miller was more specific about the degree of independence with his statement that with a very few exceptions the necessities of life were produced on the plantation.[14] Raymond E. and Marion F. Murphy called the iron plantations independent, self-supporting communities.[15] John Birkenbine asserted, "Each aggregation of houses about the iron works . . . was a settlement independent of others, often reached by long and tedious

[7] *Ibid.*, p. 30.

[8] Evarts Boutell Greene, *The Revolutionary Generation, 1763–1790* (New York: The Macmillan Company, 1943), p. 62.

[9] Freiday, *op. cit.*, p. 250.

[10] Alvin P. Stauffer and Charles W. Porter, "The National Park Service Program of Conservation," *Mississippi Valley Historical Review*, XXX, 1 (June 1943). Typescript, p. 7. Hopewell Village Library.

[11] Kurjack, *op. cit.*, p. 6.

[12] Jackson Kemper, 3rd, *American Charcoal-Making, op. cit.*, p. 1.

[13] Bining, "The Rise of Iron Manufacture in Western Pennsylvania," *op. cit.*, p. 238.

[14] Frederick K. Miller, *The Rise of an Iron Community,* published in three parts by the Lebanon County (Pennsylvania) Historical Society, 1950–1952, p. 88.

[15] Raymond E. and Marion F. Murphy, *Pennsylvania Landscapes* (State College: Penns Valley Publishers, Inc., 1954), p. 41.

journeys."[16] Kemper described the company store as supplying every need of the people from food to clothing.[17]

The analogy of the iron-making community with a Southern plantation occurred to several writers. One used the reference only in the sense of the importance of the iron industry to early American life.[18] Others saw a more specific similarity. Bining believed the iron plantations could be compared in *many* respects with the Virginia tobacco plantations.[19] Douglas A. Fisher thought that the only difference between an iron plantation and a cotton plantation was that the product was different.[20] Stevenson Whitcomb Fletcher was emphatic that the iron furnaces of central Pennsylvania were similarly organized to the great plantations of the Old South.[21]

Most of the more general accounts of charcoal-iron communities did not go beyond these stereotypes. A few supplied more details.

How large was the community? Frank H. Rowe said that a typical furnace in Scioto County, Ohio, in the 1830's employed from 100 to 250 workers.[22] Fisher thought that Hopewell Village at one time had 1,000 inhabitants.[23]

Feeding the workers and their families was an important part of the work of the furnace management. Rowe wrote that beans, bacon and fried mush were the menu on almost every table.[24] Gemmell thought the Pennsylvania workers ate better than that. He said that the furnace owner produced on his farm and sold through the company store, meat, eggs, dairy

[16] Birkinbine, "Changes in the Manufacture of Pig Iron," *op. cit.,* p. 225.
[17] Kemper, "The Making of Charcoal," *op. cit.,* no pages given.
[18] "Hopewell Village," *International Moulders' and Foundry Workers' Journal,* 94, 10 (October 1958), p. 3.
[19] Bining, *British Regulation of the Colonial Iron Industry, op. cit.,* p. 19.
[20] Douglas A. Fisher, *Steel Making in America* (United States Steel Corporation, 1949), p. 19.
[21] Fletcher, *op. cit.,* p. 336.
[22] Frank H. Rowe, *History of the Iron and Steel Industry in Scioto County, Ohio* (Columbus: State Archeological and Histroical Society, 1938), p. 10.
[23] Fisher, *op. cit.,* p. 19.
[24] Rowe, *op. cit.,* p. 19.

products, fruit and grain. He imported sugar and molasses. Neighborhood growers sold parsnips, beans, onions, cucumbers and cabbage. The workers put meat on the table by hunting and fishing.[25]

Bining said the farms produced wheat, buckwheat, corn, rye, oats, barley, flax and hemp. He thought the farms were poorly operated with an absence of crop rotation and use of fertilizer.[26]

Gemmell pointed out the numerous influences of the furnace upon the neighboring farmers. They bought iron tools and utensils and sold some of their produce at the furnace; used the roads built for furnace transportation; found off-season employment at the furnace, mine or woodlot; sold timber and iron ore; and benefited from reduced taxes because of the heavy assessments on furnace property. But the furnace was not an unmixed blessing to its neighbors. Roads were cut up by heavily laden wagons, mines ruined farm land, cut-over timber land eroded, and the furnace and coaling pits produced unpleasant gases.[27]

Birkinbine placed the work year for the furnace at eight to ten months, and he said it would be blown out early in the year when the fuel was exhausted. The furnace was relined each winter. While the repairs were going on, those miners or furnace men not engaged in the restoration work were sent into the woods to cut cordwood for coaling.[28] He said that coaling for the next blast usually began in April or May, depending upon the weather.[29] Harry Scrivenor pointed out that a furnace operated better in cold weather than in hot and thought the furnace was operated as long as possible in the winter.[30]

[25] Gemmell, *op. cit.,* p. 84.
[26] Bining, "The Iron Plantations," *op. cit.,* pp. 7–8.
[27] Gemmell, *op. cit.,* pp. 115–116.
[28] Birkinbine, *op. cit.,* p. 226.
[29] John Birkinbine, *The Manufacture of Pig Iron in Pennsylvania* (Washington: Department of Internal Affairs—Statistics, Official Document Number 10, 1894), p. 26.
[30] Scrivenor, *op. cit.,* p. 259.

Several writers noted a wide contrast between the mansions of the ironmasters and the cottages of the workers. Bining described the mansions as containing many large rooms heated by wide fireplaces and furnished with oak or mahogany furniture. The tables were set on damask cloths with pewter plates, china cups and saucers and imported Delft ware. The families slept in curtained beds. Outside, the gardens grew lilies, violets, hollyhocks, phlox and other old-fashioned flowers.[31]

Victoria Lyles said that life for the workers followed a simple pattern. The small houses were heated by a single fireplace which also served for cooking. The walls were whitewashed, and the floors were sanded. The people ate with iron knives and forks and dressed in clothing made of flannel, camblet or calico.[32] Bining wrote that the bedrooms were nearly empty and seldom contained mirrors, tables, wardrobes, drawers or even chairs.[33] Lighting was provided by tallow candles, and water was carried from a spring or well.[34] Smaller houses had two rooms with a loft above. The better homes had one or two more rooms.[35]

The store was an important feature of the iron-making village, but the authorities were not in agreement about the relationship between the store and the workers. Arthur D. Pierce said that the workers were usually in debt long before pay day.[36] According to Birkinbine, ". . . most of the pay . . . was expected to be expended at the store. . . . Some old managers would reduce the balance due a workman at the

---

[31] Bining, "The Iron Plantations," op. cit., pp. 3–4.

[32] Victoria Lyles, "Forges and Furnaces of York County," Papers of the Historical Society of York County (Pennsylvania), New Series, Number 4, no date given, p. 4.

[33] Bining, "The Iron Plantations," op. cit., p. 5.

[34] Ibid., p. 20.

[35] Bining, The Pennsylvania Iron Manufacture in the 18th Century, op. cit., p. 32.

[36] Arthur D. Pierce, Iron in the Pines (New Brunswick: Rutgers University Press, 1957), p. 17.

end of the year if it was believed that he had 'saved too much;' or rather 'traded too little.'"[37]

Other writers saw the store as more of a service than a profitable business. Gemmell believed the ironmasters were more interested in keeping their workers happy than in profiteering on prices at the store and that prices were generally cheaper than in nearby stores.[38] Borchers also found that goods were sold to employees at reasonable prices.[39]

How did the workers get along with the boss? William A. Sullivan found no evidence of union activity among the iron workers before 1840 nor any interest in the democratic forces of the Jacksonian era. He believed that many workers were close to a state of peonage.[40] Gemmell saw the worker-manager relationship as the product of the interaction of the workers' loyalty and a benevolent attitude by the ironmaster.[41]

Borchers found the wages to have been considerably below today's standards but that commodity prices were relatively still lower, producing for the iron workers a much higher standard of living than any working group in Europe.[42] Bining also thought the wages of skilled workers were higher than those paid in European countries.[43] In addition to his money wage the worker often was furnished a house, a garden, pasture for his animals and fuel for his fireplace or stove.[44]

The picture of village life on the furnace plantations presented in the literature cited was not very clear because the writers were not in agreement on most points. Such differences of view can be attributed to several circumstances: The authors were not all writing about the same communites, they were writing about different periods, they did not have the

[37] Birkinbine, *American Blast-Furnace Progress, op. cit.,* p. 292.
[38] Gemmell, *op. cit.,* p. 87.
[39] Sam Borchers, "America's Iron Industry in Colonial Times," *Forgings,* 7, 2 (March 1945), p. 7.
[40] Sullivan, *op. cit.,* p. 70.
[41] Gemmell, *op. cit.,* p. 88.
[42] Borchers, *op. cit.,* p. 7.
[43] Bining, *The Pennsylvania Iron Manufacture in the 18th Century, op. cit.,* p. 8.
[44] Sullivan, *op. cit.,* p. 59.

same data from which to draw their conclusions, some were writing from a biased view, and there was a wide difference in the competence as historians among the writers cited. Bining, Hartley, Sullivan, Miller and Kurjack were trained in historical method and in addition were able to pursue extensive research. Some of the others used only secondary sources or had little training in historical method. Harker A. Long had most personal information about Hopewell Furnace, but he erred because he relied too much upon his memory after many years had elapsed.

Bibliography

SOURCE MATERIAL

Unpublished

ABSTRACT OF DEEDS FOR HOPEWELL PROPERTY AND Correspondence Covering Acquisition by the Government of the United States, Hopewell Village Library.

Abstract of Title of the Warwick Ore Reserve Located in Berks and Chester Counties, Pennsylvania, 1790–1936; Hopewell Village Library.

American Clergy Collection, Vol. VII, Historical Society of Pennsylvania.

Archeological Reports of Work at Hopewell Village, Hopewell Village Library.

Autograph Collection, Historical Society of Pennsylvania.

Bank of North America, Minutes and Letter Book, November 2, 1781–January 21, 1792, Historical Society of Pennsylvania.

Berks and Montgomery County Papers, Historical Society of Pennsylvania.

Berks County Assessment Records, 1763–1815 (some years missing); Berks County Historical Society.

Berks County Constables' Returns of People—Estates—Servants—Stock, etc., 1756 and Miscellaneous Old Papers; Prothonotary's Office, Berks County Court House.

Berks County Court Appearance Dockets, 1800–1820; Prothonotary's Office, Berks County Court House.

Berks County Court Continuance Dockets, 1800–1820; Prothonotary's Office, Berks County Court House.

Berks County Court Pleadings and Miscellaneous Old Papers, 1752–1843; Prothonotary's Office, Berks County Court House.

Berks County Court Records Of Cases, Prothonotary's Office, Berks County Court House.

Berks County Deed Books, Office of Recorder of Deeds, Berks County Court House.

Berks County Mortgages, 1762–1888; Prothonotary's Office, Berks County Court House.

Berks County Surveyor-General's Draughts and Miscellaneous Old Papers, 1700–1800; Prothonotary's Office, Berks County Court House.

Berks County Tax Duplicates, 1829–1840; Berks County Historical Society.

Berks County Tax Lists, 1809–1819; Berks County Historical Society.

Berks County Tax Records, 1760–1864; Berks County Historical Society.

Berks County Triennial Assessments, 1846–1873; Office of the County Commissioners, Berks County Court House.

Bethesda Baptist Church, Cemetery Gravestones.

Bethesda Baptist Church Charter of Incorporation, Hopewell Village Library.

Bethesda Baptist Church Minute Book, Hopewell Village Library.

Bird, Mark, Petition in Bankruptcy, Historical Society of Pennsylvania.

Bird, William, Ledgers, 1744–1761, 3 volumes; Historical Society of Pennsylvania.

Bird, William, Papers, Berks County Historical Society.

Birdsborough Forge Book, 1821–1825; Hopewell Village Library.

Birdsborough Forge Cash Book, 1806; Hopewell Village Library.

Birdsborough Forge Journal, 1821–1824; Berks County Historical Society.

Birdsborough Forge Ledger, 1829–1831; Hopewell Village Library.

Birdsborough Forge Time Book, 1789–1810; Hopewell Village Library.

Birdsborough Store Journal, 1810, Hopewell Village Library.

Box on Iron Industry, Historical Society of Pennsylvania.

Brooke Family Letters, Hopewell Village Library.

Brooke Family Papers, Berks County Historical Society.

Buckley and Brooke, Cash Books, 1807–1810, 1829–1833, 3 volumes; Berks County Historical Society.

Buckley and Brooke, Journal Account with Clement Brooke, 1809–1814; Hopewell Village Library.

Bull, Levi, Diaries, 1806–1859, Chester County Historical Society.

Cary, Otis, Diary of a trip from New York to Pennsylvania in 1837, Microfilm at Hopewell Village Library.

Changewater Furnace Account Books, microfilm at Hopewell Village Library.

Chester County Deed Books, Office of Recorder of Deeds, Chester County Court House.

Clingan, Maria T., List of Assets, 1880, Hopewell Village Library.

Eckert and Brothers, Henry Clay Furnace Sales Book, 1867–1884; Hopewell Village Library.

Eckert and Brothers, Record of Land Purchases, 1845–1882; Hopewell Village Library.

Ege, George, Manuscripts of Mary Ann Furnace, Kemper Papers, Hopewell Furnace.

Evans, Lewis, Ledgers, 1801–1840; Hopewell Village Library.

Farmers Bank of Reading, Pennsylvania, Letter Books, 1815–1833; Hopewell Village Library.

"History of Plow Church, Robeson Township, Berks County, Pennsylvania" (unpublished, 1874) Berks County Historical Society.

Hopewell Cash Book, 1828–1830; Berks County Historical Society.

Hopewell Forge Journal, 1803–1817; Historical Society of Pennsylvania.

Hopewell Furnace and Area, Collection of old photographs, Hopewell Village Library.

Hopewell Furnace Books, 76 Volumes, some on microfilm, Hopewell Village Library. These volumes are identified as Source Material and assigned a number. They are identified in the footnotes as SM1, SM 2, etc. The originals of most of the volumes are at Hopewell. Others are at Berks County Historical Society, Chester County Historical Society and Historical Society of Pennsylvania.

Hopewell Furnace Documents, Berks County Historical Society.

Hopewell Furnace Farm Time Books, 5 volumes, Hopewell Village Library.

Hopewell Village Documents. About 8,000 loose papers on business and life at Hopewell Furnace. Some have been catalogued and assigned numbers derived from the date; *i.e.* 8161125 would mean the document was dated November 25, 1816. A letter after the number means more than one document exists for that day. Some documents were undated and some were not yet catalogued in 1962. These are identified in the footnotes by description.

Iron Masters Association, *Statistics of Iron Manufacture in Pennsylvania*. Published for the 1850 Convention of the Iron Masters Association held in Philadelphia.

James, Mrs. T. P., Manuscript Collections of Papers Relating to the Ironworks of the Potts Family, Historical Society of Pennsylvania.

Joanna Furnace Journals and Ledgers, 22 volumes, Hopewell Village Library.

Jones Keim and Company, Journals of Windsor and Schuylkill Furnaces, 1841–1845; microfilm, Hopewell Village Library.

Keen, Eli, Storebook, 1844–1845; Hopewell Village Library.

Keep, William John, "A History of Stove Making by a man who engaged in the trade for 50 years," Typescript in Hopewell Village Library.

Kemper Manuscripts on Hopewell Furnace, Hopewell Village Library.

Knox Papers, photocopy of pages in Hopewell Village Library.

Kurtz Family Bible, Berks County Historical Society.

Lake, D. J. and N. S. Beers, "Map of Vicinity of Philadelphia and Reading," Based on Actual Surveys. Philadelphia: 1860.

Lancaster County Record of County Tax and Exempt Fines, 1808; Lancaster County Historical Society.

Lightfoot Papers, Field Book, 1744–1771; Historical Society of Pennsylvania.

Lloyd Family Papers, private collection in possession of Dorothy Lloyd Collender, Pottstown, R. D., Pennsylvania.

Ledger of J. W. Patton Store, Shippensburg, Pennsylvania; private collection in possession of Henry Kauffman, Millersville, Pennsylvania.

Manada Furnace Journal, 1837–1841; microfilm at Hopewell Village Library.

Martha Furnace Diary (New Jersey), 1808–1815; microfilm at Hopewell Village Library.

Mary Ann Forge Ledger, 1810–1811; microfilm at Hopewell Village Library.

Mary Ann Furnace Journals and Ledgers, 1762–1838 (not complete for these years.) 8 volumes; microfilm at Hopewell Village Library.

McCaa, James, Pig, Coal and Cordwood Book, 1850–1868; Lancaster County Historical Society.

Miller, Daniel, Collection of Letters and Papers, Hopewell Village Library.

Miscellaneous Papers of Bucks County, Historical Society of Pennsylvania.

Montgomery Manuscripts, Hopewell Village Library.

Montgomery Manuscripts Relating to the Iron Industry in the Schuylkill Valley, Berks County Historical Society.

Morris, James L., Diary or Daily Notes of the Weather, Together with the Events of the Neighborhood, 1837–1844, 2 volumes; microfilm at Hopewell Village Library.

Mount Frisby AME Church and Cemetery.

Mount Hope Letters, microfilm at Hopewell Village Library.

Mt. Hope Furnace Ledgers and Journals, 1797–1819; microfilm at Hopewell Village Library.

Mt Hope Furnace Provision Book, 1809–1824; microfilm at Hopewell Village Library.

Mt. Hope Furnace Time Book, 1820–1822; microfilm at Hopewell Village Library.

New Pine Forge Day Book, 1759; microfilm at Hopewell Village Library.

Parsons, William, Collection, Historical Society of Pennsylvania.

Peale Papers, typescript, Historical Society of Pennsylvania.

Pennsylvania, *Proceedings of the Provincial Conference,* June 18—June 25, 1776; Historical Society of Pennsylvania.

"Posey Family History," typescript at Hopewell Village Library.

Potts and Francis, Store Ledger, 1851–1854; Hopewell Village Library.

Potts Manuscripts, 1799–1825; Historical Society of Pennsylvania.

Reber, Ira J. J., Collection, microfilm at Hopewell Village Library.

Richards, Henry M., "Map of Berks County, 1820; Constructed by Virtue of an Act of the Legislature of Pennsylvania, 19th March, 1816;" microfilm at Hopewell Village Library.

Richards, Louis, Scrapbooks, Historical Society of Berks County.

Rush Collection, Historical Society of Pennsylvania.

Rush, Dr. Benjamin, Collection of Manuscripts, Ridgeway Branch Library, Philadelphia.

Sharpe-Marshall Collection of Letters, 1830–1840; microfilm at Hopewell Village Library.

St. Gabriel's Episcopal Church Records, 1753–1901; Berks County Historical Society.

St. Marks Episcopal Church Records, 1836–1902; Berks County Historical Society.

St. Mary's Episcopal Church Records, 1806–1846; Berks County Historical Society.

St. Thomas' Episcopal Church Records, 1825–1901; Berks County Historical Society.

Stiegel Family Record Book, microfilm at Hopewell Village Library.

Stokes Collection of Documents, Hopewell Village Library.

United States Government, Census Population Schedules, Pennsylvania, Berks and Chester Counties, 1800–1870; microfilm at Hopewell Village Library.

Warwick Furnace Journals and Ledgers, 1745–1770; Historical Society of Pennsylvania.

Wilson, James, Papers, Historical Society of Pennsylvania.

Young, Alex A., "Public Lectures," handbill at Hopewell Village Library.

Ziemers, John, Day Book, 1822–1823; Lancaster County Historical Society.

Published

Aldens Appeal Record. Robert Coleman and George Dawson vs. Clement B. Brooke and Henry P. Robinson, Robert W.

Coleman and William Coleman, July Term, 1856. Equity. Reported 93 Pennsylvania 182. Philadelphia, 1878.

Barford, Joseph A., "Reminiscences of the Early Days of Stove Plate Molding and the Union," *International Molders' and Foundry Workers' Journal*, 94, 7 (July 1958), p. 8-11. Reprint from the March 1902 issue of the *Iron Molders' Journal*.

Bridgens, H. F. and A. R. Witmer, *Atlas of Chester County, Pennsylvania*. Safe Harbor, Pennsylvania : A. R. Witmer, 1873.

Colonial and State Records of North Carolina, Volume XXI. Raleigh; Department of Archives and History. Photocopy of pages on Mark Bird.

Combination Atlas Map of Lancaster County, Pennsylvania. Philadelphia : Everts and Stewart, 1875.

Documents Relating to the Manufacture of Iron in Pennsylvania. Philadelphia : General Committee of the Convention of Iron Masters, 1850.

Dudley, Dud, *Mettallum Martis*. West Bromwich, England: J. N. Bagnall, 1851.

Elsas, Madeleine (Editor), *Iron in the Making Dowlais Iron Company Letters, 1782–1860*. London: Glamorgan County Council, 1960.

Gruner, M. L., *Studies of Blast Furnace Phenomena*. Philadelphia : Henry Carey Baird, 1874.

Hemerlin, Samuel Gustof, *Report about the Mines in the United States, 1783*. Philadelphia : John Morton Memorial Museum, 1931.

Long, Harker A., *A Short History of the Hopewell Furnace Estate in Union Township, Berks County*. Reading : Reading Eagle Press, no date given.

Nicholson, John, *The Operative Mechanic,* Volume I. Philadelphia : H. C. Carey and I. Lea, 1826.

Overman, Frederick, *The Manufacture of Iron*. Philadelphia : Henry C. Baird, 1854.

Pennsylvania Archives, Third Series, Volumes XI, XII, XVIII. Harrisburg: Wm. Stanley Ray, 1897.

Pennsylvania, *Index to Local Legislation in Pennsylvania from 1700 to 1892.* Compiled to Giles D. Price. Philadephia: T. and J. W. Johnson and Company, 1894.

Pennsylvania, *Laws of the Commonwealth of Pennsylvania.* Compiled by Thomas McLean Thompson. Octarora: Francis Bailey, 1804.

Pennsylvania, *Laws of the General Assembly of the Commonwealth of Pennsylvania Passed at the Session of 1842.* Known as the Pamphlet Laws of Pennsylvania. Harrisburg: Published by Authority, 1842.

Pennsylvania, *Reports of Cases Adjudged in the Supreme Court of Pennsylvania.* Edited by Thomas Sergant and Wm. Rawle, Volume VIII. Philadelphia: Abraham Small, 1824. Volume XI, Philadelphia: M'Carty and Davis, 1826.

Pennsylvania, *Shepard's Pennsylvania Table of Cases.* New York: The Frank Shepard Company, 1925.

Pennsylvania, *Vale's Pennsylvania Digest,* Volume 44. St. Paul: West Publishing Company, 1950.

Sisco, Anneliese Grumbaldt (Editor), *Réaumier's Memoirs on Steel and Iron.* Chicago: University of Chicago Press, 1956.

United States, *Congress of the United States, Hearings Before the Joint Economic Committee, April 7–10, 1959. Historical and Comparative Rates of Production, Productivity, and Prices.* Washington: Government Printing Office, 1959.

United States, *Journals of the Continental Congress,* 34 volumes. Washington: Government Printing Office, 1904–1937.

United States House of Representatives, *House Documents,* 22nd Congress, First Session, Volume 7, Part 1. "Report of Louis McLane, Secretary of the Treasury, 1933, on Manufacturing."

Interviews With Former Hopewell Residents

(Typescripts of these Interviews are
in Hopewell Village Library.)

Boone, David, Interviewed March 22, 1941.

Boone, Sally, March 22, 1941, and February 25, 1941.

Care, Charles Sheridan, February 24, 1941.

Care, Elizabeth A., January 30, 1941.

Care, Hunter, January 26, 1941, and March 14, 1948.

Care, Morris Lyman, February 6, 1941.

Care, Nathan, Junior, January 15, 1941, and February 13, 1941.

Care, Thomas Noble, February 10, 1941.

Care, Violet, January 15, 1941, and February 13, 1941.

Freese, Samuel Wesley, September 21, 1959.

Henry, John, January 23, 1941.

Hoffman, Thomas, November 22, 1940.

House, Harry, December 10, 1940.

Huston, H. H., June 29, 1941.

Krewson, Mary, June 29, 1941.

Lacey, Charles Atwood, October 17, 1940.

Lloyd, Albert, September 15, 1962.

Long, Harker A., August 7, 8, 13, 1936, and December, 1935.

March, Mrs. Samuel, January 22, 1941.

Painter, Albert, December 12, 1947; September 24, 1950; January 16, 1956; May 9, 1958; January 8, 1959.

Painter, Charles Sheridan, April 15, 1953; February 16, 1957; April 17, 1958.

Painter, William, July 24, 1949.

Palsgrove, J. Lincoln, October 13, 1940.

Piersol, Margaret, June 6, 1961.

Rhodes, Catherine, March 4, 1941; May 13, 1941.

Sands, Rose, March 4, 1941; May 13, 1941.

Seidel, Sally Addison, January 30, 1941.

Smith, E. O., August 4, 1940.

Smith, Reginald, September 15, 1940; March 16, 1941;
August 24, 1941.
Sparr, John, October 8, 1940.
Stroley, C. W., August 14, 1940.
Styer, Grace, June 1, 1941.

Newspapers

Berks and Schuylkill Journal, Reading, Pennsylvania, 1816–
1910.
Birdsboro Dispatch, Birdsboro, Pennsylvania, 1947, 1948,
1952.
Chester and Delaware Federalist, West Chester, Pennsylvania,
1817.
The Christian Science Monitor, Boston, 1950.
Daily Local News, West Chester, Pennsylvania, 1874, 1881,
1929.
Evening Bulletin, Philadelphia, 1935–1937.
Hazard's Register of Pennsylvania, 1833–1835.
Jeffersonian, West Chester, Pennsylvania, 1867,1872.
Lancaster (Pennsylvania) *Sunday News,* 1962.
New York Times, 1937.
Norristown (Pennsylvania) *Free Press,* 1832.
Pennsylvania Gazette, Philadelphia, 1773, 1783, 1786–1787.
Pennsylvania Packet, Philadelphia, 1788.
Philadelphia Inquirer, 1932.
Reading (Pennsylvania) *Eagle,* 1915–1937.
Readinger (Pennsylvania) *Zeitung,* 1790–1791.
Village Record, West Chester, Pennsylvania, 1842.
Weekly Advertiser, Reading, Pennsylvania, 1797–1799.
West Chester (Pennsylvania) *Star,* 1913.

SECONDARY MATERIAL

Books

Agricola, Georgius, *De Re Metallica,* Translation by Herbert

Clark Hoover and Lou Henry Hoover. New York: Dover Publications, Inc., 1950.

Ashton, Thomas Southcliffe, *Iron and Steel in the Industrial Revolution.* Manchester: Manchester University Press, 1951.

Ballard, Lloyd V., *Social Institutions.* New York: D. Appleton-Century Company, 1936.

Barnes, James A., *Wealth of the American People.* New York: Prentice-Hall, 1949.

Bell, I. Lowthian, *Chemical Phenomena of Iron Smelting.* New York: D. Van Nostrand, 1872.

Bezanson, Anne, Robert D. Gray and Miriam Hussey, *Wholesale Prices in Philadelphia, 1784–1861,* 2 volumes. Philadelphia: University of Pennsylvania Press, 1937.

Bining, Arthur Cecil, *British Regulation of the Colonial Iron Industry.* Philadelphia: University of Pennsylvania Press, 1933.

Bining, Arthur Cecil, *Pennsylvania Iron Manufacture in the Eighteenth Century.* Harrisburg: Pennsylvania Historical Commission, 1938.

Bining, Arthur Cecil, *The Rise of American Economic Life.* New York: Charles Scribner's Sons, 1943.

Bogardus, Emory S., *Development of Social Thought.* New York: Longmans, Green and Company, 1940.

Bolland, Simpson, *The Art of Casting in Iron.* New York: John Wiley and Sons, 1893.

Bowen, Eli, *The Pictorial Sketch-Book of Pennsylvania.* Philadelphia: William Bromwell, 1853.

Boyer, Charles S., *Early Forges and Furnaces in New Jersey.* Philadelphia: University of Pennsylvania Press, 1931.

Brunhouse, Robert L., *The Counter-Revolution in Pennsylvania, 1776–1790.* Harrisburg: Pennsylvania Historical Commission, 1942.

Buckmaster, Henrietta, *Let My People Go.* New York: Harper and Brothers, 1941.

Burlingame, Roger *March of the Iron Men*. New York: Charles Scribner's Sons, 1940.

Campbell, Harry Huse, *The Manufacture and Properties of Iron and Steel*. New York: Hill Publishing Company, 1907.

Clark, Victor S., *History of Manufactures in the United States*, volume I, 1607–1860. New York: Peter Smith, 1949.

Committee on Historical Research, *Forges and Furnaces in the Province of Pennsylvania*. Philadelphia: Pennsylvania Society of the Colonial Dames of America, 1914.

Dictionary of American Biography, "James Wilson," Volume 20. New York: Scribners, 1936.

Diderot, Denis, *A Diderat Pictorial Encyclopedia of Trades and Industry*, Edited by Charles Caulston Gillispie. New York: Dover Publications, Inc., 1959.

Dornbusch, Charles H., *Pennsylvania German Barns*. Allentown: The Pennsylvania German Folklore Society, 1958.

Dunaway, Wayland F., *A History of Pennsylvania*. New York: Prentice Hall, Inc., 1950.

Faulkner, Harold Underwood, *American Economic History*. New York: Harper and Brothers Publishers, 1949.

Faulkner, Harold Underwod, *American Political and Social History*. New York: Appleton-Century-Crofts, 1957.

Fish, Carl Russell, *The Rise of the Common Man*. New York: The Macmillan Company, 1950.

Fisher, Douglas A., *Steel Making in America*. New York: United States Steel Corporation, 1949.

Fletcher, Stevenson Whitcomb, *Pennsylvania Agriculture and Country Life, 1640–1840*. Harrisburg: Pennsylvania Historical and Museum Commission, 1950.

Fulton, Charles Herman, *Principles of Metallurgy*. New York: McGraw-Hill Book Company, 1910.

Geigertown. Reading: Leon D. Evans, 1959.

Gemmell, Alfred, *The Charcoal Iron Industry in the Perkiomen Valley*. Morristown: Hartenstine Printing House, 1949.

Goodwin, Maud Wilder and Sidney G. Fisher, *Dutch and Quakers*. New Haven : Yale University Press, 1919.

Greeley, Horace and Others, *The Great Industries of the United States*. Hartford : J. B. Burr and Hyde, 1872.

Greene, Evarts Boutell, *The Revolutionary Generation, 1763–1790*. New York : The Macmillan Company, 1943.

Greenwood, William Henry, *Steel and Iron*. London : Cassell and Company, 1900.

Hartley, E. N., *Ironworks on the Saugus*, Norman : University of Oklahoma Press, 1957.

Hartz, Louis, *Economic Policy and Democratic Thought: Pennsylvania, 1776–1860*. Cambridge : Harvard University Press, 1948.

Herrick, Cheesman A., *History of Commerce and Industry*. New York; The Macmillan Company, 1918.

Industrial Berks County, 1748–1948. Reading : Textile Machine Works, 1948.

International Library of Technology. Scranton : International Textbook Company, 1903.

Jensen, Merrill, *The New Nation*. New York : Alfred A. Knopf, 1950.

Knollenberg, Bernhard, *Origins of the American Revolution, 1759–1766*. New York : The Macmillan Company, 1960.

Kraut, John Allen and Dixon Ryan Fox, *The Completion of Independence—1790–1830*. New York : The Macmillan Company, 1958.

Kurtz, Stephen G., *The Presidency of John Adams*. Philadelphia : The University of Pennsylvania Press, 1957.

Langdon, William Chauncy, *Everyday Things in American Life, 1607–1776*. New York : Charles Scribner's Sons, 1937.

Lesley, J. P., *A Geological Hand Atlas of the Sixy-Seven Counties of Pennsylvania*. Harrisburg : Board of Commissioners for the Second Geological Survey, 1885.

Lesley, J. P., *The Iron Manufacturers' Guide to the Furnaces, Forges and Rolling Mills of the United States*. New York : John Wiley, 1859.

MacDonald, William, *Jacksonian Democracy—1829–1837*. New York: Harper and Brothers, 1906. *American Nation Series*.

MacElree, Wilmer W., *Around the Boundaries of Chester County*. West Chester, Pennsylvania: The Author, 1934.

Martin, Robert F., *National Income in the United States, 1799–1938*. New York: National Industrial Conference Board, 1939.

Mathews, Mitford M. (Editor), *A Dictionary of Americanisms on Historical Principles*. Chicago: University of Chicago Press 1956.

McCullough, Robert and Walter Leuba, *The Pennsylvania Main Line Canal*. Martinsburg, Pennsylvania: Morrisons Cove Herald, 1962.

Mercer, Henry C., *Ancient Carpenters' Tools*. Doylestown: The Bucks County Historical Society, 1951.

Mercer, Henry C., *The Bible in Iron*. Doylestown: Bucks County Historical Society, 1914.

Montgomery, Morton L., *Historical and Biographical Annals of Berks County, Pennsylvania*, 2 volumes. Chicago, J. H. Beers and Company, 1909.

Montgomery, Morton L., *History of Berks County in Pennsylvania*. Philadelphia: Everts, Peck and Richards, 1886.

Murphy, Raymond E. and Marion Murphy, *Pennsylvania— A Regional Geography*. Harrisburg: Pennsylvania Book Service, 1937.

Murphy, Raymond E. and Marion F. Murphy, *Pennsylvania Landscapes*. State College, Pennsylvania: Penns Valley Publishers, Inc., 1954.

Nolan, J. Bennett, *Play at Reading Town*. Reading, Pennsylvania: The Feroe Press, 1935.

North, Douglas C., *The Economic Growth of the United States*. Englewood Cliffs, Prentice Hall, Inc., 1961.

One Hundred and Twenty-Five Years of Pig Iron Manufacture at Robesonia, Pennsylvania. Philadelphia: The Robesonia Iron Company, 1918.

Pearse, John B., *A Concise History of the Iron Manufacture of the American Colonies up to the Revolution and of Pennsylvania until the Present Time*. Philadelphia: Allen, Lane and Scott, 1876.

Pierce, Arthur D., *Iron in the Pines*. New Brunswick: Rutgers University Press, 1957.

The Picture Story of Steel. New York: American Iron and Steel Institute, 1952.

Porter, Burton P., *Old Canal Days*. Columbus: Herr Printing Company, 1942.

Riegel, Robert E., *Young America, 1830–1840*. Norman: University of Oklahoma Press, 1949.

Rowe, Frank H., *History of the Iron and Steel Industry in Scioto County, Ohio*. Columbus: State Archaeological and Historical Society, 1938.

Schlesinger, Arthur M., Jr., *The Age of Jackson*. Boston: Little, Brown and Company, 1945.

Schubert, H. R., *History of the British Iron and Steel Industry*. London: Routledge and Kegan Paul, 1957.

Scrivenor, Harry, *History of the Iron Trade from the Earliest Records to the Present Period*. London: Longman, Brown, Green, and Longmans, 1854.

Selsam, J. Paul, *The Pennsylvania Constitution of 1776*. Philadelphia: University of Pennsylvania Press, 1936.

Shenk, Hiram H., *A History of the Lebanon Valley in Pennsylvania*. Harrisburg: The National Historical Association, Inc., 1930.

Sim, Robert J. and Harry B. Weiss, *Charcoal-Burning in New Jersey from Early Times to the Present*. Trenton: New Jersey Agricultural Society, 1955.

Singer, Charles and Others, *A History of Technology*, volume IV. New York: Oxford University Press, 1958.

Smedley, R. C., *History of the Underground Railroad in Chester and Neighboring Counties of Pennsylvania*. Lancaster: The Journal, 1883.

Smith, Cyril Stanley, *A History of Metallography*. Chicago: University of Chicago Press, 1960.

Smith, Timothy L., *Revivalism and Social Reform in Mid-Nineteenth Century America*. New York: Abingdon Press, 1957.

Stoughton, Bradley, *The Metallurgy of Iron and Steel*. New York: Hill Publishing Company, 1908.

Strassmann, W. Paul, *Risk and Technological Innovation: American Manufacturing Methods during the Nineteenth Century*. Ithaca: Cornell University Press, 1959.

Sullivan, William A., *The Industrial Worker in Pennsylvania, 1800–1840*. Harrisburg: Pennsylvania Historical and Museum Commission, 1955.

Swank, J. M., *History of the Manufacture of Iron in all Ages and Particularly in the United States from Colonial Times to 1891*. Philadelphia: Allen, Lane and Scott, 1892.

Swank, J. M., *Introduction to a History of Ironmaking and Coal Mining in Pennsylvania*. Philadelphia: Allen, Lane and Scott, 1878.

Taylor, George Rogers, *Jackson Versus Biddle*. Boston: D. C. Heath and Company, 1949.

Transactions of the American Institute of Mining Engineers, volumes XIV and XV. New York: Published by the Institute, 1886 and 1887.

Transactions of the Historical Society of Berks County, volume III. Reading Eagle Press, 1923.

Turner, Frederick Jackson, *The United States, 1830–1850*. New York, Peter Smith, 1950.

Tyler, A. F., *Freedom's Ferment: Phases of American Social History*. Minneapolis: University of Minnesota Press, 1944.

Van Wagenen, Jaud, Jr., *The Golden Age of Homespun*. Ithaca: Cornell University Press, 1954.

Wade, Richard C., *The Urban Frontier, The Rise of Western Cities, 1790–1830*. Cambridge: Harvard University Press, 1959.

Wetzel, John C. (Editor), *200th Anniversay of Birdsboro,*

Pennsylvania. Birdsboro : The Executive Committee, 1940.

White, Mortong, *Social Thought in America.* New York : Viking Press, 1949.

Williamson, Harold F. (Editor), *The Growth of the American Economy.* New York : Prentice-Hall, 1946.

Woodward, Carl Raymond, *Ploughs and Politics : Charles Read of New Jersey and his Notes on Agriculture, 1715– 1774.* New Brunswick : Rutgers University Press, 1941.

Pamphlets

Beck, Herbert H., *Common Hill and the Hessian Ditch with Personal Reminiscences of the Furnace Hills.* Lancaster : Lancaster County Historical Society, 1940.

Bining, Arthur C., *Early Ironmasters of Pennsylvania.* Reprint from Pennsylvania History, XVIII, 2 (April 1951).

Birkinbine, John, *American Blast-Furnace Progress.* Washington : Government Printing Office, 1885.

Birkinbine, John, *The Manufacture of Pig Iron in Pennsylvania.* Washington : Department of Internal Affairs— Statistics, Official Document Number 10, 1894.

Brooke, G. Clymer, *Birdsboro Company with a Past Built to Last.* New York : The Newcomen Society in North America, 1959.

Croll, P. C., *The Tulpehocken Bi-Centennial.* Womelsdorf : Executive Committee, 1923.

Cummings, Hubertis, *The Pennsylvania Canals.* Harrisburg : Pennsylvania Historical and Museum Commission, 1949.

Hopewell Village National Historic Site Pennsylvania. Washington : United States Department of the Interior, National Park Service, 1940.

Jones, Louis C., *The Farmers' Museum.* Cooperstown : New York State Historical Association, 1948.

Kemper, Jackson, III, *American Charcoal Making in the Era of the Cold-Blast Furnace.* Washington : United States Department of the Interior, 1941.

Kurjack, Dennis C., *Hopewell Village National Historic Site.* Washington : National Park Service Handbook Series, number 8, 1950.

Miller, Frederick K., *The Rise of an Iron Community,* 3 parts. Lebanon, Pennsylvania : Lebanon County Historical Society, 1950–1952.

Schultz, George W., *Antique Iron Works and Machines of the Water Power Age.* Bowers, Pennsylvania : The Author, 1927.

Spargo, John, *Iron Mining and Smelting in Bennington, Vermont—1786–1842.* Bennington : Historical Museum, 1958.

Steel Serves the Farmer. New York : American Iron and Steel Institute, 1954.

Periodicals

Bining, Arthur Cecil, "The Early Iron Industry in Pennsylvania," *The General Magazine and Historical Chronicle, University of Pennsylvania,* XXXIV, 1 (October 1931), 51–55.

Bining, Arthur Cecil, "The Iron Plantations of Early Pennsylvania," *The Pennsylvania Magazine of History and Biography,* LVII, 2 (April 1933), 7–8.

"Bird, Barde, Brooke and Boro," *Time, The Weekly Magazine,* XXX, 1 (July 5, 1937), 48.

Birkinbine, John, "Changes in the Manufacture of Pig Iron as Illustrated by the Development of the American Blast Furnace," *Proceedings of the Engineers' Club of Philadelphia,* XIX, 3 (July 1902), 223–240.

Birkinbine, John, "The Distribution and Proportions of American Blast Furnaces," *Transactions of the American Institute of Mining Engineers,* XIV (June 1885 to May 1886), 561–575.

Borchers, Sam, "American Iron Industry in Colonial Times," *Forgings,* 7, 2 (March 1945), 6–7.

Borchers, S. J., "Forge Men of Quaker State Foremost in Revolutionary Arms Production," *Forgings,* 6, 5 (September 1944), 10–11.

"Cast Iron and Early Stoves," *International Molders' and Foundry Workers' Journal,* 94, 6 (June 1958), 9–13.

Cochran, Hamilton, "Hopewell Village—Last of the Iron Plantations," *Philadelphia Magazine,* XXXVII, 7 (July 1950), 16–18, 34.

Cook, E. S., "Management of Blast Furnaces—Transition from 'Rule of Thumb' to Application of Scientific Methods," *School of Mines Quarterly,* XIX, 3 (April 1898), 227–248.

Crockard, Frank Hearne, "Modern Iron Blast-Furnace Practice," *The Engineering Magazine* (January 1, 1902), 493–513.

D'Invilliers, E. V., "The Cornwall Iron-Ore Mines; Lebanon County, Pa.," *Transaction of the American Institute of Mining Engineers, XIV* (June 1885 to May 1886), 873–904.

"Early Iron Furnaces," *U S Steel News,* 7, 1 (January 1942), 4–15.

Eshelman, John E., "Berks County's Station on the Underground Railroad," *The Historical Review of Berks County,* VI, 4 (July 1941), 107–109.

Eshleman, H. Frank, "The Great Conestoga Road," *Papers Read Before the Lancaster County Historical Society,* XII, 6 (June 5, 1908), 215–232.

Frackenthal, B. F., Junior, "Tuyeres in the Iron Blast-Furnace," *Transactions of the American Institute of Mining Engineers,* XXVIII (1903), 673.

Freiday, Dean, "Tinton Manor: The Iron Works," *Proceedings of the New Jersey Historical Society,* LXX, 4, (October 1952), 250–261.

Garrison, L. A., "Hopewell Village Site Now Open," *Reading Automobile Club Magazine,* 18, 5 (July 1940), 7–8, 25.

Gemmell, Alfred, "On the Trail of America's First Cook

Stove," *The Historical Review of Berks County,* XV, 1 (October 1949), 142–144.

Gibson, James E., "The Pennsylvania Provincial Conference of 1776," *The Pennsylvania Magazine of History and Biography,* LVIII, 4 (October 1934), 312–341.

Handwork, Edna M., "First in Iron—Berks County's Iron Industry, 1716–1815," *The Historical Review of Berks County,* XXV, 4 (Fall 1960), 120–127.

Heathcote, Charles William, "The Iron Industries of Northern Chester County," *Bulletin of the Chester County Historical Society,* (1936), 38–50.

Heydinger, Earl J., "The Schuylkill, Lifeline to Valley Forge," *Bulletin of the Historical Society of Montgomery County, Pennsylvania,* IX, 3 (October 1954), 159–170.

Homan, Wayne E., "Pennsylvania Heritage, Our Refuge for Runaway Slaves," *Sunday Today, The Philadelphia Inquirer Magazine* (September 24, 1961), 26.

Homan, Wayne E., "The Underground Railroad," *The Historical Review of Berks County,* XXIII, 4 (Fall 1958), 112–118.

"Hopewell Village," *International Molders' and Foundry Workers' Journal,* 94, 10 (October 1958), 3–7.

"Hopewell—Where the Story of Ironmaking in Early America Comes Alive," *Lancaster Motorist,* LII, 8 (August 1962), 2, 24.

Hudson, J. Paul, "Iron Manufacturing During the Eighteenth Century," *The Iron Worker,* XXI, 4 (Autumn 1957), 9–13.

Hudson, J. Paul, "The Story of Iron at Jamestown, Virginia —Where Iron Objects Were Wrought by Englishmen almost 350 Years Ago," *The Iron Worker,* XX, 3 (Summer 1956), 2–14.

Hunter, Louis C., "Financial Problems of the Early Pittsburgh Iron Manufacturers," *Journal of Economic and Business History,* II, 3 (Mal 1930), 520–544.

Hunter, Louis C., "Influence of the Market upon Techniques in the Iron Industry in Western Pennsylvania up to 1860,"

Journal of Economic and Business History, I, 2 (February 1929), 241–281.

Hyde, Frederic G., "Built to Last," *The Philadelphia Inquirer Magazine* (May 14, 1950).

"James Wilson at Hopewell National Park," *The Historical Review of Berks County,* IV, 1 (October 1938), 16–17.

Kemper Jackson, 3rd, "American Charcoal Making in the Era of the Cold-Blast Furnace," *The Regional Review,* V, 1 (July 1940), 3–15.

Kemper Jackson, III, "The Making of Charcoal," *The Historical Review of Berks County,* II, 4 (July 1937), 98–103.

Kendig, John D., "Charcoal Burning in Hopewell," *American Forests,* 65, 10 (October 1959), 41, 59.

Kurjack, Dennis C., "Joseph Whitaker of Hopewell Furnace," second of two parts, *The Historical Review of Berks County,* XIV, 3 (April 1949), 66–73.

Livingood, James W., "The Heyday of the Schuylkill Navigation Company," *The Historical Review of Berks County,* IV, 1 (October 1938), 11–14.

Lyles, Victoria, "Forges and Furnaces of York County," *Papers of the Historical Society of York County,* New Series, number 4 (no date).

"Metals and Ancient Heating Methods," *International Molders' and Foundry Workers' Journal,* 94, 5 (May 1958), 31–33.

Montgomery, Morton L., "Early Furnaces and Forges of Berks County, Pennsylvania," *The Pennsylvania Magazine of History and Biography,* VIII, 1 (March 1884), 56–81.

Peirce, Patricia, "Iron and Copper Mining in Caernarvon Township," *The Historical Review of Berks County,* XVI, 1 (October-December 1950, 12–15, 25–31.

Rice, William S., "Mount Hope Furnace, An Early Landmark," *The American-German Review,* XVII, 5 (June 1951), 28–29.

Ruffner, Margaret C., "Hopewell Cradle of American Industry," *The Rotarian,* LXXVIII, 3 (March 1951), 21.

Sandford, Joseph E., "Charcoal Burning," *The Historian,* I, 5 (Winter 1960–1961), 25–27.

Schaeffer, Paul N., "Slavery in Berks County," *The Historical Review of Berks County,* VI, 4 (July 1941), 110–115.

Shearer, Fred W., "A Bygone Industry," *Service Letter The Pennsylvania Department of Forests and Waters,* series 7, number 11 (March 12, 1936), 1–3.

Starratt, F. Weston, "Visiting Hopewell Furnace," *Journal of Metals,* 14, 7 (July 1962), 484–485.

Stauffer, Alvin P. and Charles W. Porter, "The National Park Service Program of Conservation for Areas and Structures of National Historical Significance," *Mississipi Valley Historical Review,* XXX, 1 (June 1943). Typescript at Hopewell Village.

Thomas, Earl A., "Hopewell Iron Plantation," *The Highway Magazine* (August 1949), 171–175.

"When Charcoal Iron Industry Held Sway," *Steel* (August 3, 1942), 80 and (August 10, 1942), 78.

Whitely, Henry C., "The Principio Company," *The Pennsylvania Magazine of History and Biography,* XI, 1 (April 1887), 63.

Woodhouse, Samuel W., "Log and Journal of the Ship *United States* on a voyage to China in 1784," *"The Pennsylvania Magazine of History and Biography,* LV, 3 (July 1931), 225–258.

Unpublished Studies

Abel, Leland, "Archeological Report of Hopewell Furnace Site," typescript, 1962, Hopewell Village Library.

Apple, Russell A., "The Public Roads Serving Hopewell Furnace," typescript, 1953, Hopewell Village Library.

Apple, Russell A., "Historical Documentary Report on the

Bridge and Wheel House, Hopewell Furnace," typescript, 1956, Hopewell Village, Library.

Apple, Russel A., "The Public Serving Hopewell Furnace," typescript, 1953, Hopewell Village Library.

Appleman, Roy Edgar, "Historical Report French Creek Area," typescript, no date, Hopewell Village Library.

Appleman, Roy Edgar, "Memorandum Respecting the Historical and Archeological Importance of the French Creek Recreational Demonstration Area, Pennsylvania, and the Proposal that it Be Made a National Monument," typescript, 1939, Hopewell Village Library.

Appleman, Roy Edgar, "Proposed Restoration Plan for Old Iron Making Village," typescript, 1936, Hopewell Village Library.

Cowan, John P., "Notes on an Inventory of Buildings and Contents Hopewell, French Creek, Pennsylvania," type script, 1938, Hopewell Village Library.

Donohoe, Richard P., "The Charcoal House and Shed, Hopewell Village National Historic Site," typescript, 1956. Hopewell Village Library.

Du Hamel, William, "Historical Sketch of William Bird. Founder of Birdsboro, Pa.," typescript, 1928, Hopewell Village Library.

Fox, Cyrus T., "William Bird, Pioneer Founder of Birdsboro," typescript, no date, Hopewell Village Library.

Gale, Howard, "Report on the Furnishings and Equipment and Methods Used in the Blacksmith Shop," typescript. 1941, Hopewell Village Library.

Heydinger, Earl J., "History of French Creek Mine, 1846-1928," typescript, no date, Hopewell Village Library.

Heydinger, Earl J., "Orientation Report for Archeology in Lower Working Level at Hopewell Village NHS," typescript, 1962, Hopewell Village Library.

Heydinger, Earl J., "The Office-Store," typescript, 1959, Hopewell Village Library.

Kemper, Franklin, "J. Lincoln Palsgrove," typescript, no date, Hopewell Village Library.

Kemper, Jackson, "The Making of Charcoal as Followed by the Colliers of the Schuylkill Valley," typescript, no date, Hopewell Village Library.

Kurjack, Dennis C., "Chart of Furnace Operation, 1783–1883," typescript, no date, Hopewell Village Library.

Montgomery, Charles B., "Report on Hopewell Furnace in Berks County, Pa.," typescript, probably 1941, Hopewell Village Library.

Motz, J. C. Fisher, "The Big House," typescript, 1941, Hopewell Village Library.

Motz, J. C. Fisher, "Field Notes—Archeological Investigation of Blacksmith Shop," typescript, 1940, Hopewell Village Library.

Motz, J. C. Fisher, "Historical Base Map," typescript, 1941, Hopewell Village Library.

Motz, J. C. Fisher, "Report on Archeological Investigation of the Blacksmith Shop," typescript, 1940, Hopewell Village Library.

Motz, J. C. Fisher, "Restoration of Houck House," typescript, 1940, Hopewell Village Library.

"Restoration of Tenant Barn," typescript, 1940, Hopewell Village Library.

Ronsheim, Robert D., "Charcoal House and Charcoal Shed, Hopewell Village National Historical Site," typescript, 1957, Hopewell Village Library.

Ronsheim, Robert D., "Survey Report, Tenant House 3," typescript, 1958, Hopewell Village Library.

Ronsheim, Robert D., and Earl J. Heydinger, "Village Barn," typescript, 1961, Hopewell Village Library.

Schumacher, Paul J. F., "Archeological Exploration at the Furnace Group—1935–1951," typescript, 1951, Hopewell Village Library.

Souder, Norman M., "The Office and Store Building," typescript, 1960, Hopewell Village Library.

Sylvester, Arthur C., and Jackson Kemper, 3rd, "The Making of Charcoal as Followed by the Colliers of the Schuylkill Valley," typescript, 1937, Hopewell Village Library.

Zerbey, Benjamin J. and Earl J. Heydinger, "Anthracite Furnace, Hopewell Village National Historical Site," typescript, 1962, Hopewell Village Library.

Index

307; skills of, 242 ff; wages of, 262 ff

Collins, Andrew, 337, 347 ff, 370

Columbia (Pennsylvania), 55, 178, 223, 396, 409

Columbia County (Pennsylvania) 390

Colver Family, 274

Commissary General of Military Stores, 24

Committee of Correspondence, 27

Committee on Observation, 27

Community cooperation, 288 ff

Concord Baptist Church (Bostic, North Carolina), 34

Conestoge (Pennsylvania), 272

Confections, in store, 201

Conner, Henry, 382

Conowingo (Maryland). 178

Constables, 269, 293, 389

Continental Army, 27, 414

Continental Congress, 25 ff, 274 ff

Cook, Eliza, 320

Cook, Margaret, 321, 371

Cooks, 92, 320

Copper ore, 144

Coppersmiths, 411

Corb, Abraham, 347

Cordwood cutting, 469

Cordwood Sale, 136

Cornell Cunningham and Company, 160 ff

Corn huskings, 380

Cornwall Furnace, 34, 43, 45, 121, 210, 258, 305

Cornwall Mine. 221

Corporal punishment, 271

Cosmetics, 327

"Cosmorama," 389

Country Aurora, 278

Country castings, 36

County Poor House, 335

County Superintendent of Schools, 350

Courthouse, 388

Courting, 329 ff, 345

Court of Common Pleas of Berks County, 61

Coventry Forge, 207, 223, 364

Cows, 56. 108, 177, 315, 326; feed for, 199; price of, 129 ff, 315. See also Cattle.

Cox, Charles, 310

Cox, Peter, 21, 277, 289

Cox, Samuel, 122 ff, 277, 289

Cox, Tench, 45

Cramp, Charles, 276

Cramp, Jacob, 109, 340

"Cramps Girls," 343

Credit, 271, 397

Credit at Store, 263 ff, 288, 290

Crosby, John, 341

Croton Water Works, 393

Crutcher, Fanny, 394 (footnote)

Cummings, John, 381

Cunningham, Robert, 220

Cupola, 55

Curtin, Andrew G., 408

Curtis, Samuel, 308

Custar Family, 274

Customers for castings, 159; location of, 222 ff

Cutting wood, 229, 268; by boys, 342; by women, 323; dishonesty in, 268

Cuthbert, Thomas, 45, 275

Dale Furnace, 52, 262, 324

Dam, 21

Dampman Family, 367

Danahower Family, 367

Dances, 388 ff, 391, 394

Danfield, Isaac, 115 ff

Daniel Buckley and Company, 56, 126, 396 (footnote)

Danville (Pennsylvania), 390

Darling, William, 259, 402, 413

Davenport (Iowa), 409

David Hughs and Company, 290

Davis (Carpetweaver), 90

Davis, Anne, 294

Davis, Mathew, 43, 170, 267, 278, 347. 381 ff. 392

Dearborns, 375

Deas, James H., 163, 400 (footnote)

Deaths, 97

Debtor prisons, 279, 411

Debts, 269. 417; imprisonment for, 279, 411; payment of, 281; unpaid, 281; women, 320, 325; workers, 269

Declaration of Independence, 29

Dehaven, Abraham. 292, 410

Dehaven, Edward, 275

Dehaven Family, 366 ff

Dehart, I., 312

Dehart, John, 312